Fodor's

TORONTO

23rd Edition

Fodor's Travel Publications   New York, Toronto, London, Sydney, Auckland

www.fodors.com

FODOR'S TORONTO
Editor: Maria Hart

Writers: Shannon Kelly, Diana Ng, Sarah Richards, Nina Callaway

H14   2099   June 5, 2013.

Production Editors: Evangelos Vasilakis, Anna Birinyi
Maps & Illustrations: David Lindroth, Ed Jacobus, *cartographers;* Bob Blake, Rebecca Baer, *map editors;* William Wu, *information graphics*
Design: Fabrizio La Rocca, *creative director;* Guido Caroti, *art director;* Tina Malaney, Nora Rosansky, Chie Ushio, Jessica Walsh, *designers;* Melanie Marin, *associate director of photography*
Cover Photo: (Royal Ontario Museum): dbimages/Alamy
Production Manager: Angela L. McLean

23rd Edition

ISBN 978-0-307-92834-4

ISSN 1044-6133

SPECIAL SALES
This book is available at special discounts for bulk purchases for sales promotions or premiums. Special editions, including personalized covers, excerpts of existing books, and corporate imprints, can be created in large quantities for special needs. For more information, write to Special Markets/Premium Sales, 1745 Broadway, MD 3-1, New York, NY 10019, or e-mail specialmarkets@randomhouse.com.

AN IMPORTANT TIP & AN INVITATION
Although all prices, opening times, and other details in this book are based on information supplied to us at press time, changes occur all the time in the travel world, and Fodor's cannot accept responsibility for facts that become outdated or for inadvertent errors or omissions. So **always confirm information when it matters,** especially if you're making a detour to visit a specific place. Your experiences—positive and negative—matter to us. If we have missed or misstated something, **please write to us.** Share your opinion instantly through our online feedback center at fodors.com/contact-us.

PRINTED IN CHINA

10 9 8 7 6 5 4 3 2 1

CONTENTS

MAPS

ABOUT THIS BOOK

Our Ratings

At Fodor's, we spend considerable time choosing the best places in a destination so you don't have to. By default, anything we recommend in this book is worth visiting. But some sights, properties, and experiences are so great that we've recognized them with additional accolades. Orange Fodor's Choice stars indicate our top recommendations; black stars highlight places we deem Highly Recommended; and Best Bets call attention to top properties in various categories. Disagree with any of our choices? Care to nominate a new place? Visit our feedback center at www.fodors.com/feedback.

For expanded hotel reviews, visit **Fodors.com**

Hotels

Hotels have private bath, phone, and TV, and do not offer meals unless we specify that in the review. We always list facilities but not whether you'll be charged an extra fee to use them.

Restaurants

Unless we state otherwise, restaurants are open for lunch and dinner daily. We mention dress only when there's a specific requirement and reservations only when they're essential or not accepted—it's always best to book ahead.

Credit Cards

We assume that restaurants and hotels accept credit cards. If not, we'll note it in the review.

Budget Well

Hotel and restaurant price categories from ¢ to $$$$ are defined in the opening pages of the respective chapters. For attractions, we always give standard adult admission fees; reductions are usually available for children, students, and senior citizens.

Listings
★ Fodor's Choice
★ Highly recommended
⊠ Physical address
✛ Directions or Map coordinates
⬧ Mailing address
☎ Telephone
🖷 Fax
⊕ On the Web
✍ E-mail
💰 Admission fee
🕙 Open/closed times
Ⓜ Metro stations
▭ No credit cards

Hotels & Restaurants
🏨 Hotel
🛏 Number of rooms
♨ Facilities
🍴 Meal plans
✕ Restaurant
✍ Reservations
🕍 Dress code
⬑ Smoking

Outdoors
⛳ Golf
⛺ Camping

Other
☊ Family-friendly
⇨ See also
⊠ Branch address
☞ Take note

Experience
Toronto

TORONTO TODAY

"Toronto is a city that has yet to fall in love with itself," quipped Pier Giorgio Di Cicco, Toronto's former poet laureate. There's some truth to that, maybe because Torontonians have a hard time defining their city. It's culturally diverse, to be sure, but this, the city's most touted trait, is the polar opposite of a unifying characteristic. So what exactly is Toronto all about? It's a bit confused. Americans call Torontonians friendly and the city clean, while other Canadians say its locals are rude and egocentric. Toronto is often touted as "livable," a commendable if dull virtue. Admittedly, Toronto is not as exciting as New York, as quaint as Montréal, as glitzy as Los Angeles, as outdoorsy as Vancouver, or as historic as London. Instead, it's a patchwork of *all* of these qualities. Toronto is the complete package. And comparatively (despite what Canadian compatriots believe) Toronto *is* clean, safe, and just all-around nice. Torontonians say "sorry" when they jostle you. They recycle and compost. They obey traffic laws. Toronto is like the boy next door you eventually marry after fooling around with New York or Los Angeles. Why not cut the charade and start the love affair now?

Diverse City

Toronto is one of the most immigrant-friendly cities on the planet, and the city's official motto, "Diversity Our Strength," reflects this hodgepodge of ethnicities. More than half its population is foreign-born, and half of all Torontonians are native speakers of a foreign language. (The "other" national language of French, however, is not one of the most commonly spoken languages here, trailing Chinese, Portuguese, Punjabi, and Tagalog.) In a few hours in Toronto you can travel the globe, from Little India to Little Italy, Koreatown to Greektown, or at least eat your way around it, from Polish pierogi to Chinese dim sum to Portuguese salt-cod fritters.

A City of Neighborhoods

Every city has neighborhoods, but Toronto's are particularly diverse, distinctive, and walkable. Some were once their own villages, and many, such as the Danforth (Greektown), Little Portugal, and Chinatown, are products of the ethnic groups who first settled them. Others, like Yorkville, the Annex, and Queen West, are once-scruffy neighborhoods transformed by struggling-artist types that have grown more affluent along with their residents.

WHAT'S HOT IN TORONTO NOW?

A new mayor took office in 2011 following a divisive election. Talks of privatizing public services, hints at massive 2012 budget cuts, and Rob Ford's penchant for rapid-fire, closed-door policymaking leave Torontonians somewhat in the dark

about the future of their city for 2012 and beyond.

Promising to keep the downtown vibrant, the architectural boom of the new millennium continues, with the unveiling of the refurbished Sony Centre for the Performing Arts

in 2010, an Athlete's Village in preparation for the 2015 Pan American Games underway on King Street East, a bevy of luxury hotel construction—Ritz-Carlton and Trump International hotels in 2011 and a new Shangri-La hotel and a

Boundaries aren't fixed and are constantly evolving: on a five-minute walk down Bloor Street West you can pass a Portuguese butcher, an Ethiopian restaurant, a hip espresso bar, and a Maltese travel agency. Neighborhoods continue to crop up, with new grads and young families snapping up apartments and houses in less expensive developing areas, such as the Junction, Parkdale, and Leslieville.

On the Waterfront

Lake Ontario forms Toronto's very obvious southern border, but residents who live out of its view often forget it's there until they attend an event at the Ex or the Harbourfront Centre. It's one of the city's best features, especially in the summer, providing opportunities for boating, ferrying to the Toronto Islands, or strolling, biking, or jogging beside the water. The lakeshore is about to become more of an attraction than ever, thanks to an ongoing initiative to revitalize the waterfront and create more parks, beaches, and walkways.

Canada's Culture Center

The Toronto International Film Festival, the Art Gallery of Ontario, Canada's center for magazine and book publishing, national ballet and opera companies, the Toronto Symphony Orchestra—these are just a handful of the many reasons Toronto attracts millions of arts and culture lovers each year to live, work, and play. On any given day or night, you'll find events to feed the brain and the spirit: art gallery openings, poetry readings, theatrical releases, film revues, dance performances, and festivals showcasing the arts, from the focused JazzFest and the North by Northeast indie rock extravaganza to events marrying visual and performing arts, like Nuit Blanche and Luminato.

Gastronomical

Toronto's architecture may be evolving, but its food scene has arrived. There's no shortage of amazing restaurants in this city, and local and fresh produce is all the rage. Celebrity chefs like Susur Lee, Mark McEwan, and Jamie Kennedy give locavores street cred. Toronto's cornucopia of cultures means you can sample almost any cuisine, from Abyssinian to Yemeni. Nowhere is Torontonians' love of food more apparent, perhaps, than at St. Lawrence Market, where you can pick up nonessentials like fiddlehead ferns, elk burgers, truffle oil, and mozzarella *di bufala*. In warm weather, farmers' markets bring the province's plenty to the city.

Four Seasons refurbishment on the books for 2012—and no end in sight to condo construction downtown.

Transportation around Toronto is getting an overhaul. The city rolled out the Bixi bike-sharing system in 2011, with 1,000 bikes and 80 docking stations around the city.

At this writing, the Toronto Transit Commission (TTC) is testing shiny new subway cars with electronic displays and car-to-car access on the tracks for their mid- to late-2011 debut, replacing trains that have been in operation since the 1970s. And if you want to "ride the Rocket" via streetcar, do it in 2012: they'll be replaced with new light-rail vehicles in 2013.

WHAT'S WHERE

1 **Harbourfront, the Finan-cial District, and Old Town.** Between the waterfront and Queen Street, the city's main attractions are packed in: the CN Tower, the Harbourfront Centre, the Hockey Hall of Fame, Ontario Place amuse-ment park, the Rogers Centre, St. James Cathedral, and the St. Lawrence food market. Most of the lofty peaks in Toronto's skyline are in this epicenter of Canadian finan-cial power. A stroll through Old Town reveals the exciting Historic Distillery District entertainment complex, and a quick trip on a ferry brings you to the Toronto Islands.

2 **Chinatown, Kensington Market, and Queen West.** Tourists and locals alike battle for bargains on everything from fresh produce to vintage clothing in some of Toronto's most colorful and animated neighborhoods, centered near the intersection of Dundas and Spadina streets. West of Bathurst as far as Dufferin Street, Queen Street West draws cutting-edge artists, designers, and entrepreneurs.

3 **Queen's Park, the Annex, and Yorkville.** Toronto's polit-ical and intellectual sets, as well as some of its most afflu-ent citizens, live, work, and play around Queen's Park. Ivy-covered Gothic Revival build-ings of the 75,000-student

U of T campus are surrounded with bargain-price eateries and pubs. Heading north you'll hit the Annex, the city's academic and artsy haunt, and then the mansion Casa Loma, surrounded by leafy streets and lavish homes; southeast of here, near Avenue Road, are Yorkville's high-class designer shops, upscale groceries, and swish restaurants.

4 Dundas Square Area. This area encompasses both the square, which hosts frequent performances in summer, and the surrounding neighborhood of Broadway-style theaters, family-style restaurants, and department stores. A nudge east and north is Toronto's "queer and queer-positive" Church–Wellesley neighborhood.

5 Greater Toronto. Attractions such as Canada's Wonderland theme park, the Ontario Science Centre, and the Toronto Zoo lure visitors from downtown. Sprinkled around Toronto's major neighborhoods are pockets like residential Cabbagetown on the east side, gritty expat haven Little Portugal on the west side, and quiet High Park, a collection of Tudor brick homes surrounding downtown's largest green space.

TORONTO PLANNER

Getting Here

Most flights arrive and depart from Pearson International Airport (YYZ), about a 30-minute drive northwest of downtown. Cabs are a C$30–C$55 flat rate (varies by destination) for most downtown locations. The Toronto Transit Commission (TTC) operates the 192 Airport Rocket, a shuttle bus to the Kipling subway station; the TTC fare of C$3 applies. The Billy Bishop Toronto City Airport (YTZ), better known as the Toronto Island Airport, right in downtown, is served only by Porter Airlines, which flies to Chicago, Newark (New Jersey), Boston, and several cities in northern Ontario and in eastern Canada, including Montréal.

Amtrak and VIA Rail trains pull into Union Station, at the intersection of Bay and Front streets.

Major highways converge here: the QEW from the west (Buffalo, Detroit), the 401 from the east (Montréal, Ottawa), and the 400 from the north (Barrie, Algonquin Park).

Visitor Information

Tourism Toronto. For more information, contact Tourism Toronto. ☎ 800/363–1990, 416/203–2500 ⊕ www. seetorontonow.com.

When to Go

Toronto is most pleasant from late spring through early fall, when there are outdoor concerts, frequent festivals, and open-air dining. On the other hand, some hotels drop their prices up to 50% in the off-season. Fall through spring is prime viewing time for dance, opera, theater, and classical music. The temperature frequently falls below freezing from late November into March, when snowstorms can wreak havoc on travel plans. Winters can be cold, though Toronto's climate is one of Canada's mildest, thanks to the regulating properties of Lake Ontario. Still, snowfalls are frequent, and substantial enough to lure skiing enthusiasts to the resorts north of the city. A few underground shopping concourses, such as the PATH in the Financial District downtown, allow you to avoid the cold in the winter months.

Getting Around

Traffic is dense and parking expensive within the city core. If you have a car, leave it at your hotel. ■TIP→ In the city, take taxis or use the excellent TTC subway, streetcar, and bus system.

Car Travel. A car is helpful to access some further-flung destinations, but it isn't necessary and can be a hassle. Street parking is sometimes difficult; garages and lots usually charge C$3–C$5 per hour or C$10–C$20 per day.

Taxi Travel. Taxis here are easy to hail, or you can call ☎ 416/829–4222 for pickup. The meter starts at C$4 and you are charged C25¢ for each additional 0.155 km (roughly 1/10 mi) after the first 0.155 km.

TTC Travel. The Toronto Transit Commission operates the subway, streetcars, and buses that easily take you to most downtown attractions. The subway is clean and efficient, with trains arriving every few minutes; streetcars and buses are a bit slower. A single transferable fare is C$3; day (C$10) and week (C$36) passes are available. A day pass covers up to two adults and four children on weekend days and holidays. Most systems operate from about 6 am to 1 am Monday through Saturday and 9 am to 1 am Sunday.

Getting Oriented

The boundaries of what Torontonians consider downtown, where most of the city sights are located, are subject to debate, but everyone agrees on the southern cutoff—Lake Ontario and the Toronto Islands. The other coordinates of the rectangle that compose the city core are roughly High Park to the west, the DVP (Don Valley Parkway) to the east, and Eglinton Avenue to the north. A few sights beyond these borders make excellent half- or full-day excursions. An ideal way to get a sense of the city's layout is from one of the observation decks at the CN Tower on a clear day; the view is especially lovely at sunset.

Most city streets are organized on a grid system: with some exceptions, street numbers start at zero at the lake and increase as you go north. On the east–west axis, Yonge (pronounced "young") Street, Toronto's main north–west thoroughfare, is the dividing line: you can expect higher numbers the farther away you get from Yonge.

Making the Most of Your Time

Planning is the key to maximizing your experience. First, book a hotel near the activities that most interest you. If you're here to see a Broadway-style show, get the view from the CN Tower, stroll the lakefront, stomp your feet at a Raptors game, or soak up some culture at the ballet, opera, or symphony, go for a room in or near the Harbourfront. If food, shopping, or museums are your passion, affluent Yorkville might be better suited (bonus: it's at the axis of both major subway lines). To live like a local, wandering neighborhood streets and patronizing funky cafés and shops, consider the Queen West boutique hotels.

In a short trip you can do a lot but not everything. Decide on your priorities, and don't overbook. Allow time for wandering. Schedule coffee (or Ontario microbrew) breaks. Be realistic about your sightseeing style. If you tend to scour every inch of a museum, you could spend an entire afternoon at the ROM (Royal Ontario Museum); if you're selective, you can breeze through in an hour.

Plan your days geographically. Kensington and Chinatown make an excellent combo; High Park and the Beaches, not so much.

Ditch the car and get a TTC day pass for unlimited travel on the subways and streetcars.

Savings Tips

■ Toronto CityPASS (⊕ *www. citypass.com*) saves money and time as it lets you bypass ticket lines. Admission fees to the CN Tower, Casa Loma, the Royal Ontario Museum, the Ontario Science Centre, and the Toronto Zoo are included for a one-time fee of C$66—a savings of more than C$50, valid for nine days.

■ Buying a day or weekly pass on the TTC can save you money and make getting around the city easier.

■ Many events listed on the city's Web site (⊕ *www. toronto.ca/events*) are free. The Harbourfront Centre (⊕ *www.harbourfrontcentre. com*) hosts numerous free cultural programs and festivals year-round.

■ Some museums and art collections have free (or pay-what-you-can) admission all the time, including the Gallery of Inuit Art in the TD Centre, the Museum of Contemporary Canadian Art, and the Harbourfront Centre's Power Plant gallery. But even the major museums, including the Royal Ontario Museum, the Bata Shoe Museum, Gardiner Museum of Ceramic Art, Textile Museum of Canada, and Art Gallery of Ontario, have one or two free, pay-what-you-can, and/or half-price evening(s) per week, usually Wednesday, Thursday, or Friday, and usually beginning after 3 pm.

TORONTO
TOP ATTRACTIONS

CN Tower

(A) Since it opened as a communications tower in 1976, the CN Tower has defined Toronto's skyline and is the city's most iconic structure. Everyone has to step onto the glass floor, hovering more than 1,000 feet above the ground, at least once. You can sometimes see Niagara Falls from the Sky Pod. At nearly 1,500 feet it was the highest observation deck in the world for more than 30 years, until the Guangzhou TV & Sightseeing Tower in China crushed its record in 2009.

Historic Distillery District

(B) The 1832 Gooderham and Worts distillery was restored and revitalized in 2006 to create a pedestrian-only mini-village of cobblestone streets and brick buildings housing restaurants, shops, galleries, and theaters. The design perfectly incorporates the original Victorian industrial architecture, and the Distillery District is a great place to while away an afternoon or evening. Concerts and other events take place outdoors in summer.

Hockey Sites

(C) Canadians are as nuts about hockey as the stereotypes maintain, and to truly experience Canadian culture you should school yourself at the Hockey Hall of Fame. Its prized possession is the original 1892 Stanley Cup. The Maple Leafs are Toronto's National Hockey League team, and though they haven't won the Stanley Cup since 1967, fans are loyal and tickets are notoriously tough to get. If you can't see a game at the Air Canada Centre, see one at a sports bar: fans at Real Sports and Wayne Gretzky's downtown are always fired up.

Great Markets

(D) St. Lawrence Market is as much a destination for its brick 1844 exterior as for its city block of meats, cheeses, produce, and prepared foods inside. It's the quintessential place to grab one of the city's

famed peameal bacon sandwiches (we said "famed," not "gourmet"). Kensington Market is an entirely different beast: several blocks square of used-clothing stores, head shops, cheap ethnic and vegetarian eats, and shops selling spices, fish, and baked goods. Streets teem with browsers, buskers, and bicycles. The best time to go is when cars are prohibited, the last Sunday of every month between May and October.

Toronto Islands

(E) A short ferry ride from the Harbourfront, the car-free Islands are a relaxing respite from the concrete jungle. Take a picnic, lie on the beach, or ride a bicycle on the boardwalk. The kiddie amusement park on Centre Island attracts families. Don't forget your camera: the view of Toronto's skyline from here is unparalleled.

Top Museums

(F) An art-lover's first stop should be the Art Gallery of Ontario (AGO), with its collection of nearly 80,000 works spanning almost 2,000 years of art in a building redesigned by Toronto-born Frank Gehry in 2008. The massive Royal Ontario Museum (ROM) is one of the most impressive cultural institutions in the world. It, too, received a recent redesign: an über-modern crystalline addition in 2007. Honorable mentions: the Design Exchange and the Bata Shoe Museum.

Queen West

(G) Many a visitor falls in love with Toronto after a foray to historically bohemian Queen Street West. Though the entire strip has spirit, the ragtag artist-forged businesses keep moving west. Begin with the spiffy chain stores near Spadina and see how the record shops, boutiques, cafés, bookstores, bars, and galleries change as you head west.

TOP EXPERIENCES

Wining and Dining

Those in search of haute cuisine are pampered in Toronto, where some of the world's finest chefs vie for the attention of the city's sizable foodie population. Toronto's range of exceptional eateries, from creative Asian fusion to more daring molecular gastronomy, offers wining and dining potential for every possible palate. Aromas of finely crafted sauces and delicately grilled meats emanate from eateries in Yorkville, where valet service and designer handbags are de rigueur, and the strip of bistros in the Entertainment District gets lively with theatergoing crowds. Weekdays at lunch, the Financial District's Bay Street is a sea of Armani suits, crisply pressed shirts, and clicking heels heading to power lunches to make deals over steak frites. To conduct your own taste tests, check out some of the following places:

Bistro 990. Staff here are sure to be attentive—they're used to serving celebrities and power-wielding bigwigs who fill the tables on weekday afternoons.

Bymark. An ultramodern and ultracool spot primed for the Financial District set; chef-owner Mark McEwan aims for perfection with classy contemporary fare.

Canoe. Toronto's most famous "splurge" place. Sit back, enjoy the view, and let the waiter pair your dish with a recommended local Ontario wine.

Colborne Lane. Star chef Claudio Aprile's venture is *the* place to sample cutting-edge creations that blur the boundary between dinner and science project.

Fressen. Dimly lit, ultra-trendy vegan nouvelle cuisine with a wine list to rival any steak house.

Hot Hoods

Toronto's coolness doesn't emanate from a downtown core or even a series of town centers. The action is everywhere in the city. Dozens of neighborhoods, each with its own scene and way of life, coexist within the vast metropolitan area. Here are a few worth investigating:

West Queen West. As Queen Street West (to Bathurst Street or so) becomes more commercial and rents increase, more local artists and designers have moved farther west; it's also home to a burgeoning night scene and experimental restaurants.

Kensington Market. This well-established bastion of bohemia for hippies of all ages is a grungy and multicultural several-block radius of produce, cheese, by-the-gram spices, fresh empanadas, used clothing, head shops, and funky restaurants and cafés.

The Annex. The pockets of wealth nestled in side streets add diversity to this scruffy strip of Bloor, the favorite haunt of the intellectual set, whether starving student or world-renowned novelist.

The Beach. This bourgeois-bohemian neighborhood (also called The Beaches) is the habitat of young professionals who frequent the yoga studios and sushi restaurants along Queen Street East and walk their pooches daily along Lake Ontario's boardwalk.

Performing Arts

Refurbished iconic theaters such as the Royal Alexandra and Canon theaters host a number of big-ticket shows in elegant surroundings. More modern venues such as the Princess of Wales highlight local and Broadway performances. The Four Seasons Centre is home to both the National Ballet of Canada and the Canadian Opera Company, which shares the

music scene with the Toronto Symphony Orchestra and mainstream concerts at the Sony Centre and Massey Hall. Indie artists are attracted to the bars and grimy music venues on Queen Street West. (True theater buffs will also want to leave Toronto to hit the festivals of Stratford and Niagara-on-the-Lake.) A few of the many venues worth visiting are:

Massey Hall. Since 1894, this has been one of Toronto's premier concert halls. British royals have been entertained here and legendary musicians have performed: Charlie Parker, Dizzy Gillespie, George Gershwin, Bob Dylan, and Luciano Pavarotti, to name a few. Orchestras, musicals, dance troupes, and comedians also perform at this palpably historic venue.

Rivoli. In this multifaceted venue, you can dine while admiring local art, catch a musical act, or watch stand-up. Before they were megastars, Beck, the Indigo Girls, Iggy Pop, Janeane Garofalo, and Tori Amos all made appearances here.

Elgin and Winter Garden Theatres. These two 1913 Edwardian theaters, one stacked on top of the other, provide sumptuous settings for classical music performances, musicals, opera, and Toronto International Film Festival screenings.

The Second City. The comedic troupe here always puts on a great performance. Photo collages on the wall display the club's alumni, including Mike Myers, Dan Aykroyd, and Catherine O'Hara.

Architecture

At one point, Toronto's only celebrated icon was the CN Tower, but architects have been working hard to rejuvenate the cityscape in the new millennium—at a dizzying pace. Since 2006, the city has unveiled the transparent-glass-fronted Four Seasons Centre for the Performing Arts (Jack Diamond), the Royal Ontario Museum's deconstructed-crystal extension (Daniel Libeskind), the wood-and-glass Art Gallery of Ontario (Frank Gehry), and a 2010 Libeskind redesign of the Sony Centre for the Performing Arts with attached residential 58-story, all-glass, swooping L Tower (ETA 2013). A series of high-rises topping 50 stories—not the least of which is the 60-story, glass-spired Trump Tower, nearing completion at this writing—is changing the skyline of the city forever.

Fine examples include:

Philosopher's Walk. This scenic path winds through the University of Toronto, from the entrance between the Royal Ontario Museum and the Victorian Royal Conservatory of Music, past Trinity College's Gothic chapel and towering spires. Also look for University College, an 1856 ivy-covered Romanesque Revival building, set back from the road across Hoskin Avenue.

ROMwalks. From May to September, free themed walks organized by the Royal Ontario Museum tour some of the city's landmark buildings, such as the Church of the Redeemer, the Royal Conservatory of Music, and the Gardiner Museum.

Art Gallery of Ontario. A C$250-million renovation added thousands of square feet of gallery space in the AGO's Frank Gehry–designed building in 2008. The wooden facades, glass roofs, and four-story blue titanium wing are spectacular to admire from the outside or within.

Sharp Centre for Design. Locals are split on the eye-catching salt-and-pepper rectangle held aloft by giant colored-pencil-like stilts standing above the Ontario College of Art and Design.

TORONTO WITH KIDS

Toronto is one of the most livable cities in the world, with many families residing downtown and plenty of activities to keep them busy. *Throughout this guide, places that are especially appealing to children are indicated by a rubber-duckie icon (🦆) in the margin.*

Always check what's on at the **Harbourfront Centre,** a cultural complex with shows and workshops for ages 1 to 100. On any given day you could find a circus, clown school, musicians, juggling, storytelling, or acrobat shows. Even fearless kids' (and adults') eyes bulge at the 1,465-foot glass-elevator ride up the side of the **CN Tower,** and once they stand on the glass floor, their minds are officially blown. If you're about done with hoofing it, buckle up for a land-to-water excursion on an amphibious bus with **Toronto Hippo Tours.**

Kids won't realize they're getting schooled at the **ROM,** with its Bat Cave and dinosaur skeletons, and the **Ontario Science Centre,** with interactive exhibits exploring the brain, technology, and outer space. Not far from the Science Centre, the well-designed **Toronto Zoo** is home to giraffes, polar bears, and gorillas. Less exotic animals hang at **Riverdale Farm,** in Cabbagetown: get nose-to-nose with sheep, cows, and pigs.

Spending a few hours on the **Toronto Islands** is a good way to decompress. At the Centreville amusement park and petting zoo, geared to the under-seven set, pile the whole family into a surrey to pedal along the boardwalk, or lounge at the beach (warning: Hanlan's Point Beach is clothing-optional). The **Canadian National Exhibition (CNE),** aka "the Ex," is a huge summer fair downtown with carnival rides, games, food, puppet shows, a daily parade, and horse, dog, and cat

shows. Kids can also pet and feed horses at the horse barn or tend to chickens and milk a cow on the "farm." The waterfront **Ontario Place** amusement park has toddler-to-teen-appropriate rides, waterslides, pedal boats, shows, and an IMAX theater. But the mother of all amusement parks is a half-hour drive north of the city at **Canada's Wonderland,** home of Canada's biggest and fastest roller coaster. In winter, **ice skating** at the Harbourfront Centre is the quintessential family activity.

Young sports fans might appreciate seeing a **Blue Jays** (baseball), **Maple Leafs** (hockey), **Raptors** (basketball), or Toronto **FC** (soccer) game. To take on Wayne Gretzky in a virtual game and see the original Stanley Cup, head to the **Hockey Hall of Fame.**

Intelligent productions at the **Lorraine Kimsa Theatre for Young People** don't condescend to kids and teens, and many are just as entertaining for adults. The **Sprockets Toronto International Film Festival for Children** takes place in April, with films for ages 3 to 16. Teens and tweens who aren't tuckered out after dark might get a kick out of a retro double feature at the **Polson Pier Drive-In,** right downtown.

For the latest on upcoming shows and events, plus an overwhelming directory of stores and services, go to the Web site Toronto4Kids (⊕ *www.toronto4kids.com*).

TORONTO
LIKE A LOCAL

To get a sense of Toronto's culture and indulge in some of its pleasures, start by familiarizing yourself with the rituals of daily life. These are a few highlights—things you can take part in easily.

Leafs Nation

What do the Leafs and the *Titanic* have in common? They both look great until they hit the ice. Cue rim shot. Leafs fans—or "Leafs Nation" as they are known collectively—are accustomed to jokes, rooting as they do for a team that hasn't won the Stanley Cup since 1967. Despite heartbreak after heartbreak, they stand by every year praying for a slot in the playoffs. If the opportunity arises to attend a game (don't bank on it—nearly every one has been sold out for six decades), count yourself luckier than most Torontonians. For hockey fans or an intro to the sport, the Hockey Hall of Fame is a must. Seeing a hockey game at a sports bar is a true Canadian pastime: grab a brewski and join locals in heckling the refs on bad calls. When the Leafs score, the mirth is contagious.

International Outlook

With around half the urban population born outside Canada, and even more with foreign roots, Toronto redefines "cosmopolitan." Ethnic enclaves—Little Portugal, Greektown, Corso Italia (the "other Little Italy," on St. Clair West), and Koreatown—color downtown. It's fun to explore the unique architecture and shopping in each neighborhood, and dining out can be as exotic as you choose. Toronto's multiculturalism is evident in many of its annual festivals: the glittering Toronto Caribbean Carnival (formerly Caribana) along the waterfront; the Taste of the Danforth, featuring Greek musicians, dances, and plenty of souvlaki; the raucous celebration of Mexican Independence Day in Nathan Phillips Square; and the India Bazaar's annual festival with dancing, *chaat* (savory snacks), and henna tattooing.

Coffee, Coffee Everywhere

Morning rush hour is the best time to observe, but not participate in (lines are out the door), the ritual of caffeine and sugar intake at Tim Horton's, a coffee chain with a distinctly Canadian image and affordable prices. Go for a "double-double" (two cream, two sugar) and a box of Timbits (donut holes). But plenty of Torontonians eschew "Tim's" for more quality brews, and the city has no shortage of independently owned cafés with stellar espresso, exquisitely steamed milk, and often a fair-trade and organic options, especially along Queen Street (east of Broadview or west of Spadina) and in the Annex and Little Italy. Some of the best are Crema (Yorkville, the Junction), Sam James (the Annex, Little Italy), Dark Horse (Chinatown, Queen East, and Queen West), and Manic (Little Italy).

Lake Escapes

You don't need a car to escape Toronto's bustle and summer heat to indulge in a calm, cool day by the lake. A rite of passage for every Torontonian is a warm-weather trip to the Islands—a 15-minute ferry trip from downtown—for a barbecue, picnic, bike rides, or the Centreville amusement park. Or head to the east side of the city for strolls along the boardwalk in the Beach neighborhood. Those with wheels spend weekends on the Niagara Peninsula dallying in antiques shops in charming towns and sampling wines or head north to relax in the Muskoka Lakes cottage country or hike and camp in Algonquin Provincial Park.

TORONTO'S BEST FESTIVALS

Festivals keep Toronto lively even when cold winds blow in off Lake Ontario in winter. Themes range from art to food, Caribbean culture to gay pride. Most national championship sports events take place in and around Toronto.

Tourism Toronto. Tourism Toronto maintains an online calendar of nearly every event in the city. ☎ 416/203–2500, 800/499–2514 ⊕ www.seetorontonow.com.

January–February

WinterCity. This festival celebrates the season with citywide concerts, theater, street performers, DJ'd ice-skating parties, and **Winterlicious**, a culinary event offering discount prix-fixe menus at top restaurants as well as themed tastings and food-prep workshops. ☎ 416/395–0490 ⊕ www.toronto.ca/winterlicious.

April

Sprockets: Toronto International Film Festival for Children. Taking place in April, this children's film festival holds screenings for kids and teens aged (roughly) 3–16. ☎ 416/599–8433, 888/599–8433 ⊕ tiff.net/sprockets.

April–November

Shaw Festival. Held from late spring until fall in quaint Niagara-on-the-Lake, this festival presents plays by George Bernard Shaw and his contemporaries. Niagara-on-the-Lake is a two-hour drive south of Toronto. ☎ 905/468–2172, 800/511–7429 ⊕ www.shawfest.com.

Stratford Festival. One of the best-known Shakespeare festivals in the world, this event was created in the 1950s to revive a little town two hours west of Toronto that happened to be called Stratford (and its river called the Avon). The festival includes at least five Shakespeare plays as well as other classical and contemporary productions. Respected actors from around the world participate. ☎ 519/273–1600, 800/567–1600 ⊕ www.stratfordfestival.ca.

April–May

Hot Docs. North America's largest documentary film fest, Hot Docs takes over independent cinemas for two weeks. ☎ 416/203–2155 ⊕ www.hotdocs.ca.

CONTACT. More than 200 galleries and other venues mount photo exhibits by 1,000 different artists for this photography festival, throughout the entire month of May. ☎ 416/539–9595 ⊕ www.contactphoto.com.

June

Luminato. For 10 days, this citywide arts festival combines visual arts, music, theater, dance, literature, and more in hundreds of events, many of them free. ☎ 416/368–3100 ⊕ www.luminato.com.

North by Northeast (*NXNE*). Modeled after South by Southwest in Austin, Texas, this is a seven-day music and film festival. ☎ 416/863–6963 ⊕ nxne.com.

Pride Week. Rainbow flags fly high during Pride Week, the city's premier gay and lesbian event. It includes 10 days of cultural and political programs, concerts, a street festival, and a parade, all centered around Church–Wellesley. ☎ 416/927–7433 ⊕ www.pridetoronto.com.

Toronto Jazz Festival. For 10 days this festival brings big-name jazz artists to city jazz clubs and other indoor and outdoor venues. ☎ 416/928–2033 ⊕ torontojazz.com.

July

Beaches International Jazz Festival. In the east end Beach (aka Beaches) neighborhood, this event is a free, 10-day jazz, blues, and Latin music event and street festival. ☎ 416/698–2152 ⊕ www.beachesjazz.com.

Caribbean Carnival Toronto. A Carnival-like, 10-day cultural showcase, this festival with Caribbean music, dance, and food is put on by the West Indian communities. ☎416/391–5608 ⊕ *www.torontocaribbeancarnival.com.*

Canadian Open. One of golf's Big Five tournaments, the Canadian Open, founded in 1904, is held at the end of July. Venues change each year. ☎800/571–6736 ⊕ *www.rbccanadianopen.ca.*

Fringe of Toronto Theatre Festival. The city's largest theater festival, this 12-day event features new and developing plays by emerging artists. ☎416/966–1062 ⊕ *www.fringetoronto.com.*

Summerlicious. More than 100 restaurants in Toronto create prix-fixe menus—some at bargain prices—for this two-week culinary event. ☎416/395–0490 ⊕ *www.toronto.ca/summerlicious.*

SummerWorks. New plays are mounted at small local theaters during Summer-Works, an 11-day theater festival in early July. ☎416/504–7529 ⊕ *www.summerworks.ca.*

August

Canadian National Exhibition. With carnival rides, concerts, an air show, a dog show, a garden show, and a "Mardi Gras" parade, this 2½-week-long fair is the biggest in Canada. It's been held at the eponymous fairgrounds on the Lake Ontario waterfront since 1879. ☎416/393–6300 ⊕ *www.theex.com.*

BuskerFest. This is no ordinary street festival: aerialists, fire-eaters, dancers, contortionists, musicians, and more congregate near St. Lawrence Market for four days in August. ⊕ *www.torontobuskerfest.com.*

Rogers Cup. Founded in 1881, this is an ATP Masters 1000 event for men and a

Premier event for women. It's held on the York University campus, with the men's and women's events alternating between Toronto and Montréal each year. ☎416/665–9777, 877/283–6647 ⊕ *www.rogerscup.com.*

September

The Toronto International Film Festival. Renowned worldwide, this festival is considered more accessible to the public than Cannes, Sundance, or other major film festivals. A number of films make their world or North American premieres at this 11-day festival each year, some at red-carpet events attended by Hollywood stars. ☎416/599–8433, 888/599-8433 ⊕ *www.tiff.net.*

October

Nuit Blanche. In the downtown core, this is an all-night street festival with interactive contemporary art installations and performances. ⊕ *www.scotiabanknuitblanche.ca.*

November

Royal Agricultural Winter Fair. Held since 1922 at the Ex, this 10-day fair is a highlight of Canada's equestrian season each November, with jumping, dressage, and harness-racing competitions. ☎416/263–3400 ⊕ *www.royalfair.org.*

November–December

Cavalcade of Lights. Starting with the lighting of the city's Christmas tree at the end of November, this holiday festival continues with light displays in neighborhoods around town, fireworks, skating parties, and concerts at Nathan Phillips Square every Saturday night in December. ⊕ *www.toronto.ca/special_events/cavalcade_lights.*

SPORTS AND OUTDOORS

Toronto has a love–hate relationship with its professional sports teams, and fans can sometimes be accused of being fair-weather, except when it comes to hockey, which has always attracted rabid, sell-out crowds whether the Maple Leafs win, lose, or draw. In other words, don't count on getting Leafs tickets but take heart that sports bars will be filled with fired-up fans. It can be a cinch, however, to score tickets to Blue Jays (baseball), Raptors (basketball), Argos (football), and Toronto FC (soccer) games—depending on who they play.

StubHub. Ticket reseller StubHub is a good resource for sold-out games. ☎ 866/788–2482 ⊕ *www.stubhub.com.*

If you prefer to work up a sweat yourself, consider golf at one of the GTA's courses, ice-skating at a city rink in winter, or exploring the many parks and beaches *(see the Exploring chapter)* in warm weather.

Baseball

Toronto Blue Jays. Toronto's professional baseball team plays April through September. Interest in the team has gradually fallen since they won consecutive World Series championships in 1992 and 1993. Recent seasons have seen many young players trying to make their mark. The spectacular Rogers Centre (formerly the SkyDome) has a fully retractable roof; some consider it one of the world's premier entertainment centers. ⊠ *Rogers Centre, 1 Blue Jays Way, Harbourfront, Toronto, Ontario* ☎ *416/341–1234* ⊕ *www.bluejays.com* Ⓜ *Union.*

Basketball

Toronto Raptors. The city's NBA franchise, this team played its first season in 1995–96. For several years they struggled mightily to win both games and fans in this hockey-mad city, but the Raptors have finally come into their own, and games often sell out. Single-game tickets are available beginning in September; the season is from October through April. ⊠ *Air Canada Centre, 40 Bay St., at the Gardiner Expwy., Harbourfront, Toronto, Ontario* ☎ *416/815–5600, 416/872–5000 Ticketmaster* ⊕ *www.nba.com/raptors* Ⓜ *Union.*

Football

Toronto Argonauts. The Toronto Argonauts Canadian Football League (CFL) team has a healthy following. American football fans who attend a CFL game discover a faster, more unpredictable and exciting contest than the American version. The longer, wider field means quarterbacks have to scramble more. Tickets for games (June–November) are usually a cinch to get. ⊠ *Rogers Centre, 1 Blue Jays Way, Harbourfront, Toronto, Ontario* ☎ *416/341–2746* ⊕ *www.argonauts.on.ca* Ⓜ *Union.*

Hockey

Toronto Maple Leafs. Hockey is as popular as you've heard here, and Maple Leafs fans are particularly ardent. Even though the Leafs haven't won a Stanley Cup since 1967, they continue to inspire fierce devotion in Torontonians. If you want a chance to cheer them on, you'll have to get on the puck. ■ TIP➔ **Buy tickets at least a few months in advance or risk the game's being sold out.** No matter the stats, Leafs tickets are notoriously the toughest to score in the National Hockey League. The regular hockey season is October–mid-April. ⊠ *Air Canada Centre, 40 Bay St., at Gardiner Expwy., Harbourfront, Toronto, Ontario* ☎ *416/870–8000 Ticketmaster, 416/815–5700 information* ⊕ *www.mapleleafs.com* Ⓜ *Union.*

Soccer

Toronto's British roots combined with a huge immigrant population have helped make the Toronto Football Club (TFC), the newest addition to the city's pro sports tapestry, a success. And during events like the World Cup, Euro Cup, and Copa América (America Cup), sports bars and cafés with TVs are teeming.

Toronto FC. Canada's first Major League Soccer team and Toronto's first professional soccer team in years, Toronto FC kicked off in 2006 in a new 20,000-seat stadium. Fans get seriously pumped up for these games, singing fight songs, waving flags, and throwing streamers. Games sometimes sell out; single-game tickets go on sale a few days before the match. The season is March–October. ✉ *BMO Field, 170 Princes' Blvd., Exhibition Place, Toronto, Ontario* ☎ *416/360–4625* ⊕ *www.torontofc.ca* Ⓜ *Union, then 509 Harbourfront streetcar west; 511 Bathurst streetcar south.*

Golf

The golf season lasts only from April to late October. Discounted rates are usually available until mid-May and after Canadian Thanksgiving (early October). All courses are best reached by car.

Angus Glen Golf Club. Deemed Canada's best new course by *Golf Digest* when it opened in 1995, this club has remained one of the country's best places to play, hosting the Canadian Open in 2002 and 2007 on its par-72 South and North courses, respectively. It's a 45-minute drive north of downtown. ✉ *10080 Kennedy Rd., Markham, Ontario* ☎ *905/887–0090, 905/887–5157 reservations* ⊕ *www.angusglen.com.*

Glen Abbey Golf Club. The top course in Canada, this Jack Nicklaus–designed 18-hole, par-73 club is a real beauty. The Canadian Open was held here for the 25th time in 2009. It's in the affluent suburb of Oakville, about 45 minutes east of the city. ✉ *1333 Dorval Dr., just north of QEW, Oakville, Ontario* ☎ *905/844–1800,* ⊕ *www.clublink.ca.*

Don Valley Golf Course. About a 20-minute drive north of downtown this is a par-71, 18-hole municipal course. Despite being right in the city, it's a lovely, hilly course with water hazards and tree-lined fairways. ✉ *4200 Yonge St., North York, Toronto, Ontario* ☎ *416/392–2465* ⊕ *www.toronto.ca/parks/golf.*

Ice-Skating

Toronto Parks, Forestry & Recreation Rink Hotline. The favorite city-operated, outdoor rinks are the forested, west-side **High Park** and the tiny **Nathan Phillips Square**, surrounded by towering skyscrapers in the heart of the Financial District. City rinks are free, but skate rentals aren't always available. ☎ *311 Toronto Parks, Forestry & Recreation rink hotline* ⊕ *www.toronto.ca/parks/skating.*

Harbourfront Centre. The spacious, outdoor rink here is often voted the best in the city due to its lakeside location and DJ'd skate nights. Skate rentals are C$7. ✉ *235 Queens Quay W, at Lower Simcoe St., Harbourfront, Toronto, Ontario* ☎ *416/973–4866* ⊕ *www.harbourfrontcentre.com/skating* Ⓜ *Union.*

AROUND THE WORLD WALKING TOUR

How fast can you circumnavigate the globe? Forget 80 days—in Toronto you can do it in a mere 80 minutes (give or take). Overwhelm your senses in Chinatown and the multicultural Kensington Market, and then take your time on a leisurely walk along Little Italy's main thoroughfare. These neighborhoods are food-centric, so start out hungry.

Chinatown

Start on Chinatown's periphery with a photo op. Three of the city's most recognizable buildings are visible here: the whimsically modernist **Sharp Centre for Design**, the **CN Tower** in the distance, and the Frank Gehry–designed **Art Gallery of Ontario**. Moving west, signs of Chinatown appear, literally and immediately. At the **Chinese Bakery** fuel up with sticky rice cakes and salty pork cookies. **Ten Ren Tea** is a favorite for bubble tea, milk tea, and traditional green tea. For a full meal of noodles, try **Swatow**, and for inexpensive dim sum at any time of day (or night), drop into **Rol San**. The intersection of Dundas and Spadina is one of the busiest in the city. The **Royal Bank of Canada building** here has a colorful history. Opened as a Yiddish theater in 1921, it became a burlesque theater and then a Chinese-language cinema before closing in the 1990s. All along Spadina, sidewalks spill over with bins of exotic fruit (rambutan, durian, dragon fruit) and dried fish, stacks of rattan baskets, and racks of inexpensive clothing. Chinese restaurants are plentiful, but Thailand, Japan, and Vietnam are also represented.

Kensington Soup

Cross Spadina to **Kensington Market,** via Baldwin Street. In the early 20th century this was an overwhelmingly Jewish neighborhood; one of the few remnants is the 1930 **Minsk Synagogue**. Today Kensington is a global marketplace: side streets are crammed with colorful storefronts selling cheese, produce, clothing, and ethnic foods. Get a cupcake at **Miss Cora's Kitchen**, a pair of vintage cowboy boots at **Courage My Love**, and unique gifts at **Good Egg** and the **Blue Banana**. Or watch the carnival go 'round, coffee in hand, at **I Deal**, with a you-wouldn't-guess-it's-vegan burrito from **Hot Beans**, a "double" (chickpea sandwich) from Caribbean **Patty King**, or a fresh-squeezed juice from **Urban Herbivore.**

On the Continent

Along College Street, the passage to Little Italy, the flavors alternate between old-world European, trendy Canadian, and off the map (Ethiopian, Mexican, Persian). **Café Diplomatico** has been a Little Italy institution since 1968: its sidewalk patio is a great place to chill with a Peroni or granita. Sadly, espresso isn't its forte; hit deliberately disheveled **Manic Coffee** instead. The Italian bakeries, restaurants, gelato shops, and newsstands multiply closer to the heart of Little Italy, around College and Grace streets. End your cultural tour with a taste of Portugal: a traditional *pastel de nata* (custard pastry) at **Nova Era**, one in a chain of Portuguese bakeries around the city.

1

Where to Start:	At the Art Gallery of Ontario (AGO).
Time/Length:	Two hours at a leisurely pace; longer if you're tempted by one of the many coffee shops or restaurants along the way. About 1½ miles.
Where to Stop:	Almost anywhere in Kensington or Little Italy is suited to whiling away minutes or hours; favorites are Hot Beans and Café Diplomatico.
Best Time to Go:	Any sunny day will do, though some shops and restaurants are closed Monday. Ending up in Little Italy at tea time (or pre-dinner drinks time) is a plan.
Worst Time to Go:	In this case the early bird doesn't catch the worm: start before 10 am and you'll be faced with shuttered storefronts. After 5 pm Kensington Market starts to wind down.
Highlights:	Art Gallery of Ontario, Sharp Centre for Design, Chinatown, Kensington Market, Little Italy.

GREAT ITINERARIES

Five Days in Toronto

To really see Toronto, a stay of at least one week is ideal. However, these itineraries are designed to inspire thematic tours of some of the city's best sights, whether you're in town for one day or five. We've also included a two-to-three-day escape to the Niagara region.

One Day: Architecture and Museums

Start at Queen and Bay by pondering Finnish architect Viljo Revell's eye-shaped **City Hall** and then its regal predecessor, **Old City Hall**, across the street. From here, head south through the **Financial District** to admire the historic skyscrapers before swinging west on Front Street to the spectacular **CN Tower**. It's not hard to find—just look up. If you have more time, walk up to King and catch a streetcar east to the restored Victorian industrial buildings of the **Historic Distillery District**; choose any of the amazing restaurants here for lunch.

Begin the afternoon at the **Royal Ontario Museum**. If the steep entrance fee makes you wince, admire the modern Crystal gallery from outside before moving on to the **Gardiner Museum of Ceramic Art**, across the street, or the quirky **Bata Shoe Museum** at St. George Street. Breathtaking views from **Panorama**, on the 51st floor of the Manulife Centre at Bay and Bloor streets, set the scene for a relaxing drink or dinner.

One Day: Shopping Around the World

Before the crowds descend at lunchtime, head for the aesthetically chaotic Spadina Avenue–Dundas Street intersection, the core of **Chinatown**, to browse the stalls overflowing with exotic fruits and vegetables, fragrant herbal tonics, and flashy Chinese baubles. Either pause here for a steaming plate of fried noodles, or try one of the juice bars, vegan restaurants, or empanada stands in nearby

Kensington Market (head west on Dundas to Augusta and turn right). After lunch, browse the South American and Caribbean shops and groceries, modern cafés, and funky clothing boutiques. Take the College streetcar east to Coxwell Avenue (about a 30-minute ride), where the dazzling bejeweled saris and shiny bangles of the **India Bazaar** beckon. A fiery madras curry washed down with a mango *lassi* (yogurt drink) or Kingfisher beer is the perfect way to end the day.

One Day: With Kids

Start early at the **Toronto Zoo**, where 700-plus acres of dense forests and winding creeks are home to more than 5,000 animals and 460 species. (Allow for extra time if you are reaching the zoo by public transportation, which could take over an hour.) Or venture out to the equally enthralling indoor exhibits and demonstrations of the **Ontario Science Centre.** If your kids are sports fans, the **Hockey Hall of Fame,** at Yonge and Front streets, might be just the ticket. In the afternoon explore kid-friendly attractions on Lake Ontario, starting with either the water park and IMAX theater at **Ontario Place** or a ride up **CN Tower** to test your nerves on the glass floor that "floats" over a 1,122-foot drop and take in a view that extends far enough to let you see the mist from Niagara Falls. Dinner at **Richtree Market** in Brookfield Place is extremely kid-friendly—market-style stalls prepare burritos, pizzas, and crepes.

One Day: Island Life

Pick up picnic supplies from **St. Lawrence Market** (closed Sunday and Monday), whose stalls offer a cornucopia of imported delicacies and delicious prepared foods. From here, walk to the **docks** at the foot of Bay Street and Queen's Quay to catch one of the ferries to the **Toronto Islands;**

the view of the city skyline is an added bonus. In summer, kids have the run of **Centre Island**. **Hanlan's Point** is infamous for its nude bathing, and **Ward's Island** has great sandy beaches and a restaurant, the Rectory Café, with a lakeside patio. One of the allures of Island life is the slow pace, so spend the afternoon rambling. If you'd like to cover more ground, rent a bicycle at the ferry docks. Winter is not without charms—namely, cross-country skiing and snowshoeing. When you're back downtown in the evening, keep the outdoorsy theme going with an alfresco dinner in the **Danforth, Little Italy**, or the **Historic Distillery District**—Toronto's only pedestrian-friendly entertainment village.

One Day: Neighborhood Watching

Begin the day window-shopping along the rows of restored Victorian residences on **Yorkville Avenue**, or reading at a sidewalk café along **Cumberland Street**. In the 1960s, before the country's most exclusive shops settled here, Yorkville was a hippie haven, attracting emerging Canadian musical artists like Joni Mitchell and Gordon Lightfoot. The shops spill onto **Bloor Street West**, and the strip between Yonge Street and Avenue Road is sometimes referred to as Toronto's Fifth Avenue. The **Royal Ontario Museum** is worth a peek, even if just from the street, to admire the shiny crystal-inspired modern structure. In stark contrast to Yorkvillian sophistication, the grungy shops along Bloor, west of Spadina, are housed in less lovingly restored turn-of-the-20th-century storefronts. Rest your legs in either **Future Bakery & Café**, a student-friendly outpost for comfort food, or the more upscale, Mediterranean spot **Splendido**. In the evening, take in a play, a concert, or a comedy show downtown at the **Second City**.

A Few Days: Niagara Getaway

If you have a few days to spare, start by succumbing to the force and brilliance of **Niagara Falls**. A ride on the **Maid of the Mist** is highly recommended, and in the afternoon—especially if you have kids—you may want to experience **Clifton Hill** in all its tacky, amusement-filled glory. Alternatively, head along the scenic Niagara Parkway to visit the **Botanical Gardens** or **White Water Walk**, more peaceful and natural attractions. Get dressed up for dinner at the Skylon Tower or another restaurant overlooking the falls and tuck in for a night at the slots. Admire the **fireworks** at 10 pm (Friday and Sunday in summer) from either your falls-view hotel room or the **Table Rock Centre**. The next day, a good breakfast is essential, perhaps at one of the many options in the Fallsview Casino Resort, to prepare for a day of wine tasting and strolling in bucolic **Niagara-on-the-Lake**. You'll need a car to follow the beautiful Niagara Parkway north to Niagara-on-the-Lake's **Queen Street** for shopping. Nibble and tipple the day away along the **Wine Route**, which follows Highway 81 as far west as Grimsby. Dinner at one of the wineries or the excellent restaurants, such as **Peller Estates Winery Restaurant**, then a night in one of the region's boutique hotels or luxurious B&Bs is an indulgent end to a great weekend. If you're here during the **Shaw Festival** (April–December), book a ticket for a play by George Bernard Shaw or one of his contemporaries.

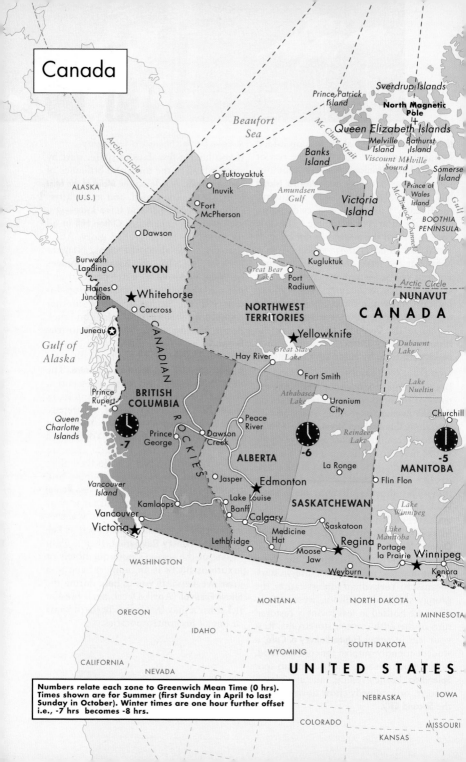

Canada

Beaufort
Sea

Arctic Circle

ALASKA
(U.S.)

○ Tuktoyaktuk
○ Inuvik
○ Fort
McPherson

○ Dawson

Prince Patrick
Island

Sverdrup Islands

**North Magnetic
Pole** ✛

Queen Elizabeth Islands

Melville
Island

Bathurst
Island

Viscount Melville
Sound

Somerset
Island

Prince of
Wales
Island

BOOTHIA
PENINSULA

Banks
Island

Amundsen
Gulf

Victoria
Island

Mc Clure Strait

McClintock Channel

Gulf

Burwash
Landing○

YUKON

○ Dawson

Haines
Junction ○

★ **Whitehorse**
○ Carcross

Juneau ✪

*Gulf of
Alaska*

Great Bear
Lake

Kugluktuk ○

Port
Radium

**NORTHWEST
TERRITORIES**

★ Yellowknife

Hay River ○

Great Slave
Lake

○ Fort Smith

Arctic Circle

NUNAVUT

C A N A D A

Dubawnt
Lake

Lake
Nueltin

Prince
Rupert ○

**BRITISH
COLUMBIA**

*Queen
Charlotte
Islands*

CANADIAN

ROCKIES

Prince
George ○

Dawson
Creek ○

Peace
River ○

*Athabasca
Lake*

○ Uranium
City

Reindeer
Lake

Churchill ○

-7 🕐 (clock)

Jasper ○

○ Lake Louise

ALBERTA

Banff ○

★ Edmonton

Calgary

La Ronge ○

-6 🕐 (clock)

Flin Flon ○

Lake
Winnipeg

-5 🕐 (clock)

MANITOBA

*Vancouver
Island*

Kamloops ○

Vancouver ○

Victoria ○ ★

Lethbridge ○

Medicine
Hat ○

Moose
Jaw ○

SASKATCHEWAN

Saskatoon ○

★ Regina

Weyburn ○

Lake
Manitoba

Portage
la Prairie ○

★ Winnipeg

Kenora ○

WASHINGTON

OREGON

MONTANA

IDAHO

WYOMING

NORTH DAKOTA

SOUTH DAKOTA

MINNESOTA

U N I T E D   S T A T E S

NEBRASKA

IOWA

CALIFORNIA

NEVADA

COLORADO

KANSAS

MISSOURI

**Numbers relate each zone to Greenwich Mean Time (0 hrs).
Times shown are for Summer (first Sunday in April to last
Sunday in October). Winter times are one hour further offset
i.e., -7 hrs becomes -8 hrs.**

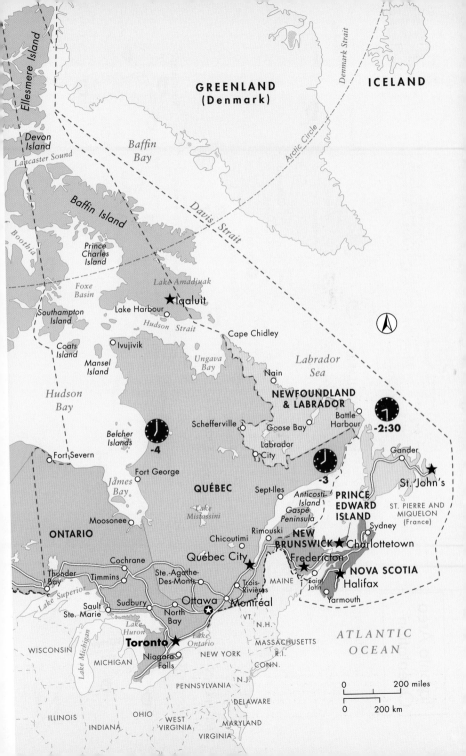

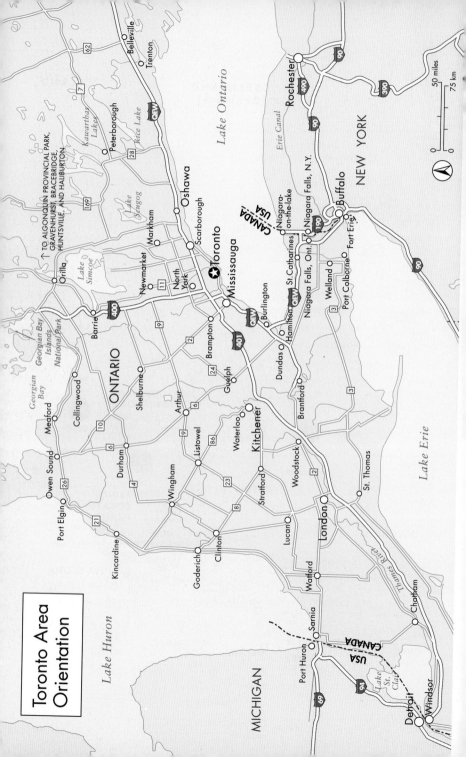

Toronto Area Orientation

Exploring Toronto

WORD OF MOUTH

"I love the Harbourfront area . . . stroll around, have a cone and/ or fries, bring your bike and ride all along the lakeshore, take the ferry over to the islands, have a picnic, take some great photos looking across the lake at downtown Toronto."

—OceanBreeze1

Updated by
Sarah Richards

"Toronto is like New York, as run by the Swiss," actor Peter Ustinov is rumored to have said. Indeed, this is a big, beautiful, and efficient city, one that has emerged from relative obscurity over the past half-century to become the center of culture, commerce, and communications in Canada. With its colorful ethnic mix, rich history, and breathtaking architecture, Toronto is nonstop adventure, from the top of the CN Tower to as far as the eye can see.

More than half of the 2.5 million residents who now live in Toronto were born and raised somewhere else, often very far away. Nearly 500,000 Italians give Greater Toronto one of the largest communities outside Italy; while South Asians, the biggest visible minority group inside Toronto, account for 12% of the population (nearly 300,000 people). It's also the home of the largest Chinese community in Canada and the largest Portuguese community in North America. The city hosts close to 200,000 Jewish people, nearly as many Muslims, and tens of thousands of Germans, joined by Greeks, Hungarians, East Indians, West Indians, Vietnamese, Maltese, South Americans, and Ukrainians—more than 80 ethnic groups in all, speaking more than 80 different languages. Toronto is also the home of Canada's largest gay and lesbian community.

Although the assimilation of these various cultures into the overall fabric of the city is ongoing, several ethnic neighborhoods have become attractions for locals and visitors. These include Kensington Market (west of Spadina Avenue between College and Dundas), Chinatown (around the Spadina Avenue and Dundas Street intersection), Greektown (Danforth Avenue between Chester and Jones), Little Italy (College Street between Euclid and Shaw), Little Poland (Roncesvalles Avenue between Queen and Dundas), Portugal Village (Dundas Street West, west of Bathurst), India Bazaar (Gerrard Street between Coxwell and Greenwood), and Koreatown (Bloor Street West between Bathurst and Christie).

A BRIEF HISTORY OF TORONTO

The city officially became Toronto on March 6, 1834, but its roots are much older. In the early 1600s a Frenchman named Etienne Brûlé was sent into the not-yet-Canadian wilderness by the famous explorer Samuel de Champlain to see what he could discover. He found the river and portage routes from the St. Lawrence to Lake Huron, possibly Lakes Superior and Michigan, and eventually Lake Ontario. The native Huron peoples had known this area between the Humber and Don rivers for centuries—and had long called it "Toronto," believed to mean "meeting place."

A bustling village called Teiaiagon grew up here, which became the site of a French trading post. After the British won the Seven Years' War, the trading post was renamed York in 1793. More than 40 years later the city again took the name Toronto. Following an unsuccessful American invasion in 1812, several devastating fires, and a rebellion in 1837, there was a slow but steady increase in the population of white Anglo-Saxon Protestants leading into the 20th century. Since World War II, Toronto has attracted residents from all over the world. Unlike the American "melting pot," Toronto is more of a "tossed salad" of diverse ethnic groups.

What this immigration has meant to Toronto is the rather rapid creation of a vibrant mix of cultures that echoes turn-of-the-20th-century New York City—but without the slums, crowding, and tensions. Torontonians embrace and take pride in their multicultural character, their tradition of keeping a relatively clean and safe city, and their shared belief in the value of everyone getting along and enjoying the basic rights of good health care, education, and a high standard of living.

Toronto is also filled with boutiques, restaurants, and cafés, and there are plenty of shops, both aboveground and on the PATH, Toronto's underground city—an 11-km-long (7-mi-long) subterranean walkway lined with eateries, shops, banks, and medical offices.

And then there are the oft-overlooked gems of Toronto, such as the beach-fringed Toronto Islands. These eight tree-lined islands—and more than a dozen smaller islets—that sit in Lake Ontario just off the city's downtown have been attracting visitors since 1833, especially during summer, when their more than 550 acres of parkland are most irresistible. From any of the islands you have spectacular views of Toronto's skyline, especially as the setting sun turns the skyscrapers to gold, silver, and bronze.

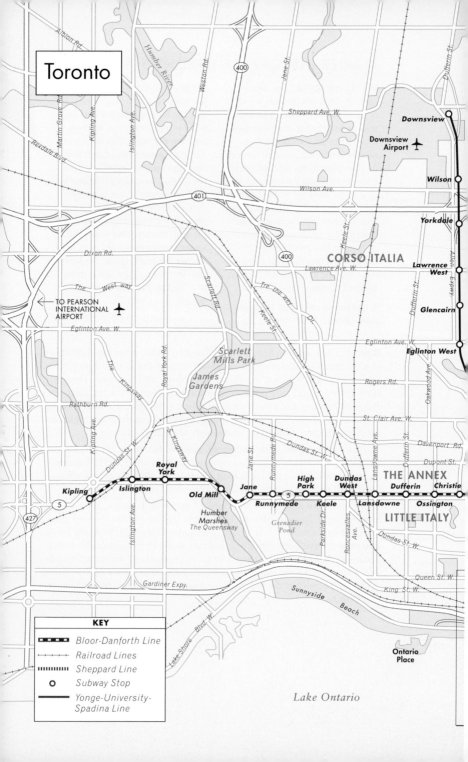

Toronto

TO PEARSON
INTERNATIONAL
AIRPORT

Downsview
Downsview
Airport

Wilson

Yorkdale

CORSO ITALIA

Lawrence
West

Glencairn

Eglinton West

THE ANNEX

Kipling   Islington   Royal
York

Old Mill   Jane   High   Dundas   Dufferin   Christie
Park   West

Runnymede   Keele   Lansdowne   Ossington

LITTLE ITALY

Humber
Marshes
The Queensway   Grenadier
Pond

Ontario
Place

Lake Ontario

KEY

- Bloor-Danforth Line
- Railroad Lines
- Sheppard Line
- ○ Subway Stop
- Yonge-University-
  Spadina Line

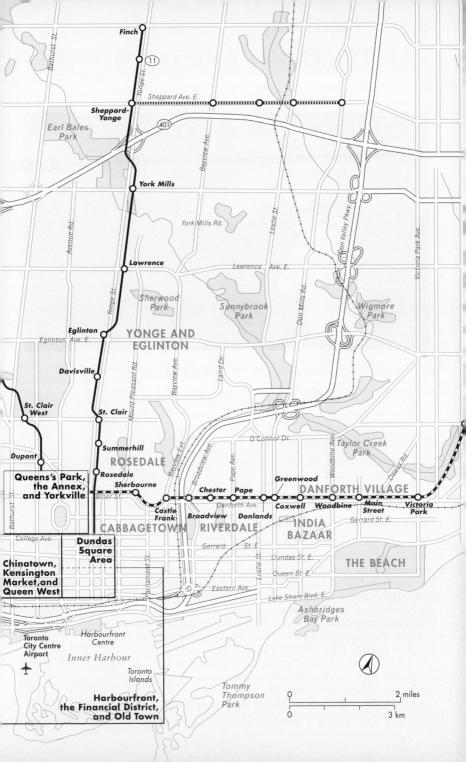

Finch

(11)

Sheppard-Yonge

Sheppard Ave. E.

Earl Bales Park

401

York Mills

York Mills Rd.

Lawrence

Lawrence Ave. E.

Sherwood Park

Sunnybrook Park

Wigmore Park

Eglinton

Eglinton Ave. E.

YONGE AND EGLINTON

Davisville

St. Clair West

St. Clair

Dupont

Summerhill

ROSEDALE

Queens's Park, the Annex, and Yorkville

Rosedale

Sherbourne

Bloor St.

Chester **Pape**

Greenwood

DANFORTH VILLAGE

O'Connor Dr.

Taylor Creek Park

Victoria Park

Castle Frank

Danforth Ave.

Coxwell **Woodbine**

Main Street

Broadview **Donlands**

CABBAGETOWN **RIVERDALE**

INDIA BAZAAR

Gerrard St. E.

THE BEACH

Dundas Square Area

College Ave.

Gerrard St. E.

Chinatown, Kensington Market, and Queen West

Dundas St. E.

Queen St. E.

Eastern Ave.

Lake Shore Blvd. E.

Ashbridges Bay Park

Toronto City Centre Airport

Harbourfront Centre

Inner Harbour

Toronto Islands

Harbourfront, the Financial District, and Old Town

Tommy Thompson Park

| 0 | | | 2 miles |
| 0 | | | 3 km |

HARBOURFRONT AND THE ISLANDS

The new century has brought renewed interest to Toronto's Harbourfront. Cranes dot the skyline as condominium buildings seemingly appear overnight. Pedestrian traffic increases as temperatures rise in spring and summer. Everyone wants to be overlooking, facing, or playing in Lake Ontario.

Above: Enjoying the skyline from one of Toronto's ferries; top right: A performance of the Luminato Cirque du Soleil; bottom right: One of the Toronto ferries.

The lakefront is appealing for strolls, and myriad recreational and amusement options make it ideal for those craving fresh air and exercise or with kids in tow. Before the drastic decline of trucking due to the 1970s oil crisis reduced the Great Lakes trade, Toronto's waterfront was an important center for shipping and warehousing. It fell into commercial disuse and was neglected for a long time. The Gardiner Expressway, Lake Shore Boulevard, and a network of rusty rail yards stood as hideous barriers to the natural beauty of Lake Ontario; the area overflowed with grain silos, warehouses, and malodorous towers of malt, used by local breweries. In the 1980s the city began to develop the waterfront for people-friendly purposes, and the trend continues today.

BEST TIME TO GO

If it's sun and sand you're looking for, you'll want to aim for a visit in June, July, or August. The cool breeze coming off Lake Ontario can be the perfect antidote to one of Toronto's hot and humid summer days, but in the off-season it can make things a little chilly if you aren't packing an extra layer.

WAYS TO EXPLORE

BOAT

The best way to enjoy the waterfront is to get right onto Lake Ontario. There are many different boat tours—take your pick from the vendors lining the Harbourfront's lakeside boardwalk—but most offer the same deal: a pleasant, hour-long jaunt around the harbor for about C$20. More extravagant packages include dinner and dancing at sunset.

To soak up the sun and skyline views, use the public ferry to head for the **Toronto Islands.** The best beaches are those on the southeast tip of Ward's Island, Centre Island Beach, and the west side of Hanlan's Point. The most secluded and natural beach on the Islands is Hanlan's Beach, backed by a small dunes area, a portion of which is clothing-optional. Most families with kids head for Centre Island Beach.

BIKE AND STROLL

To get away from busy downtown and stretch your legs, the Toronto Islands are the perfect destination. This car-free open space has paved trails for biking, in-line skating, or strolling; miles and miles of green space to explore; and picture-perfect vistas of the surrounding lake and skyline.

Bicyclists, power-walkers, and Sunday strollers alike enjoy the **Martin Goodman Trail,** the Toronto portion of the 219-mi Lake Ontario Waterfront Trail. The string of beaches along the **eastern waterfront** (east of Coxwell Avenue) is connected by a continuous boardwalk that parallels the Martin Goodman Trail. At the western end of this walking and biking trail is **Sunnyside Park Beach,** once the site of a large amusement park, and now a favorite place for a swim in the "tank" (a huge heated pool) or a snack at the small restaurant inside the handsomely restored 1922 Sunnyside Bathing Pavilion. Between the eastern and western beaches is the downtown stretch of the trail that hugs the waterfront and passes by a sewage treatment plant (no, it's not all pretty), marinas, a waterfowl conservation area, a sugar refinery, the Harbourfront, and the Toronto Island ferry terminal.

FESTIVALS AND EVENTS

The **Canadian National Exhibition** (CNE, or "the Ex") takes place the last two weeks of August and Labor Day weekend, attracting more than 3 million people each year. It began in 1879 primarily as an agricultural show and today is a collection of carnival workers pushing C$5 balloons, midway rides, bands, horticultural and technological exhibits, parades, dog swims, horse shows, and (sometimes) top-notch performances. Stick around for nightly fireworks at 10. Throughout the year, the **Harbourfront Centre** hosts a dizzying array of festivals, covering cultural celebrations such as Kuumba (February) and the Mexican Day of the Dead (November), foodie-friendly fêtes like the Hot & Spicy Festival (August) and Vegetarian Food Fair (September), and literary events such as the International Festival of Authors (October).

HARBOURFRONT, THE FINANCIAL DISTRICT, AND OLD TOWN

Packed into this area, which runs from Bay Street east to Parliament Street and from Queen Street south to Lake Ontario, you'll find the city's main attractions and historical roots and the financial hub of the nation. As many of its attractions are outdoors, this downtown core is especially appealing during warm weather, but should a sudden downpour catch you off guard, shelter can be found in the area's museums and underground shopping city.

In fair weather, the Harbourfront area is appealing for strolls, and myriad recreational and amusement options make it ideal for those traveling with children. The nearby Toronto Islands provide a perfect escape from the sometimes stifling summer heat of downtown.

Farther north lies the Financial District with its unique and wonderful architectural variety of skyscrapers. Most of the towers have bank branches, restaurants, and retail outlets on their ground floors and are connected to the PATH, an underground city of shops and tunnels.

East of the Financial District is Old Town, where the city got its municipal start as the village of York in 1793. A pleasing natural disorder now prevails in this neighborhood, which blends old and new buildings, residential and commercial space. At the far east end of Old Town is one of Toronto's hottest entertainment destinations, the Historic Distillery District, in which contemporary galleries, bustling pubs, and chic restaurants fill restored Victorian-era factories.

GETTING HERE

The Financial District is at Queen, King, and Union stations. To get to the Harbourfront, take the 509 Queens Quay streetcar from Union Station. Use the 503 King streetcar to explore Old Town, including the Historic Distillery District.

TORONTO DAY TOURS

BOAT TOURS

If you want to get a glimpse of the skyline, try a boat tour. There are many boat-tour companies operating all along the boardwalk of Harbourfront.

Toronto Harbour Tours. Toronto Tours runs one-hour, narrated tours of the waterfront from mid-April through late October, which cost C$25. ☎ 416/869–1372 ⊕ www.torontotours.com.

Great Lakes Schooner Company. To further your appreciation for man-made beauty, Great Lakes Schooner Company lets you see Toronto's skyline from the open deck of the 165-foot three-mastered *Kajima*. Two-hour tours are available early June to the end of September and cost C$22. ☎ 416/203–2322 ⊕ www.tallshipcruisestoronto.com.

BUS TOURS

For a look at the city proper, take a bus tour around the city. If you want the freedom to get on and off the bus when the whim strikes, take a hop-on, hop-off tour.

Toronto City Tours. Affiliated with Toronto Harbour Tours, Toronto City Tours offers two-hour guided tours in 24-passenger buses for C$40. ☎ 416/869–1372 ⊕ www.torontotours.com.

Gray Line Sightseeing Bus Tours. Gray Line Sightseeing Bus Tours has London-style double-decker buses and turn-of-the-20th-century trolleys. ✉ 610 Bay St., north of Dundas St., Dundas Square Area, Toronto, Ontario ☎ 800/594–3310 ⊕ www.grayline.ca.

Toronto Hippo Tours. Toronto Hippo Tours gives amphibious narrated land–water tours hourly every afternoon from May to October (C$38). Take in the downtown sights in what's basically a boat with wheels that retract in time to splash into the lake and float along the waterfront. ☎ 877/635–5510, 416/703–4476 ⊕ www.torontohippotours.com.

SPECIAL-INTEREST TOURS

Toronto Field Naturalists. Toronto Field Naturalists schedules about 150 guided tours during the year, each focusing on an aspect of nature, such as geology or wildflowers, and with starting points accessible by public transit. ☎ 416/593–2656 ⊕ www.torontofieldnaturalists.org.

WALKING TOURS

Heritage Toronto. To get a feel for Toronto's outstanding cultural diversity, check out Heritage Toronto, which has free guided walking tours on weekends and occasional holidays from May to early October. They last 1½ to 2 hours and cover one neighborhood or topic. ☎ 416/338–3886 ⊕ www.heritagetoronto.org.

Royal Ontario Museum. The Royal Ontario Museum runs 1½- to 2-hour ROMwalk tours on such topics as Rosedale, the city's upper-crust neighborhood. Several free walks are given weekly. ☎ 416/586–8097 ⊕ www.rom.on.ca/programs.

A Taste of the World. A Taste of the World runs food-, literary-, and ghost-theme tours of various lengths in several neighborhoods. Reservations are essential; prices range from C$25–45. ☎ 416/923–6813 ⊕ www.torontowalksbikes.com.

TIMING

If you have kids in tow, plan on spending a whole day in the Harbourfront area. If you're going to the Toronto Islands, add 45 minutes total traveling time just to cross the bay and return on the same ferry. Museum buffs will want to linger for at least an hour each in the Hockey Hall of Fame and the Design Exchange. In Old Town, if you want to catch the farmers setting out their wares at the St. Lawrence Market, you should arrive as early as 5 am on Saturday.

TOP ATTRACTIONS

Fodor's Choice ★

CN Tower. The tallest freestanding tower in the Western Hemisphere, this landmark stretches 1,815 feet and 5 inches high and marks Toronto with its distinctive silhouette. The CN Tower is tall for a reason: prior to the opening of this telecommunications tower in 1976, so many tall buildings had been built over the previous decades that lower radio and TV transmission towers had trouble broadcasting. The C$63 million building weighs 130,000 tons and contains enough concrete to build a curb along Highway 401 from Toronto to Kingston, some 262 km (162 mi) to the east. It's worth a visit if the weather is clear, despite the steep fee. Six glass-front elevators zoom up the outside of the tower at 20 feet per second, and the ride takes less than a minute—a rate of ascent similar to that of a jet taking off. Each elevator has one floor-to-ceiling glass wall—three opaque walls make the trip easier on anyone prone to vertigo—and at least one now has glass floor panels.

There are four observation decks. The **Glass Floor Level,** which is exactly what it sounds like, is about 1,122 feet above the ground. This may be the most photographed indoor location in the city—lie on the transparent floor and have your picture taken from above like countless visitors before you. Don't worry—the glass floor can support 85,000 pounds. Above is the **Look Out Level,** at 1,136 feet; one floor more, at 1,150 feet, is the excellent **360 Revolving Restaurant.** If you're here to dine, your elevator fee is waived. At an elevation of 1,465 feet, the **Sky Pod** is the world's highest public observation gallery. All the levels provide spectacular panoramic views of Toronto, Lake Ontario, and the Toronto Islands. On really clear days you may see Lake Simcoe to the north and the mist rising from Niagara Falls to the south. Adrenaline junkies can try the new **EdgeWalk** attraction, which allows harnessed tower-goers to roam "hands free" around a 5-foot ledge outside the tower's main pod. Reservations are required.

On the ground level, the **Marketplace at the Tower** has 12,500 square feet of shopping space with quality Canadian travel items and souvenirs, along with a shop selling Inuit art. There's also the **Far Coast Cafe,** with seating for 300; the **Maple Leaf Cinema,** which screens the 20-minute documentary *The Height of Excellence*, about the building of the Tower; and the **Themed Arcade,** with the latest in virtual-game experiences and the Himalamazon motion picture ride based loosely on the Himalayan and Amazon regions. ■TIP➔ **Peak visiting hours are 11 to 4; you may wish to work around them, particularly on weekends.** Ticket packages get more expensive with more attractions included. ⊠ *301 Front St. W, at Bremner Blvd., Harbourfront, Toronto, Ontario* ☎ *416/868–6937, 416/362–5411 restaurant, 416/601–3833 EdgeWalk*

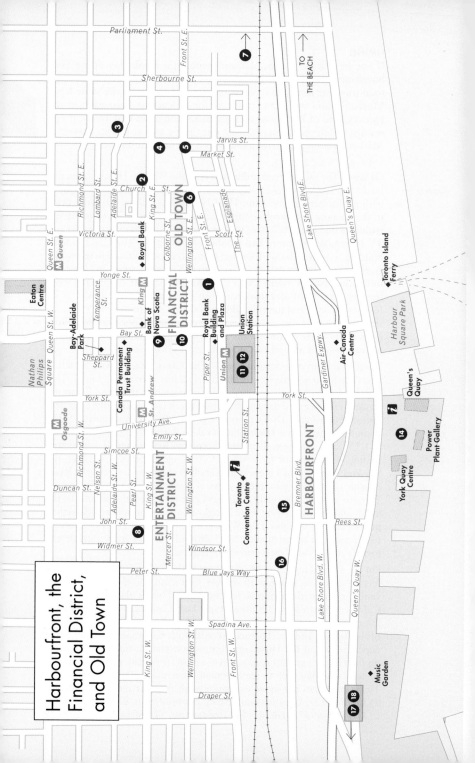

Harbourfront, the
Financial District,
and Old Town

Parliament St.

Sherbourne St.

Front St. E.

7

TO
THE BEACH

3

Richmond St. E.

Lombard St.

Adelaide St. E.

4

5

Jarvis St.

Market St.

Church St.

2

King St. E.

6

The Esplanade

Colborne St.

Wellington St. E.

Front St. E.

Scott St.

OLD TOWN

Lake Shore Blvd. E.

Queen's Quay E.

Queen St. E.

Ⓜ Queen

Victoria St.

◆ Royal Bank

Toronto Island
Ferry ◆

Harbour
Square Park

Yonge St.

Ⓜ King

FINANCIAL
DISTRICT

1

Bay-Adelaide
Park

Temperance St.

◆ Bank of
Nova Scotia

9

10

◆ Royal Bank
building
and Plaza

Union
Station

Ⓜ Union

11 **12**

Gardiner Expwy.

Air-Canada
Centre ◆

Queen's Quay

Eaton
Centre

Bay St.

Canada Permanent
Trust Building ◆

Sheppard
St. ◆

Piper St.

Ⓘ

14

Power
Plant Gallery

Nathan
Philips
Square

Queen St. W.

York St.

St. Andrew Ⓜ

University Ave.

Station St.

York St.

York Quay
Centre

Ⓜ
Osgoode

Richmond St. W.

Emily St.

Bremner Blvd.

HARBOURFRONT

Simcoe St.

Nelson St.

Adelaide St. W.

Pearl St.

King St. W.

Wellington St. W.

◆ Toronto
Convention Centre

7

15

Duncan St.

ENTERTAINMENT
DISTRICT

Rees St.

John St.

Mercer St.

8

16

Queen's Quay W.

Widmer St.

Windsor St.

Peter St.

Blue Jays Way

Lake Shore Blvd. W.

Wellington St. W.

Spadina Ave.

Music
Garden ◆

Front St. W.

King St. W.

17 **18**

Draper St.

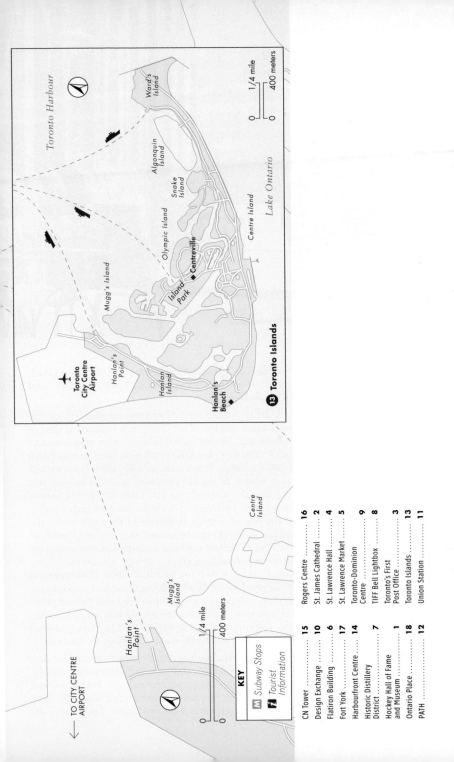

TO CITY CENTRE
AIRPORT

Toronto Harbour

Lake Ontario

Toronto City Centre Airport

Hanlan's Point

Mugg's Island

Olympic Island

Algonquin Island

Snake Island

Ward's Island

Hanlan's Island

Island Park

Centreville

Centre Island

Hanlan's Beach

Mugg's Island

Hanlan's Point

Centre Island

🔟③ Toronto Islands

0   1/4 mile

0   400 meters

KEY

Ⓜ Subway Stops

ℹ️ Tourist
   Information

CN Tower **15**
Design Exchange **10**
Flatiron Building **6**
Fort York **17**
Harbourfront Centre **14**
Historic Distillery
District **7**
Hockey Hall of Fame
and Museum **1**
Ontario Place **18**
PATH **12**

Rogers Centre **16**
St. James Cathedral **2**
St. Lawrence Hall **4**
St. Lawrence Market **5**
Toronto-Dominion
Centre **9**
TIFF Bell Lightbox **8**
Toronto's First
Post Office **3**
Toronto Islands **13**
Union Station **11**

The cobblestoned Historic Distillery District is now home to more than 100 upscale galleries, shops, and restaurants.

⊕ *www.cntower.ca* ✉ *First 2 observation levels C$23, Sky Pod C$29, combined packages start at C$35* ⊙ *Sun.–Thurs., 9 am–10 pm; Fri. and Sat., 9 am–10:30 pm* Ⓜ *Union.*

★ **Design Exchange.** A delightful example of streamlined moderne design (a later and more austere version of art deco), this building is clad in polished pink granite and smooth buff limestone, with stainless-steel doors. Between 1937 and 1983 the DX (as it's now known) was home to the Toronto Stock Exchange. Don't miss the witty stone frieze carved above the doors—a banker in top hat marching behind a laborer and sneaking his hand into the worker's pocket. Only in Canada, where socialism has always been a strong force, would you find such a political statement on the side of a stock exchange. In the early 1990s the building reopened as a nonprofit center devoted to promoting Canadian design. The permanent collection contains examples of contemporary and older decorative arts, furniture, graphic design, housewares, lighting, and tableware. Check the Web site for information about rotating exhibits which make good use of the old trading floor. And stop into the Design Exchange shop to browse witty gifts like stackable "totem pole" mugs or kerchiefs with stenciled mustaches. ✉ *234 Bay St., at King St., Financial District, Toronto, Ontario* ☎ *416/363–6121* ⊕ *www.dx.org* ✉ *C$10* ⊙ *Weekdays 10–5, weekends noon–5* Ⓜ *King, St. Andrew.*

Fodor's Choice **Historic Distillery District.** Utterly charming, this excellently restored collec-
★ tion of Victorian industrial buildings, complete with interlinking cobble-stone lanes, has become a hub of independent eateries, boutiques, and galleries. The carefully preserved former Gooderham and Worts Distillery (founded in 1832) has been reborn as a cultural center. The 13-acre site

includes 45 19th-century buildings and a pedestrian-only village that houses more than 100 tenants— including galleries, artist studios and workshops, boutiques, a brewery, upscale restaurants, bars, and cafés. In 2011, Ontario Spring Water Sake Company, Toronto's first sake distillery, opened. It uses local (Huntsville) water, highly regarded by the brewery's *toji* (brewmaster), and

> **DOWN TOWN**
>
> According to the *Guinness Book of World Records*, the PATH is the biggest underground shopping complex in the world. Maps to guide you through this labyrinth are available in many downtown news and convenience stores.

imported specialty rice. Other delicious detours include the Soma Chocolatemaker, Mill Street Brewpub, and Brick Street Bakery. Live music, outdoor exhibitions, fairs, and special events take place year-round, but summer months are the best time to visit. Hour-long walking tours (C$19) take place every day at 11:30 am and 3:30 pm; or you can join one of the once-hourly (11 am–6 pm) Segway lesson-tours (C$39–69) at Segway of Ontario (in Building 37). ⊠ *55 Mill St., south of Front St. and east of Parliament St., Old Town, Toronto, Ontario* ☎ *416/364–1177* ⊕ *www. thedistillerydistrict.com* 🅿 *Parking from C$5* ⊙ *Mon.–Thurs. 11–7, Fri. 11–9, Sat. 10–9, Sun. 11–6; individual tenant hrs may vary, including restaurants, cafés, and boutiques* Ⓜ *King, then streetcar 504 east.*

☾ **Hockey Hall of Fame and Museum.** Even if you're not a hockey fan, it's
★ worth a trip here to see this shrine to Canada's favorite sport. Exhibits include the original 1893 Stanley Cup, as well as displays of goalie masks, skate and stick collections, great players' jerseys, video displays of big games, and a replica of the Montréal Canadiens' locker room. Grab a stick and test your speed and accuracy in the "shoot out" virtual experience, or strap on a goalie mask and field shots from big-name players like Wayne Gretzky and Mark Messier with the "shut out" computer simulation. It's also telling that this museum is housed in such a grand building, worthy of any fine art collection. A former Bank of Montréal branch designed by architects Darling & Curry in 1885, the building is covered with beautiful ornamental details. Note the richly carved Ohio stone and the Hermès figure supporting the chimney near the back. At the corner of Front and Yonge streets, the impressive statue—a seventeen-foot bronze entitled "Our Game"—is a busy photo-op. ■ TIP→ Entrance is through Brookfield Place on the lower level of the east side. ⊠ *30 Yonge St., at Front St., Financial District, Toronto, Ontario* ☎ *416/360–7765* ⊕ *www.hhof.com* 🅿 *C$15* ⊙ *Sept.– June, weekdays 10–5, Sat. 9:30–6, Sun. 10:30–5; July and Aug., Mon.– Sat. 9:30–6, Sun. 10–6* Ⓜ *Union.*

■ QUICK
BITES

Brookfield Place. A modern office and retail complex cleverly designed to incorporate the facades of the Bank of Montréal and other older buildings under a vaulted glass roof, Brookfield Place is one of the most impressive architectural spaces in Toronto. The atrium under the glass canopy makes a lovely place to sit and enjoy a cup of coffee and pastry from Richtree Market, or a snack at the mozzarella bar, Obikà. ⊠ *181 Bay St., between Front St. W and Wellington St. W, Financial District, Toronto, Ontario* Ⓜ *Union.*

Fodor's Choice ★ **St. Lawrence Market.** Both a lovely landmark and an excellent place to sample Canadian bacon, this market was originally built in 1844 as the first true Toronto city hall. The building now has an exhibition hall upstairs—the Market Gallery—where the council chambers once stood. The food market, which began growing up around the building's square in the early 1900s, is considered one of the world's best.

Local and imported foods such as fresh shellfish, sausage varieties, and cheeses are renowned. Stop and snack on Canadian bacon, also known as "peameal bacon," at the Market's Carousel Bakery. The plain brick building across Front Street, on the north side, is open on Saturday mornings for the 200-year-old farmers' market; it's a cornucopia of fine produce and homemade jams, relishes, and sauces from farms just north of Toronto. On Sunday the wares of more than 80 antiques dealers are on display in the same building. ⊠ *Front and Jarvis sts., Old Town, Toronto, Ontario* ☎ *416/392–7219* ⊕ *www.stlawrencemarket. com* ☉ *Tues.–Thurs. 8–6, Fri. 8–7, Sat. 5–5; farmers' market Sat. 5–2; antiques market Sun. 5–5* Ⓜ *Union.*

TIFF Bell Lightbox. A five-story architectural masterpiece in the city's center, this glass-paneled building houses the year-round headquarters of the internationally acclaimed, wildly popular Toronto International Film Festival. Throughout the year—except in September when TIFF fever paralyzes the city—visitors can attend film-related lectures, watch screenings, and enjoy smaller film festivals, including Sprockets, a celebration of children's film that takes place each April. A stellar educational program includes summer camps, ongoing workshops—how to produce a stop-motion movie, for example—and gallery exhibitions that highlight big-shot filmmakers such as Tim Burton and Federico Fellini; faculty and post-secondary students get free admission to special TIFF offerings every Friday (a limited number of tickets is available one hour before each event). The TIFF Cinematheque, open to the public, plays world cinema classics and contemporary art house films all year. Hit the concession stand for gourmet treats far beyond the standard popcorn fare, or head to one of the two restaurants in the complex for the traditional dinner-and-a-movie pairing. ⊠ *Reitman Square, 350 King St. W, at John St., Entertainment District, Toronto, Ontario* ☎ *416/599–8433, 888/599–8433* ⊕ *www.tiff.net/tiffbelllightbox* ☉ *box office 10 am–10 pm* Ⓜ *St.Andrew.*

☼ ★ **Toronto Islands.** These eight narrow, tree-lined islands, plus more than a dozen smaller islets, just off the city's downtown in Lake Ontario, provide a gorgeous green retreat with endless outdoor activities. The more than 550 acres of parkland are hard to resist, especially in the summer, when they're usually a few degrees cooler than the city.

Sandy beaches fringe the islands; the best are on the southeast tip of Ward's Island, the southernmost edge of Centre Island, and the west side

The outstanding St. Lawrence food market, one of the finest in the world, sells a huge variety of local and imported specialties.

of Hanlan's Island. In 1999 a portion of Hanlan's Beach was officially declared "clothing-optional" by Toronto's City Council. The declaration regarding Ontario's only legal nude beach passed without protest—perhaps a testament to the city's live-and-let-live attitude. The section frequented by gays and lesbians is at the east end; the straight section is more westerly. There are free changing rooms near each side. Lake Ontario's water is declared unfit for swimming a few days every summer, so call ☎ 416/392–7161 or check ⊕ *www.toronto.ca/beach* for water-quality reports. Swimming in the lagoons and channels is prohibited. In summer, Centre Island has rowboat and canoe rentals. Bring picnic fixings or something to grill in one of the park's barbecue pits, or grab a quick (and expensive) bite at one of the snack bars. Note that the consumption of alcohol in a public park is illegal in Toronto. There are supervised wading pools, baseball diamonds, volleyball nets, tennis courts, and even a disc-golf course. The winter can be bitterly cold on the islands, but snowshoeing and cross-country skiing with downtown Toronto over your shoulder are appealing activities.

All transportation is self-powered: no private cars are permitted. The boardwalk from Centre Island to Ward's Island is 2½ km (1½ mi) long. Centre Island gets so crowded that no bicycles are allowed on its ferry from the mainland during summer weekends. Consider renting a bike for an hour or so once you get there and working your way across the islands. Bike rentals can be found south of the Centre Island ferry docks on the Avenue of the Islands.

You may want to take one of the equally frequent ferries to Ward's or Hanlan's Island. Both islands have tennis courts and picnic and

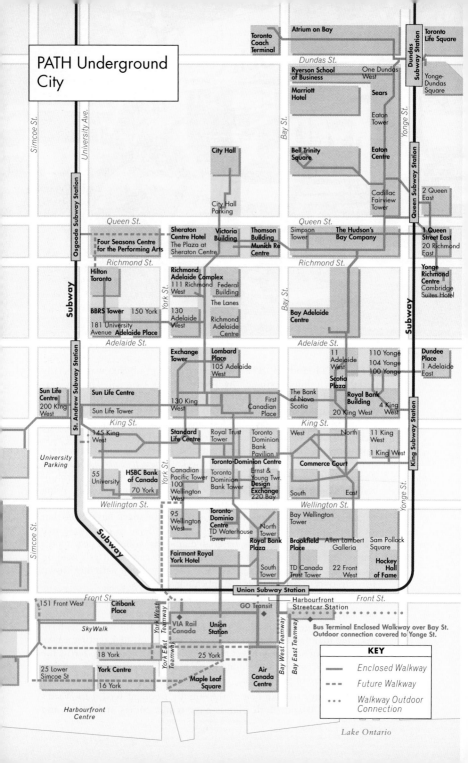

sunbathing spots. Late May through early September, the ferries run between the docks at the bottom of Bay Street and the Ward's Island dock between 6:35 am and 11:45 am; for Centre and Hanlan's islands, they begin at 8 am. Ward's Island Ferries run roughly at half-hour intervals most of the working day and at quarter-hour intervals during peak times such as summer evenings. On Canada Day (July 1) the lines are slow moving. In winter the ferries run only to Ward's Island on a limited schedule. There are more than a dozen rides, including a restored 1890s merry-go-round with four dozen-plus hand-carved animals, at the children's amusement park **Centreville** (☎ *416/203–0405* ⊕ *www. centreisland.ca ⊠ Day Pass C$31 ☉ June weekdays 10:30–6, weekends 10:30–8; May and Sept., weekends 10:30–5; July and Aug., daily 10:30–8).* It's modeled after a late-19th-century village, complete with shops, a town hall, and a small railroad station. Among the rides are a kiddie roller coaster, swan paddleboats, a sky ride, a kid-size antique train ride, a log-flume ride, pony rides, games, and more. Older kids may enjoy the paddleboats and log flume ride—if not, the beach and bike rentals aren't far away. The free Far Enough Farm has all kinds of animals to pet and feed, including piglets, geese, and cows. There's no entrance fee to the modest 14-acre park, although there's a charge for rides. ■TIP➔ **A day pass is worthwhile instead of tickets for more than two rides.** ⊠ *Ferries at foot of Bay St. and Queen's Quay, Harbourfront, Toronto, Ontario* ☎ *416/392–8186 for island information, 416/392–8193 for ferry information* ⊕ *www.toronto.ca/parks/island* ⊠ *Ferry C$6.50 round-trip* Ⓜ *Union, then streetcar 509 or 510.*

★ **Toronto-Dominion Centre.** Ludwig Mies van der Rohe, a virtuoso of modern architecture, designed this five-building masterwork, though he died before its completion in 1985. As with his acclaimed Seagram Building in New York, Mies stripped the TD Centre's buildings to their skin and bones of bronze-color glass and black-metal I-beams. The tallest building, the Toronto Dominion Bank Tower, is 56 stories high. The only decoration consists of geometric repetition, and the only extravagance is the use of rich materials, such as marble counters and leather-covered furniture. In summer, the exterior central courtyard, Oscar Peterson Square, is full of office workers eating lunch and listening to one of many free outdoor concerts. Inside the low-rise square TD banking pavilion at King and Bay streets is a virtually intact Mies interior. Inside the TD Centre's Waterhouse Tower is the **Gallery of Inuit Art** (⊠ *79 Wellington St. W* ☎ *416/982–8473 ⊠ Free ☉ Weekdays 8–6; weekends 10–4).* Their collected works, equal to that of the Smithsonian, focus on the bank's renowned collection of Inuit art from the vast Arctic region in northern Canada: Over 200 pieces are on display in glass cases. ⊠ *55 King St. W, at Bay St., Financial District, Toronto, Ontario* Ⓜ *St. Andrew.*

WORTH NOTING

Flatiron Building. One of several wedge-shape buildings scattered all over North America, Toronto's Flatiron occupies the triangular block between Wellington, Scott, and Front streets. It was erected in 1892 as the head office of the Gooderham and Worts distilling company. ⊠ *Front St. between Church and Scott sts., Old Town, Toronto, Ontario* Ⓜ *King.*

A popular destination for families, Ontario Place features downtown Toronto's only water park.

Fort York. The most historic site in Toronto is a must for anyone interested in the origins of the city. Toronto was founded in 1793 when the British built Fort York to protect the entrance to the harbor during Anglo-American strife. Twenty years later the fort was the scene of the bloody Battle of York, in which explorer and general Zebulon Pike led U.S. forces against the fort's outnumbered British, Canadian, and First Nations defenders. The Americans won this battle—their first major victory in the War of 1812—and burned down the provincial buildings during a six-day occupation. A year later British forces retaliated when they captured Washington, D.C., and torched its public buildings, including the Executive Mansion. Exhibits include restored barracks, kitchens, and gunpowder magazines, plus changing museum displays. There are guided tours, marching drills, and cannon firings daily during the summer months. ⊠ *250 Fort York Blvd., between Bathurst St. and Strachan Ave., Harbourfront, Toronto, Ontario* ☎ *416/392–6907* ⊕ *www.fortyork.ca* ⊠ *C$9* ☉ *Mid-May–Aug., daily 10–5; Sept.–mid-May, weekdays 10–4, weekends 10–5* Ⓜ *Bathurst, then streetcar 511 south.*

☺ **Harbourfront Centre.** Stretching from just west of York Street to Spadina Avenue, the original Harbourfront opened in 1974, rejuvenating more than a mile of city. Today Harbourfront Centre, a streamlined version of the original concept, draws more than 3 million visitors to the 10-acre site each year. At Harbourfront Centre, **Queen's Quay Terminal** (⊠ *207 Queen's Quay W* ☎ *416/203–0510* ⊕ *www.qqterminal.com*) is a former Terminal Warehouse building, where goods shipped to Toronto were stored before being delivered to shops in the city. In 1983 it was transformed into a magnificent, eight-story building with specialty shops, eateries, the 450-seat Fleck Dance Theatre—and harbor views. Exhibits of contemporary painting, sculpture, architecture, video, photography, and design are mounted at the **Power Plant** (⊠ *231 Queen's Quay W* ☎ *416/973–4949* ⊕ *www.thepowerplant.org* ⊒ *C\$6; tours are free* ⊙ *Tues. and Thurs.–Sun. noon–6, Wed. noon–8*). It was built in 1927 as a power station for the Terminal Warehouse's ice-making plant and can be spotted by its tall red smokestack. Sunday Scene tours at 2 pm, given by experts in the field, provide an in-depth look at the current exhibition; more general, staff-led guided tours of the gallery start at 7 pm on Wednesday and 2 pm on Saturday. ■ TIP→ **On Wednesday from 5 pm to 8 pm admission is free.** Developed by renowned cellist Yo-Yo Ma and garden designer Julie Moir Messervy, the **Music Garden** on the south side of Queen's Quay was planned for Boston, but when that venue fell through, Toronto was the pair's next choice. The garden is Yo-Yo Ma's interpretation of Johann Sebastian Bach's *Cello Suite No. 1* (which consists of six movements—Prelude, Allemande, Courante, Sarabande, Minuet, and Gigue). Each movement is reflected in the park's elaborate design: undulating riverscape, a forest grove of wandering trails, a swirling path through a wildflower meadow, a conifer grove, a formal flower parterre, and giant grass steps. Among the seasonal events in Harbourfront Centre are the Ice Canoe Race in late January, Winterfest in February, a jazz festival in June, Canada Day celebrations and the Parade of Lights in July, the Authors' Festival and Harvest Festival in October, and the Swedish Christmas Fair in November. The **York Quay Centre** (⊠ *235 Queen's Quay W* ☎ *416/973–4000, 416/973–4866 rink info, 416/973–4963 craft studio*) is center hosts concerts, theater, readings, and even skilled artisans. The Craft Studio, for example, has professional craftspeople working in ceramics, glass, metal, and textiles from February to December (Tuesday through Sunday), in full view of the public. A shallow pond outside is used for canoe lessons in warmer months and has the largest artificial ice-skating rink in North America in more wintry times. At the nearby Nautical Centre, many private firms rent boats and give lessons in sailing and canoeing. ⊠ *410 Queen's Quay W, Harbourfront, Toronto, Ontario* ☎ *416/973–4000 event hotline, 416/973–4600 offices* ⊕ *www.harbourfrontcentre.com* Ⓜ *Union, then streetcar 509 or 510 west.*

QUICK BITES

There are plenty of places inside **Queen's Quay** for a quick sandwich, freshly squeezed juice, or ice-cream concoction. You can also check out one of the food trucks outside, selling french fries.

Ontario Place. The waterfront entertainment complex stretches along three man-made islands and includes Soak City, downtown Toronto's only water park complete with tube rides, a sandy beach, and lounge pool; pedal boats at Bob's Boat Yard; the Wilderness Adventure Ride; and the Mars Simulator Ride. The **Cinesphere,** an enclosed dome with a six-story movie screen, uses the world's first IMAX projection system, a Canadian invention. The 16,000-seat outdoor **Molson Amphitheatre** stages performances by singers and rock groups throughout summer, and the **Atlantis Pavilions** is a 32,000-square-foot entertainment and dining facility. Live children's entertainment on two stages is included in the admission price to the park. *The Big Comfy Couch, Toopy and Binoo,* and other children's favorites are featured. ■ TIP→ **The Play All Day Pass allows unlimited use of most rides and attractions, including daytime Cinesphere IMAX and large-format films.** Weekends in September bring several annual events to this venue: the Great White North Dragon Boat Challenge, the Toronto In-Water Boat Show, and the Fall Fishing Festival and Kids' Fishing Derby. ⊠ *955 Lake Shore Blvd. W, across from Exhibition Place, Harbourfront, Toronto, Ontario* ☎ *866/663–4386 recording* ⊕ *www.ontarioplace.com* 🎫 *Pass C$29* ⊙ *May and mid-Sept.–late Sept., weekends 10–6; June, weekdays 10–6, weekends 10–8; July–early Sept., daily 10–8* Ⓜ *Union, then streetcar 509 southwest.*

PATH. This subterranean universe emerged in the mid-1960s partly to replace the retail services in small buildings that were demolished to make way for the latest skyscrapers and partly to protect office workers from the harsh winter weather. As each major building went up, its developers agreed to build and connect their underground shopping areas with others and with the subway system. You can walk from beneath Union Station to the Fairmont Royal York hotel, the Toronto-Dominion Centre, First Canadian Place, the Sheraton Centre, the Bay, Eaton Centre, and City Hall without ever seeing the light of day, encountering everything from art exhibitions to buskers (the best are the winners of citywide auditions, who are licensed to perform throughout the subway system) and walkways, fountains, and trees. There are underground passageways in other parts of the city—one beneath Bloor Street and another under College Street (both run from Yonge to Bay Street)—but this is the city's most extended subterranean network.

Ⓒ **Rogers Centre.** One of Toronto's most famous landmarks, the Rogers Centre is home to baseball's Blue Jays and was the world's first stadium with a fully retractable roof. Rogers Communications, the owner of the Blue Jays, bought the stadium, formerly known as the SkyDome, in February 2005 for a mere C$25 million. A new playing surface and a state-of-the-art integrated scoring and display system were added, including two color screens that display the action on either side of the outfield wall. One way to see the 52,000-seat stadium is to buy tickets for a Blue Jays or Argos game or one of the many other events that take place here. You might watch a cricket match, Wrestlemania, a monster-truck race, a family ice show, or a rock concert—even the large-scale opera *Aïda* has been performed here. You can also take a one-hour guided walking tour. Depending on several factors, you may find yourself in the middle of the field, in a press box, in the dressing rooms, or, if a roof tour is available, 36 stories above home plate on a catwalk. ⊠ *1 Blue Jays Way, tour entrance at Front and John sts., between Gates 1 and 2, Harbourfront, Toronto, Ontario* ☎ *416/341–2770 for tours, 416/341–3663 for events and shows, 416/341–1234, 888/654–6529 for Blue Jays information* ⊕ *www.rogerscentre.com* 🎫 *Tour C$16* ⊙ *Tours 11 am, 1 pm, 3 pm daily (canceled during special events)* Ⓜ *Union.*

St. James Cathedral. Even if bank towers dwarf it now, this Anglican church with noble Gothic revival spires has the tallest steeple in Canada.

Its illuminated clock once guided ships into the harbor. This is the fourth St. James Cathedral on this site; the third burned down in the Great Fire of 1849. Stand near the church most Sundays after the 9 am service ends (about 10:10 am) and be rewarded with a glorious concert of ringing bells. ⊠ *65 Church St., at King St., Old Town, Toronto, Ontario* ☎ *416/364–7865* ⊕ *www.stjamescathedral.on.ca* Ⓜ *King.*

St. Lawrence Hall. Erected on the site of the area's first public meeting space, the St. Lawrence Hall, built in 1850–51, demonstrates Renaissance Revival architecture at its finest. Erected for musical performances and balls, it is here that famed opera soprano Jenny Lind sang, where antislavery demonstrations were held, and where P. T. Barnum first presented the midget Tom Thumb. Take time to admire the exterior of this architectural gem, now used for everything from concerts to wedding receptions and graduation parties. If there's no event scheduled, you can take a peek at the photos in the East Room on the third floor; the various notable figures displayed once performed or lectured here. ⊠ *157 King St. E, Old Town, Toronto, Ontario* ☎ *416/392–7130* ⊕ *www.stlawrencemarket.com/hall/index.html* Ⓜ *Union.*

Ⓒ **Toronto's First Post Office.** Dating from 1833, this small working post office continues to use quill pens, ink pots, and sealing wax. Exhibits include reproductions of letters from the 1820s and 1830s. Distinctive cancellation stamps are used on all outgoing cards and letters. ⊠ *260 Adelaide St. E, Old Town, Toronto, Ontario* ☎ *416/865–1833* ⊕ *www. townofyork.com* 🖃 *Free* ⊙ *Weekdays 9–4, weekends 10–4* Ⓜ *King.*

Union Station. Historian Pierre Berton wrote that the planning of Union Station recalled "the love lavished on medieval churches." Indeed, this train depot can be regarded as a cathedral built to serve the god of steam. Designed in 1907 and opened by the Prince of Wales in 1927, it has a 40-foot-high Italian tile ceiling and 22 pillars weighing 70 tons apiece. The main hall, with its lengthy concourse and light flooding in from arched windows at each end, was designed to evoke the majesty of the country that spread out by rail from this spot. The names of the towns and cities across Canada that were served by the country's two railway lines, Grand Trunk (incorporated into today's Canadian National) and Canadian Pacific, are inscribed on a frieze along the inside of the hall. As train travel declined, the building came very near to being demolished in the 1970s, but public opposition eventually proved strong enough to save it, and Union Station is now a vital transport hub. Commuter, subway, and long-distance trains stop here. ⊠ *65–75 Front St. W, between Bay and York sts., Financial District, Toronto, Ontario* Ⓜ *Union.*

2

CHINATOWN, KENSINGTON MARKET, AND QUEEN WEST

The areas along Dundas and Queen streets typify Toronto's ethnic makeup and vibrant youthfulness. To many locals, the Dundas and Spadina intersection means Chinatown and Kensington Market, while Queen West, which was the home of 1990s comedy troupe Kids in the Hall and pop-rockers Barenaked Ladies, has always been a haven for shoppers and trendsetters. On the western fringe, the rejuvenated West Queen West neighborhood is quickly becoming Toronto's newest hot spot.

Chinatown and Kensington Market, often explored together, are popular destinations for tourists and locals alike. On a weekend morning, the sidewalks are jam-packed with pedestrians shopping for cheap produce and Chinese trinkets, lining up for a table at one of Chinatown's many restaurants, or heading to "the Market" for a little afternoon shopping. On the last Sunday of each month (May–October), Kensington Market goes car-free, and the streets explode with live entertainment, street performances, and vendors selling handicrafts and clothing.

Queen West is busy any time of the year, mostly with teenagers hanging out at the MuchMusic building and young fashionistas-in-training shopping up a storm. Beyond Bathurst Street, the scene changes drastically. Gone is the more mainstream vibe, to be replaced by artsy types, hipsters, and the occasional young bohemian family, leisurely making their way in and out of small independent boutiques, cutting-edge art galleries, and laid-back cafés. Trinity Bellwoods Park punctuates the neighborhood at the center and provides a beautiful setting for a picnic or a bench break.

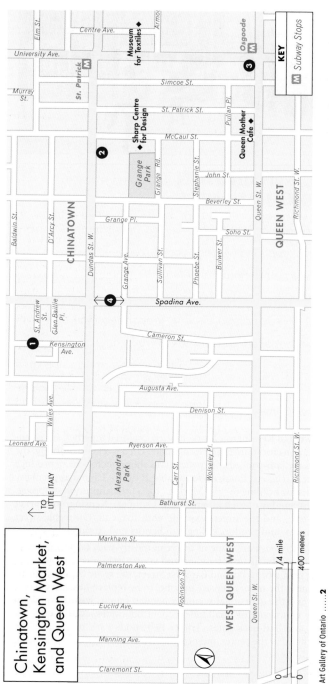

Chinatown, Kensington Market, and Queen West

CHINATOWN

QUEEN WEST

WEST QUEEN WEST

← TO LITTLE ITALY

Elm St.
Centre Ave.
University Ave.
Murray St.
St. Patrick Ⓜ
Museum for Textiles ◆
Armoury
Osgoode
Ⓜ Osgoode
❸
Simcoe St.
St. Patrick St.
Sharp Centre ◆ for Design
McCaul St.
Grange Park
Grange Rd.
Stephanie St.
John St.
Beverley St.
Soho St.
Bulwer St.
Phoebe St.
Sullivan St.
Grange Ave.
Dundas St. W.
Grange Pl.
Baldwin St.
D'Arcy St.
Pullan Pl.
Queen Mother Cafe ◆
Queen St. W.
Richmond St. W.
❷
❹ Spadina Ave.
St. Andrew St.
Glen Baillie Pl.
Kensington Ave.
Wales Ave.
❶
Cameron St.
Augusta Ave.
Denison St.
Leonard Ave.
Ryerson Ave.
Carr St.
Wolseley Pl.
Richmond St. W.
Alexandra Park
Bathurst St.
Markham St.
Palmerston Ave.
Robinson St.
Euclid Ave.
Manning Ave.
Claremont St.
Queen St. W.

1/4 mile
400 meters
0
0

KEY
Ⓜ Subway Stops

Art Gallery of Ontario **2**
Campbell House **3**
Kensington Market **1**
Spadina Avenue **4**

GETTING HERE

The Osgoode subway station is ideal for getting to Queen West. Alternatively, the 501 streetcar will take you through Queen West, all the way to the end of West Queen West. The 510 Spadina streetcar (which originates at the Spadina subway station) services Chinatown and Kensington Market.

TIMING

In Queen West, the Campbell House merits at least a half hour; the Art Gallery an hour or more. Chinatown is at its busiest (and most fun) on Sunday, but be prepared for very crowded sidewalks and much jostling. Kensington is great any time, although it can feel a bit sketchy at night, and it gets mobbed on weekend afternoons. Just strolling around any of these neighborhoods can gobble up an entire afternoon.

TOP ATTRACTIONS

Fodor's Choice ★ **Art Gallery of Ontario.** In 2008, a transformed AGO opened to the public with a major expansion designed by world-renowned architect and Toronto native son Frank Gehry. Now it's hard to miss; the monumental glass and titanium facade hovering over the main building is a stunning beauty. Near the entrance, you'll find visitors of all ages climbing in and around Henry Moore's large *Two Forms* sculpture, on the corner of Dundas and McCaul streets. Inside, the collection, which had an extremely modest beginning in 1900, is now in the big leagues, especially in terms of its exhibitions of landscape paintings from the 19th and 20th centuries. Be sure to take a pause in the light and airy Walker Court, to admire Gehry's spiraling Baroque Stair; climb the staircase and look straight up for the best view.

The Canadian Wing includes major works by such northern lights as Emily Carr, Cornelius Krieghoff, David Milne, and Homer Watson, plus the Thomson Collection with pieces by Paul Kane, Tom Thomson, and Lawren Harris. The AGO also has a growing collection of works by such world-famous artists as Rembrandt, Hals, Van Dyck, Hogarth, Reynolds, Chardin, Renoir, de Kooning, Rothko, Oldenburg, Picasso, Rodin, Degas, Matisse, and many others. A rediscovered early-17th-century piece by Flemish painter Peter Paul Rubens, *Massacre of the Innocents*, was unveiled in 2008. The brand-new Weston Family Learning Centre offers art courses, camps, lectures, and interactive exhibitions for adults and children alike. If you have time, take a peek at the open excavation of buried artifacts sealed in the foundations of the Grange, the original site of the Art Gallery of Toronto, which was built in 1817. Themed tours take in unusual sites, such as the Grange kitchen, or specific genres, like Canadian art; check the Web site for dates and times. AGO Highlights tours run daily at 1 pm. ✉ *317 Dundas St. W, at McCaul St., Chinatown, Toronto, Ontario* ☎ *416/979–6648* ⊕ *www.ago.net* ☞ *C$19.50; permanent collection free on Wed. after 6 pm* ⊙ *Tues. and Thurs.–Sun. 10–5:30, Wed. 10–8:30* Ⓜ *St. Patrick.*

Chinatown. Compact and condensed, Toronto's Chinatown—which is actually the main or original Chinatown in the city, as five other areas with large Chinese commercial districts have sprung up elsewhere—covers much of the area of Spadina Avenue from Queen Street to College

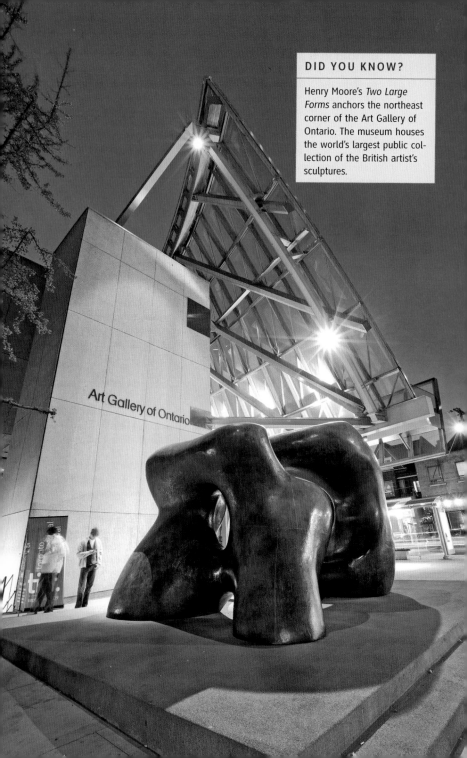

Art Gallery of Ontario

Street, running along Dundas Street nearly as far east as Bay Street. The population is more than 100,000, which is especially impressive when you consider that just over a century ago there was only a single Chinese resident, Sam Ching, who ran a hand laundry on Adelaide Street.

Especially jumbled at its epicenter, the Spadina–Dundas intersection, Chinatown's rickety storefronts selling (real and fake) jade trees, lovely sake sets, Chinese herbs, and fresh fish are packed every day of the week. On Sunday, Chinese music blasts from storefronts, cash registers ring, and bakeries, markets, herbalists, and restaurants do their best business of the week. ☒ *Spadina Ave., at Dundas St. W, Chinatown, Toronto, Ontario* ⊕ *www.chinatownbia.com* Ⓜ *St. Patrick, then streetcar 505 west.*

QUICK BITES

Queen Mother Café. Queen Street West is lined with cafés and restaurants, and one solid choice is the Queen Mother Café, a neighborhood institution popular with art students and broadcast-media types. Serving Lao-Thai and Italian cuisine, the "Queen Mum" is open until 1 am (Sunday until midnight) for wholesome meals and rich desserts at reasonable prices. ☒ *208 Queen St. W, at St. Patrick St., Queen West, Toronto, Ontario* ☎ *416/598–4719* Ⓜ *Osgoode.*

Kensington Market. This collection of colorful storefronts, crumbling brick houses, delightful green spaces, and funky street stalls titillates all the senses. On any given day you can find Russian rye breads, barrels of dill pickles, fresh fish, imported cheese, and ripe fruit. Kensington's collection of vintage-clothing stores is the best in the city.

The site sprang up in the early 1900s, when Russian, Polish, and Jewish inhabitants set up stalls in front of their houses. Since then the district, or "market"—named after the area's major street—has become a sort of United Nations of stores. Unlike the members of the UN, however, these vendors get along well with one another. Jewish and Eastern European shops sit side by side with Portuguese and Caribbean ones, as well as with a sprinkling of Vietnamese and Chinese establishments. ■TIP→ Saturday or Sunday are the best days to visit, preferably by public transit; parking is difficult. ☒ *Bordered by College St. on the north, Spadina Ave. on the east, Dundas St. on the south, and Bellevue Ave. on the west, Kensington Market, Toronto, Ontario* ☉ *Daily dawn–dusk* Ⓜ *St. Patrick, then streetcar 505 west.*

QUICK BITES

King's Café. In a neighborhood where the bohemian vegetarian lifestyle is the norm, King's Café has become a mainstay for diners seeking healthy grub with an Asian accent. Artists, students, and young professionals flock to this serene and airy interior with wide windows overlooking bustling Augusta Avenue. Specialties include enoki mushrooms in seaweed and spinach and King's Special Vegetable Soup, a hearty broth with homemade veggie nuggets, taro, and fried tofu. ☒ *192 Augusta Ave., Kensington Market, Toronto, Ontario* ☎ *416/591–1340* Ⓜ *St. Patrick, then streetcar 505 west.*

WORTH NOTING

Campbell House. The Georgian mansion of Sir William Campbell, the sixth chief justice of Upper Canada, is now one of Toronto's best house museums. Built in 1822 in another part of town, the Campbell House was moved to this site in 1972. It has been restored with elegant early-19th-century furniture. Costumed guides detail the social life of the upper class. Note the model of the town of York as it was in the 1820s and the original kitchen. ✉ *160 Queen St. W, Queen West, Toronto, Ontario* ☎ *416/597–0227* ⊕ *www.campbellhousemuseum.ca* 🖾 *C$6* ⊙ *Oct.–mid-May, Tues–Fri., 9:30–4:30; mid-May–Sept., Tues–Fri., 9:30–4:30, weekends noon–4:30* Ⓜ *Osgoode.*

> **WORD OF MOUTH**
>
> "I'd recommend Chinatown— Kensington Market is nearby . . . and has Wanda's Pie in the Sky. [Enjoy] people watching from their patio on a sunny corner and all sorts of REALLY GOOD pies." —morningglory47

Old City Hall. Opened in 1899, and used until 1965 when "new" City Hall was built across the street, the old municipal building is still the home of the provincial courts, county offices, and marriage bureau. This imposing building was designed by E. J. Lennox, who was also the architect for Casa Loma and the King Edward Hotel. Note the huge stained-glass window as you enter. The fabulous gargoyles above the front steps were apparently the architect's witty way of mocking certain turn-of-the-20th-century politicians; he also carved his name under the eaves on all four faces of the building. The building has appeared in countless domestic and international TV shows and feature films. It's been made even more famous by the hundreds of gay and lesbian marriages that have been performed here since the summer of 2003. ✉ *60 Queen St. W, Downtown, Toronto, Ontario* ⊙ *Weekdays 8:30–5* Ⓜ *Queen.*

Spadina Avenue. Spadina (pronounced "Spa-*dye*-nah"), running from the lakeshore north to College Street, has never been chic. For decades it has housed a collection of inexpensive stores, factories that sell wholesale if you have connections, ethnic food stores, and eateries, including some first-class, if modest-looking, Chinese restaurants. Each new wave of immigrants—Jewish, Chinese, Portuguese, East and West Indian, South American—has added its own flavor to the mix, but Spadina–Kensington's basic bill of fare is still bargains galore. Here you can find discounts of up to half off the prices of Yorkville stores, yards of remnants piled high in bins, designer clothes minus the labels, and the occasional rock-and-roll nightspot and interesting greasy spoon. A streetcar line runs down the wide avenue to Front Street. ✉ *from Queen's Quay W. to College St. Toronto, Ontario.*

Toronto's network of streetcars provide an excellent method of transportation for getting around downtown.

**EN
ROUTE** **Leslieville.** Perhaps because of its location, far from much-hyped and highly publicized West Queen West and Ossington, Leslieville has been quietly gentrifying into a colorful and exciting strip of interior design shops, hip eateries, funky boutiques, and independent cafés that is often labeled by trend-spotters (much to the disdain of locals) as Toronto's Brooklyn. Interior design shops stand out, but the vibe has more of a community feel due to a tight-knit collection of shop owners with regular customers. And like the nearby Beach neighborhood, the sidewalks are often filled with baby strollers and dog walkers.

It's quaint at times, with dusty antiques shops, old-fashioned ice cream parlors, and the occasional old-school appliance shop thrown into the mix, but the offerings lean more toward local designer boutiques, cute bakeries, organic butcher shops, cheese emporia, homey diners, chic eateries, and, in keeping with the chilled-out vibe of the area, an unusually large selection of independent coffee shops.

To explore Leslieville, take the 501 Queen streetcar east from downtown to Coxwell Avenue and walk west along Queen Street East.

Neighborhood Watch: W. Queen West and Beyond

West Queen is home to an increasing number of trendy boutiques and cutting-edge galleries.

Grunge meets chic along Queen Street west of Bathurst, dubbed "West Queen West" by locals. While it's still possible to find a run-down hardware store shouldering a high-end hipster bar, more of the latter are moving in these days. Almost completely devoid of the familiar chains that plague older sister Queen West, this area is instead filling with vegan spa resorts, trendy ethnic restaurants, and European kitchenware shops; much farther west a bustling art scene is blossoming.

The neighborhood's landmarks, the **Drake Hotel** and the **Gladstone Hotel,** enjoy much success for their creative, eclectic decor and their happening nightlife. Businesses like these, which revolutionized the once-shabby district and gave it its current über-cool image, helped pave the way for a second wave of émigrés. An eclectic smattering of restaurants and more than 300 art galleries vie for real estate with fair-trade coffee shops and boutiques featuring Canada's hottest new designers.

The previously shady strip along Ossington Street, north of Queen West, is Toronto's newest *it* spot. Fashion designers, artists and musicians, and creative restaurateurs have flooded the street, and the area now attracts attention for its sudden and celebrated gentrification.

Even farther west, after the overpass next to the Gladstone Hotel, is Parkdale, a once crime-infested and still fairly run-down neighborhood that has become home to North America's largest Tibetan community. Apartment buildings streaked with prayer flags and shops offering everything from beef *momos* (dumplings) to singing bowls have been a welcome improvement over the previously derelict storefronts.

Boundaries: From Bathurst west along Queen Street West.

Getting Here: Take the subway to Queen or Osgoode TTC stop, then the streetcar 501 west.

CLOSE UP

Neighborhood Watch: The Beach

2

Although the area has been officially renamed The Beach, it actually comprises four separate beaches.

The Beach. Queen Street West represents the city's of-the-moment trends, but the Beach neighborhood, 15 minutes east of the Queen subway stop, is old-school bohemian. This pricey area is bounded by Neville Park Road to the east and Woodbine Avenue to the west. The main strip, Queen Street East, has a funky flair *and* a small-town feel, and it's easy to spend an afternoon strolling the delightful yet crowded (in summer) boardwalk along the shore of Lake Ontario. Musicians often perform at the parks fronting the boardwalk, where you're also likely to see artists selling their wares. You could also do some window-shopping on Queen Street East, which is lined with antiques stores and specialty boutiques and shops. An annual jazz festival in July attracts more than 400 musicians and thousands of listeners to this laid-back community.

This neighborhood's official name has been a source of controversy since the 1980s. It boils down to whether you view the four separate beaches—Woodbine, Balmy, Kew, and Scarboro—as one collective entity or plural. When the area decided to welcome tourists with fancy, emblematic street signs, the long-running debate surfaced. "The Beach" folks won, but not before the dispute was settled fairly with a democratic vote in spring 2006.

Big Dog Bakery. One of the more unusual neighborhood stores is this bakery for dogs. ⊠ *2014 Queen St. E, The Beach, Toronto, Ontario* ☎ *416/551–0234* ⊕ *www.bigdogbakery. com.* **Murphy's Law.** For something to drink, stop at one of several Irish pubs such as this local favorite. ⊠ *1702 Queen St. E, The Beach, Toronto, Ontario* ☎ *416/690–5516* ⊕ *www. murphyslaw.ca.* **Licks.** This neighborhood institution is great for burgers and ice cream. ⊠ *1962 Queen St. E, The Beach, Toronto, Ontario* ☎ *416/362–5425* ⊕ *www.lickshomeburgers.com.*

Boundaries: Queen Street East, between Woodbine Avenue and Neville Park Road.

Getting Here: From Queen or Osgoode subway station, take Queen streetcar 501 east.

QUEEN'S PARK, THE ANNEX, AND YORKVILLE

This vast area that encompasses a huge chunk of Toronto's downtown core holds several important attractions, but it couldn't feel further from a tourist trap if it tried, bringing together Toronto's upper crust, Ontario's provincial politicians, and Canada's intellectual set. Take a break in one of The Annex's many casual spots and you could be rubbing shoulders with a student cramming for an exam, a blocked author looking for inspiration, or a busy civil servant picking up a jolt of caffeine to go.

The large, oval Queen's Park circles the Ontario Provincial Legislature and is straddled by the sprawling, 160-acre downtown campus of the University of Toronto. Wandering this neighborhood will take you past century-old colleges, Gothic cathedrals, and plenty of quiet benches overlooking leafy courtyards and student-filled parks.

The University of Toronto's campus overflows west into The Annex, where students and scholarly types while away the hours after class. This frantic section of Bloor Street West abounds with ethnic restaurants and plenty of student-friendly cafés and bars, plus two of the city's must-see attractions: the Bata Shoe Museum and Casa Loma.

At the eastern end of The Annex, near St. George Street, Bloor Street West morphs into Yorkville, an affluent neighborhood characterized by the Royal Ontario Museum at its northern tip. Big-name boutiques and elegant cafés are tucked into the Victorian houses that line the small, tidy back streets to the north—Yorkville Avenue and Cumberland Street.

GETTING HERE

Use the subway to reach Yorkville (Museum and Bay stations), the University of Toronto (St. George and Queen's Park stations), Casa Loma (Dupont station), The Annex (Spadina and Bathurst stations), and Queen's Park (Queen's Park station).

TIMING

The Queen's Park, Annex, and Yorkville area is a nice place to take a stroll any time of year because many of the attractions bring you indoors. A visit to the legislature and one or two of the museums or libraries would make a nice half-day (or more) program; allot at least one hour each for the Royal Ontario and Gardiner museums. Give yourself at least a few hours for a full tour of Casa Loma and about an hour for the Bata Shoe Museum.

TOP ATTRACTIONS

The Annex. Born in 1887, when the burgeoning town of Toronto engulfed the area between Bathurst Street and Avenue Road north from Bloor Street to the Canadian Pacific Railway tracks at what is now Dupont Street, the countrified Annex soon became an enclave for the well-to-do; today it attracts an intellectual set. Timothy Eaton of department-store fame built a handsome structure at 182 Lowther Avenue (since demolished). The prominent Gooderham family, owners of a distillery, erected a lovely red castle at the corner of St. George Street and Bloor Street, now the home of the exclusive York Club.

As Queen Victoria gave way to King Edward, old money gave way to new money and ethnic groups came and went. Upon the arrival of developers many Edwardian mansions were demolished to make room for bland 1960s-era apartment buildings.

Still, the Annex, with its hundreds of attractive old homes, can be cited as a prime example of Toronto's success in preserving lovely, safe streets within the downtown area. Examples of late-19th-century architecture can be spotted on Admiral Road, Lowther Avenue, and Bloor Street, west of Spadina Avenue. Round turrets, pyramid-shape roofs, and conical spires are among the pleasures shared by some 20,000 Torontonians who live in this vibrant community, including professors, students, writers, lawyers, and other professional and artsy types. Bloor Street between Spadina and Palmerston keeps them fed and entertained with its bohemian collection of used-record stores, whole-foods shops, juice bars, and restaurants from elegant Italian to aromatic Indian. ⊠ *From Bathurst St. to Spadina Ave. along Bloor St. W, The Annex, Toronto, Ontario* Ⓜ *Bathurst, Spadina.*

★ **Bata Shoe Museum.** Created by Sonja Bata, wife of the founder of the Bata Shoe Company, this shoe museum holds a permanent collection of 10,000 varieties of foot coverings and, through the changing fashions, highlights the craft and sociology of making shoes. Some items date back more than 4,000 years. Pressurized skydiving boots, iron-spiked shoes used for crushing chestnuts, and smugglers' clogs are among the items on display. Elton John's boots have proved wildly popular, but Marilyn Monroe's red leather pumps give them a run for their money. Ongoing exhibits such as "Chronicles of the Riches" have featured the bear-fur shoes of samurai and Napoléon Bonaparte's black silk socks. Admission is free every Thursday from 5 to 8 pm. ✉ *327 Bloor St. W, at St. George St., The Annex, Toronto, Ontario* ☎ *416/979–7799* ⊕ *www. batashoemuseum.ca* ✉ *C\$14* ⊗ *Mon.–Wed., Fri., and Sat. 10–5, Thurs. 10–8, Sun. noon–5* Ⓜ *St. George.*

⟳ **Casa Loma.** A European-style castle, Casa Loma was commissioned by Sir Henry Pellatt, a soldier and financier. This grand display of extravagance has 98 rooms, two towers, creepy passageways, and lots of secret panels. The home's architect, E. J. Lennox, also designed Toronto's Old City Hall and the King Edward Hotel. Pellatt spent more than C\$3 million to construct his dream (that's in 1913 dollars), only to lose his house to the tax man just over a decade later. Some impressive details are the giant pipe organ; the reproduction of Windsor Castle's Peacock Alley; the majestic, 60-foot-high ceiling of the Great Hall; the mahogany-and-marble stable, reached by a long, underground passage; and the extensive, 5-acre estate gardens (open May–October). The rooms are copies of those in English, Spanish, Scottish, and Austrian castles. This has been the location for many a horror movie and period drama, an episode of the BBC's *Antiques Roadshow*, and several Hollywood blockbusters, including *Chicago* and *X-Men*. Self-guided audio tours are available in eight languages for C\$3. Admission includes a docudrama about Pellatt's life. ■ TIP→ A tour of Casa Loma is a good 1½-km (1-mi) walk, so wear sensible shoes. And if you're traveling with young children, note strollers must be left on the first floor. ✉ *1 Austin Terr., The Annex, Toronto, Ontario* ☎ *416/923–1171* ⊕ *www. casaloma.org* ✉ *C\$20* ⊗ *Daily 9:30–5, last admission at 4* Ⓜ *Dupont.*

Hart House. A neo-Gothic student center built in 1911–19, Hart House represents the single largest gift to the University of Toronto. Vincent Massey, a student here at the turn of the 20th century, regretted the absence of a meeting place and gym for students and convinced his father to build one. It was named for Vincent's grandfather, Hart, the founder of Massey-Ferguson, once the world's leading supplier of farm equipment. Originally restricted to male students, Hart House has been open to women since 1972.

Keep your eyes peeled for artwork scattered throughout the building, including a revolving collection of works by famed Canadians like Emily Carr and evocative landscape paintings by the Group of Seven. Hart House founder Vincent Massey filled the walls of the house with artwork so that the students would "consciously or unconsciously . . . develop an interest in it." The project to build a permanent collection, which holds more than 600 important works by both emerging and established Canadian

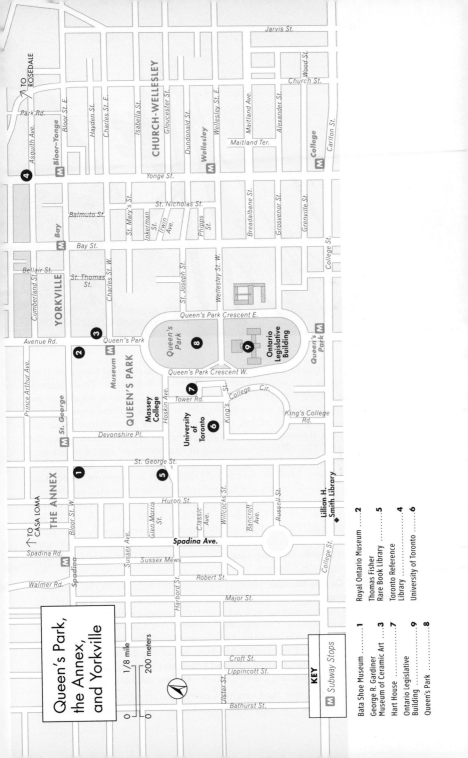

Queen's Park, the Annex, and Yorkville

0   1/8 mile
0   200 meters

TO ROSEDALE
TO CASA LOMA

THE ANNEX

YORKVILLE

QUEEN'S PARK

CHURCH-WELLESLEY

Queen's Park

Ontario Legislative Building

Massey College

University of Toronto

Lillian H. Smith Library

KEY

Ⓜ Subway Stops

Bata Shoe Museum 1
George R. Gardiner
Museum of Ceramic Art ...3
Hart House 7
Ontario Legislative
Building 9
Queen's Park 8

Royal Ontario Museum 2
Thomas Fisher
Rare Book Library 5
Toronto Reference
Library 4
University of Toronto 6

Jarvis St.
Wood St.
Church St.
Park Rd.
Bloor St. E.
Hayden St.
Charles St. E.
Isabella St.
Gloucester St.
Dundonald St.
Wellesley St. E.
Maitland Ave.
Alexander St.
College St.
Carlton St.
Maitland Ter.
Wellesley
Asquith Ave.
Bloor-Yonge Ⓜ
Bay Ⓜ
Yonge St.
Balmuto St.
St. Nicholas St.
Inkerman St.
Twin Ave.
Phipps St.
Breadalbane St.
Grosvenor St.
Grenville St.
College St.
Bellair St.
Cumberland St.
St. Thomas St.
Charles St. W.
St. Joseph St.
Wellesley St. W.
Bay St.
St. Mary's St.
Avenue Rd.
Prince Arthur Ave.
Queen's Park
Museum Ⓜ
Queen's Park Crescent E.
Queen's Park Crescent W.
Queen's Park Ⓜ
Hoskin Ave.
Tower Rd.
College St.
Cir.
King's College Rd.
Devonshire Pl.
St. George Ⓜ
St. George St.
Bloor St. W.
Glen Morris St.
Huron St.
Classic Ave.
Willcocks St.
Bancroft Ave.
Russell St.
Spadina Ⓜ
Spadina Rd.
Sussex Ave.
Sussex Mews
Robert St.
Major St.
Harbord St.
College St.
Walmer Rd.
Spadina Ave.
Croft St.
Lippincott St.
Ulster St.
Bathurst St.
King's College

A striking modern addition showcases some of the 6 million items in the Royal Ontario Museum's collection.

artists, began in 1922 with the purchase of the painting *Georgian Bay, November,* by Group of Seven member A. Y. Jackson. Two hundred works are on display throughout the building, most of which can be viewed by anyone willing to wander in and out of the rooms. Each year a new piece is added, carefully chosen by a committee made up of mainly students, and today the collection is reported to be worth close to C$17 million. Comprised of two rooms of mixed-media art, the **Justina Barnicke Gallery** (☎ *416/978–8398 ⊙ Mon.–Wed. and Fri. 11–5, Thurs. 11–7, weekends 1–5*) showcases homegrown talent. The stained-glass windows and vaulted ceiling in the Great Hall are impressive, but so is chef Suzanne Baby's cuisine at the resident **Gallery Grill** (☎ *416/978–2445 ⊙ Sept.–June, weekdays 11:30–1:30, Sun. 11–1*). Try one of the grilled fish dishes, a juicy steak, or a creative vegetarian torte while enjoying the elegant surroundings. ⊠ *U of T, 7 Hart House Circle, Queen's Park, Toronto, Ontario* ☎ *416/978–2452* ⊕ *www.harthouse. utoronto.ca* Ⓜ *Museum.*

🕐 **Royal Ontario Museum.** Since its inception in 1912, the ROM, Canada's
★ largest museum, has amassed more than 6 million items. What sets the ROM apart is that science, art, and archaeology exhibits are all appealingly presented in one gigantic complex. A C$200-million refurbishment project, envisioned by world-renowned architect Daniel Libeskind (the designer of the Jewish Museum in Berlin), added 40,000 square feet and the ultramodern **Michael Lee-Chin Crystal** gallery in 2009—a series of interlocking prismatic cubes spilling out onto Bloor Street.

Highlights include the **Learning Centre**—a state-of-the-art educational facility for the 220,000 schoolchildren expected annually—and the

Crystal Court, a four-story atrium slashed on all sides by sliver-thin windows through which light pours into the open space. A look through the windows reveals parts of the treasures inside, such as the frightful creatures from the **Age of Dinosaurs** exhibit standing guard. The **Institute for Contemporary Culture** hangs 110 feet over Bloor Street from its fourth-floor perch. The **Crystal Five Bistro,** "C5" for short, on the fifth floor feels a bit

WORD OF MOUTH

"It is always fun to take the Hop-on Hop-off trolley to get an overview of the city so you can return to spots that take your interest. If the weather is good, sit on the upper deck to get the best experience."

—prinret

like the lounge on Star Trek's Enterprise, and turns out a selection of perfectly presented tapas and the region's finest wines.

The **Herman Herzog Levy Gallery** exhibits a stunning range of large and colorful textiles, paintings, and prints from the museum's acclaimed Asian collection; the **Chinese Sculpture Gallery** in the Matthews Family Court displays 25 stone Buddhist sculptures dating from the 2nd through 16th centuries; and the **Gallery of Korean Art** is North America's largest permanent gallery devoted to Korean art and culture. The **Patricia Harris Gallery of Textiles and Costume** houses a selection of Chinese imperial court garments, early Canadian quilts, and a survey of European fashions from the 18th century to the present. ■TIP➔ Admission is free after 3:30 on Wednesday and reduced to C$12 on Friday after 4:30. ✉ *100 Queen's Park, Yorkville, Toronto, Ontario* ☎ *416/586–8000* ⊕ *www.rom.on.ca* 🎟 *C$24* ☉ *Mon.–Thurs. and weekends 10–5:30, Fri. 10–8:30* Ⓜ *Museum.*

University of Toronto. Almost a city unto itself, U of T has a staff and student population of around 60,000. The institution dates to 1827, when King George IV signed a charter for a "King's College in the Town of York, Capital of Upper Canada." The Church of England had control then, but by 1850 the college was proclaimed nondenominational, renamed the University of Toronto, and put under the control of the province. Then, in a spirit of Christian competition, the Anglicans started Trinity College, the Methodists began Victoria, and the Roman Catholics began St. Michael's; by the time the Presbyterians founded Knox College, the whole thing was a bit out of hand. Now the 10 schools and faculties are united, and they welcome anyone who can meet the admission standards and afford the tuition, which, thanks to government funding, is still somewhat reasonable. The architecture is interesting, if uneven, as one might expect on a campus that's been built in bits and pieces over 150 years. From June to August there are historical campus walks in addition to general daily tours. Walking tours leave from the Nona Macdonald Visitors Centre. ✉ *Visitors Centre, 25 King's College Circle, Queen's Park, Toronto, Ontario* ☎ *416/978– 5000* ⊕ *www.utoronto.ca* 🎟 *Tours free* ☉ *Walking tours weekdays at 11 and 2, weekends at 11; historical tours June–Aug., weekdays 2:30* Ⓜ *St. George, Queen's Park.*

Neighborhood Watch: Little Italy

Dining and people-watching draw locals and tourists to Little Italy.

Once a quiet strip of College Street with just a few unfrequented clothing shops and the odd, obstinate pizzeria, Little Italy has become one of the hippest haunts in Toronto. This is the southern edge of the city's Italian community, and though not much remains of this heritage—most Italians now live in the suburbs and throughout the city—the flavor lingers on many a table and in a few food markets.

Whether you're in the mood for old-school Italian trattorias (think checkered tablecloths) or polished martini bars, Little Italy won't disappoint. Pasta and pizza are not the only things on the menus here—new ethnic restaurants open monthly, and every corner holds fashionable cafés and diners to match.

Café Diplomatico. At the epicenter of Little Italy, the "Dip" is one of the few old-school establishments still standing in Little Italy. Since 1968 locals have flocked to its large streetside patio, which offers perfect people-watching opportunities, to sip cappuccinos or savor a pint of beer and spicy mussels. ⊠ 594 College St., at Clinton St., Little Italy, Toronto, Ontario ☎ 416/534–4637 ⊕ www. diplomatico.ca.

Bar Italia. Enjoy a taste of Southern Italy inside, or on the raucous sidewalk patio that is packed all day in fine weather. ⊠ 582 College St., Toronto, Ontario ☎ 416/535–3621 ⊕ www.bar-italia.ca.

Surprisingly, this edge of downtown has a nightlife that rivals the clubs and bars of the Entertainment District (around Adelaide Street West). Bars and coffeehouses are busy into the night, and summer months bring out booming cruise-mobiles, patio revelers, and plenty of pedestrian animation.

Boundaries: College Street, west of Bathurst Street, between Euclid Avenue and Shaw Street.

Getting Here: From Queen's Park subway station, take streetcar 506 west.

Yorkville. Toronto's equivalent to Fifth Avenue or Rodeo Drive, Yorkville, and Bloor Street in particular, is a dazzling spread of high-price stores stocked with designer clothes, furs, and jewels along with restaurants, galleries, and specialty boutiques. It's also where much of the excitement takes place in September during the annual Toronto International Film Festival, reportedly the world's largest and most people-friendly film festival, where the public actually gets to see premieres and hidden gems and attend industry seminars. Klieg lights shine over skyscrapers, bistros serve alcohol until 2 am, cafés teem with the well-heeled, and everyone practices air kisses. Yorkville is also home to a unique park on Cumberland Street, designed as a series of gardens along old property lines and reflecting both the history of the Village of Yorkville and the diversity of the Canadian landscape. ⊠ *From Avenue Rd. to Yonge St., north of and including Bloor St. W, Toronto, Ontario* Ⓜ *Bay.*

A STROLL THROUGH PARADISE

The posh residential neighborhood northeast of Yorkville has tree-lined curving roads (it's one of the few neighborhoods to have escaped the city's grid pattern), many small parks, and a jumble of oversized late-19th-century and early-20th-century houses in Edwardian, Victorian, Georgian, and Tudor styles. An intricate ravine system weaves through this picturesque corner of downtown, its woodsy contours lined with "old money" and Old World majesty. The neighborhood is bounded by Yonge Street, Don Valley Parkway, St. Clair Avenue, and Rosedale Ravine.

WORTH NOTING

George R. Gardiner Museum of Ceramic Art. This collection of rare ceramics includes 17th-century English delftware and 18th-century yellow European porcelain; its pre-Columbian collection dates to Olmec and Maya times. Other galleries feature Japanese Kakiemon-style pottery and Chinese white-and-blue porcelain. If your visit coincides with lunchtime, hit the museum's café for light, seasonal cuisine by local celebrity chef Jamie Kennedy. Free guided tours take place at 2 Sunday–Thursday; to embellish your tour with afternoon tea for C$5, come on Monday or Wednesday. ■ TIP→ Admission is half-price on Friday after 4. ⊠ *111 Queen's Park Crescent, Yorkville, Toronto, Ontario* ☎ *416/586–8080, 416/362–1957 Restaurant reservations* ⊕ *www.gardinermuseum.on.ca* 🎫 *C$12* ☼ *Mon.–Thurs. 10–6, Fri. 10–9, weekends 10–5* Ⓜ *Museum.*

Lillian H. Smith Branch of the Toronto Public Library. Honoring the memory of the city's first children's librarian, this branch maintains nearly 60,000 items in three children's collections, ranging from the 14th century to the present. In addition, the Merril Collection of Science Fiction, Speculation and Fantasy includes about 50,000 items, on everything from parapsychology to UFOs. The Electronic Resource Centre has 32 public terminals for online access. ⊠ *239 College St., between Spadina Ave. and St. George St., Downtown, Toronto, Ontario* ☎ *416/393–7746* ⊕ *www.torontopubliclibrary.ca* 🎫 *Free* ☼ *Library Mon.–Thurs. 9–8:30, Fri. 9–6, Sat. 9–5, Sun. 1:30–5 (from Sun. after Labor Day to 3rd Sun.*

*in June, excluding Sun. adjacent to holidays); children's and Merril col-
lections Mon.–Fri. 10–6, Sat. 9–5* Ⓜ *Queen's Park.*

Ontario Legislative Building. Like City Hall, this home to the provincial
parliament was the product of an international contest among architects, in this case won by a young Briton residing in Buffalo, New York.
The 1893 Romanesque Revival building, made of pink Ontario sandstone, has a wealth of exterior detail; inside, the huge, lovely halls echo
half a millennium of English architecture. The long hallways are hung
with hundreds of oils by Canadian artists, most of which capture scenes
of the province's natural beauty. Take one of the frequent tours to see
the chamber where the 130 MPPs (members of Provincial Parliament)
meet. The two heritage rooms—one each for the parliamentary histories
of Britain and Ontario—are filled with old newspapers, periodicals,
and pictures. The many statues dotting the lawn in front of the building, facing College Street, include one of Queen Victoria and one of
Canada's first prime minister, Sir John A. Macdonald. The lawn is also
the site of Canada Day celebrations and the occasional political protest.
These buildings are often referred to simply as Queen's Park, after the
park surrounding them. ✉ *1 Queen's Park, Queen's Park, Toronto,
Ontario* ☎ *416/325–7500* ⊕ *www.ontla.on.ca* 🎟 *Free* ☉ *Guided tour
mid-May–mid-Sept., daily 9–4; mid-Sept.–mid-May, weekdays 10–4*
Ⓜ *Queen's Park.*

Thomas Fisher Rare Book Library. Early writing artifacts such as a Bab-
ylonian cuneiform tablet, a 2,000-year-old Egyptian papyrus, and
books dating to the beginning of European printing in the 15th century are shown here in rotating exhibits, which change three times
annually. Subjects of these shows might include William Shakespeare,
Galileo Galilei, Italian opera, or contemporary typesetting. Registra-
tion is required upon entry, so bring some form of identification with
you. ✉ *U of T, 120 St. George St., Queen's Park, Toronto, Ontario*
☎ *416/978–5285* ⊕ *www.library.utoronto.ca/fisher* 🎟 *Free* ☉ *Weekdays 9–4:45* Ⓜ *St. George.*

Toronto Reference Library. Designed by one of Canada's most admired
architects, Raymond Moriyama, who also created the Ontario Science
Centre, this five-story library is arranged around a large atrium, afford-
ing a wonderful sense of open space. There is a small waterfall in the
foyer, and glass-enclosed elevators glide swiftly and silently up and
down. One-third of the more than 4 million items—spread across 45
km (28 mi) of shelves—are open to the public. Audio carrels are available for listening to nearly 30,000 music and spoken-word recordings.
The largest Performing Arts Centre in a public library in Canada is on
the fifth floor, as is the **Arthur Conan Doyle Room** (*Tues., Thurs., and
Sat. 2–4, and by appointment*), which is of special interest to Baker
Street regulars. It houses the world's finest public collection of Holm-
esiana, including records, films, photos, books, manuscripts, letters,
and even cartoon books starring Sherlock Hemlock of *Sesame Street.*
✉ *789 Yonge St., Yorkville, Toronto, Ontario* ☎ *416/395–5577* ⊕ *www.
torontopubliclibrary.ca* ☉ *Mon.–Thurs. 9:30–8:30, Fri. 9:30–5:30, Sat.
9–5, Sun. 1:30–5 (Sept.–June only)* Ⓜ *Bloor-Yonge.*

MACDONALD

DUNDAS SQUARE AREA

Yonge Street is the central vein of Toronto, starting at Lake Ontario and slicing the city in half as it travels through Dundas Square and north to the suburbs. Tourists gather below the enormous billboards and flashy lights in Dundas Square, especially in the summer, when the large public area comes alive with outdoor festivals and entertainment. The few sights in this neighborhood, namely the Eaton Centre and Nathan Phillips Square, get a lot of attention from both locals and visitors.

Tourists always end up here, whether they want to or not. Usually it's the enticement of nonstop shopping in the Eaton Centre, Toronto's biggest downtown shopping mall, or the shops lining Yonge Street, nearby. Others see the allure of outdoor markets, ethnic food festivals, and street concerts in the bright and lively, larger-than-life Dundas Square.

To catch a glimpse of what locals are up to, grab lunch and dine alfresco at Nathan Phillips Square. Under the omnipresent gaze of City Hall—the two curving buildings were designed to resemble a watchful eye—nearby suits from the Financial District and spent shoppers populate the benches in all weather. During the winter, the water fountain at Nathan Phillips Square becomes an ice-skating rink that draws in gaggles of giggling teenage girls, young couples holding hands, and little ones testing out their skates for the first time.

There's also a selection of distinct museums. History buffs will enjoy the MacKenzie House, the former home of Toronto's first mayor; contemporary fashion and design are highlighted at the Museum for Textiles; and at the Toronto Police Museum, kids can hop aboard a 1914 paddy wagon or examine their own fingerprints.

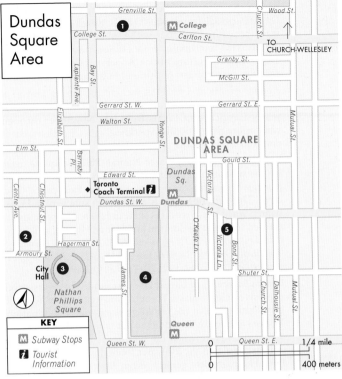

GETTING HERE

The subway stations Dundas and Queen, conveniently at either end of the Eaton Centre, are the main transportation hubs for this part of the city. There are also streetcar lines running along Dundas and Queen streets, linking this area to Chinatown and Kensington Market, and Queen West respectively.

TIMING

Depending on your patience and the contents of your wallet, you could spend anywhere from one to ten hours in the colossal Eaton Centre, literally shopping until you drop. The MacKenzie House, Museum for Textiles, and Toronto Police Museum merit an hour each; and you could easily while away an afternoon people-watching in Dundas Square or Nathan Phillips Square.

TOP ATTRACTIONS

City Hall. Toronto's modern city hall resulted from a 1958 international competition to which some 520 architects from 42 countries submitted designs. The winning presentation by Finnish architect Viljo Revell was controversial—two curved towers of differing height—but logical: an aerial view of City Hall shows a circular council chamber sitting like an eye between the two tower "eyelids," which contain the offices of 44 municipal wards, with 44 city councillors. A remarkable mural within the main entrance, *Metropolis,* was constructed by sculptor David Partridge from 100,000 nails. Revell died before his masterwork was opened in 1965, but within months City Hall became a symbol of a thriving metropolis, with a silhouette as recognizable as the Eiffel Tower. Robert Fulford's book *Accidental City* details the positive influence the development of this building has had on Toronto's civic life.

Annual events at City Hall include the Spring Flower Show in late March; the Toronto Outdoor Art Exhibition in early July; and the yearly Cavalcade of Lights from late November through Christmas, when more than 100,000 sparkling lights are illuminated across both new and old city halls.

In front of City Hall, 9-acre **Nathan Phillips Square** (named after the mayor who initiated the City Hall project) has become a gathering place, whether for royal visits, protest rallies, picnic lunches, or concerts. The reflecting pool is a delight in summer, and even more so in winter, when office workers skate at lunch. The park also holds a Peace Garden for quiet meditation and Henry Moore's striking bronze sculpture *The Archer.* ⊠ *100 Queen St. W, at Bay St., Dundas Square Area, Toronto, Ontario* ☎ *416/338–0338, 416/338–0889 TDD* ⊕ *www.toronto.ca* ⊙ *Weekdays 8:30–4:30* Ⓜ *Queen.*

Dundas Square. A public square surrounded by oversize billboards and explosive light displays, Toronto's answer to New York's Times Square is becoming one of the fastest-growing tourist destinations in the city. Visitors and locals converge on the tables and chairs that are scattered across the square when the weather is fine, and kids (and the young at heart) frolic in the 20 water fountains that shoot out of the cement floor like miniature geysers. From May to October, there's something happening every weekend—it could be an artisan market, an open-air film viewing, a summertime festival, or a live musical performance. ⊠ *Yonge St., at Dundas St., Dundas Square Area, Toronto, Ontario* ⊕ *www.ydsquare.ca* Ⓜ *Dundas.*

Eaton Centre. The 3-million-square-foot Eaton Centre shopping mall has been both praised and vilified since it was built in the 1970s, but it remains incredibly popular. From the graceful glass roof, arching 127 feet above the lowest of the mall levels, to artist Michael Snow's exquisite flock of fiberglass Canada geese floating poetically in open space, there is plenty to appreciate.

Such a wide selection of shops and eateries can be confusing, so here's a simple guide: Galleria Level 1 contains two food courts; popularly priced fashions; photo, electronics, and music stores; and much "convenience" merchandise. Level 2 is directed to the middle-income shopper; Level 3, suitably, has the highest fashion and prices. Named for the store (Eaton's) that once anchored it, its biggest tenants are now Sears and H&M. The southern end of Level 3 has a skywalk that connects the Centre to the seven floors of the Bay (formerly Simpsons) department store, across Queen Street.

Safe parking garages with spaces for some 1,800 cars are sprinkled around Eaton Centre. The building extends along the west side of Yonge Street all the way from Queen Street up to Dundas Street (with a subway stop at each end). ⊠ *220 Yonge St., Dundas Square Area, Toronto, Ontario* ☎ *416/598–8560* ⊕ *www.torontoeatoncentre.com* ☉ *Weekdays 10–9, Sat. 9:30–7, Sun. 11–6* Ⓜ *Dundas, Queen.*

Mackenzie House. Once home to journalist William Lyon Mackenzie, Toronto's first mayor (elected in 1834) and designer of the city's coat of arms, this Greek Revival row house is now a museum. Among the period furnishings and equipment preserved here is an 1845 printing press, which visitors may try. Mackenzie served only one year as mayor. In 1837, he gathered some 700 supporters and marched down Yonge Street to try to overthrow the government, but his minions were roundly defeated, and he fled to the United States with a price on his head. When Mackenzie was pardoned by Queen Victoria years later, he returned to Canada and was promptly elected once again to the legislative assembly. By this time, though, he was so down on his luck that a group of friends bought his family this house. Mackenzie enjoyed the place for only a few years before his death in 1861. His grandson, William Lyon Mackenzie King, became the longest-serving prime minister in Canadian history. ⊠ *82 Bond St., at Dundas St. W, Dundas Square Area, Toronto, Ontario* ☎ *416/392–6915* ⊠ *C$6* ☉ *Jan.–Apr., weekends noon–5; May–Sept., Tues.–Sun. noon–5; Sept.–Dec., Tues.–Fri. noon–4, weekends noon–5* Ⓜ *Dundas.*

QUICK BITES

Trinity Square Café. The Trinity Square Café at the Church of the Holy Trinity is a charming eatery serving sandwiches, soups, pastries, and tea. It's open for lunch weekdays 11:30 am to 2:30 pm. The church itself is fully operational and available for quiet contemplation in the midst of one of downtown Toronto's busiest sections. ⊠ *19 Trinity Sq., facing Bay St., Dundas Square Area, Toronto, Ontario* ☎ *416/598–2010* ⊕ *www.trinitysquarecafe.webs.com* Ⓜ *Dundas.*

WORTH NOTING

Museum for Textiles. Ten galleries showcase over 12,000 cultural artifacts—men's costumes from northern Nigeria and ceremonial masks from Papua New Guinea, for example—as well as the latest in contemporary design. Rugs, cloth, and tapestries from around the world are exhibited. Wednesday evenings (after 5) admission is pay what you can. ⊠ *55 Centre Ave., at Dundas St. W, Dundas Square Area, Toronto, Ontario* ☎ *416/599–5321* ⊕ *www.textilemuseum.ca* ⊠ *C$15* ☉ *Thurs.–Tues. 11–5, Wed. 11–8* Ⓜ *St. Patrick.*

WORD OF MOUTH

"I've never been but I hear the Textile Museum is supposed to be great. It's very central—around Dundas and University."
—goddesstogo

↻ **Toronto Police Museum and Discovery Centre.** A replica of a 19th-century police station, a collection of firearms, and exhibits about infamous crimes are the highlights at this museum devoted exclusively to the Toronto police. Interactive displays include law-and-order quizzes and the opportunity to study your own fingerprints. Kids have fun with the 1914 paddy wagon, car-crash videos, and, especially, a Harley-Davidson they can jump on. They also enjoy climbing in and out of a car sliced in half and hearing a dispatcher squawk at them. Tours are self-guided only. ✉ *40 College St., at Bay St., Dundas Square Area, Toronto, Ontario* ☎ *416/808–7020* ⊕ *www. torontopolice.on.ca/museum* ✉ *Donations accepted* ⊗ *Weekdays 8–4* Ⓜ *College.*

OFF THE
BEATEN
PATH

Cabbagetown. Mockingly named by outsiders for the cabbages that grew on tiny lawns and were cooked in nearly every house, the term is used with a combination of inverse pride and almost wistful irony today. Although it has few tourist attractions per se, it's fun to stroll around and enjoy the architectural diversity of this funky residential area. The enclave extends roughly from Parliament Street on the west—about 1½ km (1 mi) due east of Yonge Street—to the Don River on the east, and from Bloor Street on the north to Queen Street East on the south.

The St. James Cemetery at the northeast corner of Parliament and Wellesley streets contains interesting burial monuments, including the small yellow-brick Gothic **Chapel of St. James-the-Less** with a handsome spire rising from the church nave. Built between 1859 and 1860, it is still considered one of the most beautiful church buildings in the country. Also nearby is **Necropolis Cemetery**, the resting place of many of Toronto's pioneers—including Toronto's first mayor, William Lyon Mackenzie. The 1872 chapel, gate, and gatehouse of the nonsectarian burial ground constitute one of the most attractive groupings of small Victorian buildings in Toronto. **Riverdale Farm** (✉ *201 Winchester St.* ☎ *416/392–6794* ⊕ *www.friendsofriverdalefarm.com* ✉ *Free* ⊗ *Daily 9–5*), which once hosted the city's main zoo, is now home to this farm, a free farm museum that is a special treat for children, who may enjoy brushing the horses or attempting to milk the goats. Demonstrations of crafts such as quilting and spinning are offered daily. Permanent residents include Clydesdale horses, cows, sheep, goats, pigs, donkeys, ducks, geese, chickens, and a small assortment of other domestic animals. The park adjacent to the farm has a wading pool. On Tuesdays (3–7 pm) from mid-May to late October, a farmers' market makes good use of the grounds.

GREATER TORONTO

Toronto's wealth of diverse neighborhoods and fascinating attractions cater to most tastes, but explore beyond downtown to find the ethnic enclaves, parks, museums, and attractions that make this city even more intriguing. Most of these must-sees are accessible by public transportation, although a car would make the journey to some of the more far-flung destinations more convenient.

To experience a community in diaspora, try Little India in the city's east end, where, for a few blocks, shiny sequined saris and tantalizing scents of spicy curries and *dosas* (thin pancakes stuffed with vegetables) make you forget all about the CN Tower. Greektown, along Danforth Avenue, is the place to go for souvlaki—usually served up with a healthy amount of buttery roasted potatoes, fluffy rice, and Greek salad. If you're hankering for a little Eastern European flavor, head west to Bloor West Village, a strip of delis, bakeries, and shops mere blocks from the green, leafy expanse of High Park.

Outdoor enthusiasts will want to check out High Park, almost 400 acres of green space in the city's west end, and for those with a vehicle, the Kortright Centre for Conservation is the perfect getaway. For a phenomenal display of flowers and other botanical beauties, spend a summer afternoon at Edwards Gardens in North York.

If the Art Gallery of Ontario didn't fully satisfy your thirst for Canadian art, then take a stab at the phenomenal collection of Group of Seven pieces at the McMichael Canadian Art Collection, in the quaint village of Kleinburg. Black Creek Pioneer Village, a living-history museum, and Canada's Wonderland, an enormous theme park, are extremely kid-friendly. The Ontario Science Centre is just minutes from downtown, and the sprawling Toronto Zoo, set in the beautiful Rouge River Valley, makes an unforgettable day trip.

2

GETTING HERE

Little India is accessible by the College streetcar (eastbound) or the Bloor–Danforth subway line, which also services Greektown and High Park. Buses run from various downtown subway stations to Edwards Gardens, the Ontario Science Centre, the Toronto Zoo, and Black Creek Pioneer Village. You'll need a car to visit the Kortright Centre for Conservation and the McMichael Canadian Art Collection. A special GO Transit bus serves Canada's Wonderland in summer.

TIMING

You can explore each Greater Toronto sight independently or combine a couple of sights in one trip. The Ontario Science Centre and Edwards Gardens are very close together, for example, and would make a manageable day trip; Greektown and Little India are both in the east end, just a short bus ride apart; and, if you're driving from the city, you could visit Black Creek Pioneer Village and the Kortright Centre for Conservation on the way to the McMichael Canadian Art Collection.

TOP ATTRACTIONS

Canada's Wonderland. Yogi Bear, Fred Flintstone, and Scooby Doo are part of Canada's first theme park, filled with more than 200 games, rides, restaurants, and shops. Favorite attractions include Kidzville, home of the Rugrats, and the SkyRider stand-up looping inverted roller coaster. The newest attraction, Windseeker, which opened in 2011, features thirty-two 301-foot swings. At Planet Snoopy, nine rides star Peanuts characters Charlie Brown, Snoopy, Lucy, and Linus. The Whitewater Bay wave pool, the Black Hole waterslide, and a children's interactive water-play area are all a part of Splash Works, the 20-acre on-site water park. Look for the strolling *Star Trek* characters and the Fun Shoppe, arcade, miniature golf, and batting cages. Other entertainment includes concerts, musicals, light shows, fireworks, and cliff divers. Check newspapers, chain stores, and hotels for discount coupons. ■TIP→ The park is about 30 minutes north of downtown Toronto by car or via the "Wonderland Express" GO Bus from the Yorkdale and York Mills subway stations. ✉ *9580 Jane St., Vaughan, Ontario* ☎ *905/832–7000, 905/832–8131 Kingswood Theatre tickets* ⊕ *www.canadaswonderland.com* ▣ *C$45* ⊙ *Late May–June, weekdays 10–6, Sat. 10–10, Sun. 10–8; late June–Aug., daily 10–10; Sept., weekends 10–8; Oct., weekends 10–5.*

★ **McMichael Canadian Art Collection.** On 100 acres of lovely woodland in Kleinburg, 30 km (19 mi) northwest of downtown, the McMichael is the only major gallery in the country with the mandate to collect Canadian art exclusively. The museum holds impressive works by Tom Thomson, Emily Carr, and the Group of Seven landscape painters, as well as their early-20th-century contemporaries. These artists were inspired by the wilderness and sought to capture it in bold, original styles. First Nations art and prints, drawings, and sculpture by Inuit artists are well represented. Strategically placed windows help you appreciate the scenery as you

WORD OF MOUTH

"The Ontario Science Centre has lots of hands-on exhibits for kids from 2 yrs and up. A great place, especially on a rainy day."

—laverendrye

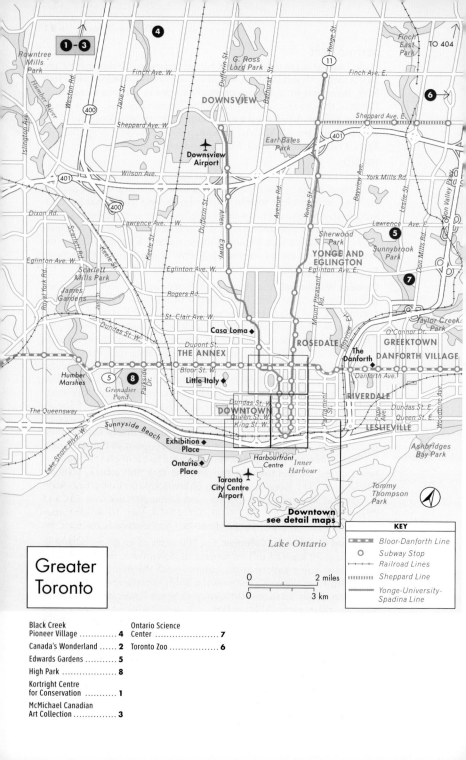

Greater
Toronto

KEY

Bloor-Danforth Line

Subway Stop

Railroad Lines

Sheppard Line

Yonge-University-
Spadina Line

view art that took its inspiration from the vast outdoors. Inside, wood walls and a fireplace set a country mood. Free guided tours take place every Saturday and Sunday at 12:30 (museum) and 2 (special exhibits). ⊠ *10365 Islington Ave., west of Hwy. 400 and north of Major Mackenzie Dr., Kleinburg, Ontario* ☎ *888/213–1121, 905/893–1121* ⊕ *www.mcmichael.com* ✉ *C$15, parking C$5* ⊙ *Daily 10–4.*

☺ **Ontario Science Centre.** It has been called a museum of the 21st century,
★ but it's much more than that. Where else can you stand at the edge of a black hole, work hand-in-clamp with a robot, or land on the moon? Even the building itself is extraordinary: three linked pavilions float gracefully down the side of a ravine and overflow with exhibits that make space, technology, and communications fascinating. The 25,000-square-foot Weston Family Innovation Centre, rife with hands-on activities, is all about experience and problem solving. Make a music soundtrack, take a lie-detector test, and measure fluctuations in your body chemistry as you flirt with a virtual celebrity. Younger visitors learn through play in KidSpark, a space specially designed for children eight and under to enjoy and explore. The CA Technologies Planetarium, Toronto's only public planetarium, uses state-of-the-art technology to take participants on a trip to the outer reaches of the universe. Demonstrations of glassblowing, papermaking, lasers, electricity, and more take place daily; check the schedule when you arrive. The museum has a cafeteria, a restaurant, and a gift store with a cornucopia of books and scientific doodads. ⊠ *770 Don Mills Rd., at Eglinton Ave., North York, Ontario* ☎ *416/696–1000* ⊕ *www.ontariosciencecentre.ca* ✉ *C$20, parking C$10 (cash only)* ⊙ *Daily 10–5* Ⓜ *Eglinton, then No. 34 Eglinton East bus to Don Mills Rd. stop; then walk ½ block south.*

☺ **Toronto Zoo.** With its varied terrain, from river valley to dense forest,
★ the Rouge Valley was an inspired choice of site for this 710-acre zoo in which mammals, birds, reptiles, and fish are grouped according to their natural habitats. Enclosed, climate-controlled pavilions have botanical exhibits, such as the Africa pavilion's giant baobab tree. Look over an Events Guide, distributed at the main entrance, to help plan your day; activities might include chats with animal keepers and animal and bird demonstrations. An "Around the World Tour" takes approximately three hours and includes the Africa, Americas, Australasia, Indo-Malayan, and "Canadian Domain" pavilions. From late April through early September, the Zoomobile can take you through the outdoor exhibit area.

The African Savanna is the country's finest walking safari, a dynamic reproduction that brings rare and beautiful animals and distinctive geological landscapes to the city's doorstep. You can also dine in the Savanna's Safari Lodge and camp overnight in the Serengeti Bush Camp (reservations required). The zoo is a 30-minute drive east from downtown. ⊠ *Meadowvale Rd., Exit 389 off Hwy. 401, Scarborough, Ontario* ☎ *416/392–5929, 416/392–5947 for camping reservations* ⊕ *www.torontozoo.com* ✉ *C$23, parking C$10* ⊙ *Mid-Mar.–late May and early Sept.–mid-Oct., daily 9–6; late May–early Sept., daily 9–7:30; mid-Oct.–Dec., daily 9:30–4:30* Ⓜ *Kennedy, then bus 86A or Don Mills, then bus 85.*

WORTH NOTING

🐾 **Black Creek Pioneer Village.** Less than a half-hour drive from downtown is a rural, mid-19th-century living-history-museum village that makes you feel as though you've gone through a time warp. Black Creek Pioneer Village is a collection of 40 buildings from the 19th and early-20th centuries, including a town hall, a weaver's shop, a printing shop, a blacksmith's shop, and a school complete with a dunce cap. The mill dates from the 1840s and has a 4-ton wooden waterwheel that grinds up to a hundred barrels of flour a day (bags are available for purchase).

As men and women in period costumes go about the daily routine of mid-19th-century Ontario life, they explain what they're doing and answer questions. Visitors can see farm animals; take free wagon rides, Victorian dance classes, and 19th-century baseball lessons; and explore a hands-on discovery center. There's a great brewery-restaurant for lunch or afternoon tea (reservation required). In winter you can also skate, toboggan, or hop on a sleigh ride. ⊠ *1000 Murray Ross Pkwy., near the intersection of Jane St. and Steeles Ave., North York, Ontario* 📞 *416/736–1733* ⊕ *www.blackcreek.ca* 🎫 *C$7, parking C$7* ⊙ *May and June, weekdays 9:30–4, weekends 11–5; July and Aug., weekdays 10–5, weekends 11–5; Sept.–Dec., weekdays 9:30–4, weekends 11–4:30* Ⓜ *Finch, then bus 60 west or Jane, then bus 35.*

🐾 **Toronto Botanical Garden and Edwards Gardens.** The beautiful 17 contem-
★ porary botanical garden areas and adjacent estate garden (once owned by industrialist Rupert Edwards) flow into one of the city's most visited ravines. Paths wind along colorful floral displays and exquisite rock gardens. Refreshments and picnic facilities are available, but no pets are allowed. There's also a signposted "teaching garden." Free general tours between May and early September depart Tuesdays at 10 am or Wednesday at 7:30 pm; additional guided tours (fee) can be arranged for small groups of seniors, children, ESL students, or adults with a special interest (history, eco-nature, etc.). For a great ravine walk, start at the gardens' entrance and head south through Wilket Creek Park and the winding Don River valley. Pass beneath the Don Valley Parkway and continue along Massey Creek. After hours of walking (or biking or jogging) through almost uninterrupted park, you reach the southern tip of Taylor Creek Park on Victoria Park Avenue, just north of the Danforth. From here you can catch a subway back to your hotel. ⊠ *777 Lawrence Ave. E, entrance at southwest corner of Leslie St. and Lawrence Ave. E, North York, Ontario* 📞 *416/397–1340, 416/397–1366 tours* ⊕ *www. torontobotanicalgarden.ca* ⊙ *Daily dawn–dusk* Ⓜ *Eglinton, then bus 54 or 54A.*

🐾 **High Park.** One of North America's loveliest parks, High Park (at one
★ time the privately owned countryside "farm" of John George Howard, Toronto's first city architect) is especially worth visiting in summer, when the many special events include professionally staged Shakespeare productions. Hundreds of Torontonians and guests arrive at dinnertime and picnic on blankets before the show (High Park Amphitheatre). Admission is by donation; shows run Tuesday to Sunday.

The futuristic Ontario Science Centre engages visitors of all ages with hands-on exhibits and workshops.

Grenadier Pond in the southwest corner of the park is named after the British soldiers who, it is said, crashed through the soft ice while rushing to defend the town against invading American forces in 1813.

In summer there are concerts on Sunday afternoons; in winter, there's ice-skating. Wear durable shoes for free guided tours every first and third Sunday of the month at 10:30 am (departing from the Grenadier Cafe and Teahouse), which are led by volunteer naturalists, scientists, and historians. Other highlights of the 398-acre park are a large swimming pool, tennis courts, fitness trails, and hillside gardens with roses and sculpted hedges. There's limited parking along Bloor Street north of the park, and along the side streets on the eastern side. At the south end of High Park, near Colborne Lodge, is **High Park Zoo** (☎ 416/392–8186 ☒ Free ☉ Daily 7–dusk). It's more modest than the Toronto Zoo but a lot closer to downtown and free. Even young children won't tire walking past the paddocks that are home to American bison, Barbary sheep, emus, yaks, llamas, peacocks, and deer. Built more than 150 years ago by High Park's architect, **Colborne Lodge** (☎ 416/392–6916 ☒ C$6 ☉ Jan.–Apr., Fri.–Sun. noon–4; May–Aug., Tues.–Sun. noon–5; Sept., weekends noon–5; Oct.–Dec., Tues.–Sun. noon–4), a Regency style cottage, contains its original fireplace, bake oven, and kitchen, as well as many of John George Howard's drawings and paintings. ☒ Bordered by Bloor St. W, Gardiner Expressway, Parkside Dr., and Ellis Park Rd. Main entrance off Bloor St. W at High Park Ave., Greater Toronto, Toronto, Ontario ☎ 416/392–1111, 416/392–1748 walking tours ⊕ www.highparktoronto.com Ⓜ High Park.

CLOSE UP

Neighborhood Watch: The Danforth

The Danforth neighborhood serves some of the best Greek food in North America.

Once English-settled, this area along Danforth Avenue named after Asa Danforth, an American contractor who cut a road into the area in 1799, has a dynamic ethnic mix, although it's primarily a Greek community. You'll now find bright organic juice bars, boisterous patios overflowing with late-night revelers, and some of the best souvlaki this side of the Atlantic.

The western end, between Broadview and Chester subway stations, is a health nut's haven. Juice bars, vegetarian food emporia, yoga studios, and stores devoted to holistic healing, naturopathic medicine, and environmentally friendly clothing and cleaning products abound.

East of Chester subway station is the area referred to as "Greektown." Late-night taverns, all-night fruit markets, and some of the best Greek food in North America keep this neighborhood busy at all hours. A number of bakeries offer mouthwatering baklava, *tyropita* (cheese pie), and *touloumbes* (fried cinnamon-flavored cakes soaked in honey) if you prefer to snack and stroll. ■TIP➔ Summer is the best season to visit, as most eateries have patios open and are busy until the wee hours of morning.

Taste of the Danforth. Every August this local festival pays tribute to the little nook of foodie paradise here. More than a million visitors come to sample the fare—mainly dolmades, souvlaki, and other Greek specialties— for C$1 to C$5 per taste. The festival motto—"Don't eat for a week before coming"—is helpful advice.

But it's not just about food. Between bites, you might want to check out the independent, original boutiques in the neighborhood that offer everything from fair-trade gifts to funky kitchenware. For those who like to live on the edge, there's even a shop that sells nothing but hot sauce, with samplers ranging from mild to "smack my ass." ☎ 416/469–5634 ⊕ www. tasteofthedanforth.com.

Boundaries: The Danforth is bounded by Broadview Avenue to the west and Donlands Avenue to the east.

Getting Here: Take the subway to the Broadview (west end of the neighborhood), Chester or Pape (heart of Greektown), or Donlands (eastern end) TTC stops.

CLOSE UP

Neighborhood Watch: India Bazaar

2

You can eat, shop, and experience Indian culture in Little India.

"Little India" and "Indian Village" all refer to Gerrard India Bazaar, the largest collection of South Asian restaurants, sari stores, and Bollywood movie-rental shops in North America. Follow your nose through the sweets shops, food stalls, and curry restaurants, and allow your eyes to be dazzled by storefront displays of jewelry, Hindu deities, and swaths of sensuous fabrics ablaze with sequins.

Mornings are generally quiet. Afternoons see a trickle of visitors, but the area really comes alive in the evening, when those with hungry bellies stroll in search of a fiery madras, creamy korma, or hearty masala curry. Many of the restaurants offer buffet lunches and dinners for around C$10 per person, which draw huge crowds on the weekends. Sunday afternoons set the familiar scene of Indian families crowding the sidewalks, enjoying corn on the cob and *paan* (an Indian street food of spices, fruits, and sometimes sugar wrapped in leaves of the betel pepper), and window-shopping their way up and down Gerrard Street.

As this area represents such a diverse group of people, there are many

festivals throughout the year. During the biggest event, the three-day **Festival of South Asia** in August, stages are set for colorful music and dance performances, and the streets fill with the tantalizing scents of snack stalls and the calls of vendors peddling everything from henna tattoos to spicy corn on the cob. In late autumn, the **Hindu Festival of Lights** (Diwali) and the end of **Ramadan** (Eid) are celebrated together with another fun and fiery street fête. For more information on the festivals, contact ☎ *416/465–8513*.

Boundaries: This little piece of Bombay is crammed into the strip of Gerrard Street between Coxwell and Greenwood avenues.

Getting Here: Use the College streetcar east to get here from downtown.

Kortright Centre for Conservation. Only 15 minutes north of the city, this delightful conservation center has three aquariums, more than 16 km (10 mi) of hiking trails through forest, meadow, river, and marshland, and a renewable-energy cottage that demonstrates what life would be like off the grid. In winter some of the trails are reserved for cross-country skiing (C$18 to use the trail; equipment rentals available). In the magnificent woods there have been sightings of foxes, coyotes, rabbits, deer, wild turkeys, pheasants, chickadees, finches, and blue jays. Seasonal events include a dogsled race, a spring maple-syrup festival, and a Christmas crafts fair. Nature day camps and day-long energy conservation workshops are offered throughout the year for an extra fee. To get here, drive 3 km (2 mi) north along Highway 400, exit west at Major Mackenzie Drive, and continue south 1 km (½ mi) on Pine Valley Drive to the gate. ⊠ *9550 Pine Valley Dr., Woodbridge, Ontario* ☎ *905/832–2289, 416/667–6295 for workshops and camps* ⊕ *www. kortright.org* ⊠ *C$6.50, special events C$9* ⊙ *Daily 10–4:30.*

Tommy Thompson Park. This park comprises a peninsula that juts 5 km (3 mi) into Lake Ontario. It was created from the sand dredged for a new port of entry and the landfill of a hundred skyscrapers. It has quickly become one of the best areas in the city for cycling, jogging, walking, sailing, photography, and, especially, bird-watching. The strange, artificial peninsula is home (or stopover) to the largest colony of ring-billed seagulls in the world and dozens of species of terns, ducks, geese, and snowy egrets. At the end of the spit, you'll find a red-and-white lighthouse, in addition to amazing views of downtown and an awesome sense of isolation in nature. Bird-watching is best from mid-May to mid-October. To get here, head east along Queen Street to Leslie Street, then south to the lake. No private vehicles are permitted in the park. ⊠ *Entrance at the foot of Leslie St., Southeast Toronto, Toronto, Ontario* ☎ *416/661–6600* ⊙ *Weekends Apr.–Nov., daily 9–6; Dec.–Mar., daily 9–4:30* Ⓜ *Queen, then streetcar east.*

Where to Eat

WORD OF MOUTH

"The great thing about Toronto is that it is multicultural and that reflects the restaurant scene. If you want hip, go downtown. If you want Italian go to College/Bathurst street. Indian? Gerard St. in the East end."

—sarajane

THE ENTERTAINMENT DISTRICT

The Entertainment District is under constant renovation these days, and the ongoing condo boom along this downtown strip is echoed in a restaurant boom, which is good news for the area's young bucks with money to burn and any visitors, spoiled for choice.

Above: Locals enjoy dining alfresco in warm weather; top right: A feast at Victor, in the Hôtel Le Germain; bottom right: A dish of the house specialty at Smoke's Poutinerie.

Though extremely close to Queen Street West, this strip has a whole different personality that's noticeable as soon as you walk out of the subway station. While Queen Street West is funky and artsy, Entertainment District restaurants adopt a more chic attitude, in tune with the many clubs. At night, the streets come to life with lineups of patrons dressed to impress.

Looking for entertainment with your meal? Supper clubs and social clubs such as The Fifth and The Roosevelt cater to the more discriminating palate. For something with an Asian flair, Lee and Spice Route offer great food with ingredients that you may not be able to pronounce.

POUTINE

A Québécois classic traditionally made from french fries, cheese curds, and gravy is getting dressed up and refined. Modern takes might include pulled pork and other meats, as well as different sauces and ethnic spices. Poutini (www.poutini.com) and Smoke's Poutinerie (www.smokespoutinerie.com) are restaurants dedicated to it. Caplansky's (www.caplanskys.com) makes the gravy with their famous smoked meat.

KING WEST TWO DIFFERENT WAYS

	DAY	NIGHT
Noodles or Pasta?	Japanese-style noodle house **Liberty Noodle** (✉ 171 East Liberty St. ☎ 416/588–4100) takes the Asian approach to comfort food.	The Rustic Italian cuisine at **Buca** (✉ 604 King St. W ☎ 416/865–1600 ✛ B:5, see full review) makes you feel like you're in someone's home.
Light Bites	**Oro Caffe** (✉ 171 East Liberty St. ☎ 416/588–7688) has a European café menu, including panini, pizzas, and salads.	Great for lunch and dinner, **Mildred's Temple Kitchen** (✉ 85 Hanna Ave. ☎ 416/588–5695) dishes up Continental flavor pairings.
Asian Flavors	You'll find a modern interpretation of sushi in a casual setting at **Toshi Sushi** (✉ 565 King St. W ☎ 416/260–8588 ✛ 6:G, see full review).	Using Asian ingredients with western techniques **Lee** (✉ 603 King St. W ☎ 416/504–7867 ✛ B:6, see full review) served up tapas-style small plates.
Euro-Inspired	Serving up fun variations on familiar treats **School Bakery and Café** (✉ 70 Fraser Ave. ☎ 416/588–0005) has a fan following for their McMuffins.	The vast selection of wine at **Crush Wine Bar** (✉ 455 King St. W ☎ 416/977–1234 ✛ 6:C, see full review) pairs well with their English food.

BOUTIQUE HOTEL DINING

Traditionally, hotel restaurants are grand and regal, but stuffy and boring. That is not true of the trendy boutique hotels on King Street West, where the restaurants are not to be missed.

✕ **Victor.** Just off of King Street within Hôtel Le Germain, Victor has a different four-course menu every night of the week, as well as à la carte dishes, all with international influences dominated by Mediterranean flavors, like marinated sardines with shaved bean salad. ✉ 30 Mercer St. ☎ 416/883–3431.

✕ **Senses Restaurant.** At Senses Restaurant, within the SoHo Metropolitan Hotel, award-winning chef Patrick Lin uses perfectly executed Asian cooking methods on familiar ingredients, as demonstrated by dishes like crispy duck breast on pan-fried king oyster and shitake mushrooms, and torched sashimi. ✉ 318 Wellington St. W ☎ 416/935–0400. Also see **Toca** in the Ritz Carlton. See full reviews.

QUEEN WEST

Queen West keeps moving farther west, so much so that now there's an area known as West Queen West. It's a boisterous 'hood of cafés, organic food shops, galleries, funky clothing stores, and lots of good restaurants at manageable price points.

Above: Sample sweet and savory treats at Café Crepe; top right: Excellent sushi is available throughout Toronto; bottom right: The Black Hoof specializes in house-made charcuterie.

Artsy and bohemian, there is more to this strip besides galleries and boutiques. Urban, young, and laid-back bistros line the street, adding to the inviting atmosphere of the area. The variety of restaurants is as diverse as the crowd—from Nota Bene, which serves a pre-theater menu for the art-loving crowd, to Fressen's vegan menu for the urban herbivore.

CHARCUTERIE

Charcuterie is the art of preparing and preserving meats. Many chefs in the city are ordering whole animals and curing and brining them into house-made delicacies. With a name inspired by Spanish sparkling wine, Cava lives up to expectations with their superb platter of chorizo, duck *bresaola*, and Iberico ham. Black Hoof does it so well that it has become synonymous with the term. (*See their full reviews.*)

QUEEN WEST TWO WAYS

	DAY	NIGHT
Cheap to chic	**Arepa** (✉ 490 Queen St. W ☎ 416/362–4111) is a sunny Latin American snack shop that serves cheesy sandwiches in fluffy bread.	First-class food at **Nota Bene** (✉ 180 Queen St. W ☎ 416/977–6400 ✛ E:5, see full review) fits the sophisticated and artsy setting.
So hip it hurts	Ultrachic **Tequila Bookworm Café** (✉ 512 Queen St. W ☎ 416/504–7335) has a piano and patio, with books for those who like to curl up with a good read.	You might miss the faded sign of **Czehoski** (✉ 678 Queen St. W ☎ 416/366–6111), but this hip yet casual spot dishes out haute but simple food that's not to be missed.
Sweet tooth	Take home some desserts or stay for a light savory snack at **Dufflet Pastries** (✉ 787 Queen St. W ☎ 416/504–2870). Whatever you order, this place will brighten your afternoon.	Laid-back **Café Crepe** (✉ 246 Queen St. W ☎ 416/260–2205) serves just as many tasty savory crepes as dessert crepes to satisfy any craving.

SUSHI LUNCH

Satisfy that mid- or post-shopping hunger with a sushi meal at one of the many Japanese restaurants in the area.

✕ **Aji Sai.** For great value, try the all-you-can-eat lunch at Aji Sai Japanese Restaurant. ✉ *467 Queen St. W* ☎ *416/603–3366.*

✕ **Omi.** Owner John Lee moved Omi to Cabbage-town where he continues to whip up delicious sushi, using sustainable fish, in this narrow, brightly colored space. ✉ *243 Carlton St., Cabbagetown* ☎ *416/920–8991.*

✕ **Sushi Time.** Sushi Time offers familiar sushi and sashimi choices. Try the sushi pizza—a fried rice patty topped with salmon, green onions, *tobiko* (flying fish roe), and mayo. ✉ *325 Queen St. W* ☎ *416/977–2222.*

✕ **To-ne Sushi.** There may not be bells and whistles, but come here for beautifully presented fresh sushi and the seared tuna salad at a very reasonable price. ✉ *414 Queen St. W,* ☎ *416/866–8200* ▭ *No credit cards.*

Updated by
Diana Ng

Toronto's calling card—its ethnic diversity—offers up a potent mix of cuisines. But with that base, the city's chefs are now pushing into new territory. A key example could be Guu Izakaya, bringing forward not just a cuisine, but an entire cultural experience of Japanese small plates. And just as crucial, the farm-to-table movement has connected diners directly with local farms and vineyards in the Niagara region. Many chefs even grow their own spring greens and make their own bread, condiments, or preserves.

A slew of restaurants are also flexing their butchery skills with nose-to-tail cooking, the best of which is The Black Hoof, presenting dishes that use all parts of an animal. It points to a larger sense of individuality from restaurants, some unabashedly luxurious and classic, in the case of Chiado and Canoe, and some who let ingredients shine in the simplest way possible, like Origin and Queen Margherita Pizza. Gastro-pubs like The Gabardine are also popular as a happy medium between formulaic dingy pubs and stuffy upscale spots.

The diners themselves are also evolving. With the click of a few buttons, photos and narratives are uploaded onto the Internet, sharing and relaying dining experiences with a global community. Chefs recognize they must compete on an international level, and keep up with new tastes and demands. Toronto's cuisine is reflective of these changes and continues to lead.

With locally grown talent and ingredients, traditional techniques, and modern bravado, the dining scene is more exciting than it's ever been.

PLANNING

With new restaurants and shops opening up farther away from the downtown core, tourists have a lot more area to cover. We make it easy by sorting restaurants by price, cuisine, and neighborhood, with

THE ANNEX
Cheap eats, great ethnic food

YORKVILLE
Discerning tastes for heavy wallets

DANFORTH
Traditional Greek fare

LITTLE ITALY
From red-sauce joints to sleek and modern

CHINATOWN AND KENSINGTON MARKET
Noodle shops and hippie havens

DUNDAS SQUARE AREA
Flashy chains and sporty bars

QUEEN WEST
Funky and bohemian eateries with an ethnic edge

OSSINGTON
Up-and-coming casual spots

ENTERTAINMENT DISTRICT
Trendy and hip, bustling at night

FINANCIAL DISTRICT AND HARBOURFRONT
High end business dining: steak houses to take-out sushi

QUEEN'S PARK

University of Toronto

Queen's Park

Ontario Legislative Building

City Hall

Nathan Phillips Square

Toronto Coach Terminal

King's Coll. Cir.

Madison Ave.
Sussex Ave.
Huron St.
Willcocks St.
St. George St.
College St.
Hoskin Ave.
Bloor St. W.
Cumberland St.
Charles St. E.
St. Joseph St.
Wellesley St. W.
Maitland Ave.
Alexander St.
Grosvenor St.
Grenville St.
College St.
Carlton St.
Cecil St.
Baldwin St.
D'Arcy St.
Dundas St. W.
Sullivan St.
Grange Park
Renfrew Pl.
Pullan Pl.
Queen St. W.
Queen St. E.
Nelson St.
Richmond St. E.
Adelaide St. E.
King St. W.
King St. E.
Wellington St. W.
Front St. W.
Brennner Blvd.
Gardiner Expy.
Lake Shore Blvd. E.
Queens Quay W.
Queens Quay E.
Harbour St.
Pearl St.
Avenue Rd.
Bay St.
Yonge St.
Bay St.
University Ave.
Elizabeth St.
Chestnut St.
Simcoe St.
St. Patrick St.
McCaul St.
Henry St.
Beverley St.
Spadina Ave.
Huron St.
Bellevue Ave.
Augusta Ave.
Brunswick Ave.
Major St.
Soho St.
Beverley St.
Peter St.
John St.
Duncan St.
Widmer St.
York St.
Bay St.
Yonge St.
Victoria St.
Mutual St.
Jarvis St.
Church St.
Elm St.
Edward St.
Gould St.
Shuter St.
Dundas St. E.
Park Rd.
Spadina Ave.
Gardiner Expy.

St. George
Museum
Bay
Bloor-Yonge
Wellesley
College
Queen's Park
St. Patrick
Dundas
Queen
Osgoode
Union

0   1/4 mile
0   400 meters

spotlight features focused on specific interests. Search "Best Bets" for top recommendations. But good eats aren't limited to the city core. *For recommended restaurants in the Greater Toronto Area, refer to the Greater Toronto section near the end of the chapter.*

DISCOUNTS

For 2½ weeks between January and February, more than 100 of the city's best restaurants offer the **Winterlicious** Program, where a fixed-price, three-course lunch is C$15 to C$20, and dinner is C$20 to C$30, and the regular menu is still served. Similarly, **Summerlicious** runs for around two weeks in July. For more details, see ⊕ *www.toronto.ca/special_events.*

DRESS

With the exception of high-end restaurants, the dining atmosphere in Toronto is generally cool and relaxed, with patrons donning trendy and polished attire. In the more elegant and upscale restaurants, or around the Financial District, men are likely to feel more comfortable wearing a jacket. Conversely, in the Kensington Market area, casual comfort is the style of choice. In the aggressively air-conditioned summer months, women are advised to bring a light sweater or jacket when heading out, especially in the evening. We mention dress only when men are required to wear a jacket or a jacket and tie.

FOODIE FESTIVALS

Because of long winters, weekends in the summer are celebrated to their fullest. What better way than food festivals to showcase Canadian culture?

The annual **Taste of the Danforth Festival** celebrates the mouthwatering diversity of the city as it welcomes millions to the Danforth strip each August. ⊕ *www.tasteofthedanforth.com.*

A smaller event when compared to the Danforth Festival, **Taste of Little Italy** takes place in June on College Street, where Italian-centric cuisine and live music are celebrated. ⊕ *www.tasteoflittleitaly.ca.*

MEALTIMES

Lunch typically starts at 11:30 or noon, and dinner service begins around 5:30 or 6. Many restaurants close between lunch and dinner (roughly 2:30 to 5:30). On weekdays, kitchens usually close around 10:30 pm. Chinatown, Yorkville, and Danforth have some late-night spots. There are few all-night restaurants in the city. Unless otherwise noted, the restaurants listed in this guide are open daily for lunch and dinner. *In the Exploring chapter, look for "Quick Bites" places—perfect for a snack while sightseeing.*

ORIENTATION

Throughout the chapter, you'll see mapping symbols and coordinates (✠ 3:F2) after property names or reviews. To locate the property on a map, turn to the Toronto Dining maps within this chapter. The first number after the ✠ symbol indicates the map number. Following that are the property's coordinates on the map grid.

RESERVATIONS

Reservations are always a good idea; we mention them only when they're essential or not accepted. Book as far ahead as you can. (Large parties should always call to check the reservations policy.) Many restaurants have lounges and sections for walk-ins only.

SMOKING

Toronto restaurants prohibit smoking, including areas outdoors under an awning or overhang. Some let diners get away with smoking in open-air outdoor dining areas.

TIPPING AND TAXES

There is no hard and fast rule when it comes to tipping; it is optional but customary, and some restaurants include gratuities on the bill for parties of six or more. It's common to leave 15%–20% for standard or good service and 20% or more for exceptional service. If you have brought your own wine or cake for a special occasion, it's proper etiquette to tip more for the extra service. The percentage of tips is generally calculated on the subtotal. As of July 2010, Goods and Services Tax and Provincial Sales Tax were combined into the Harmonized Sales Tax of 13%, meaning the tax on alcohol was lowered, and food and alcohol are no longer taxed separately.

WHAT IT COSTS

Credit cards are widely accepted in Toronto restaurants though some may accept only MasterCard and Visa. Cafés and burger joints may accept debit cards as well.

WHAT IT COSTS IN CANADIAN DOLLARS					
	¢	$	$$	$$$	$$$$
AT DINNER	under C$8	C$8–C$12	C$13–C$20	C$21–C$30	over C$30

Restaurant prices are based on the median main course price at dinner.

RESTAURANT REVIEWS

Listed alphabetically within neighborhoods.

HARBOURFRONT, THE FINANCIAL DISTRICT, AND OLD TOWN

THE FINANCIAL DISTRICT

$$
CONTINENTAL
✕ **Beer Bistro.** A culinary tribute to beer, the creative menu here incorporates its star ingredient in every dish, even dessert, in subtle and clever ways without causing a malted flavor overload. Start the hoppy journey with a taster of three draft beers, chosen from almost 20 options, arranged from mild to bold. Follow that with a beer-bread pizza made with oatmeal stout; a mussel bowl, available in eight different broths; pulled-pork *primanti* (sandwich) with beer-braised, house-smoked pork, or Dragon Stout and Skor ice cream. The warm, modern interior includes a huge angled mirror on the wall above the kitchen, which

BEST BETS FOR TORONTO DINING

Where can I find the best food the city has to offer? Fodor's writers and editors have selected their favorite restaurants by price, cuisine, and experience *in the lists below.* In the first column, the Fodor's Choice properties represent the "best of the best" across price categories. You can also search by area—just peruse our complete reviews on the following pages.

Fodor's Choice ★

The Black Hoof, p. 122
C5, p. 114
Canoe, p. 99
Crêpes à GoGo, p. 117
Foxley, p. 123
The Gabardine, p. 100
The Gardiner Café, p. 114
Globe Bistro, p. 120
Globe Earth, p. 124
Guu Izakaya, p. 119
La Palette, p. 111
Lai Wah Heen, p. 108
Lee Garden, p. 110
Mistura, p. 125
Origin, p. 102
Pangaea, p. 118
Pastis, p. 125
Queen Margherita Pizza, p. 120
Quince, p. 126
Splendido, p. 113
Starfish, p. 100

By Price

¢

Crêpes à GoGo, p. 117

Future Bakery & Café, p. 111

$

7 West Cafe, p. 114
Duff's Famous Wings, p. 122
The Gardiner Café, p. 114
Spadina Garden, p. 110
Swatow, p. 110

$$

The Gabardine, p. 100
Guu Izakaya, p. 119
Lee Garden, p. 110
Live Organic Food Bar, p. 112
Queen Margherita Pizza, p. 120
Quince, p. 126
Origin, p. 102

$$$

The Black Hoof, p. 122
Foxley, p. 123
Globe Bistro, p. 120
Globe Earth, p. 124
La Palette, p. 111
Lai Wah Heen, p. 108
Mistura, p. 125

Pastis, p. 125
Quince, p. 126
Splendido, p. 113
Starfish, p. 100

$$$$

C5, p. 114
Canoe, p. 99
Lai Wah Heen, p. 108
Pangaea, p. 118

By Cuisine

CHINESE

Lai Wah Heen, $$$, p. 108
Spadina Garden, $, p. 110
Swatow, $, p. 110

FRENCH

Bistro 990, $$$, p. 118
The Fifth, $$$, p. 106
La Palette, $$$, p. 111
Pastis, $$$, p. 125

ITALIAN

Mistura, $$$, p. 125
Quince, $$$, p. 126
Sotto Sotto, $$$, p. 118

Terroni, $$, p. 101
Zucca, $$$, p. 126

MODERN CANADIAN

Bymark, $$$$, p. 99
Canoe, $$$$, p. 99
Colborne Lane, $$$, p. 102
Far Niente, $$$, p. 99
The Gardiner Café, $, p. 114
Lucien, $$$$, p. 102
Toca, $$$$, p. 108

By Experience

BUSINESS DINING

Bymark, $$$$, p. 99
Canoe, $$$$, p. 99
FOUR, $$, p. 99
Pangaea, $$$$, p. 118
Reds Bistro & Bar, $$$$, p. 100
Starfish, $$$, p. 100
Vertical, $$$, p. 101

CELEB-SPOTTING

Bistro 990, $$$, p. 118
One, $$$, p. 117
Sotto Sotto, $$$, p. 118
Studio Café, $$$, p. 118

CHILD-FRIENDLY

Duff's Famous Wings, $, p. 122
Spadina Garden, $, p. 110
Terroni, $$, p. 101

MOST ROMANTIC

C5, $$$$, p. 114
The Fifth, $$$, p. 106
La Palette, $$$, p. 111

allows a peek into the heart of the restaurant. The patio is a joy in summer. ⊠ *18 King St. E, Financial District, Toronto, Ontario* ☎ *416/861–9872* ⊕ *www.beerbistro.com* ☉ *Closed Sun.* Ⓜ *King* ✛ *1:G6.*

$$$$
MODERN
CANADIAN

✕**Bymark.** Wood, glass, and water create drama in a space anchored by a 5,000-bottle wine "cellar" inside a two-story glass column. Mark McEwan's refined modern menu showcases sophisticated seafood dishes like butter-poached lobster and simply prepared meats like the signature 8-ounce burger with molten Brie de Meaux and grilled king mushrooms. The glass-encased bar upstairs oozes extreme comfort and has a good view of architect Ludwig Mies van der Rohe's Toronto Dominion Centre Plaza. Bar dishes are as luxurious as they are casual, as exhibited by halibut tacos with hot pickled red onions. Upscale service matches the food, and in summer patio tippling and dining are dreamy. ⊠ *66 Wellington St. W, concourse level, Financial District, Toronto, Ontario* ☎ *416/777–1144* ⊕ *www.bymark.ca* ⌂ *Reservations essential* ☉ *Closed Sun.* Ⓜ *St. Andrew* ✛ *1:G6.*

$$$$
MODERN
CANADIAN
Fodor's Choice
★

✕**Canoe.** Look through huge windows on the 54th floor of the Toronto Dominion Bank Tower and enjoy the breathtaking view of the Toronto Islands and the lake while you dine. Begin with dishes like Yarmouth lobster terrine with octopus and pickled cabbage. Entrées like roasted pheasant supreme with quinoa and double-smoked bacon nod to both tradition and trend. Traditional desserts such as sticky toffee pudding and firewood honey butter tart round out the exceptional meal. ■TIP➡ The restaurant and lounge is a great place to sample Niagara wines. ⊠ *Toronto-Dominion Centre, 66 Wellington St. W, 54th fl., Financial District, Toronto, Ontario* ☎ *416/364–0054* ⊕ *www.oliverbonacini. com* ⌂ *Reservations essential* ☉ *Closed weekends* Ⓜ *King* ✛ *1:G6.*

$$$
MODERN
CANADIAN

✕**Far Niente.** Classic fine dining gets a face-lift at this opulent, yet comfortable, New York–inspired restaurant. Since the late 1990s, this stalwart has stayed current with oversized hanging lamp shades, flattering lighting, banquettes, and a color scheme that's all black and camel. Chef Gordon Mackie takes simple ingredients and creates luxurious inventions like seafood bouillabaisse salad, lobster potpie, and stuffing crusted pork chop with bourbon barbeque sauce. Belgian chocolate s'mores are the perfect finale to the meal. The impressive wine selection is heavily California-focused, with more than 4,400 bottles total. ⊠ *187 Bay St., Financial District, Toronto, Ontario* ☎ *416/214–9922* ⊕ *www. farnienterestaurant.com* ⌂ *Reservations essential* ☉ *Closed Sun. No lunch Sat.* Ⓜ *King* ✛ *1:F6.*

$$
CANADIAN

✕**FOUR.** While other eateries are busy curing and preserving in their kitchens, FOUR zones in on another trend, healthful eating, with a menu of dishes that are all under 650 calories. Directly below sister restaurant Far Niente, it has a buoyant atmosphere of high-top tables and a three-sided bar in the center of the dining room. Dishes are either steamed, grilled, or broiled to deliver big and bold flavors like those in the grilled calamari with black bean sauce made from scratch and the cuts-like-butter beef tenderloin in horseradish vinaigrette. Don't think for a second that you will refrain from dessert, as each decadent choice comes in a shot glass—the perfect portion to leave you craving a return visit. ⊠ *187 Bay St., Financial District, Toronto, Ontario*

3

Canoe puts a modern spin on traditional Canadian fare.

☎ *416/368–1444* ⊕ *www.fourtoronto.com* ⚓ *Reservations essential* ☉ *Closed weekends* Ⓜ *King* ✛ *1:F6.*

$$
BRITISH
Fodor'sChoice
★

✕ **The Gabardine.** Cozy and unpretentious, this gastro-pub stands out from the other restaurants in the area that cater mostly to suits with a corporate AmEx. A light space of white walls, ceilings, and counters is the backdrop for pub classics like chicken liver pâté and salt cod cakes, but updated with gourmet touches like smoked paprika aioli for the latter. Moist and juicy roasted brined pork with creamed polenta is comforting, as is the house-ground sirloin bacon cheeseburger with aioli. ✉ *372 Bay St., Financial District, Toronto, Ontario* ☎ *647/352–3211* ⊕ *www.thegabardine.com* ☉ *Closed weekends* ✛ *1:G5.*

$$$$
AMERICAN

✕ **Reds Bistro & Bar.** A clubby and vibrant decor emphasizes natural materials as a backdrop for chef Michael Steh's wine-inspired American classics. Catering to the office-tower set, the bustling ground-floor bar is the place to sample international picks from the broad wine list (80 by the glass), and the charcuterie tasting plate. Visit the upstairs dining room for starters like beef tartar, or entrées like roast duck breast with fennel and anise scented farro. ✉ *77 Adelaide St. W, Financial District, Toronto, Ontario* ☎ *416/862–7337* ⊕ *www.redsbistro.com* ☉ *Closed Sun. No lunch Sat.* Ⓜ *King* ✛ *1:F6.*

$$$
SEAFOOD
Fodor'sChoice
★

✕ **Starfish.** Patrick McMurray—a walking encyclopedia of shellfish lore and winner of the 48th World Oyster Opening Championship in Galway, Ireland (won by shucking 30 oysters in under four minutes)—brings you the most unusual tastes from the sea in the most diverse Oyster Bar in North America. Oysters from Ireland, England, Scotland, as well as North America are all available in this casual bistro with simple wooden tables and chairs, a maritime themed bar, and walls covered with small pictures. Ingredients used are local and sustainable. Choose a dancing pink scallop or an Emerald Cove, Belon, or Malpeque oyster. From the kitchen, the oven-roasted organic black cod, boiled East Coast lobsters, crisp salads, and homemade desserts will make you fall for Starfish hook, line, and sinker. ✉ *100 Adelaide St. E, Financial District, Toronto, Ontario* ☎ *416/366–7827* ⊕ *www.starfishoysterbed. com* ⊛ *Reservations essential* ⊗ *No lunch weekends* Ⓜ *King* ✛ *1:H6.*

$$
ITALIAN
☺

✕ **Terroni.** This cool pizza joint whose open shelving is lined with Italian provisions has a menu to suit one and all—from the simple Margherita to the gourmet Polentona of tomato, mozzarella, fontina, speck (smoked prosciutto), and pine nuts. The thin-crust pies, bubbled and blistered, are the best in town, and generous panini are also *buono*. Daily specials are hit and miss, but desserts—like a flourless wedge of Nutella chocolate cake—are almost universally delicious. Try the other location if you are in the Queen Street West area at *720 Queen St. W.* ✉ *57 Adelaide St. E, Financial District, Toronto, Ontario* ☎ *416/504– 1992* ⊕ *www.terroni.ca* Ⓜ *Queen* ✛ *1:H6.*

$$$
JAPANESE

✕ **Takesushi.** Dramatic black and deep-blue decor with a central grove of bamboo sets the stage for a food experience that focuses on presentation, with both a sushi bar and table service. Master chefs thrill customers with an array of spectacular items: black cod with miso paste and king crab salad roll—just to start. Progress on to fresh and beautifully made sushi and sashimi for the main. You can pair those with a vast selection of sake and sake cocktails. ✉ *22 Front St. W, Financial District, Toronto, Ontario* ☎ *416/862–1891* ⊕ *www.takesushi.ca* ⊛ *Reservations essential* ⊗ *Closed Sun. No lunch Sat.* Ⓜ *King* ✛ *1:H6.*

$$$
ITALIAN

✕ **Vertical.** Tucked away off First Canadian Place's food court, the slick, crimson-lit substantial and symmetrical dining room demands your attention. A starter of seared scallops with pancetta vinaigrette introduces you to the rich signature flavors. Other highlights on the Italian menu include house-made pastas like pappardelle with Ontario lamb ragu, whole fish on the grill, and other sustainable seafood selections. The patio is hidden within the building, a secret gem well known to those in the area. ✉ *First Canadian Place, 100 King St. W, main mezzanine, Financial District, Toronto, Ontario* ☎ *416/214–2252* ⊕ *www. verticalrestaurant.ca* ⊗ *Closed weekends* Ⓜ *King* ✛ *1:F6.*

HARBOURFRONT

$$$
AMERICAN

✕ **E11even.** This New York–style restaurant of wooden tables and booths serves well-executed dishes from its predominantly American menu. The double-cut bacon with maple sherry glaze is the perfect example of sweet and savory, and the slow-roasted prime rib is a model piece of steak that's tender and flavorful. Wine choices are presented on an iPad, where a full description of the characteristics of each option is given. ✉ *15 York St., Harbourfront, Toronto, Ontario* ☎ *416/815–1111* ⊕ *www.e11even.ca* ⊗ *Closed Sun.*

$$$$
STEAKHOUSE

✕ **Harbour Sixty Steakhouse.** When you are eating the finest foods, you want an opulent setting to match, and you won't be disappointed as you walk up stone steps to the grand entrance of the restored Harbour Commission building. A baroque-inspired foyer leads to a sleek marble bar. On the lower level is the wall-to-wall wine storage that houses the goods from their 36-page wine list. Whet your appetite with the zesty shrimp cocktail. Bone-in rib steak is a specialty, and dover sole runs out quickly. The comfortable high-backed armchairs and spacious, curved booths are particularly hard to abandon after the tab is settled. ⊠ *60 Harbour St., Harbourfront, Toronto, Ontario* ☎ *416/777–2111* ⊕ *www.harboursixty.com* ⊗ *No lunch weekends* Ⓜ *Union* ✚ *1:F6.*

OLD TOWN

$$$
MODERN
CANADIAN

✕ **Colborne Lane.** Claudio Aprile, recognized as one of the most innovative chefs in Canada, proves that he is more than just a master of kitchen pyrotechnics and liquid nitrogen in his fun and funky domain, housed in a modern room with whitewashed walls and raw, industrial beams. Choose four or five delicious and complex dishes from a list of several on the à la carte menu, like arctic char with butter-poached lobster, beluga lentils, and braised leeks; or enjoy a 10-course dining-room tasting menu that includes seven savory courses and three desserts. A 15-course chef's table tasting menu is also available, served only at an enclosed, semiprivate table in the kitchen. ⊠ *45 Colborne La., Old Town, Toronto, Ontario* ☎ *416/368–9009* ⊕ *www.colbornelane.com* ⊗ *No lunch* Ⓜ *King* ✚ *1:H6.*

$$
IRISH

✕ **Irish Embassy Pub & Grill.** Popular both with the après-work crowd and late-night carousers, this handsome pub is the place for hearty homemade food and a proper pint. The soaring ceilings and columns and mahogany wood make an authentic backdrop for the approachable lineup of imported beers, such as Guinness, Smithwick's, Harp, and Kilkenny. As for the pub food, both the sausage platter with grainy mustard and the bowl of fries with curry sauce satisfy traditional and nontraditional palates. ⊠ *49 Yonge St., Old Town, Toronto, Ontario* ☎ *416/866–8282* ⊕ *www.irishembassypub.com* ⊗ *Closed Sun.* Ⓜ *King* ✚ *1:G6.*

$$$$
MODERN
CANADIAN

✕ **Lucien.** The Gothic-inspired backlit filigree, red ceiling, sparkly chandeliers, heavy curtains, and contemporary menu are not what you would expect from just a restaurant rooted in classic French cusine. While you wait at the bar, have a nibble of shrimp cocktail or *poutine* of smoked beef bacon. Berkshire pork belly served with kimchi, clams, and cuttlefish harmonizes an unusual pairing. Finish with the chocolate complex of four chocolate selections from around the world, a little lesson in being a cocoa connoisseur. ⊠ *36 Wellington St. E, Old Town, Toronto, Ontario* ☎ *416/504–9990* ⊕ *www.lucienrestaurant. com* ⊗ *Closed Sun. No lunch* Ⓜ *King* ✚ *1:H6.*

$$
CONTINENTAL
Fodor'sChoice
★

✕ **Origin.** Another spot helmed by chef Claudio Aprile, Origin is practically on the other end of the spectrum as his venture Colborne Lane. In this sleek space of wooden floors and black decor with playful touches like the chandelier of monster figures, ingredients are allowed to star without being overworked. Great examples are beets with goat cheese and pickled red onions in sherry dressing, fried calamari with caramelized peanut sauce, and wonderfully tender braised pork back ribs in sweet chili sauce. ⊠ *107 King St. E, Old Town, Toronto, Ontario* ☎ *416/603-8009* ⊕ *www.origintoronto.com* ⊗ *No lunch weekends* ✚ *1:H6.*

$$ ✕ **PJ O'Brien.** This traditional pub will make you feel like you're in
IRISH Dublin the second you set foot on its wooden floors. Unlike the legions
of cookie-cutter imitation Irish pubs, with token Irish beers, phony
Irish names, and shamrocks galore, this is the real deal. Tuck into an
authentic meal of Irish Kilkenny Ale–battered fish-and-chips, beef and
Guinness stew, or corned beef and cabbage, ending with bread pud-
ding steeped in whiskey and custard, just like Gran made. The bar
upstairs is even cozier than the one on the main floor. ✉ *39 Colborne
St., Old Town, Toronto, Ontario* ☎ *416/815–7562* ⊕ *www.pjobrien.
com* ☽ *Closed Sun.* Ⓜ *King* ✛ *1:H6.*

$$ ✕ **Toshi Sushi.** Toshi caters to lovers of both raw and cooked Japanese
JAPANESE food in this simple, well-kept room with small tables, light-colored
walls, and hanging lanterns. The daily lunch special is an implausibly
good deal (C$9.50) for warming miso and a bento box loaded with al
dente green beans in luscious sesame-mirin sauce, crunchy shrimp and
vegetable tempura, ginger-tinged green salad, proper sticky rice topped
with chicken teriyaki, and orange wedges to finish. Don't bypass the
stellar sushi lineup, including European-influenced torched foie gras or
buttered bread-crumb oysters, and chef's specials such as tuna carpaccio
and crispy flounder. ■**TIP**➔ **Call ahead for the omakase (chef's choice)
menu and join the in-the-know Japanese businesspeople at the eight-
seat bar at the back.** ✉ *565 King St. W, Old Town, Toronto, Ontario*
☎ *416/260–8588* ⊕ *www.toshisushi.ca* ☽ *Closed Sun.* Ⓜ *King* ✛ *1:D6.*

ENTERTAINMENT DISTRICT

$$$ ✕ **Buca.** Amidst an abundance of extremes in this neighborhood—stodgy
ITALIAN pasta drowned in marinara or authentic dishes in super formal dining
rooms—this rustic yet stylish Italian restaurant that makes everything
in-house is refreshing. Tucked into an alleyway just off King Street, the
repurposed boiler room has exposed brick walls, metal columns, and
wooden tables that reflect the natural philosophy behind the food by
Chef Rob Gentile. Start with the selection of cured meats, including
cinnamon and clove–rubbed pancetta or *nodini,* warm bread knots
seasoned with rosemary and sea salt. For the lightest pasta dish you can
imagine, order the agnolotti *dal plin,* stuffed with buffalo ricotta, in a
sauce of chopped sweet peas, sweet butter, and aged ricotta. End your
meal with an insanely luscious dessert, such as basil gelato made with
duck eggs. Wines are meticulously procured from Italy by the sommelier
to complement the dishes. ✉ *604 King St. W, Entertainment District,
Toronto, Ontario* ☎ *416/865–1600* ⊕ *www.buca.ca* ⌘ *Reservations
essential* ☽ *Closed Sun. No lunch Sat.* Ⓜ *Osgoode* ✛ *1:C6.*

$$$ ✕ **Crush Wine Bar.** Polished hardwood floors in this old building give it a
MODERN fresh veneer, and an open kitchen lets you see the corps of chefs at work
CANADIAN at this wine bar. The locally sourced menu is a dreamscape of the chefs'
expertise. Lighter dishes to start the meal include seared scallops on
celery root puree and charcuterie board. For entrées, the selections are
straightforward and well executed, like pork chop with brussels sprouts
and curried apple sauce, and duo of lamb. A sommelier does wine pairings by the glass with panache, suggesting just the right tipple for ricotta
and spinch agnolotti in Pernod cream. ✉ *455 King St. W, Entertainment*

District, Toronto, Ontario ☎ 416/977–1234 ⊕ www.crushwinebar.com
⚘ *Reservations essential* ⊙ *Closed Sun.* Ⓜ *St. Andrew* ✛ *1:D6.*

$$$ ✕ **The Fifth.** Enter through the Easy Social Club, a main-floor dance
FRENCH club, and take a freight elevator to this semiprivate dining club and
loft space with the right balance of formality and flirtation. The mood
is industrial-strength romantic. In winter, sit on a sofa in front of a
huge fireplace; in summer, dine on the gazebo terrace. Entrées include
a wide variety of steaks, miso-glazed salmon, and rack of lamb with
rosemary jus. Vegetarian offerings include the risotto of the day and
mushroom ravioli. ✉ *225 Richmond St. W, Entertainment District,
Toronto, Ontario* ☎ 416/979–3005 ⊕ www.thefifthgrill.com ⚘ *Reservations essential* ⊙ *Closed Sun.–Wed. No lunch* Ⓜ *Osgoode* ✛ *1:F5.*

$$$ ✕ **Lee.** Everyone looks beautiful here, on pink pedestals in the glow of
ASIAN fuchsia Lucite tables, in a room hung with transparent copper screens.
Famed Toronto chef Susur Lee's creations mix Asian and European
sensibilities and are served on handmade plates from mainland China
and Hong Kong. Small, perfect dishes like spicy Hunan chicken wings
that fill your nose with heady aromas; Asian-style salmon ceviche with
pickled daikon and ponzu sauce; and duck confit roll with oven-dried
pineapples and ice-wine syrup all tickle your senses. ✉ *603 King St. W,
Entertainment District, Toronto, Ontario* ☎ 416/504–7867 ⊕ www.
susur.com ⚘ *Reservations essential* ⊙ *Closed Sun.* Ⓜ *St. Andrew*
✛ *1:C6.*

$$$ ✕ **Luma.** Duck out of a double-feature at the TIFF Bell Lightbox to grab
MODERN lunch at Luma. Consistent with the artistic nature of the glass-paneled
CANADIAN film festival and film education venue, this restaurant plays with global
flavors and mostly Canadian ingredients. Try the grilled octopus with
smoked paprika, preserved lemons, and candied olives; roasted cod with
seared sweetbreads; and free-range chicken with semolina and braised
garlic. ✉ *330 King St. W, Entertainment District, Toronto, Ontario*
☎ 647/288–4715 ⊙ *No dinner Sun.* ✛ *1:E6.*

$$ ✕ **Rodney's Oyster House.** A den of oceanic delicacies, this playful basement
SEAFOOD raw bar is frequented by dine-alones and showbiz types. Among
the options are soft-shell steamer clams, a variety of smoked fish, and
"Oyster Slapjack Chowder," plus Merigomish oysters from Nova Scotia
or perfect Malpeques from owner Rodney Clark's own oyster beds
on Prince Edward Island. A zap of Rodney's in-house line of condiments
or a splash of vodka and freshly grated horseradish are eye-openers.
■TIP→ Shared meals and half orders are okay. Be sure to ask
about the daily "Grace's soup" and "white-plate" specials. ✉ *469 King St.
W, Entertainment District, Toronto, Ontario* ☎ 416/363–8105 ⊕ www.
rodneysoysterhouse.com ⊙ *Closed Sun.* Ⓜ *St. Andrew* ✛ *1:D6.*

$$$ ✕ **The Roosevelt Room.** Many swanky and soulless establishments call
FRENCH themselves supper clubs, but few manage to deliver both food and
entertainment. Enter the Roosevelt Room—a space elegantly inspired
by the Roaring '20s, with dark fixtures, peacock feathers, a curved
ceiling, and gold trim. Exclusive events with celebrity appearances are
common here, as are themed music nights with DJs. Drinks range from
traditional cocktails like the sidecar and manhattan to unusual French
wines. In the kitchen, Chef Trevor Wilkinson dishes out familiar flavors

CLOSE UP

Local Chains Worth a Taste

Torontonians head to the numerous Second Cup cafés for their caffeine fix.

For those times when all you want is a quick bite, consider these local chains where you're assured of fresh, tasty food and good value.

Freshii: A healthier choice (formerly Lettuce Eatery) where baseball-capped salad artists get through the lunch rush like a championship team. The interior is all steely white and blond wood, and designer greens and custom-made sandwiches clearly appeal to the masses. The Cobb is a standout. ⊕ *www.freshii.com*

Harvey's: Harvey's says it makes a hamburger a beautiful thing, and we agree—whether it's a beef, salmon, or veggie burger. Made-to-order toppings will please even the most discerning kids. The fries are a hit, too. ⊕ *www. harveys.ca*

Lick's: Great Homeburgers and turkey burgers, plus the best veggie burger you'll ever taste. Onion rings, fresh fries, extra-thick milk shakes, and frozen yogurt will keep you coming back for more. ⊕ *www.lickshomeburgers.com*

Milestones: Duck into the cool comfort of this very happening spot for Cajun popcorn shrimp or stone-oven pizza. Spit-roasted half chicken with curly fries and gloriously spicy cornbread muffins may be the kitchen's best. ⊕ *www.milestonesrestaurants.com*

Second Cup: You'll find coffees plain and fancy, as well as flavored hot chocolates, a variety of teas, Italian soft drinks, and nibbles that include muffins, bagels, and raspberry–white chocolate scones. ⊕ *www.secondcup.com*

Spring Rolls: For Asian favorites on the fly: appealing soups and spiced salads, savory noodle dishes, and spring rolls all satiate lunchtime hunger pangs. ⊕ *www.springrolls.ca*

Swiss Chalet Rotisserie and Grill: Children are welcome at this Canadian institution known for its rotisserie chicken and barbecued ribs, in portions that suit every family member. ■TIP→ **Ask for extra sauce for your french fries.** ⊕ *www. swisschalet.ca*

Tim Horton's: It never closes, and coffee is made fresh every 20 minutes. Check out the variety of fresh donuts, muffins, bagels, and soup-and-sandwich combos. The Canadian Maple donut is an obvious frontrunner. ⊕ *www.timhortons.com*

using local ingredients. Truffled scented mac and cheese is an updated version of comfort food, while the herb-roasted chicken supreme pays homage to classic French cuisine. ⊠ *2 Drummond Pl., Entertainment District, Toronto, Ontario* 🕾 *416/599–9000* ⊕ *www.therooseveltroom. ca* ⌕ *Reservations essential* ⊘ *Closed Sun.–Wed.* Ⓜ *St. Andrew* ✛ *1:E6.*

$$
ASIAN
✕ **Spice Route.** This massive hodgepodge of Asian Zen furnishings, such as a 16-foot rotating vertical waterfall, screen-printed images, and statues of Buddha scattered throughout, is the place to go for both the trendy and not-so-trendy. Entrées, which include mussels steamed in red Thai curry and Kaffir lime and the surf and turf of Kobe and tempura soft shell crab mini burgers, are meant to be shared. End your meal with the banana tempura and apple-mango dragon roll, or try one of the tasty beverages such as a lychee martini or a hot or cold spiked tea. The DJ's nightly music can get loud, so request a table in a corner if possible. ⊠ *499 King St. W, Entertainment District, Toronto, Ontario* 🕾 *416/849–1808* ⊕ *www.spiceroute.ca* ⊘ *No lunch weekends* Ⓜ *St. Andrew* ✛ *1:D6.*

$$$$
MODERN
CANADIAN
✕ **Toca.** The swanky Ritz Carlton dining experience comes to Toronto in the form of Toca, where chef Tom Brodi invents dishes like avocado frites, venison loin with fava vines, and crab marrow with cheese and fennel pollen, in addition to dishes like ricotta ravioli and well-aged steaks for the traditionalists. The dining room, a blend of tasteful beige and brown, has a curvaceous wood-beamed ceiling and a glass-enclosed cheese-cave. High rollers can dine at the chef's table, inside a private dining nook in the kitchen. ⊠ *181 Wellington St. W, Entertainment District, Toronto, Ontario* 🕾 *416/572–8008* ▭ *No credit cards* ✛ *1:F6.*

CHINATOWN, KENSINGTON MARKET, AND QUEEN WEST

CHINATOWN

$$
CHINESE
✕ **Asian Legend.** With wall coverings that depict ancient explorers' maps, stone floor tiles, and white paper lanterns, this restaurant looks both modern and sleek, and its efficient servers know the menu well, though it covers many regions of a vast country. Best are the Northern and Szechuan dishes like soft, soup-filled meat dumplings and the unusual and tasty tea-smoked duck. If you like fish, a whole bass smothered in a sauce of chili, garlic, black bean, and vinegar is memorable. ⊠ *418 Dundas St. W, Chinatown, Toronto, Ontario* 🕾 *416/977–3909* ⌕ *Reservations essential* Ⓜ *St. Patrick* ✛ *1:E4.*

$$$$
CHINESE
Fodor's Choice
★
✕ **Lai Wah Heen.** In an elegant room with a sculpted ceiling, etched-glass turntables, and silver serving dishes, the service is formal; here mahogany-color Peking duck is wheeled in on a trolley and presented with panache as it's cut into paper-thin slices. Excellent choices from the 100-dish inventory include wok-fried shredded beef and vegetables in a crisp potato nest, and dried seafood delicacies like dried scallops with fried garlic on a bed of vegetables. Dim sum is divine for lunch: meat–filled morsels and translucent dumplings burst with juicy fillings of shark's fin sprinkled with bright-red lobster roe and in shrimp dumplings with green tops reminiscent of baby bok choy. Sister restaurant **Lai Toh Heen**, in the Yonge and Eglinton neighborhood (⊠ *692 Mt. Pleasant Rd.* 🕾 *416/489–8922* ⊕ *www.laitohheen.com*), also wins fans

CLOSE UP

Vegetarian Restaurants

The days when a vegetarian had few menu options other than a limp iceberg salad are past. Today meatless options in Toronto abound, and vegetarian restaurants are increasingly creative and delicious.

Fresh by Juice for Life. The continental fare from Asian Buddha bowl to Middle Eastern starter plate, and great selection of energy elixirs and smart drinks at Fresh by Juice for Life will make meat look boring. ⊠ *326 Bloor St. W, The Annex, Toronto, Ontario* ☎ *416/531–2635* ⊕ *www. freshrestaurants.ca.*

Fressen. Queen Street West has always been ahead of the curve, and there have been vegetarian restaurants there for years. These days, the best is Fressen, *(see full review)* where diners can remain true to their vegan souls. Tofu with an exotic turn and exceptionally tasty pasta dishes appeal even to carnivores. ⊠ *478 Queen St. W, Toronto, Ontario* ☎ *416/504–5127* ⊕ *www. fressenrestaurant.com.*

Full Moon Vegetarian. Another herbivore option is this restaurant, offering delicious faux meaty dishes such as lemon "chicken" and stir-fried "beef" made with bean curd and texturized vegetable protein. ⊠ *638 Dundas St. W, Chinatown, Toronto, Ontario* ☎ *416/213–1210* ☺ *Closed Wed.*

Kings Café. In Kensington Market, this café is spacious and open. This Chinese vegetarian- and health-oriented center of calm in the bustling market offers vegan delights like mushroom, cabbage, and ginger dumplings, and eggplant and broccoli stir-fry. Hot ginger tea is a must. Pick up some quality tea leaves in the little shop inside the restaurant.

⊠ *192 Augusta Ave., Toronto, Ontario* ☎ *416/591–1340* ⊕ *www. kingscafe.com* ⊟ *No credit cards.*

Live Organic Food Bar. If you want to try something completely different, check out "live food" at this restaurnt. The unique vegetarian dishes are completely raw and free of dairy, wheat, and preservatives. Try the lasagna of zucchini layered with cashew ricotta; the buckwheat pizza with guacamole, tomatoes, and olives; and the butterscotch hemp mousse. Choose from a good selection of organic wines, cocktails, and beer to go with the meal. ⊠ *264 Dupont St., at Spadina Ave., The Annex, Toronto, Ontario* ☎ *416/515–2002* ⊕ *www.livefoodbar. com* ⊟ *No credit cards* ☺ *Closed Sun. and Mon.*

Udupi Palace. If you visit the India Bazaar area, dine on authentic south Indian *dosas* (pancakes) at Udupi Palace. Paper-thin, and crisp on the outside and soft on the inside, they are stuffed with potato, onions, mustard seeds, and lentils. The mild spicing will appeal to all ages. Soups are loaded with veggies and sing of coconut and coriander. It's gently priced, with complete dinners for C$12 per person. ⊠ *1460 Gerrard St. E, Toronto, Ontario* ☎ *416/405–8138* ⊕ *www.udupipalace.ca.*

Urban Herbivore. Inside an old house with an exposed-brick open kitchen, you'll dine on stools at high tables and try rustic daily soups or design your own salads and sandwiches on house-made flax bread. ⊠ *64 Oxford St., Kensington Market, Toronto, Ontario* ☎ *416/927–1231* ⊕ *www.fressenrestaurant.com.*

3

with a similar menu. ✉ *Metropolitan Hotel, 108 Chestnut St., 2nd fl., Chinatown, Toronto, Ontario* ☎ *416/977–9899* ⊕ *www.laiwahheen. com* ♨ *Reservations essential* Ⓜ *St. Patrick* ✛ *1:F4.*

$$ ✗ **Lee Garden.** Always packed, this Cantonese eatery with printouts of
CHINESE recommended dishes taped on green walls does everything well. Oys-
Fodor'sChoice ters steamed in black bean sauce are meaty and flavorful, Grandfa-
★ ther's smoked chicken is aromatic and moist, and flash-fried salt and pepper shrimp is addictive. Avoid lines by going early. ✉ *331 Spadina, Avenue, Chinatown, Toronto, Ontario* ☎ *416/593–9524* ⊕ *www. leegardenrestaurant.ca* ✛ *1:D4.*

$$ ✗ **Matahari Grill.** It's hard to pass up any of the Southeast Asian dishes
MALAYSIAN here, so you might use size as a decision-making tool. If you have a taste for adventure, order the platter for two: a sampling of satays, spring rolls, deep-fried wontons, *keropok*, and *achar achar*. Then get into more exotic flavors with the *sambal udang*—grilled tamarind-scented prawns in sweet, sour-and-spicy tamarind-shallots *sambal.* The seafood curry grill is scallops, prawns, calamari, tomatoes, and okra served in a tanta-lizing coconut-curry broth. In summer there's a tiny outdoor patio, but most people prefer the sophisticated green-and-white decor inside. ✉ *39 Baldwin St., Chinatown, Toronto, Ontario* ☎ *416/596–2832* ⊕ *www. mataharigrill.com* ♨ *Reservations essential* ◷ *Closed Mon. No lunch weekends* Ⓜ *St. Patrick* ✛ *1:E4.*

$ ✗ **Spadina Garden.** The Chen family has owned Spadina Garden for
CHINESE more than a decade, and the restaurant's dishes are Toronto classics.
ↈ This is largely the cuisine of inland northwest China, so there is no tank of finny creatures to peruse. Start with barbecued honey-garlic spareribs or hot-and-sour soup before moving on to entrées. Try the chili chicken and the crispy ginger beef along side steamed rice. The room itself is calm, with standard black lacquer, high-back chairs and red paper lanterns. ✉ *114 Dundas St. W, Chinatown, Toronto, Ontario* ☎ *416/977–3413, 416/977–3414* Ⓜ *St. Patrick or Dundas* ✛ *1:G4.*

$ ✗ **Swatow.** If there is an equivalent to a fast-paced casual Hong Kong–
CHINESE style diner in Chinatown, this would be it; here you'll find cheap, hon-est, and authentic food. In bright and clean surrounds, communal diners enjoy heaping bowls of congee and customized noodle soups, including the best fish balls and shrimp dumpling bowl in town. Rice dishes are also a filling specialty, the best of which, *fuk-kin*, tosses fried rice together with shrimp, crab, scallops, chicken, and egg. ✉ *309 Spa-dina Ave., Chinatown, Toronto, Ontario* ☎ *416/977–0601* Ⓜ *Dundas* ✛ *1:D4.*

$$ ✗ **Wah Sing Seafood Restaurant.** Just one of a jumble of Asian eateries
CHINESE clustered on a tiny Kensington Market street, this newly renovated, meticulously clean and spacious restaurant has two-for-one lobsters (in season, which is almost always). They're scrumptious and tender, with black-bean sauce or ginger and green onion. You can also choose giant shrimp Szechuan-style or one of the lively queen crabs from the tank. Chicken and vegetarian dishes are good, too. ✉ *47 Baldwin St., Chinatown, Toronto, Ontario* ☎ *416/599–8822* Ⓜ *College* ✛ *1:E4.*

KENSINGTON MARKET

$$$ ✕ **La Palette.** Formerly in Kensington Market, this bright spot moved to
FRENCH the hip and trendy Queen West area, and continues to stake its claim as
Fodor's Choice one of Toronto's truly authentic bistros. The updated location ditched
★ old checkered tablecloths and vinyl chairs, and went for simple decor
of exposed brick interior and wooden floors and chairs. Favorite dishes
include luscious Camembert fritters with maple-glazed pumpkin seeds,
garlicky escargots, good steak frites, rack of lamb, and many quaffable
wines, including a long list of European choices. A three-course prix-fixe
(C$32) is available; it's a great spot for brunch, too. ⊠ *492 Queen St.
W, Queen West, Toronto, Ontario* ☎ *416/929–4900* ⊕ *www.lapalette.
ca* Ⓜ *College* ✛ *1:D3.*

QUEEN WEST

$ ✕ **Fressen.** In forward-thinking Queen West, a feast of herbivorous cui-
VEGETARIAN sine jumps off the vegan menu at this relaxing amber-lit café. Besides
being meat- and dairy-free, dishes are also noted as gluten- or wheat-
free. Pan-fried cornmeal polenta is suited up with herbed tomato sauce;
handmade pasta dishes are plump with wild mushrooms and vegeta-
bles. Cleanse your palate with innovative fresh juice cocktails and local
organic wines. ⊠ *478 Queen St. W, Queen West, Toronto, Ontario*
☎ *416/504–5127* ⊕ *www.fressenrestaurant.com* ⊙ *No lunch weekdays*
Ⓜ *Osgoode* ✛ *1:D5.*

$$$ ✕ **Nota Bene.** Chef David Lee and partners, the team behind high-end
MODERN stalwart Splendido, have moved on to create this more affordable
CANADIAN option—and if the pedigree doesn't get you, the crispy duck salad with
green papaya slaw will. A stone's throw from the Four Seasons Opera
House, the modern dining room is all clean lines in Brazilian cherry
wood, chartreuse leather banquettes, and panels of contemporary art.
Chef Lee turns out finely wrought Continental dishes with seasonal
Canadian ingredients. Jalapeños add zip to a refreshing yellowtail cevi-
che, and the Mediterranean sea bass with beurre noisette is substan-
tial without being heavy. ⊠ *180 Queen St. W, Queen West, Toronto,
Ontario* ☎ *416/977–6400* ⊕ *www.notabenerestaurant.com* ⊙ *Closed
Sun. No lunch Sat.* Ⓜ *Osgoode* ✛ *1:F5.*

$$ ✕ **Oyster Boy.** Whether you get them baked (in one of 12 different ways),
SEAFOOD fried, or raw, oysters are the thing at this casual neighborhood spot. A
chalkboard spells out what's fresh and available, along with sizing and
price for the beauties. There's a pleasing array of house condiments
with which to slurp your choices. Other treats include beer-battered
fish and chips and oyster potpie, and excellent onion rings. A nice
selection of wines and beers, as well as cool, friendly servers, makes for
a fun night out. ⊠ *872 Queen St. W, Queen West, Toronto, Ontario*
☎ *416/534–3432* ⊕ *www.oysterboy.ca* ⊙ *No lunch* Ⓜ *Queen* ✛ *1:A5.*

QUEEN'S PARK, THE ANNEX, AND YORKVILLE

THE ANNEX

¢ ✕ **Future Bakery & Café.** Aside from European-style baked goods, this
CAFÉ spot also serves Old World recipes like beef borscht, buckwheat cab-
bage rolls, and potato-cheese pierogi slathered with thick sour cream.

It's a place beloved by the pastry-and-coffee crowd, students wanting great value, and people-watchers, from 7 am to 2 am. Health-conscious foodies looking for fruit salad with homemade yogurt and honey get their sweet fix, while those who like to indulge order the *dulce de leche* cheesecake. A St. Lawrence Market branch (⊠ *95 Front St. E*) sells just bread and pastries and closes early in the evening. ⊠ *483 Bloor St. W, The Annex, Toronto, Ontario* ☎ *416/922–5875* ⊕ *www.futurebakery. com* ⌂ *Reservations not accepted* Ⓜ *Bathurst* ✢ *1:C1.*

$$ ✕ **Le Paradis.** This is the kind of comfortable neighborhood place you'd
FRENCH find in Paris—checkerboard floors, sunny walls with murals and black-and-white photographs, and waiters rushing around in white aprons. A mixed crowd comes to this authentic French bistro-on-a-budget for the ambience, daily menu, and gently priced wine list. Almost everything on the menu of seasonal offerings is under $20; popular menu items include Blaff à la Martiniquaise, mixed fish, calamari, and shrimp braised in tomato broth; Coq au Riesling, rooster or chicken in white wine sauce; Couscous Royale; and classic dessert options like flourless cake and crème caramel. ⊠ *166 Bedford Rd., The Annex, Toronto, Ontario* ☎ *416/921–0995* ⊕ *www.leparadis.com* ⌂ *Reservations essential* Ⓜ *Dupont* ✢ *1:F1.*

$$ ✕ **Live Organic Food Bar.** Sunny decor will charm you, but the real draw
VEGETARIAN here is the imaginative (and enthusiastic) owners and the amazing raw-foods they create. A lasagna of ground cashews, marinated tomatoes, and basil pesto, between layers of zucchini, is a crowd favorite. The stove is used ever so slightly for "roasting" root vegetables served over mixed greens with balsamic drizzle and for warm tomato soup. A long list of seriously fresh–squeezed juices is served. Be aware: service is casual. ⊠ *264 Dupont St., The Annex, Toronto, Ontario* ☎ *416/515–2002* ⊕ *www.livefoodbar.com* ⊘ *Closed Mon. No dinner Sun.* Ⓜ *Spadina* ✢ *1:C1.*

$$$ ✕ **Loire.** A close-to-perfect neighborhood bistro, this spot is named for
FRENCH the place where the French owners grew up and formed their palates. Now it's where locals enjoy lightly finessed dishes of seasonal ingredients like oysters with horseradish mignonette made interesting with the addition of apples, slow-braised pork belly served unusually with a quail egg, mac and cheese with braised lamb, a spectacular Loire lamb burger with tomato jam and Québec brie, and wonderful wines, many from the Loire Valley. End the meal with one of the cheese plates featuring Québec and French selections. The spare dining room has warmth, thanks to soft lighting, and the service is impeccable (it's usually the owner–sommelier dancing about the narrow space). Overall, you can't help but be enchanted. ⊠ *119 Harbord St., The Annex, Toronto, Ontario* ☎ *416/850–8330* ⊕ *www.loirerestaurant.ca* ⊘ *Closed Sun. and Mon. No lunch Sat.* Ⓜ *Spadina* ✢ *1:D2.*

$$ ✕ **Messis.** Skillful chef-owner Eugene Shewchuk presents fresh, pretty
MODERN dishes in a light and airy space with accents of wood and linen. Basil-
CANADIAN crusted roast rack of New Zealand lamb with polenta and creamy curried coconut risotto with jumbo shrimp exemplify the inspired comfort food. Messis is a favorite for small celebrations because of lovely desserts like a phyllo package of wild blueberries and white chocolate.

Diners enjoy sophisticated cuisine made with local ingredients at Nota Bene.

The summer patio twinkles with lights at night. ⊠ *97 Harbord St., The Annex, Toronto, Ontario* ☎ *416/920–2186* ⊕ *www.messisrestaurant. ca* ⊗ *No lunch Sat.–Mon.* Ⓜ *Spadina* ✛ *1:D2.*

$$
SOUTHERN

✕ **Southern Accent.** On a street lined with antiques shops, bookstores, and galleries sits this funky Cajun and Creole restaurant. Perch at the bar, order a martini and hush puppies, and chat with the resident psychic. Whimsical knickknacks adorn every inch of the place, and dining rooms on two floors offer a market-driven menu. Some constants are Bourbon Street chicken (blackened boneless chicken breast in lemon butter sauce), cracker catfish (a fillet coated with spiced crackers) served with jalapeño tartar sauce, and shrimp étouffée with caramelized vegetables. ⊠ *595 Markham St., The Annex, Toronto, Ontario* ☎ *416/536–3211* ⊕ *www.southernaccent.com* ⊗ *Closed Mon. No lunch* Ⓜ *Bathurst* ✛ *1:C1.*

$$$
MODERN
CANADIAN
Fodor's Choice
★

✕ **Splendido.** Current chef Victor Barry, a disciple of former owner and superstar chef David Lee, ensures that even the hardest to please will be thrilled by the tasting menus here. The selection might include maple syrup charred mackerel, poached white asparagus with tarragon and preserved lemon, and pancetta-wrapped water buffalo. The kitchen is peerless, and the front of the house functions like a fine Swiss watch. A huge iron chandelier serves as the focal point in one of the city's most beautifully balanced dining rooms. Special touches include a champagne trolley and purse stools for the ladies. ⊠ *88 Harbord St., The Annex, Toronto, Ontario* ☎ *416/929–7788* ⌂ *Reservations essential* ⊗ *Closed Mon.* Ⓜ *Spadina* ✛ *1:D2.*

QUEEN'S PARK

$ ✕ **7 West Cafe.** No late-night craving goes unsatisfied at this 24-hour
ECLECTIC haven for the hip and hungry. Snacks, pastas, sandwiches, soups, and
drinks are all served in this eclectic, three-story, dimly lit café. Everything is homemade and comes with a green salad. Soups like Moroccan
or vegetarian chili are comforting and filling, and dinner-size sandwiches like the grilled herbed chicken breast with honey mustard are
huge. The menu of basic foods sets the tone for simple wine, beer,
and cocktail choices. It's not fancy, but there's plenty to choose from.
⊠ *7 Charles St. W, Queen's Park, Toronto, Ontario* ☎ *416/928–9041*
⊕ *www.7westcafe.com* Ⓜ *Bloor-Yonge* ✛ *1:G2.*

$$$$ ✕ **C5.** You can't miss the angular, Daniel Libeskind–designed crys-
MODERN talline extension to the Royal Ontario Museum, which juts out over
CANADIAN Bloor Street; and you shouldn't miss dining at C5, the starkly designed,
Fodor'sChoice unapologetically modernist restaurant on the addition's fifth floor. Visi-
★ tors enjoy panoramic city views, while savvy locals know to arrive early
for a drink in the stylish lounge, whose black furnishings juxtapose
with the adjacent brightly lighted, white dining room. An underrated
house-made charcuterie platter and a famous boutique cheese platter
best demonstrate the focus on regional cuisine, complemented further
by Ontario and Canadian wines. The tasting menu showcases the chef's
inspirations and seasonal ingredients beautifully. Brunch is just as popular as dinner, though drawing a more varied crowd with families and
larger groups. ■ TIP➔ If you're coming for dinner, time your reservation for
sunset. ⊠ *100 Queen's Park, 5th fl., enter from Bloor St., Queen's Park,
Toronto, Ontario* ☎ *416/586–7928* ⊕ *www.c5restaurant.ca* ⌔ *Reservations essential* ⊗ *No dinner Sun.–Wed.* Ⓜ *Museum* ✛ *1:F1.*

$ ✕ **The Gardiner Café.** Well-known local- and seasonal-cuisine advocate
MODERN chef Jamie Kennedy is still at the helm here, although his name is no
CANADIAN longer in the title. All limestone, slate, blond oak, and glass, the airy
Fodor'sChoice dining room is a fitting accompaniment to a simple focus on sandwiches
★ and salads. The lunch crowd (dinner is not served) enjoys seasonal starters before more substantial offerings like a smooth Ontario sweet corn
bisque with a plump, seared scallop. Count on excellent signature frites
with cider mayo, fabulous cheese plates and charcuterie, the daily poutine, and bulgur wheat salad. Wines are matched with each dish, including many from Ontario's Niagara region—home, too, to the berries in
the pleasingly retro strawberry shortcake. To enjoy Jamie Kennedy's
creations in the evening, head to Gilead Café at the less accessible neighborhood of Corktown. ⊠ *111 Queen's Park, Queen's Park, Toronto,
Ontario* ☎ *416/362–1957* ⊕ *www.jamiekennedy.ca* ⊗ *Open for lunch
7 days, for private functions only in the evening* Ⓜ *Museum* ✛ *1:F1.*

YORKVILLE

$$ ✕ **Asuka.** Among hip and often pretentious establishments, this sunken
JAPANESE space stands out for its simplicity and coziness and proves that celebrity
spotting and fine Asian cuisine are not exclusive to upscale restaurants.
You won't find any avant-garde dishes here, but you will find well-
crafted and fresh sushi and sashimi at a reasonable price for the area.
Try substituting soybean wrapper for nori for hand rolls and sushi.

CLOSE UP

Alfresco Dining

From the first sign of warm weather until September's cool evenings, Torontonians hit the deck, the patio, the courtyard, and the rooftop terrace.

YORKVILLE

Amber. The patio at Amber rocks with cool, late-night people. ✉ *119 Yorkville Ave., Yorkville, Toronto, Ontario* ☎ *416/926–9037* ⊕ *www.amberinyorkville.com.*

Hemingway's. Throngs of people are attracted to Hemingway's colorful and bustling roof garden. ✉ *142 Cumberland St., Yorkville, Toronto, Ontario* ☎ *416/968–2828* ⊕ *www.hemingways.to.*

MBCo. Gourmet sandwiches, pizza, and soups are served up here to eat on the patio or in the park. ✉ *100 Bloor St. W, Yorkville, Toronto, Ontario* ☎ *416/961–6226* ⊕ *www.mbco.ca.*

Roof Lounge. Enjoy lunch or sip a cosmo and watch the sunset at the quiet and lesser known Roof Lounge. ✉ *Park Hyatt Hotel, 4 Avenue Rd., Yorkville, Toronto, Ontario* ☎ *416/924–5471* ⊕ *www.parktoronto.hyatt.com.*

Summer's Ice Cream. This is the spot to grab homemade ice cream in just-made waffle cones, then stroll in Yorkville Park. ✉ *101 Yorkville Ave., Yorkville, Toronto, Ontario* ☎ *416/944–2637* ⊕ *www.summersicecream.com.*

KENSINGTON MARKET

Christina's. The sidewalk patio at Christina's is a good place to check out the scene. ✉ *513 Danforth Ave., Danforth, Toronto, Ontario* ☎ *416/465–1751* ⊕ *www.christinas.ca.*

Jumbo Empanadas. Savor oversized empanadas and corn pie on the tented patio at this empanadas joint. ✉ *245 Augusta Ave., Kensington Market, Toronto, Ontario* ☎ *416/977–0056.*

Supermarket. Tasty Asian tapas and a boisterous patio are two of the offerings here. ✉ *268 Augusta Ave., Kensington Market, Toronto, Ontario* ☎ *416/840–0501* ⊕ *www.supermarkettoronto.com* ⊘ *Closed Monday.*

Torito. One of the first authentic tapas restaurants in the city, Torito has excellent *patatas bravas* and sangria. ✉ *276 Augusta Ave., Kensington Market, Toronto, Ontario* ☎ *647/436–5874* ⊕ *www.toritorestaurant.com.*

THE ENTERTAINMENT DISTRICT

Black Bull Tavern. One of the largest and most affordable local patios can be found here. ✉ *298 Queen St. W, Queen West, Toronto, Ontario* ☎ *416/593–2766.*

Drake Hotel. Way west, the Drake Hotel has a swanky rooftop prime for people-watching. ✉ *1150 Queen St. W, Queen West, Toronto, Ontario* ☎ *416/531–5042* ⊕ *www.thedrakehotel.ca.*

Queen Mother Café. The garden at the Queen Mother Café is a cool place for East–West dishes. ✉ *208 Queen St. W, Queen West, Toronto, Ontario* ☎ *416/598–4719* ⊕ *www.queenmothercafe.ca.*

Rivoli. A hot outdoor spot for people watching, this lounge is located on cool Queen St. ✉ *322 Queen St. W, Queen West, Toronto, Ontario* ☎ *416/596–1908* ⊕ *www.rivoli.ca.*

3

C5, in the Royal Ontario Museum, treats guests to sleek design, stunning city views, and top-quality regional food and wine.

✉ 108 Yorkville Ave., Yorkville, Toronto, Ontario ☎ 416/975–9084 ⊙ No lunch Sun. Ⓜ Bay ✛ 1:F1.

$$$
ITALIAN
✕ **Bellini's Ristorante.** Never wavering from its focus on elegance, good taste, classic food, and professional service, Bellini's has stood the test of time. The sense of class and air of formality can be felt as soon as you set foot in the regally furnished restaurant with high-backed chairs, wooden wall panels and moldings, and gold light fixtures. If you can't choose among dishes such as roasted pistachio-crusted sea bass, Provimi veal osso buco with saffron risotto and lemon-thyme jus, and lobster risotto with honey mushrooms, mascarpone cheese, and chervil, then there are several set three-course menus to assist you. This is a romantic haven and a quiet oasis for visiting celebs. *✉ 101 Yorkville Ave. W, Yorkville, Toronto, Ontario ☎ 416/929–9111 ⊕ www.bellinis.sites. toronto.com ⊙ No lunch Ⓜ Bay ✛ 1:F1.*

$$
ITALIAN
✕ **Ciao Wine Bar.** This 2010 addition to the Yorkville scene is swanky, yet soulful. A modern staircase greets you upon entrance to a dimly lighted space, filled with put-together patrons; you can sit either on the sleek upper level or the rustic lower level with wooden tables and exposed brick walls. The wine selection is extensive, dominated by European classics and many Italian regional choices. Regulars enjoy reliable and familiar choices like capellini with tomatoes, capers, anchovies, and olives; oven-baked whole fish with lemon and parsley; and the Caprese pizza with cherry tomatoes, *bocconcini* cheese, arugula, and shaved Grana Padano cheese. *✉ 133 Yorkville Ave., Yorkville, Toronto, Ontario ☎ 416/925–2143 ⊕ www.ciaowinebar.com Ⓜ Bay ✛ 1:F1.*

¢ ✕**Crêpes à GoGo.** In this casual bistro, proprietress Veronique and
FRENCH crew turn out simple sandwiches and buckwheat crepes, also known
Fodor's Choice as galettes, using a technique that has been passed down for generations.
★ Signature items include the cheese crepe, a crisped crepe folded around
☺ the sharpness of red onion, the fatty nuttiness of Swiss, a herbaceous
hit of parsley, and a bit of tangy sour cream; and the Veronique, made
of Brie, strawberries, baby spinach, and maple syrup. Apple cider, a
traditional Breton beverage of fruit juice fermented in the bottle just
like champagne, is also served. Crepes are presented in the distinctive square Bretonne-style fold, whereupon Veronique tears down the
paper bag's edges, looks you in the eye, and says, "*Bon appétit.*" ✉ *18
Yorkville Ave., Yorkville, Toronto, Ontario* ☎ *416/922–6765* ⊕ *www.
crepesagogo.com* Ⓜ *Bay* ✛ *1:G1.*

$$ ✕**The Host.** Dine in the garden room among flowering plants or in the
INDIAN handsome dining room at this well-established curry spot. Waiters rush
around carrying baskets of hot naan. Tandoori *machi* (whole fish baked
in a tandoor oven and served on a sizzling plate with onion and cori-
ander) is an excellent dish. Tender sliced lamb is enfolded in a curry of
cashew nuts and whole cardamom. End your meal with such classic
Indian desserts as *golabjabun*, little round cakes soaking in rosewater-
scented honey. ✉ *14 Prince Arthur Ave., Yorkville, Toronto, Ontario*
☎ *416/962–4678* ⊕ *www.welcometohost.com* ⌐ *Reservations essential*
☾ *Closed Mon.* Ⓜ *Bay* ✛ *1:F1.*

$$$$ ✕**Morton's.** Just when you thought this top-notch international chain
STEAKHOUSE couldn't possibly get better, it added glorious additional steak variations
to its repertoire, including steak au poivre, with yummy peppercorn-
cognac sauce; and filet Oskar, topped with crab, asparagus, and béar-
naise. You can still dine on a New York strip or a 48-ounce porterhouse.
All beef is shipped chilled, not frozen, from one Chicago supplier. The
interior has a handsome, wood-panel clubbiness. ✉ *4 Avenue Rd., Yor-
kville, Toronto, Ontario* ☎ *416/925–0648* ⊕ *www.mortons.com* Ⓜ *Bay*
✛ *1:F1.*

$$$ ✕**One.** In the hot Hazelton Hotel, chef-owner Mark McEwan's One
MODERN becomes a celeb-spotting free-for-all during September's Film Festival.
CANADIAN The modern and elegant dining room—rich woods, smoked glass, cow-
hide, and onyx—is the brainchild of designer Yabu Puschelberg (whose
work also includes Bymark and North 44 restaurants). McEwan's ingre-
dient-driven cuisine runs from a first course of ruby tuna sashimi with
yuzu (fragrant citrus) and chili to the deeply satisfying Prime burger
with aged cheddar and smoked bacon. Many dishes, like the USDA
Prime strip loin, arrive perfectly cooked but simply prepared and are
meant to be accompanied by baked bone marrow and watercress. The
all-Canadian cheese lineup is an especially proud menu moment. The
chef ages his own beef, and many agree his steaks are the best in the city.
✉ *The Hazelton Hotel Toronto, 118 Yorkville Ave., Yorkville, Toronto,
Ontario* ☎ *416/963–6300* ⊕ *www.onehazelton.com* ⌐ *Reservations
essential* Ⓜ *Bay* ✛ *1:F1.*

118 < **Where to Eat**

$$$$ ✕ **Pangaea.** Living up to its name, Pangaea harmonizes global-inspired
MODERN cuisine with local ingredients. A long skylight by the bar and private
CANADIAN dining rooms give the loft an ethereal quality, but even the decor has
Fodor'sChoice a regional connection in Toronto-made chairs. The menu concentrates
★ on sustainable seafood. Curried mussels set the stage for refined entrees
like pan-roasted duck breast with *rösti* (Swiss potato pancake), and pan-
seared Ontario pickerel with sauteed fiddleheads, ramps, and mushrooms in a bacon butter sauce. Vegetarian dishes can be requested
and are just as thoughtful and substantial as the rest of the menu.
Desserts made by pastry chef Colen Quinn uphold the high standard;
a standout is warm citrus doughnuts with Asian spices like cardamom.
✉ *1221 Bay St., Yorkville, Toronto, Ontario* ☎ *416/920–2323* ⊕ *www.
pangaearestaurant.com* Ⓜ *Bay* ✥ *1:G1.*

$$$ ✕ **Sotto Sotto.** A coal cellar in a turn-of-the-20th-century home was dug
ITALIAN out, its stone walls and floor polished, and what has emerged is a dining
oasis for locals and international jet-setters alike. The menu of more
than 20 pasta dishes gives a tantalizing tug at the taste buds. Gnoc-
chi is made daily. The orecchiette ("ear-shape" disks of pasta) tossed
with prosciutto, mushrooms, black olives, and fresh tomatoes is a sym-
phony of textures. Cornish hen is marinated, pressed, and grilled to a
juicy brown, and the swordfish and fresh fish of the day are beautifully
done on the grill. ✉ *116-A Avenue Rd., Yorkville, Toronto, Ontario*
☎ *416/962–0011* ⊕ *www.sottosotto.ca* ☺ *No lunch* Ⓜ *Bay* ✥ *1:F1.*

$$$ ✕ **Studio Café.** At this well-lighted, comfortable eatery—a combination
CAFÉ hotel coffee shop, restaurant, and contemporary glass-and-art gallery—
you can have classic brunch fare like eggs Benedict or more exotic flavors like the tandoori chicken with cilantro chutney and naan. Trendy
dishes include Ontario goat-cheese fritter with shallots, blueberry mar-
malade and basil, and lobster mac and cheese with white cheddar. There
is also a daily three-course prix fixe dinner, for those who like variety.
✉ *Four Seasons Toronto hotel, 21 Avenue Rd., Yorkville, Toronto,
Ontario* ☎ *416/964–0411* ⊕ *www.fourseasons.com* Ⓜ *Bay* ✥ *1:F1.*

CHURCH-WELLESLEY AND DUNDAS SQUARE AREA

CHURCH-WELLESLEY

$$$ ✕ **Bistro 990.** A superior kitchen is seamlessly paired with bistro infor-
FRENCH mality. Start your experience with traditional *pâté de maison* (liver
pâté partnered with quince marmalade, wine preserves, and plenty of
homemade croutons). Seared east coast scallops with truffled mush-
room risotto is a treat, and a roasted half chicken with herb garlic *au jus*
crackles with crispness and Provençal flavor. Ask about the wild-game
dish of the day. Faux stone walls stenciled with Jean Cocteau-esque
modernist designs, sturdily upholstered chairs, and a tiled floor make
the dining area sophisticated but comfortable. ✉ *990 Bay St., Church–
Wellesley, Toronto, Ontario* ☎ *416/921–9990* ⊕ *www.bistro990.ca*
🍴 *Reservations essential* ☺ *No lunch weekends* Ⓜ *Bloor-Yonge, Welles-
ley* ✥ *1:G2.*

DUNDAS SQUARE AREA

$$$$ ✕**Barberian's.** A Toronto landmark where wheeling, dealing, and lots of
STEAK eating have gone on since 1959, Barberian's is also romantic: Elizabeth
Taylor and Richard Burton got engaged here (the first time). The menu
is full of steak-house classics, like starters of tomato and onion salad
and jumbo shrimp cocktail. Mains are all about the meat, be it a perfectly timed porterhouse, New York strip loin, or rib steak. Fresh fish
of the day and grilled free-range capon also hold their charms. One of
the oldest steak houses in the city, Barberian's offers a selection of 3,000
labels in its underground two-story wine cellar. ✉ *7 Elm St., Dundas
Square Area, Toronto, Ontario* ☎ *416/597–0335* ⊕ *www.barberians.
com* ⌕ *Reservations essential* Ⓜ *Dundas* ⟊ *1:G4.*

$$ ✕**Guu Izakaya.** Torontonians went crazy when Guu opened in 2009, and
JAPANESE for good reason. There simply isn't another place like it here. The pas-
Fodor'sChoice sionate staff shouts greetings at the top of their lungs before patrons sit
★ down. It's noisy, rowdy, and ultra-friendly—very much in line with the
traditional *izakaya* (bar with drinks and small plates), complete with an
open space and communal tables. The salmon *natto yukke* (a mixture
of chopped salmon, *natto* (fermented soybeans), wonton chips, garlic
chips, and egg yolk wrapped in crunchy nori) makes the introduction
to natto a pleasant experience and offers amazing textural differences
among its elements. For a hot dish, the *kakimayo* (grilled oysters with
spinach and garlic mayo topped with cheese) is savory and creamy. Even
amid a menu of small plate items, you'll still find excellent rice dishes.
Kinoko cheese *bibimbap*, rice and garlic sautéed mushrooms with sea-
weed sauce and cheese in hot stone bowl, take this humble ingredient to
new heights. Choose from an array of sake cocktails to sip. ■TIP➜ **Line
up early outside to secure a table. There is a two-hour seating limit.** ✉ *398
Church St., Dundas Square Area, Toronto, Ontario* ☎ *416/977–0999*
⊕ *www.guu-izakaya.com/toronto.html* ⌕ *Reservations not accepted*
⊗ *No lunch* Ⓜ *College* ⟊ *1:H4.*

GREATER TORONTO

Pockets of good restaurants are to be found across Greater Toronto,
including great neighborhood haunts in Cabbagetown and the Yonge
and Eglinton area (nicknamed "Young and Eligible" for its lively single
young professionals). Little Italy, meanwhile, is an enduring hot spot for
people-watching from a sunny patio while consuming everything from
pizza and vino to gelato in the area that while almost fully gentrified,
still maintains its neighborly charms. While the Danforth is also known
as Greektown—the street signs are even translated into Greek—things
have been changing on this restaurant-heavy strip. The area has always
been alive with the buzz of people, chic meze spots, family-style souvlaki
emporiums, and lots of places for drinks and gelato, but now there's
everything from sushi to bakeshops, upscale Canadian, and old-school
burgers. The annual Taste of the Danforth street festival combines live
music with a wide range of food vendors.

DANFORTH

$$$ ✕**Allen's.** Slide into a well-worn wood booth or sit at a blue-and-white-
AMERICAN checkered table at this New York–style saloon, complete with oak bar
and pressed-tin ceiling. If the traditional interior isn't your style, per-
haps the famous willow-shaded patio is. With 340 varieties of whiskey,
it is home to one of the best selections in the city. The beer selection lags
behind some, with 140 options in bottles and 16 on draft. All meats on
the menu include their place of origin. The braised lamb shank with
mashed potatoes and the liver and onions get raves. Servers may recom-
mend the chocolate bread pudding with caramel sauce, bourbon, and
pecans; trust them. ✉ *143 Danforth Ave., Danforth, Toronto, Ontario*
☎ *416/463–3086* ⊕ *www.allens.to* ⌂ *Reservations essential* Ⓜ *Broad-
view* ✛ *2:C5.*

$$ ✕**Christina's.** Who doesn't have a foodie love affair with Greek dips?
GREEK Here they're served individually or as a large platter combination,
♻ *pikilia mezedakia,* which comes with warm pita. Try a bottle of Greek
wine and specials like *saganaki* (an iron plate of Kefalograviera cheese
flamed in brandy), and you may shout "*Opa*" with the waiters. Order
a fish or mixed-meat grill, and the tray of food almost covers the table.
This cheery place, with the colors of the Aegean Sea and sun on the
walls, has live music and belly dancers on Friday and Saturday evenings.
✉ *492 Danforth Ave., Danforth, Toronto, Ontario* ☎ *416/463–4418*
⊕ *www.christinas.ca* Ⓜ *Chester* ✛ *2:D4.*

$$$ ✕**Globe Bistro.** The motto here is "Think global. Eat local." Chef Kevin
MODERN McKenna does justice to locally raised animals by letting the main
CANADIAN ingredient shine in the international-inspired dishes, from head-to-tail,
Fodor's Choice like the elk dish of seared loin and foie gras elk sausage with lentils and
★ celeriac puree. Ivory and taupe neutral tones and soft lights enhance the
open dining room and give it a luxurious feel, but, weather permitting,
you may want to enjoy the swanky rooftop patio. ✉ *124 Danforth Ave.,
Danforth, Toronto, Ontario* ☎ *416/466–2000* ⊕ *www.globebistro.com*
⊙ *No lunch Sat.* Ⓜ *Chester* ✛ *2:C4.*

$$$ ✕**Provence Delices.** With a potbellied stove and a delightful summer
FRENCH patio, this French-style villa has been a Cabbagetown landmark since
1980. Classics like French marinated herring, cassoulet of pork shoulder, sausage, and duck confit, as well as global flavors like shiitake scallop and shrimp risotto can all be enjoyed here. If classic Provençal fish
soup appeals, this is the place to try it. Duck confit with olive sauce is
crisp and juicy at the same time. Authentic patisserie, including tarte
tatin, with caramelized apples and a buttery crust, makes a fine ending.
✉ *12 Amelia St., Greater Toronto, Toronto, Ontario* ☎ *416/924–9901*
⊕ *www.provencerestaurant.com* Ⓜ *Sherbourne, College* ✛ *2:C5.*

LESLIEVILLE

$$ ✕**Queen Margherita Pizza.** One of the newest and best pizza places in
PIZZA town, Queen Margherita is all about authenticity. Inside this small
Fodor's Choice space with dark wooden floors and tables, the Neapolitan pizza oven,
★ hauled in by crane prior to restaurant opening, churns out daily selec-
tions like Margherita pizza made simply, with just tomato sauce, moz-
zarella, and basil; burrata, of just burrata cheese and tomato sauce; and
Calabrese, made with tomato sauce, mozzarella, Italian sausage, and

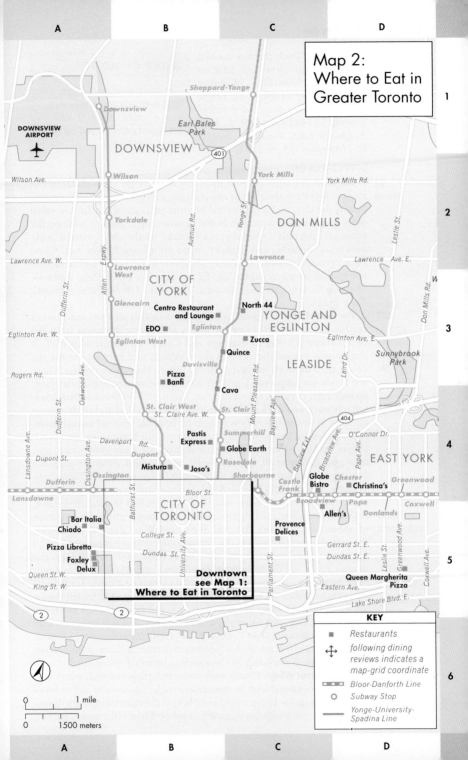

Map 2:
Where to Eat in
Greater Toronto

1

DOWNSVIEW
AIRPORT

Downsview

Sheppard-Yonge

Earl Bales
Park

DOWNSVIEW   401

Wilson Ave.   Wilson   York Mills   York Mills Rd.

2

Yorkdale   DON MILLS

Lawrence Ave. W.   Lawrence   Lawrence Ave. E.

Dufferin St.   Allen Expwy.   Lawrence
West

CITY OF
YORK   Centro Restaurant
and Lounge   ■   ■ North 44

Glencairn   EDO ■   Eglinton   YONGE AND
EGLINTON   Eglinton Ave. E.   Leslie St.   Don Mills Rd.

Eglinton Ave. W.   Eglinton West   ■ Zucca   Sunnybrook
Park

Rogers Rd.   Oakwood Ave.   Davisville   ■ Quince   LEASIDE   Laird Dr.

Pizza
Banfi ■

■ Cava

St. Clair West
St. Claire Ave. W.   St. Clair   Mount Pleasant Rd.   Bayview Ave.   404

Lansdowne Ave.   Dufferin St.   Davenport   Rd.   Summerhill   O'Connor Dr.

Pastis
Express ■   Dupont   Pape Ave.   EAST YORK

Dupont St.   Mistura ■   ■ Globe Earth   Bayview Ext.   Broadview Ave.

Ossington Ave.   ■ Joso's   Rosedale   Sherbourne

Dufferin   Bathurst St.   Bloor St.   Castle
Frank   Globe
Bistro ■   Chester   Greenwood

Lansdowne   CITY OF
TORONTO   ■ Christina's   Pape   Coxwell

Bar Italia ■   College St.   Broadview   Donlands

Chiado ■   Allen's ■

Pizza Libretto ■   Dundas St.   Provence
Delices ■

Foxley ■   University Ave.   Gerrard St. E.   Leslie St.   Greenwood Ave.   Coxwell Ave.

Delux ■   Queen St. W.   Dundas St. E.

King St. W.   Downtown
see Map 1:
Where to Eat in
Toronto   Queen Margherita
Pizza ■

Eastern Ave.

2   2   Lake Shore Blvd. E.

KEY

■   Restaurants

↔   following dining
reviews indicates a
map-grid coordinate

▨▨▨   Bloor-Danforth Line

○   Subway Stop

———   Yonge-University-
Spadina Line

0   1 mile
0   1500 meters

1

2

3

4

5

6

hot peppers. Each pizza is cooked quickly at an ultra-high heat to give it that beautifully blistering crust. Request a table in the bright loft upstairs for more comfortable seating. ✉ *1402 Queen St. E, Unit 8, Queen East, Toronto, Ontario* ☎ *416/466–6555.* ✛ *2:D5.*

WORD OF MOUTH

"The charcuterie at the Black Hoof is incredible and they also have a decent take on St. John Restaurant's marrow and parsley salad." —JMWF

LITTLE ITALY

$$
ITALIAN

✗ **Bar Italia.** A fixture in Little Italy, this is where the city's glitterati can be found getting their fix of the classics: well-prepared pasta, risotto, fish of the day, and a traditional favorite of sautéed mushroom salad with arugula and Parmesan. In the summer, sip a glass of wine on the patio and dig into a specialty: the Cubano sandwich of roasted pork, avocado, pancetta, and garlicky mayo on a huge Italian bun. Close your eyes and pretend you're in southern Italy; you'll still hear Italian spoken at many tables. ✉ *582 College St., Little Italy, Toronto, Ontario* ☎ *416/535–3621* ⊕ *www.bar-italia.ca* Ⓜ *Bathurst, Queen's Park* ✛ *2:A5.*

$$$
MODERN
CANADIAN
Fodor's Choice
★

✗ **The Black Hoof.** A typical evening spent in this narrow head-to-tail cuisine hot spot features exotic meats and loving attention from the two owners: Jen Agg as manager and Grant van Gameren as chef. A chalkboard behind the bar lists the selection, and patrons can see the cooks hard at work at the tiny stove just to the left of the bar where hot foods are prepared. The must-have house-made charcuterie plates include bites of rabbit rillettes terrine, cured venison *bresaola* (air-dried, salted meat), and duck prosciutto, plus octopus salad and roasted bone marrow. A house specialty is tongue on brioche; smoked sweetbreads; and *tapas*-sized horse tartare, a first for many in Toronto and not available in the United States. The tartare is delicious: a somehow clean, lean meat, not gamey at all, like the purest, lightest beef. Monthly cocktails are listed on a huge mirror by the bar. ✉ *928 Dundas St. W, Little Italy, Toronto, Ontario* ☎ *416/551–8854* ⊜ *Reservations not accepted* ▭ *No credit cards* ☾ *Closed Tues. and Wed. No lunch* Ⓜ *St. Patrick* ✛ *1:B4.*

$$$$
PORTUGUESE

✗ **Chiado.** It's all relaxed elegance here, beginning with the fine selection of appetizers at Senhor Antonio Tapas and Wine Bar and continuing through the French doors to the dining room, which has polished wood floors and plum-velvet armchairs. The exquisite fish, which form the menu's basis, are flown in from the Azores and Madeira. You might have monkfish, grouper, or *peixe espada* (scabbard fish). Traditional Portuguese dishes include *assorda*, in which seafood is folded into a thick, custardlike soup made with bread and eggs. There's much for meat eaters, too—for example, a roasted rack of lamb sparkles with Douro wine sauce. ✉ *864 College St. W, Little Italy, Toronto, Ontario* ☎ *416/538–1910* ⊕ *www.chiadorestaurant.com* ⊜ *Reservations essential* ☾ *No lunch weekends* Ⓜ *Ossington, Queen's Park* ✛ *2:A5.*

$
AMERICAN
☺

✗ **Duff's Famous Wings.** Plump with meat and crisp-skinned, wings and drumettes are served with pristine celery sticks and creamy dill or blue-cheese dressing. Ordering a pitcher of beer is the right thing to do. If you go with the hot wings (as opposed to other flavors like honey garlic), which you should, Duff's wing sauces are measured in Scoville heat units (SHU), the standard for measuring the heat of a pepper: 0 plain, 800 mild, 10,000 medium (their most popular), 500,000 death, and 850,000 Armageddon. If you take the kids, they can have burgers, hot dogs, or deep-fried mac-and-cheese nuggets. ⊠ *558 College St. W, Little Italy, Toronto, Ontario* ☎ *416/963–4446* ⊕ *www.duffsfamouswings.ca* Ⓜ *Queen's Park* ✛ *1:B3.*

$ ✕**Young Thailand.** Chef Wandee Young impressed Toronto's taste buds
THAI   when she launched Canada's first Thai restaurant in 1980. Her gently spiced authentic staples are just as delicious now. Within the open dining room with white walls and black accents and small Thai decorations, you can order from a traditional menu of chicken satay with peanut sauce, Thai-spiced calamari with sweet chili, and refreshing salad rolls are a nice start. Move on to zingy lemon chicken soup and shared mains like green mango salad, red-curry beef, spicy basil chicken, and Thai-style eggplant. It's pretty hard to order wrong here. ⊠ *936 King St. W, Little Italy, Toronto, Ontario* ☎ *416/366–8424* ⊕ *www. youngthailand.com* ☉ *No lunch weekends* Ⓜ *Dundas* ✛ *1:A6.*

OSSINGTON

$$$ ✕**Delux.** This better-than-average neighborhood bistro is a worthwhile
FRENCH   stop on Ossington. With its welcoming yet slightly edgy room, streamlined service, and a menu full of comforting French classics, it's a busy local favorite that's full every night. There are oysters on the half shell with a playful Granny Smith mignonette, steak frites, and tender short ribs with horseradish crème; chef-owner Corinna Mozo's chicken is roasted to juicy perfection. Hot-from-the-oven chocolate-chip cookies with a milk kicker keep the kids coming back for more. ⊠ *92 Ossington Ave., Ossington, Toronto, Ontario* ☎ *416/537–0134* ☉ *No lunch* Ⓜ *St. Patrick* ✛ *2:A5.*

$$$ ✕**Foxley.** Like the appealingly bare-bones aesthetic of its space (exposed
ECLECTIC   brick, hardwoods, candlelight), this creative bistro offers unadorned
Fodor's Choice   dishes that are jammed with flavor. After traveling for a year, chef-
★   owner Tom Thai returned to Toronto with newfound inspiration from places like Asia, Latin America, and the Mediterranean. There are daily ceviches like Spanish bonito with pomegranate and crispy capers, as well as a couple dozen other *tapas*-style offerings, including spicy blue crab and avocado salad, lamb and duck prosciutto dumplings, and grilled side ribs with sticky shallot glaze. All can be paired with an impressive list of red, white, and sparkling wine, sake and soju, from dry Hungarian Tokaji to a bold Barolo—most modestly priced. ■ TIP➔ **The restaurant doesn't take reservations, and it does get busy. Plan accordingly and go early or late.** ⊠ *207 Ossington St., Ossington, Toronto, Ontario* ☎ *416/534–8520* ⚐ *Reservations not accepted* ☉ *No lunch* ✛ *2:A5.*

$$ ✕**Pizzeria Libretto.** Authentic Neapolitan pizzas are fired in a wood-
PIZZA   burning oven imported from Italy to this pizza joint on the Ossington strip. Amid the communal wood tables, exposed brick, chalkboard paint, and Banksy artwork, owner Max Rimaldi adheres to the rules of classic pizza set by the Associazione Verace Pizza Napoletana. Starters include charcuterie and cheeses like house-made duck prosciutto and four-year-old Parmigiano-Reggiano, but the pizza's the thing. Try the

pizza Margherita D.O.P. with San Marzano tomatoes, fresh basil, and local (nearby Ingersoll) Fiore di Latte Mozzarella, or duck confit pizza for something more unconventional. Service is both speedy and charming. ⊠ *221 Ossington Ave., Ossington, Toronto, Ontario* ☎ *416/532–8000* ⊕ *www.pizzerialibretto.com* ⤳ *Reservations not accepted* ⊗ *No lunch* Ⓜ *St. Patrick* ✚ *2:A5.*

YONGE AND EGLINTON

$$
SPANISH
✕ **Cava.** After spending 11 years creating 12-course, high-concept "adventure menus," chef Chris McDonald traded his restaurant Avalon for this *tapas* place. A *salumi* (cured meat) bar serving house-cured meats is rounded out by a menu with a couple of dozen small plates like chickpeas with morilla and smoked pork hock, and cauliflower and kabocha squash tagine. The drinks list offers Spanish sparkling wines and lots of sherries. Desserts are the evening's biggest treat, especially spiced-plum clafouti with pistachio ice cream. ⊠ *1560 Yonge St., Yonge and Eglinton, Toronto, Ontario* ☎ *416/979–9918* ⊕ *www.cavarestaurant.ca* ⤳ *Reservations essential* ⊗ *No lunch* Ⓜ *St. Clair* ✚ *2:B4.*

$$$$
ECLECTIC
✕ **Centro Restaurant and Lounge.** Showpiece chandeliers and 28-foot ceilings with pillars of cream suede complement the brown-suede chairs in this drop-dead gorgeous, 138-seater with attitude. The New American cuisine encompasses Italian, French, Asian—but not on one plate. Try pastas such as gnocchi with lemon, Parmesan and spinach, or bucatini pasta with duck ragout. Mains are simple and elegant, like rainbow trout with sunchoke and green butter, and Atlantic cod with citrus and honey. Desserts and cheeses are divine. ■TIP➔ **A downstairs lounge has buzz, its own small, less-expensive menu ($$), and live music weekends.** ⊠ *2472 Yonge St., at Eglinton Ave., Yonge and Eglinton, Toronto, Ontario* ☎ *416/483–2211* ⊕ *www.centro.ca* ⤳ *Reservations essential* ⊗ *Closed Sun. No lunch* Ⓜ *Eglinton* ✚ *2:B3.*

$$
JAPANESE
✕ **EDO.** Aficionados of Japanese food may have to stop themselves from ordering everything on the menu. Even the uninitiated are mesmerized by the intriguing dishes here, including plates of black cod marinated in *saikyo* miso sauce, dynamite roll with giant shrimp and dynamite sauce, and miso-glazed eggplant. If soft-shell crab is on the menu, it's a worthy choice. The chef is an artist with sushi and sashimi, but if you can't decide, the kitchen menus give you a balanced and exciting array of dishes. ⊠ *484 Eglinton Ave. W, Yonge and Eglinton, Toronto, Ontario* ☎ *416/481–1370* ⊕ *www.edosushi.com* ⊗ *No lunch* Ⓜ *Eglinton* ✚ *2:B3.*

$$$
MODERN
CANADIAN
Fodor'sChoice
★
✕ **Globe Earth.** Many restaurateurs believe this location is cursed, as predecessors always floundered, but not owner Ed Ho, owner of the equally excellent Globe Bistro, who is passionate about knowing and sharing the origin of foods. Situated in the affluent Rosedale area, Earth is a neighborhood bistro that is surprisingly laid-back, with cool black-and-gray furniture, wooden floors, and a marble bar, and offers great value. The use of whole animals in creative ways is introduced via bacon-infused whiskey on the bar menu. Elk is used extensively, especially in cooler months, for hearty dishes like elk onion soup and elk venison shepherd's pie. A tender piece of pork belly set atop maple

chili glaze with chopped kimchi on the side is succulent, not greasy or cloying. Many meat dishes are prepared in the wood-burning oven, like the Tamworth suckling pig roast and whole roasted daily Ontario fish. ⊠ *1055 Yonge St., Rosedale, Toronto, Ontario* ☎ *416/551–9890* ⊕ *www.globeearth.ca* ⌂ *Reservations essential* Ⓜ *Rosedale* ✛ *2:B4.*

$$$
SEAFOOD
✕ **Joso's.** Artistic *objets,* sensuous paintings of nudes and the sea, and signed celebrity photos line the walls at this two-story seafood institution that might catch you off-guard with its eccentricity. The kitchen prepares dishes from the Dalmatian side of the Adriatic Sea, and members of the international artistic community who frequent the place adore the unusual and healthy array of seafood and fish. The black risotto with squid is a must. A dish of grilled prawns, their charred tails pointing skyward, is often carried aloft by speed-walking servers. ⊠ *202 Davenport Rd., Yonge and Eglinton, Toronto, Ontario* ☎ *416/925–1903* ⌂ *Reservations essential* ⊘ *Closed Sun. No lunch Sat.* Ⓜ *Dupont* ✛ *2:B4.*

$$$
ITALIAN
Fodor'sChoice
★
✕ **Mistura.** Mistura's combination of comfort and casual luxury and its innovative menu make for an ongoing buzz. A bright dining room with wooden pillars, black chairs and curtains, and white tablecloths set the tone for a straightforward meal without fuss or nonsense. Choose from more than a dozen delectable starters, like beef carpaccio with Grana Padano shavings and black truffle over arugula. Balsamic glazed lamb ribs, square-cut spaghetti with lobster, and boneless Cornish hen stuffed with fresh herbs are specialties. Parmigiano-crusted veal scallopine is always a hit, as are homemade pastas like braised duck agnolotti with sour cherries. Daily whole fish is a carefully thought-out triumph. Vegetarians are given their due with signature dishes like beet risotto. **Sopra** ($$–$$$), a second-floor Italian lounge and jazz bar, offers full-sized meals as well as bite-size delights. Conceived as a million-dollar playroom for grown-ups, it's all zebrawood and onyx, complete with a grand piano. ⊠ *265 Davenport Rd., ½ block west of Avenue Rd., Yonge and Eglinton, Toronto, Ontario* ☎ *416/515–0009* ⊕ *www.mistura.ca* ⊘ *Closed Sun. No lunch* Ⓜ *Dupont* ✛ *2:B4.*

$$$$
MODERN
CANADIAN
✕ **North 44.** The lighting here creates a refined, sophisticated environment, and the appetizers match: medley of lobster, crab and prawns with spiced crème fraîche, and crispy soft-shell crab with white asparagus, grapefruit, and hollandaise awaken your taste buds. It's hard to choose from chef-owner Marc McEwen's creative and exciting main courses, including pan-seared Dover sole in brown butter, and roasted lamb loin with minted spring pea ravioli, and cauliflower puree. There are more than 50 wines sold by the glass, enough to complement any dish. ⊠ *2537 Yonge St., 4½ blocks north of Eglinton Ave., Yonge and Eglinton, Toronto, Ontario* ☎ *416/487–4897* ⊕ *www.north44restaurant. com* ⊘ *Closed Sun. No lunch* Ⓜ *Eglinton* ✛ *2:C3.*

$$$
FRENCH
Fodor'sChoice
★
✕ **Pastis.** Menu items etched into the frosted-glass windows and plastered walls the color of the dawn in Provence bring a Gallic mood to Yonge Street. The food is good, but this place could run on the charm of owner George Gurnon alone. Expect pure bistro fare here, like mussels and foie gras terrine to start, traditional steak frites, and butter roasted lobster. The wine list is short and simple, with something for every palate. End

the perfect meal with crème brûlée or profiteroles. ⊠ *1158 Yonge St., at Summerhill, Yonge and Eglinton, Toronto, Ontario* ☎ *416/928–2212* ☉ *Closed Sun. and Mon. No lunch* Ⓜ *Summerhill* ✛ *2:B4.*

$$ ✕ **Pizza Banfi.** No matter what day or time, there's usually a line for
ITALIAN two reasons: it doesn't take reservations, and the classic Italian food is
☺ really good. The decor is slightly cliché, with wall paintings over light colored bricks, but the pizzas are the main attraction here. Thin-crust pizzas are tossed in full view, then baked with aplomb, especially the popular pesto, chicken, and roasted red pepper combo. Pastas, generously portioned, are just as good, and the stellar Caesar salad tops just about every table. ⊠ *333B Lonsdale Rd., Forest Hills, Toronto, Ontario* ☎ *416/322–5231* ⬧ *Reservations not accepted* ☉ *Closed Sun.* Ⓜ *Eglinton West* ✛ *2:B3.*

$$$ ✕ **Quince.** Looking around the narrow earth-toned dining room on the
MEDITERRANEAN main level, you will soon realize that this Mediterranean bistro serves a
Fodor'sChoice straightforward and candid assembly of ingredients, without fuss or any
★ type of distraction. The wood-burning oven near the back of the restaurant is the highlight of the space, churning out not only pizza, but daily flatbread, roasted salmon with peas, and roasted sea bream. Martinis like the Lychee Sakitini and Quince are a great way to start the meal. Go on Monday or Tuesday and there's no corkage fee. ⊠ *2110 Yonge St., Yonge and Eglinton, Toronto, Ontario* ☎ *416/488–2110* ⊕ *www.quincetoronto.com* ☉ *Closed Sun.* Ⓜ *Eglinton* ✛ *2:C3.*

$$$ ✕ **Zucca.** Chef-owner Andrew Milne-Allan delivers the purest made-
ITALIAN from-scratch Italian food in a modern, sleek, and friendly room. The wine list of more than 150 labels, all Italian varieties, is beautifully paired with pasta, all handmade and hand-rolled. Options include semolina pasta with rapini and fresh peperoncino, wide black olive noodles with ragout of rabbit, and squid-ink pasta with seafood. In addition to meats, grilled fish is a specialty here. Finish the meal with Amaretto crème caramel. ⊠ *2150 Yonge St., Yonge and Eglinton, Toronto, Ontario* ☎ *416/488–5774* ⊕ *www.zuccatrattoria.com* ⬧ *Reservations essential* Ⓜ *Eglinton* ✛ *2:C3.*

Where to Stay

WORD OF MOUTH

"I ended up LOVING the energy of this far Queen West area and the Drake is such a jewel, an artsy hotel unlike anything I've EVER stayed at in my life. Innovative art-deco room design for the so-called "Crash Pad" I've stayed at, front desk staff were unbelievable (bending over backward with a smile to every request."
—Daniel_Williams

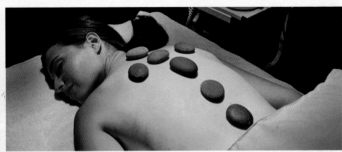

Updated by
Sarah Richards

Given that more than 100 languages and dialects are spoken in the Greater Toronto area, it's not surprising that much of the downtown hotel market is international-business-traveler savvy. Wi-Fi connections are standard at most high-end properties, and business services abound. But these same core hotels are close to tourist attractions — Harbourfront and the Toronto Islands, the cavernous Rogers Centre, the Air Canada Centre, the Four Seasons Centre for the Performing Arts, and the Royal Ontario Museum.

Not wanting to miss out on potential customers, hotels like the Delta Chelsea have instituted perks for the younger set, such as complimentary milk and cookies, kid-size bathrobes, and children's day camp. Another key trend in Toronto's downtown lodgings is the emergence of small, upscale boutique hotels, such as the Hotel Le Germain, the Pantages and Cosmopolitan hotels, and the swank SoHo Metropolitan. There is also a growing number of bed-and-breakfasts and hostels.

City-center accommodations are usually within a few minutes' walk of Yonge Street and the glittering lights of the Entertainment District, the soaring office towers of the Financial District, the shops of the Dundas Square Area, and the bars and art galleries of Queen West. Within a 15-minute drive west of downtown are the forested High Park and the meandering Humber River, an area where there are few major hotels but an ample array of B&Bs and the lovely Old Mill Inn. The growing West Queen West area has some unique places to stay, such as the restored Gladstone and Drake hotels, as well as funky restaurants and galleries. Lester B. Pearson International Airport is 29 km (18 mi) northwest of downtown; airport hotels are airport hotels, but staying in this area also means quick connections to cities beyond, such as Niagara Falls.

WHERE SHOULD I STAY?

	Neighborhood Vibe	Pros	Cons
Harbourfront, The Financial District, and Old Town	This tourist hub includes Toronto's first buildings in Old Town, the towering skyscrapers of the Financial District, and the many activities of Harbourfront.	Good eats in the St. Lawrence Market and Historic Distillery District, close to Island escapes in Lake Ontario, and surrounded by the city's top attractions.	Quiet at night and a bit removed from the action of Toronto's livelier neighborhoods. Rooms are often smaller and more expensive than in other areas.
The Entertainment District	Toronto's highest concentration of nightclubs and the city's thriving theater district.	Hotels here cater to more adventurous pleasure-seekers. Plenty of restaurants serve pre- and post-theater dinners and lots of late-night conveniences.	When the clubs let out at around 3 am, it can get extremely noisy and rowdy on the streets.
Queen's Park, The Annex, and Yorkville	Abundant ethnic restaurants and secondhand bookstores line Bloor Street West. Farther south is the airy Queen's Park; while to the east, upscale shops fill sophisticated Yorkville.	Beautifully restored Victorian houses make for unique B&B accommodations. Alternatively, splash out in one of the big, luxurious hotels in Yorkville.	High prices in Yorkville could clean out your wallet, and the area's central artery, Bloor Street West, attracts many panhandlers.
Church-Wellesley and Dundas Square Area	Dundas Square, Toronto's hottest new events center, faces the mammoth Eaton Centre shopping mall. Farther northeast is Canada's largest gay community, Church-Wellesley.	These areas have a festival-like atmosphere, and patios teem at sunset.	Things can get slightly sketchy late at night, and there aren't many recommended restaurants in the immediate vicinity.
Queen West	Funky boutiques, cutting-edge design shops, and experimental restaurants and hotels.	This area sets the trends in Toronto, the restaurants and bars attract diverse clientele, and the Queen Street streetcar is frequent and runs 24 hours.	The western end of the neighborhood feels shady after dark, and there aren't many parking options.
Greater Toronto	Most hotels in the northwest end of the city surround its great green expanse, High Park, and this area feels like a pleasant resort town with interesting shops and restaurants.	Safe, quiet, and relatively inexpensive area of Toronto, set against the 400-acre High Park.	Unlike central Toronto, the vibe here is more small-town. It can take up to a half hour to get to Toronto's attractions by subway or car.

4

PLANNING

Where should you stay? With hundreds of Toronto hotels, it may seem like a daunting question. But fret not—our expert writers and editors have done most of the legwork. The 50-plus selections here represent the best the city has to offer—from the best budget motels to the sleekest boutique hotels. Scan "Best Bets" on the following pages for top recommendations by price and experience. Or find a review quickly in the listings. Search by neighborhood, then alphabetically. Happy Hunting!

RESERVATIONS

Hotel reservations are a necessity—rooms fill up quickly, so book as far in advance as possible. Summer is the busiest time, and if you plan on visiting during the Pride Festival (late June), Caribbean Carnival Toronto (late July), or Toronto International Film Festival (September), note that hordes of visitors will be joining you in a search for a room, especially anywhere in the downtown area. At these times it doesn't hurt to search farther afield, but look for places along the subway lines to the north, west, or east, unless you have a car.

FACILITIES

Unless otherwise noted in individual descriptions, all the hotels listed have private baths, central heating, and private phones. Almost all hotels have Wi-Fi and phones with voice mail. Most large hotels have video or high-speed checkout capability, and many can arrange babysitting. Web TV, in-room video games, DVD players, and CD players are also provided in many hotels.

Bringing a car to Toronto can be a headache unless your hotel provides free parking. Garages cost around C$20 per day, and street-side parking is not available in most neighborhoods, but many city-owned parking lots have favorable rates on weekends and holidays.

WITH KIDS

Many of the downtown chain hotels offer free stays for kids under 12, but it would be best to check in advance when making reservations. Boutique hotels and B&Bs won't impose any rules against bringing children, but they will be considerably less accommodating. In the listings, look for the ☾, which indicates a property that we recommend for when you're traveling with children.

DISCOUNTS AND DEALS

When booking, remember first to ask about discounts and packages. Even the most expensive properties regularly reduce their rates during low-season lulls and on weekends. If you're a member of a group (senior citizen, student, auto club, or the military), you may also get a deal. Downtown hotels regularly have specials that include theater tickets, meals, or museum passes. It never hurts to ask for these kinds of perks up front.

PRICES AND PRICE CHART

The lodgings we list are the cream of the crop in each price category. Properties are assigned price categories based on the price of a standard double room during Toronto's busy summer season. We always list the facilities that are available, such as in-house spas or gym access, but we don't specify whether they cost extra. When pricing accommodations, always ask what's included and what costs extra.

Although paying with U.S. dollars no longer gives you the advantage it has in the past, there are other ways to save money during a visit. Many hotels that cater to business travelers cut rates for weekends, and these hotels typically have special packages for couples and families. Toronto hotels usually slash rates a full 50% in January and February. Smaller hotels and apartment-style accommodation downtown are also moderately priced (and, therefore, popular in summer).

WHAT IT COSTS IN CANADIAN DOLLARS					
	¢	$	$$	$$$	$$$$
For two people	under C$75	C$75–C$125	C$126–C$175	C$176–C$250	over C$250

Prices are for two people in a standard double room in high season, excluding service and 13% hotel tax.

HOTEL REVIEWS

Listed alphabetically within neighborhoods.

Throughout the chapter, you'll see mapping symbols and coordinates (✛ F2) after property names or reviews. To locate the property on a map, turn to the Where to Stay Toronto map within this chapter. The numbers after the ✛ symbol indicate its coordinate on the map grid.

For expanded hotel reviews, visit Fodors.com.

HARBOURFRONT, FINANCIAL DISTRICT, AND OLD TOWN

Situating yourself here is a good idea for exploring the greatest concentration of Toronto's must-see attractions, such as St. Lawrence Market, the Historic Distillery District, the Rogers Centre, Ontario Place, and the CN Tower. You'll find that, while boisterous during the day, these areas really quiet down after the sun sets.

HARBOURFRONT

$$$ ⬚ **Hôtel Le Germain Maple Leaf Square.** Inside the Maple Leaf Square complex, which includes a Longos grocery store and Starbucks, this ultra-★ stylish hotel is perfectly poised to receive traffic from the Air Canada Centre across the street, the Rogers Centre just minutes away on foot, or any of the Harbourfront's other myriad distractions. **Pros:** free welcome treats for kids and pets (mention when booking); intimate service; spacious lobby for guests with free coffee; attached to PATH network. **Cons:** area is boisterous only when events are happening at nearby Air Canada Centre. ✉ 75 Bremner Blvd., Harbourfront, Toronto, Ontario ☎ 416/649–7575, 888/940–7575 ⊕ www.germainmapleleafsquare. com ⇥ 167 rooms ⬚ In-room: a/c, safe, Internet, Wi-Fi. In-hotel: bar, gym, business center, parking, some pets allowed ⊺⊙⏐ Breakfast Ⓜ Union ✛ E6.

BEST BETS FOR TORONTO LODGING

Fodor's offers a selective listing of quality lodging experiences at every price, from the city's best budget motel to its most sophisticated luxury hotels. Here, we've compiled our top recommendations by price and experience. The very best properties—those that provide a particularly remarkable experience in their price range—are designated in the listings with a Fodor's Choice logo.

Fodor's Choice ★

Hazelton Hotel, p. 141
Hôtel Le Germain Toronto, p. 137
Residence Inn by Marriott, p. 139

By Price

¢

Global Village Backpackers, p. 137
Hostelling International, p. 136

$

Annex Quest House, p. 140
Bonnevie Manor Bed & Breakfast Place, p. 142

$$

Hilton Garden Inn City Centre, p. 142
Hotel Victoria, p. 136
Suite Dreams, p. 1140

$$$

Drake Hotel, p. 143
Gladstone Hotel, p. 143
Hôtel Le Germain Maple Leaf Square, p. 131
One King West Hotel & Residence, p. 136
Residence Inn by Marriott, p. 139

$$$$

Fairmont Royal York, p. 133
Hazelton Hotel, p. 141
Hôtel Le Germain Toronto, p. 137
Ritz-Carlton, Toronto, p. 136
SoHo Metropolitan Hotel, p. 140

By Experience

BEST FOR ROMANCE

Cosmopolitan Toronto Hotel, p. 133
Hazelton Hotel, p. 141
Hôtel Le Germain Toronto, p. 137
Park Hyatt Toronto, p. 141

BEST FOR BUSINESS

Fairmont Royal York, p. 133
InterContinental Toronto Centre, p. 139
Westin Harbour Castle, p. 133
Ritz-Carlton, Toronto, p. 136

BEST FOR FAMILIES

Delta Chelsea Hotel, p. 142
Radisson Plaza Hotel Admiral Toronto-Harbourfront, p. 133
Renaissance Toronto Hotel Downtown, p. 139
Residence Inn by Marriott, p. 139

BEST VIEWS

Four Seasons Toronto, p. 140
Radisson Plaza Hotel Admiral Toronto–Harbourfront, p. 133
Sheraton Centre, p. 139
One King West Hotel & Residence, p. 136
Westin Harbour Castle, p. 133

BEST CELEBRITY RETREAT

Cosmopolitan Toronto Hotel, p. 133
Four Seasons Toronto, p. 140
Hazelton Hotel, p. 141
Park Hyatt Toronto, p. 141
Sutton Place, p. 140

BEST INTERIOR DESIGN

Drake Hotel, p. 143
Gladstone Hotel, p. 143
Hazelton Hotel, p. 141
Hôtel Le Germain Maple Leaf Square, p. 131

BEST SPA

Hazelton Hotel, p. 141
Park Hyatt Toronto, p. 141
Ritz-Carlton, Toronto, p. 136

$$$ **Radisson Plaza Hotel Admiral Toronto–Harbourfront.** You can't get much closer to Toronto's waterfront, and unobstructed Lake Ontario and verdant Toronto Islands vistas come standard. **Pros:** good value for its location; easy access to Toronto Islands ferries and convention center; now entirely smoke-free; free Wi-Fi. **Cons:** quiet and seems out of the way in winter and spring. ✉ *249 Queen's Quay W, at York St., Harbourfront, Toronto, Ontario* ☎ *416/203–3333, 800/395–7046* ⊕ *www.radisson.com/torontoca_admiral* ⌁ *157 rooms* ⌂ *In-room: a/c, Wi-Fi. In-hotel: restaurant, bar, pool, gym, parking* Ⓜ *Union* ✛ *E6.*

$$$$ **Westin Harbour Castle.** On a clear day you can see the skyline of Rochester, New York, across the sparkling blue Lake Ontario from most rooms at this elegant, high-end hotel. **Pros:** very comfortable beds; bustling lobby. **Cons:** not right in downtown; hotel can feel overwhelmingly large and very spread out. ✉ *1 Harbour Sq., at Bay St., Harbourfront, Toronto, Ontario* ☎ *416/869–1600, 800/937–8461* ⊕ *www.westinharbourcastletoronto.com* ⌁ *977 rooms* ⌂ *In-room: a/c, Wi-Fi. In-hotel: restaurant, bar, pool, tennis court, gym, business center, parking* Ⓜ *Union* ✛ *F6.*

FINANCIAL DISTRICT

$$$ **Cambridge Suites.** With just 12 suites per floor, this self-dubbed boutique hotel focuses on high-quality service: rooms are cleaned twice daily, and there's same-day dry cleaning and laundry, free access to a downtown fitness club, and a complimentary airline boarding pass kiosk in the lobby. **Pros:** central location; extras like free shoe shines; in-and-out parking privileges mean no extra fee to access your car. **Cons:** some services are expensive, like parking and Internet (in lower-priced rooms). ✉ *15 Richmond St. E, at Victoria St., Financial District, Toronto, Ontario* ☎ *416/368–1990* ⊕ *www.cambridgesuitestoronto.com* ⌁ *229 suites* ⌂ *In-room: a/c, safe, kitchen, Internet, Wi-Fi. In-hotel: restaurant, gym, laundry facilities, parking* Ⓜ *Queen* ✛ *F5.*

$$$ **Cosmopolitan Toronto Hotel.** Tucked away on a side street in the heart of Toronto, this überboutique hotel opened in 2005, seamlessly blending an Eastern aesthetic and spirituality with typical Western hotel amenities. **Pros:** private and quiet; hipness factor; great breakfast buffet. **Cons:** side street dark at night; trendiness may get stale for some. ✉ *8 Colborne St., at Yonge St., Financial District, Toronto, Ontario* ☎ *416/945–5455, 800/958–3488* ⊕ *www.cosmotoronto.com* ⌁ *95 suites, 2 penthouse suites* ⌂ *In-room: a/c, kitchen, Wi-Fi. In-hotel: restaurant, bar, gym, spa, parking* Ⓜ *King* ✛ *F6.*

$$$$ **Fairmont Royal York.** Like a proud grandmother, the Royal York stands serenely on Front Street in downtown Toronto, surrounded by gleaming skyscrapers and the nearby CN Tower. **Pros:** grand royal experience; excellent health

> **WORD OF MOUTH**
>
> "We stayed at the [Westin Harbour] Castle in June 2010 for our anniversary. Perfect location for summertime. The waterfront is a great spot to relax, enjoy a meal or a drink. Our room overlooked the lake (33rd floor). Well appointed, clean. Very friendly staff. We didn't eat at the hotel, but the menu looked great."
> —Tanya

Where to Stay in Toronto

KEY

☐ Hotels

Ⓜ Subway Stops

✛ following lodging reviews
   indicates a map-grid
   coordinate

A   **B**   **C**   **D**

0   1/4 mile

0   400 meters

THE ANNEX

☐ Suite Dreams

☐ Annex Quest House

ST. GEORGE Ⓜ

←☐ Old Mill Inn & Spa
☐ Sandman Signature Toronto Airport
☐ Sheraton Gateway Hotel
☐ Islington Bed & Breakfast House

Bloor St. W.   SPADINA Ⓜ

Lennox St.

←☐ By the Park B&B

Herrick St.

← TO AIRPORT STRIP

Massey College
Student Residence ☐

Hoskin Ave.

Harbord St.

UNIVERSITY OF TORONTO

Ulster St.

Willcocks St.

Russell St.

LITTLE ITALY

College St.

Oxford St.

Nassau St.

Leonard Ave.

CHINATOWN

Baldwin St.

D'Arcy St.

Dundas St. W.

Alexandra Park

Grange Park
Grange Rd.

←☐ The Drake Hotel

Robinson St.

Carr St.

Sullivan St.

Bulwer St.

Renfrew Pl.

Wolseley St.

←☐ Gladstone Hotel

Queen St. W.

QUEEN WEST

Richmond St. W.

Camden St.

Adelaide St. W.

←☐ Bonnevue Manor
Bed & Breakfast Place

King St. W.

Global Village
Backpackers ☐

Hyatt
Regency
Toronto ☐

Hôtel Le
Germain
☐ Toronto

Mercer St.

SoHo Metropolitan ☐
Hotel

☐
Residence Inn

Wellington St. W.

Front St. W.

Renaissance Toronto ☐
Hotel Downtown

Street labels: St. George St., Walmer Rd., Spadina Ave., Huron St., Devonshire Pl., Croft St., Howland Ave., Brunswick Ave., Sussex Ave., Sussex Mews, Spadina Ave., Robert St., Major St., Ross St., Henry St., Cecil St., King's College Rd., College St., Clinton St., Euclid Ave., Palmerston Blvd., Markham St., Bathurst St., Lippincott St., Bellevue Ave., Augusta Ave., Denison Ave., Ryerson Ave., Augusta Ave., Grange Pl., Beverley St., Tecumseth St., Bathurst St., Brant St., Spadina Ave., Peter St., Widmer St., John St., Brant Pl., Portland St., Blue Jays Way, Windsor St.

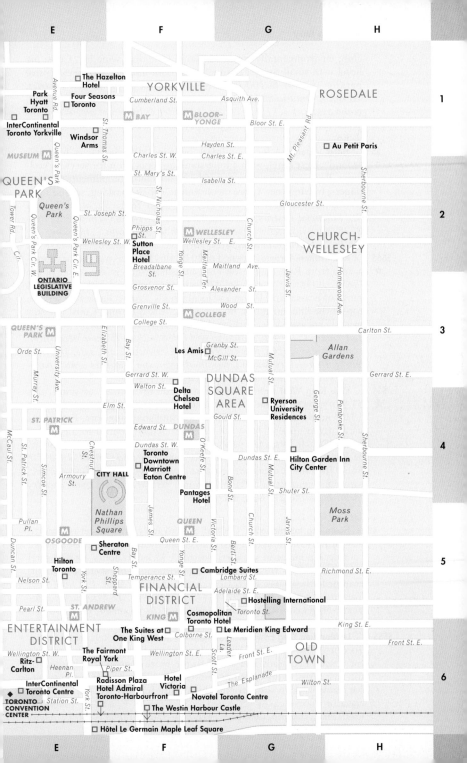

club; environmentally conscious; large Canadian wine list. **Cons:** big hotel with small rooms; charge for in-room Internet access; expensive parking (C$40). ✉ *100 Front St. W, at York St., Financial District, Toronto, Ontario* ☎ *416/368–2511, 800/441–1414* ⊕ *www.fairmont. com/royalyork* ⤻ *1,304 rooms, 61 suites* ♿ *In-room: a/c, Wi-Fi. In-hotel: restaurant, bar, pool, gym, spa, business center, parking* Ⓜ *Union* ✛ *E6.*

$$ 🏨 **Hotel Victoria.** A local landmark built in 1909, the Vic is Toronto's second-oldest hotel, with a long-standing reputation for service excellence. **Pros:** gym privileges at nearby health club; complimentary newspapers; free Internet. **Cons:** inconvenient, off-site parking; second-floor rooms noisy from street; slow elevator. ✉ *56 Yonge St., at Wellington St., Financial District, Toronto, Ontario* ☎ *416/363–1666, 800/363–8228* ⊕ *www.hotelvictoria-toronto.com* ⤻ *56 rooms* ♿ *In-room: a/c, Wi-Fi. In-hotel: restaurant, gym, business center, parking* Ⓜ *King* ✛ *F6.*

$$$$ 🏨 **Ritz-Carlton, Toronto.** Opened in 2010, this Ritz has a great location—
★ across from Roy Thompson Hall and smack-dab in the center of the Financial District—and a solid elegance, embellished with a Canadian motif of brass maple leaves and local woods. **Pros:** reliable Ritz service; top-of-the-line amenities; no check-in/check-out time. **Cons:** five-star prices; expensive valet parking (C$42). ✉ *181 Wellington St. W, Financial District, Toronto, Ontario* ☎ *416/585–2500* ⊕ *www.ritzcarlton. com/toronto* ⤻ *208 rooms, 59 suites* ♿ *In-room: a/c, safe, Internet, Wi-Fi. In-hotel: restaurant, bar, pool, gym, spa, business center, parking, some pets allowed* Ⓜ *St. Andrew, Union* ✛ *E6.*

$$$ 🏨 **One King West Hotel & Residence.** Made up entirely of suites, this
★ 51-story tower is attached to the old Dominion Bank of Canada (circa 1912) in the city's downtown business and shopping core. **Pros:** great views from upper floors; self-catering facility; central locale. **Cons:** small 27-inch TVs; valet parking only (C$30 per day). ✉ *1 King St. W, at Yonge St., Financial District, Toronto, Ontario* ☎ *416/548–8100, 866/470–5464* ⊕ *www.onekingwest.com* ⤻ *340 suites* ♿ *In-room: a/c, safe, kitchen, Internet, Wi-Fi. In-hotel: restaurant, bar, gym, laundry facilities, parking* Ⓜ *King* ✛ *F6.*

OLD TOWN

¢ 🏨 **Hostelling International.** Central and no-frills, this hostel is open to adventurers of all ages. **Pros:** convenient location; international feel; roof deck popular in summer; electronic locks on doors. **Cons:** hostel environment not for everyone; neighborhood a bit sketchy at night; cramped when busy. ✉ *76 Church St., at Adelaide St. E, Old Town, Toronto, Ontario* ☎ *416/971–4440, 877/848–8737* ⊕ *www.toronto-youth-hostel.com* ⤻ *35 rooms, 154 beds* ♿ *In-room: a/c, no TV, Wi-Fi. In-hotel: laundry facilities, business center* Ⓜ *Union* ✛ *G5.*

$$$$ 🏨 **Le Meridien King Edward.** Managed by Starwood Hotels and Resorts, Toronto's "King Eddy" Hotel continues to be a landmark property for special occasions and a nod to the more genteel grand hotels of the past. **Pros:** great location; historic; friendly service. **Cons:** no mirror above sink in some rooms; high daily Internet fee (C$14); brass elevator doors heavily scratched. ✉ *37 King St. E, east of Yonge St., Old Town, Toronto, Ontario* ☎ *416/863–9700, 800/543–4300* ⊕ *www.*

starwoodhotels.com ⟲*292 rooms, 29 suites* △ *In-room: a/c, Internet. In-hotel: restaurant, bar, gym, spa, business center, parking* Ⓜ *King* ⟐ *G6.*

$$ Ⓗ **Novotel Toronto Centre.** A good-value, few-frills, modern hotel, the Novotel is in the heart of the animated, bar-lined Esplanade area, near the St. Lawrence Market, the Air Canada Centre, Union Station, and the Entertainment District. **Pros:** excellent location; good value; laptop-size in-room safes. **Cons:** small in-hotel parking spaces; spotty service and housekeeping; noisy neighborhood. ✉ *45 The Esplanade, at Church St., Old Town, Toronto, Ontario* ☎ *416/367–8900, 800/668–6835* ⊕ *www.novotel. com* ⟲*262 rooms* △ *In-room: a/c, Wi-Fi. In-hotel: restaurant, bar, pool, gym, parking* Ⓜ *Union* ⟐ *F6.*

4

THE ENTERTAINMENT DISTRICT

It's hard to imagine the quiet, empty-looking warehouses in the Entertainment District spontaneously exploding with activity, but when the sun goes down this neighborhood is party central. The bustle and excitement generated by Toronto's clubbers, theatergoers, and night owls keep the action alive until 3 am most nights.

¢ Ⓗ **Global Village Backpackers.** Formerly known as the Spadina Hotel, this centrally located hostel is filled with international students roaming the world. **Pros:** spirited atmosphere with live music in the bar; fun extras. **Cons:** some groups may be noisy; on western edge of Entertainment District; must have valid hostelling or student ID card for low rates. ✉ *460 King St. W, at Spadina Ave., Entertainment District, Toronto, Ontario* ☎ *416/703–8540, 888/844–7875* ⊕ *www.globalbackpackers. com* ⟲*30 rooms with 165 beds* △ *In-room: a/c. In-hotel: bar, laundry facilities, business center* Ⓜ *St. Andrew or Union, then streetcar 504 or 508 west* ⟐ *D5.*

$$$$ Ⓗ **Hôtel Le Germain Toronto.** The Germain Group is known for beautiful, Fodor's Choice chic, upscale boutique hotels, and this downtown Toronto model is no ★ exception. **Pros:** complimentary breakfast; attentive staff; on a quiet street in a bustling neighborhood. **Cons:** spotty temperature controls; hotel's popularity means that rooms fill up fast. ✉ *30 Mercer St., at John St., Entertainment District, Toronto, Ontario* ☎ *416/345–9500, 866/345–9501* ⊕ *www.germaintoronto.com* ⟲*118 rooms, 4 suites* △ *In-room: a/c, safe, Wi-Fi. In-hotel: restaurant, gym, laundry facilities, parking, some pets allowed* ❶ *Breakfast* Ⓜ *St. Andrew* ⟐ *D6.*

$$$$ Ⓗ **Hyatt Regency Toronto.** Request views of Lake Ontario, the downtown skyline, or the Rogers Centre at this recently rebranded luxury hotel smack in the middle of the pulsating Entertainment District. **Pros:** closest large hotel to King Street West theaters; dozens of excellent

The Hazelton Hotel

Hotel Le Germain Toronto

restaurants and cinemas nearby. **Cons:** in-hotel restaurant is pricey; guest rooms on lower floors facing King Street may be especially noisy; service is hit and miss. ✉ *370 King St. W, Entertainment District, Toronto, Ontario* ☎ *416/343–1234, 800/633–7313 in U.S.* ⊕ *www. torontoregency.hyatt.com* ➟ *394 rooms, 32 suites* ⚒ *In-room: a/c, safe, Wi-Fi. In-hotel: restaurant, bar, pool, gym, laundry facilities, business center, parking* Ⓜ *St. Andrew* ✛ *D6.*

$$$ ⌂ **InterContinental Toronto Centre.** Attached to the Metro Toronto Convention Centre, this large but unassuming hotel is a good bet for visiting businesspeople, but the leisure traveler will also find some deals on weekends or during slower periods. **Pros:** atypical convention hotel; bright and airy lobby restaurant; haberdashery in lobby. **Cons:** no shopping nearby; neighborhood streets quiet at night. ✉ *225 Front St. W, west of University Ave., Entertainment District, Toronto, Ontario* ☎ *416/597–1400, 800/422–7969* ⊕ *www.torontocentre. intercontinental.com* ➟ *440 rooms, 136 suites* ⚒ *In-room: a/c, safe, Internet, Wi-Fi. In-hotel: restaurant, bar, pool, gym, spa, business center, parking* Ⓜ *Union* ✛ *E6.*

$$$ ⌂ **Renaissance Toronto Hotel Downtown.** Where else can you watch a base-
☺ ball game, pop-star concert, or monster-truck rally from the comfort of your room? **Pros:** likable staff; free lobby Internet; guest rooms best place to watch Blue Jays baseball games. **Cons:** very long hallways; little natural light in guest rooms overlooking field; hotel's public spaces and rooms due for a makeover. ✉ *1 Blue Jays Way, at Front St. W, Entertainment District, Toronto, Ontario* ☎ *416/341–7100, 800/237–1512* ⊕ *www.renaissancehotels.com* ➟ *313 rooms, 35 suites* ⚒ *In-room: a/c, Wi-Fi. In-hotel: restaurant, bar, gym, laundry facilities, business center, parking* Ⓜ *Union* ✛ *D6.*

$$$ ⌂ **Residence Inn By Marriott.** A big hit with families and long-term visitors
☺ to Toronto, the very modern suites (built in 2007) at the Residence Inn
Fodor's Choice come with full kitchens, spacious living and dining rooms, and very
★ comfortable bedrooms. **Pros:** close to Toronto's major attractions; a smart choice for large families; no minimum stay. **Cons:** valet parking only; street is very quiet at night; breakfast buffet gets very crowded during peak season. ✉ *255 Wellington St. W, at Windsor St., Entertainment District, Toronto, Ontario* ☎ *416/581–1800* ⊕ *www.marriott. com* ➟ *256 suites* ⚒ *In-room: a/c, safe, kitchen, Internet, Wi-Fi. In-hotel: restaurant, pool, gym, laundry facilities, parking, some pets allowed* Ⓜ *Union* ✛ *D6.*

$$$$ ⌂ **Sheraton Centre.** Views from this hotel in the city center are marvelous—to the south are the CN Tower and the Rogers Centre; to the north, both new and old city halls. **Pros:** underground access to shopping in PATH network; pool open until late evening; walk to Four Seasons Centre for Performing Arts. **Cons:** slightly sterile; expensive parking (C$45 per day) and Internet (C$15 per day); hotel is overwhelmingly massive. ✉ *123 Queen St. W, at Bay St., Entertainment District, Toronto, Ontario* ☎ *416/361–1000, 800/325–3535* ⊕ *www. sheratontoronto.com* ➟ *1,302 rooms, 75 suites* ⚒ *In-room: a/c, Wi-Fi. In-hotel: restaurant, bar, pool, gym, spa, business center, parking* Ⓜ *Osgoode* ✛ *E5.*

$$$$ SoHo Metropolitan Hotel. Saturated in pampering detail, the SoHo Met conjures luxury with Frette linens, European down duvets, walk-in closets, marble bathrooms with heated floors, and Molton Brown bath products. **Pros:** no detail left to chance, including electric do-not-disturb signs and curtains; stylish but not showy. **Cons:** lap pool only three feet deep; toiletries not restocked daily; located slightly away from main streets. ⊠ *318 Wellington St. W, east of Spadina Ave., Entertainment District, Toronto, Ontario* ☎ *416/599–8800, 800/668–6600* ⊕ *www. soho.metropolitan.com* ⤳ *72 rooms, 19 suites* ♿ *In-room: a/c, safe, Wi-Fi. In-hotel: restaurant, bar, pool, gym, spa, business center, parking* Ⓜ *St. Andrew* ✚ *D6.*

QUEEN'S PARK, THE ANNEX, AND YORKVILLE

Thanks to its neighbor, the University of Toronto, the Queen's Park area has numerous budget options and dormitory lodgings. The Annex may bustle along Bloor Street West, but the long residential streets running north hide quiet B&Bs that lend a small-town feel to the middle of the city. Yorkville, in keeping with its lofty image as Toronto's most upscale neighborhood, boasts a handful of glamorous, ultradecadent hotels.

QUEEN'S PARK

$$$ Sutton Place Hotel. Visiting film and stage stars still stay here because of the hotel's commitment to service and privacy. **Pros:** quiet location; helpful concierges; valet parking. **Cons:** pricey Internet (C$18.50 per day); limited room-service menu; slightly faded glamour. ⊠ *955 Bay St., at Wellesley St. W, Queen's Park, Toronto, Ontario* ☎ *416/924– 9221, 866/389–8866* ⊕ *www.toronto.suttonplace.com* ⤳ *230 rooms, 53 suites, 28 apartments* ♿ *In-room: a/c, Wi-Fi. In-hotel: restaurant, bar, pool, gym, parking* Ⓜ *Wellesley* ✚ *F2.*

THE ANNEX

$ Annex Quest House. Ecologically friendly and following the eastern
★ design rules of *Vastu* (a sort of Hindu feng shui), the 18 rooms at this Victorian house are decked out in colorful Asian textiles, wooden sculptures and furniture, and splashes of sequined silk. **Pros:** good value; excellent location; striking yet soothing decor. **Cons:** Vastu decor not for everyone; no breakfast. ⊠ *83 Spadina Rd., The Annex, Toronto, Ontario* ☎ *416/922–1934* ⊕ *www.annexquesthouse.com* ⤳ *18 rooms* ♿ *In-room: a/c, Internet, Wi-Fi. In-hotel: laundry facilities, parking* ✚ *D1.*

$$ Suite Dreams. At the western end of the Annex, almost bordering the
★ trendy area dubbed "Little Korea," this elegant B&B has four lovely suites that remain in high demand among B&B enthusiasts. **Pros:** interesting location; owner is wealth of tourist information. **Cons:** only four rooms means reserve well in advance. ⊠ *390 Clinton St., at Bloor St. W, The Annex, Toronto, Ontario* ☎ *416/538–0417* ⊕ *www.suitedreamstoronto. com* ⤳ *4 rooms, 3 with bath* ❢❍❙ *Breakfast* Ⓜ *Christie* ✚ *B1.*

YORKVILLE

$$$$ Four Seasons Toronto. Some of Toronto's most tasteful guest rooms are here, in fashionable Yorkville, with Four Seasons touches like antique-style writing desks, oversize towels, and twice-daily housekeeping. **Pros:**

movie-star hangout; desirable neighborhood. **Cons:** movie-star prices; rooms are not stylish; a trifle pretentious. ⊠ *21 Avenue Rd., at Bloor St. W, Yorkville, Toronto, Ontario* ☎ *416/964–0411, 800/819–8053* ⊕ *www.fourseasons.com/toronto* ⤳ *230 rooms, 150 suites* ⚲ *In-room: a/c, safe, Wi-Fi. In-hotel: restaurant, bar, pool, gym, laundry facilities, business center, parking* Ⓜ *Bay* ✢ *E1.*

$$$$
Fodor's Choice
★
Hazelton Hotel. A lot can be surmised by the Hazelton's opening in 2007, which was timed right before the Toronto International Film Festival, signaling Hollywood to move in and the rest of us to enjoy the same celebrity treatment. **Pros:** Toronto's hottest address and Hollywood hot spot; well-equipped techno gym; private spa; great in-room amenities. **Cons:** Toronto's hottest address with prices to reflect it; screening room and other perks may not be available to average guests. ⊠ *118 Yorkville Ave., at Avenue Rd., Yorkville, Toronto, Ontario* ☎ *416/963–6300, 866/473–6301* ⊕ *www.thehazeltonhotel.com* ⤳ *62 rooms, 15 suites* ⚲ *In-room: a/c, safe, Wi-Fi. In-hotel: restaurant, pool, gym, spa, business center, parking, some pets allowed* Ⓜ *Bay* ✢ *E1.*

$$$
InterContinental Toronto Yorkville. Handsome and intimate, this outpost of the respected InterContinental chain is a two-minute walk from the Yorkville shopping area and directly across from the Royal Ontario Museum's stunning Crystal addition. **Pros:** close to the Royal Ontario and Gardiner museums; knowledgeable concierges; ultracool lobby bar. **Cons:** some front-desk staff inexperienced; expensive Internet. ⊠ *220 Bloor St. W, west of Avenue Rd., Yorkville, Toronto, Ontario* ☎ *416/960–5200, 800/267–0010* ⊕ *www.toronto.intercontinental.com* ⤳ *185 rooms, 23 suites* ⚲ *In-room: a/c, safe, Wi-Fi. In-hotel: restaurant, bar, pool, gym, laundry facilities, business center, parking* Ⓜ *Museum* ✢ *E1.*

$$$$
Park Hyatt Toronto. The experience here is *très* New York Park Avenue, with elegant guest rooms (a generous 350 to 400 square feet) overlooking Queen's Park and Lake Ontario. **Pros:** large marble baths; Davies Gate toiletries; free Internet; impeccably appointed. **Cons:** inexpensive breakfasts unavailable; locker rooms for paying spa guests only. ⊠ *4 Avenue Rd., at Bloor St. W, Yorkville, Toronto, Ontario* ☎ *416/925–1234, 800/778–7477* ⊕ *www.parktoronto.hyatt.com* ⤳ *291 rooms, 45 suites* ⚲ *In-room: a/c, safe, Wi-Fi. In-hotel: restaurant, bar, gym, spa, business center, parking* Ⓜ *Museum* ✢ *E1.*

$$$$
Windsor Arms. Service is the motto here, with a staff-to-guest ratio of 1 to 5 and 24-hour butler service. **Pros:** high repeat business due to privacy and personal service; ultracomfortable beds; complimentary Continental breakfast. **Cons:** some fourth-floor rooms noisy due to downstairs functions; complaints about service slipping in recent years; rooms ready for an update. ⊠ *18 St. Thomas St., at Bloor St. W, Yorkville, Toronto, Ontario* ☎ *416/971–9666, 877/999–2767* ⊕ *www.windsorarmshotel.com* ⤳ *2 rooms, 26 suites* ⚲ *In-room: a/c, Internet. In-hotel: restaurant, bar, pool, gym, spa, business center* ⦿ *Breakfast* Ⓜ *Bay* ✢ *E1.*

CHURCH-WELLESLEY AND DUNDAS SQUARE AREA

Once a run-down strip of downtown, the Dundas Square Area near the tourist-centric Eaton Centre and bright lights of the square has undergone a renaissance in recent years. Similarly, the Church-Wellesley neighborhood is sprucing up its image, restoring historic houses and giving them an energetic, youthful vibe. Hotels in this neighborhood are centrally located, making perfect bases for exploring the city.

$$$ 🛏 **Delta Chelsea Hotel.** Canada's
🐣 largest hotel has long been popular with families and tour groups, so be prepared for a flurry of activity. **Pros:** all-inclusive cruise-ship-like atmosphere; excellent service; adults-only floors. **Cons:** many children in public areas; busy and noisy lobby at times; unmemorable guest rooms. ✉ *33 Gerrard St., at Yonge St., Dundas Square Area, Toronto, Ontario* ☎ *416/595–1975, 800/243–5732* ⊕ *www.deltachelsea.com* ⤢ *1,590 rooms, 46 suites* ♿ *In-room: a/c, Wi-Fi. In-hotel: restaurant, bar, pool, gym, children's programs, laundry facilities, parking* Ⓜ *College* ⟐ *F3.*

$$ 🛏 **Hilton Garden Inn City Centre.** Suites at this hotel, an incarnation of the popular Hilton chain's lower-end brand, are modern and simple with basic furniture and spacious bathrooms. **Pros:** close to the Eaton Centre; advance reservations are heavily discounted. **Cons:** run-down neighborhood with panhandlers. ✉ *200 Dundas St. E, Dundas Square Area, Toronto, Ontario* ☎ *416/362–7700* ⊕ *www.hiltongardeninn.hilton.com* ⤢ *151 suites* ♿ *In-room: a/c, Internet, Wi-Fi. In-hotel: restaurant, bar, pool, gym, laundry facilities, business center, parking* Ⓜ *Dundas* ⟐ *G4.*

$$$ 🛏 **Pantages Hotel.** Clean lines, gleaming hardwood flooring, and brushed-steel accents exude contemporary cool at this hotel. **Pros:** quiet but very central location for shopping; excellent spa; great for long stays. **Cons:** smallish TVs; lobby can be noisy; dark hallways. ✉ *200 Victoria St., at Shuter St., Dundas Square Area, Toronto, Ontario* ☎ *416/362–1777, 866/852–1777* ⊕ *www.pantageshotel.com* ⤢ *95 suites* ♿ *In-room: a/c, kitchen, Wi-Fi. In-hotel: restaurant, bar, gym, spa, laundry facilities, parking* ⦿ *Breakfast* Ⓜ *Queen* ⟐ *F4.*

$$$ 🛏 **Toronto Downtown Marriott Eaton Centre.** Guest rooms at the Marriott's flagship hotel in Canada are connected to Eaton Centre through an aboveground walkway. **Pros:** knowledgeable employees; good value; large guest rooms. **Cons:** may be noisy; parking area can be full. ✉ *525 Bay St., at Dundas St. W, Dundas Square Area, Toronto, Ontario* ☎ *416/597–9200, 800/905–0667* ⊕ *www.marriotteatoncentre.com* ⤢ *435 rooms, 24 suites* ♿ *In-room: a/c, Wi-Fi. In-hotel: restaurant, bar, pool, gym, parking* Ⓜ *Dundas* ⟐ *F4.*

QUEEN WEST

While some of the large chains, like Hilton, have branches near this very trendy strip of Queen Street West, most of the hotels in this area are beyond Bathurst Street in West Queen West. In this up-and-coming neighborhood, experimental, cutting-edge hotels featuring local art, music, and food thrive.

$ 🛏 **Bonnevue Manor Bed & Breakfast Place.** True craftsmen created this 5,000-square-foot house, and it shows in every enchanting nook and cranny, in the high plastered ceilings, and in the richly aged hardwood

The Drake is both a boutique hotel and a fixture of Toronto's humming nightlife.

floors. **Pros:** safe and comfortable neighborhood; excellent breakfasts. **Cons:** two-night minimum stay; old heating system may have problems; no Internet. ⊠ *33 Beaty Ave., south of Queen St. W, Queen West, Toronto, Ontario* ☎ *416/536–1455* ⊕ *www.bonnevuemanor.com* ⇆ *4 rooms* ⚄ *In-room: a/c, no TV. In-hotel: restaurant, parking* ⦿ *Breakfast* Ⓜ *Osgoode, then streetcar 501 west* ✛ *A5.*

$$$ 🔢 **The Drake Hotel.** Once a notorious flophouse, this 19th-century building is now an ultra-hip hotel peppered with contemporary art and attracting a chic, creative crowd. **Pros:** attracts Toronto's hippest crowds; food consistently good; forward-thinking; complimentary access to off-site gym. **Cons:** slightly seedy neighborhood; can be noisy at night; not great for children. ⊠ *1150 Queen St. W, at Beaconsfield Ave., Queen West, Toronto, Ontario* ☎ *416/531–5042, 866/372–5386* ⊕ *www.thedrakehotel.ca* ⇆ *19 rooms, 1 suite* ⚄ *In-room: a/c, safe, Wi-Fi. In-hotel: restaurant, bar, business center* Ⓜ *Osgoode, then streetcar 501 west* ✛ *A5.*

$$$ 🔢 **Gladstone Hotel.** The Canadian newspaper the *Globe and Mail* called the Gladstone the "anti-chain-hotel Toronto experience" in 2006, and that's still an apt description for this bohemian beacon. **Pros:** every guest room is designed differently; friendly, bohemian place; truly a one-of-a-kind property and experience. **Cons:** rooms are on the smaller side; downtrodden neighborhood; long walk or transit to downtown core. ⊠ *1214 Queen St. W, at Gladstone Ave., Queen West, Toronto, Ontario* ☎ *416/531–4635* ⊕ *www.gladstonehotel.com* ⇆ *34 rooms, 3 suites* ⚄ *In-room: a/c, kitchen. In-hotel: restaurant, bar* Ⓜ *Osgoode, then streetcar 501 west* ✛ *A5.*

$$$ 🔢 **Hilton Toronto.** Everything that you'd expect from a Hilton, this Queen West outpost is decorated in golds and browns in the lobby and

Toronto Lodging Alternatives and Resources

Massey College Student Residence is an affordable alternative to a hotel during the summer.

APARTMENT RENTALS
If you want a home base that's roomy enough for a family and comes with cooking facilities, consider a furnished rental. Home-exchange directories sometimes list rentals as well as exchanges.

Hideaways International. A four-month membership is US$49. ☎ 603/430–4433, 800/843–4433 ⊕ www.hideaways.com.

LOCAL AGENTS
Apartments International Inc.
Apartments International Inc. provides upper-end furnished apartments for executives visiting for a month or more. ☎ 416/410–2400, 888/410–2400 ⊕ www.apts-intl.com.

BED-AND-BREAKFASTS
Toronto Bed & Breakfast. A free registry, this organization lists more than a dozen private homes, all in and around downtown. ☎ 705/738–9449, 877/922–6522 ⊕ www.torontobandb.com.

The Downtown Toronto Association of Bed & Breakfast Guest Houses. This organization represents privately owned B&Bs. ☎ 416/410–3938 ⊕ www.bnbinfo.com.

Au Petit Paris. A great alternative to big chain hotels in this area, this B&B is just east of Yorkville and north of the Church-Wellesley district. Vegetarian breakfasts, served on the rooftop (weather permitting) are memorable. ✉ 3 Selby St., Church–Wellesley, Toronto, Ontario ☎ 416/928–1348 ⊕ www.bbtoronto.com/aupetitparis.

By the Park B&B. This B&B consists of two buildings (a B&B and an apartment-style accommodation in a separate house), the brainchildren of a married couple who happen to be alumni of the Ontario College of Art and Design; their attention to detail is evident. ✉ 92 & 89 Indian Grove., at Bloor St. W, Greater Toronto, Toronto, Ontario ☎ 416/761–9778, 416/520–6102 ⊕ www.bythepark.ca.

Islington Bed & Breakfast House.
At this B&B, paintings and tapestries reflect the local landscape. ✉ *1411 Islington Ave., Greater Toronto, Toronto, Ontario* ☎ *416/236–2707* ⊕ *www.islingtonhouse.com.*

Les Amis. The charming Parisian host Paul-Antoine fills Les Amis with beautiful photos of his travels through South America and Africa and the tantalizing aromas of his legendary fruit crepes and Belgian-style waffles. ✉ *31 Granby St., at Yonge St., Dundas Square Area, Toronto, Ontario* ☎ *416/928–1348* ⊕ *www.bbtoronto.com.*

COLLEGE RESIDENCES
You can crash at these college residences, which are affordable summertime alternatives to hotels.

Massey College Student Residence.
Between early May and mid-August, this student residence at the University of Toronto provides budget lodging. Single and double junior suites have shared bathrooms, and single and double senior suites have private bathrooms—all rooms are spartan, but linens, towels, and housekeeping services are provided, as well as breakfast. ✉ *4 Devonshire Pl., south of Bloor St. W, Queen's Park, Toronto, Ontario* ☎ *416/946–7843* ⊕ *www. masseycollege.ca.*

Ryerson University Residences.
These residences consist of two adjacent buildings with dormitory-style guest rooms available to nonstudents during the summer months (early May to late August). In Pitman Hall, bathroom and kitchen facilities are shared, and Continental breakfast is included; larger single or double bedrooms in the International Centre have en suite baths and cable TV but no breakfast. ✉ *160 [Pitman] and 133 [International Centre] Mutual St., north of Dundas St. E, Dundas Square Area, Toronto, Ontario* ☎ *416/979–5296, 888/592–8882 in Canada only* ⊕ *www.ryerson.ca/conference.*

HOSTELS
With some 4,500 locations in more than 70 countries, Hostelling International (HI), the umbrella group for a number of national youth-hostel associations, has single-sex, dorm-style beds and, at many hostels, including those in Toronto, rooms for couples and accommodations for families. Membership in any HI national hostel association, open to travelers of all ages, allows you to stay in HI-affiliated hostels at member rates; one-year membership is about C$28 for adults (C$35 for a two-year membership in Canada); hostels charge about C$10 to C$30 per night.

Organizations Hostelling International—USA ✉ *8401 Colesville Rd., Ste. 600, Silver Spring, Maryland, USA* ☎ *301/495–1240* ⊕ *www.hiusa.org.* **Hostelling International—Canada** ✉ *205 Catherine St., Suite 400, Ottawa, Ontario* ☎ *613/237–7884, 800/663–5777* ⊕ *www.hihostels.ca.*

4

wooden floors, subtle earth tones, and modern furniture in the guest rooms. **Pros:** popular on-site steak house; safe and walkable neighborhood; Crabtree & Evelyn toiletries. **Cons:** rooms generally on the small side; service can lag at times. ⊠ *145 Richmond St. W, at University Ave., Queen West, Toronto, Ontario* ☎ *416/869–3456, 800/267–2281* ⊕ *www.hilton.com* ⇘ *601 rooms, 47 suites* ☐ *In-room: a/c, Wi-Fi. In-hotel: restaurant, bar, pool, gym, laundry facilities, business center, parking* Ⓜ *Osgoode* ✢ *C5.*

GREATER TORONTO

A breath of fresh air, West End hotels are closer to natural beauty but still well-situated on the subway line.

$$$ 🔲 **The Old Mill Inn & Spa.** Tucked into the Humber River valley, the Old Mill is the only country inn within the city limits of Toronto. **Pros:** whirlpool tubs; subway and bus stop very close; live jazz music (Friday). **Cons:** residential neighborhood is sometimes too quiet; no shopping nearby; can be very busy with weddings. ⊠ *21 Old Mill Rd., at Bloor St. W, Greater Toronto, Toronto, Ontario* ☎ *416/236–2641, 866/653–6455* ⊕ *www.oldmilltoronto.com* ⇘ *44 rooms, 13 suites* ☐ *In-room: a/c, Internet, Wi-Fi. In-hotel: restaurant, bar, gym, spa, business center, parking* Ⓜ *Old Mill* ✢ *A1.*

THE AIRPORT STRIP

If you have an early-morning departure or late-night arrival at Pearson International Airport, staying nearby might be the best option, considering the drive from downtown Toronto can take up to two hours when traffic is at its worst.

$$ 🔲 **Sandman Signature Toronto Airport.** Reasonable prices, great parking
Ⓒ deals, and quiet, modern rooms are the assets of this Sandman property just down the road from Pearson International Airport. **Pros:** best value along the Airport Strip; unexpectedly excellent service; free Internet. **Cons:** on-site restaurant is pricey. ⊠ *55 Reading Court, Airport Strip, Toronto, Ontario* ☎ *416/798–8840* ⊕ *www.sandmansignature.com/toronto.html* ⇘ *256 rooms* ☐ *In-room: a/c, Internet, Wi-Fi. In-hotel: restaurant, bar, pool, gym, business center, parking, some pets allowed.*

$$$$ 🔲 **Sheraton Gateway Hotel.** For business travelers and quick layovers, it's hard to beat the location this mid-range hotel—right inside Pearson International Airport. **Pros:** inside the airport; totally soundproof. **Cons:** room service prices don't match quality of food; only wired Internet is available; Internet is pricey (C$15 per day). ⊠ *Terminal 3, Toronto AMF, PO Box 3000, Airport Strip, Toronto, Ontario* ☎ *905/672–7000* ⊕ *www.starwoodhotels.com* ⇘ *474 rooms* ☐ *In-room: a/c, Internet. In-hotel: restaurant, bar, pool, gym, business center, parking.*

Nightlife and the Arts

WORD OF MOUTH

"I don't try to see galas, or stars [at the Toronto Film Festival], I try to see really wonderful movies, that I might not otherwise see."

—bxb52

Updated by
Shannon Kelly
and Nina
Callaway

In terms of culture, Toronto truly is Canada's New York—the city to which artists immigrate to make a name for themselves. And the rest of us reap the rewards. With all of the options available, these days the biggest obstacle to arts and culture in Toronto is deciding what to experience while you're here. The capital of the performing arts in English-speaking Canada, Toronto has world-class resident symphony, opera, and ballet companies. The city's nightlife is just as diverse as its culture. From indie-rock mash-ups and live bluegrass to popular bars, lounges, and nightclubs, Toronto *rocks* after dark.

Toronto is growing, with new performance venues opening and old ones being refurbished. The current flurry of artistic activity shows no signs of abating. The city has more than 50 dance companies; film festivals and retrospectives overtake screens year-round; and the numerous theatrical troupes and big-budget musicals staged here have earned it the nickname "Broadway North." Theater is where it really shines, from spit-and-chewing-gum new works to Broadway-style, no-expenses-spared extravaganzas. In fact, Toronto is the largest center for English-speaking theater in the world after New York and London—not bad for a city that's only the fifth largest in North America by population.

Its compact downtown means that if you really wanted to, you could hear jazz with dinner, sip a single malt with a view of the skyline, catch an indie band, and get low on the dance floor all in one (very busy) night. Torontonians are out on the town every night of the week. When a popular band is playing or when the weather is unseasonably warm, you might confuse a Tuesday for a Saturday with all the people milling about after midnight. Thursday is unofficially locals' night out and the best night to check out the local scene: it's lively but not sardine-can packed.

PLANNING

WHAT'S ON NOW?

Check free alternative newsweeklies *NOW* (⊕ *www.nowtoronto. com*) and *The Grid* (⊕ *www.thegridto.com*) and monthly magazine *Toronto Life* (⊕ *www.torontolife.com*) for reviews, concerts, movie times, and events. *Whole Note* (⊕ *www.thewholenote.com*) publishes classical, jazz, opera, and world music concert dates and news online and in its free monthly print publication. There are also the Thursday "What's On" section of the *Toronto Star* (⊕ *www.thestar.com/ entertainment/whatson*) and the arts sections of the *Globe and Mail* (⊕ *www.theglobeandmail.com/news/arts*) and *National Post* (⊕ *www. nationalpost.com/arts*).

LATE-NIGHT TRANSPORTATION

Subway and streetcar service ends at 1 am, so for late-night outings, hailing a cab is your best bet. Some streetcars and buses along major streets (including Queen, Bloor, and Yonge) run 24 hours but pick up only every half hour.

TOP EXPERIENCES

Rub elbows with Hollywood types at the Toronto International Film Festival. See star-studded premieres and discover the next big thing with independent films.

Laugh it up. In Canada's breeding ground for comedy, Second City is the cream of the crop, and there are about a dozen stand-up venues around town.

See a major musical. Catch a performance of *War Horse* or *Sister Act* at one of the grand, historic theaters in Toronto—the next best thing to Broadway.

Partake in patio life. Torontonians are notorious in Canada for being cold, but when the sun comes out, they're giddy, and come 5:15 on a warm-weather weekday April through October, bar and restaurant patios are teeming.

Root for your team. Sports fans run rampant in the T-Dot; if you can't get to the pitch, catch NHL matches, Premier League games, or even cricket and curling at Hemingways, Wayne Gretzky's, the Queen and Beaver, or the mother of them all, Real Sports Bar.

TICKETS

Ticketmaster. Tickets for almost any event can be obtained through Ticketmaster. ☎ *855/985–5000* ⊕ *www.ticketmaster.ca.*

T.O. Tix booth. For half-price theater, dance, music, and comedy tickets on the day of a performance, visit the T.O. Tix booth, open Tuesday to Saturday noon to 6:30 pm, weather permitting. Tickets for Sunday and Monday performances are sold on Saturday. In summer the wait can be 45 minutes or more. ■ TIP→ Arrive by around 11:15 for the best chance of getting the tickets you want. Visa, MasterCard, and cash are accepted. ✉ *Yonge and Dundas sts., Dundas Square Area, Toronto, Ontario, Canada* ☎ *800/541–0499, 416/536–6468* ⊕ *www.totix.ca* Ⓜ *Dundas.*

TORONTO'S FILM SCENE

Toronto loves the movies, and the feeling is mutual. So many films are shot here (the city has posed as everywhere from Paris to Vietnam) that Toronto has earned the nickname "Hollywood North." The highlight of the cinematic year is the world-renowned Toronto International Film Festival.

North America's third-largest film production center after L.A. and New York, Toronto keeps cameras rolling with its excellent local crews and production facilities and plenty of filmmaker tax credits. It helps, too, that Toronto's chameleonic streets easily impersonate other cities and time periods. Credits include: Yonge Street as Harlem (*The Incredible Hulk*), the Distillery District as Prohibition-era Chicago (*Chicago*), Casa Loma as the school for young mutants in *X-Men*, and the U of T campus as Harvard (*Good Will Hunting*). Spotting Toronto "tells" in films is fun, but locals get even more jazzed when the city represents itself for a change, as in 2010's *Scott Pilgrim vs. the World*.

WHERE TO WATCH

Oddball series and theme nights: Revue

Documentaries: Bloor Cinema

Pure cinephelia: TIFF Bell Lightbox

IMAX: Scotiabank, AMC Yonge & Dundas Square, Ontario Place

3-D: Scotiabank, TIFF Bell Lightbox, Varsity and Varsity VIP, AMC Yonge-Dundas Square

Summer films al fresco: Harbourfront Centre (✉ 235 Queens Quay W; Polson Pier Drive-In (✉ 176 Cherry St., Harbourfront); TIFF in the Park (✉ King and Simcoe sts., next to Roy Thompson Hall).

TORONTO INTERNATIONAL FILM FESTIVAL

Widely considered the most important film festival in the world after Cannes, TIFF is open to the public with even star-studded galas accessible to the average joe. More than 300 of the latest works of great international directors and lesser-known independent-film directors from around the world are shown. Movies premiered at TIFF have gone on to win Academy Awards and launch the careers of emerging actors and directors. In recent years, TIFF audiences have been among the first in the world to see *The Hurt Locker, Slumdog Millionaire,* and *Juno,* to mention just a few. The red carpet is rolled out, and paparazzi get ready for big-budget, star-studded premieres ("galas"), for which actors and directors may be on hand afterward for Q&As. Along with the serious documentaries, foreign films, and Oscar contenders, TIFF has fun with its Midnight Madness program, screening campy horror films, comedies, and action movies into the wee hours. ☎ 416/968–3456, 877/968–3456 ⊕ www.tiff.net.

DOING THE FESTIVAL

When: The 10-day festival begins in early September
Where: Screenings are at movie theaters and concert halls throughout the city, as are ticket booths, but the festival HQ is the TIFF Bell Lightbox building, at ✉ *363 King St. W (at Peter St.).*
Tickets: If you plan to see 10 or more films, consider a festival pass or package. These go on sale in July; the somewhat complicated lottery process is fully explained on the TIFF Web site. Individual tickets go on sale four days before screenings. You may not get your first choice, but discovering something new is part of the fun. (No, really!) Ticket prices are about C$20 per film. Popular films sell out early, but tickets are almost always available for *something,* even at the last minute, and even sold-out shows have a rush line.

TIPS

■ Book a hotel as early as possible: some hotels near the theaters are booked by May.

■ Read ticket-buying instructions carefully; fixing something that's gone awry is difficult.

■ Arrive 30 minutes to an hour before the film; at least two hours early for rush lines.

■ Most films have two or three screenings, so don't despair if you miss the first one.

■ Visa is the official TIFF sponsor, and Visa holders get numerous perks—including being the only credit card accepted for purchases.

FILM FESTIVALS

Among the scores of Toronto film festivals (full list at ⊕ wx.toronto.ca/festevents.nsf) these are our faves.

Hot Docs is the largest documentary film festival in North America. ⊕ www.hotdocs.ca.

Sprockets: Toronto International Film Festival for Children features new and classic films aimed at the 4-to-14-year-old crowd. ⊕ sprockets.ca.

Toronto After Dark is a festival of horror, sci-fi, and thrillers. ⊕ www.torontoafterdark.com.

★ The city's most hyped annual event is September's **Toronto International Film Festival** (⇨ See left).

Worldwide Short Film Festival is five days of shorts from around the world. ⊕ www.worldwideshortfilmfest.com.

Left: Fans outside the Roy Thomson Hall during the Toronto Film Festival. Above: Actor Jeff Bridges at a TIFF premiere.

THE ARTS

Toronto is the capital of the performing arts in English-speaking Canada, but it hasn't always been this way. Before 1950, Toronto had no opera company, no ballet, and very little theater worthy of the title "professional." Then came the Massey Report on the Arts, and money began to pour in from government grants. The Canada Council, the Canadian Opera Company, CBC television, and the National Ballet of Canada were born. A number of small theaters began to pop up as well, culminating in an artistic explosion throughout the 1970s in every aspect of the arts.

FREE CONCERTS

Free Concert Series. The Canadian Opera Company's Free Concert Series takes place September through June with music and dance performances most Tuesdays and Thursdays at noon and some Wednesday evenings, in the Four Seasons Centre's Richard Bradshaw Amphitheatre. ⊠ *145 Queen St. W., Queen West, Toronto, Ontario, Canada* ☎ *416/363-6671* ⊕ *www.coc.ca* Ⓜ *Osgoode Station.*

(This was also when the Toronto International Film Festival, which has since become one of the top film festivals in the world next to Cannes, was born.) Adding fuel to the fire was a massive spike in immigration from England and Eastern and Central Europe, a recognition that if Canadians did not develop their own arts the Americans would do it for them, and a severing of the political apron strings tying Canada to England, resulting in a desire to cement Canada's independence from the mother country and to encourage homegrown talent.

CLASSICAL MUSIC AND OPERA

CLASSICAL MUSIC

★ **Glenn Gould Studio.** A variety of classical, folk, jazz, and world-music companies perform at this 341-seat shoebox concert hall named for the famed Torontonian pianist and designed for the Canadian Broadcasting Centre (CBC). Studio recordings are done here as well, a testament to its excellent acoustics. Gould would have expected nothing less. ⊠ *Canadian Broadcasting Centre, 250 Front St. W, at John, Entertainment District, Toronto, Ontario, Canada* ☎ *416/205–5000 Tours and Information, 416/872-4255 Tickets* ⊕ *www.cbc.ca/glenngould* Ⓜ *Union, St. Andrews.*

★ **Koerner Hall.** Artists and audiences quickly fell in love with this handsome 1,135-seat concert hall with rich acoustics and undulating wood "strings" floating overhead when it opened in 2009. Performers have included such greats as Yo-Yo Ma, Chick Corea, Ravi Shankar, Concha Buika, and Savion Glover. The hall is part of The Royal Conservatory's arts-education facility, the TELUS Centre for Performance and Learning. ⊠ *273 Bloor St. W, at Avenue Rd., Yorkville, Toronto, Ontario, Canada* ☎ *416/408–0208* ⊕ *www.rcmusic.ca* ☉ *Box Office open Mon.– Fri. 10–6, Sat. noon–6* Ⓜ *St. George.*

With its circular shape and striking glass canopy, Roy Thomson Hall is a classic of Toronto architecture.

Tafelmusik. Internationally renowned as one of the world's finest period ensembles, Tafelmusik presents baroque and classical music on original instruments. Most performances are in the historic Trinity–St. Paul's Church. ⊠ *Trinity–St. Paul's United Church, 427 Bloor St. W, The Annex, Toronto, Ontario, Canada* ☎ 416/964–6337 ⊕ *www.tafelmusik.org* Ⓜ *Spadina.*

Toronto Mendelssohn Choir. This group of 150 vocalists, which often performs with the Toronto Symphony Orchestra, was formed in 1894 and performs at various venues including the Royal Conservatory's lovely Koerner Hall. The choir sings Handel's *Messiah* annually at Christmastime. ☎ 416/598–0422 ⊕ *www.tmchoir.org.*

Toronto Symphony Orchestra. Since 1922 this orchestra has achieved world acclaim with music directors such as Seiji Ozawa, Sir Thomas Beecham, and Sir Andrew Davis. Canadian-born Peter Oundjian helped return the ensemble to an international level when he took over as musical director in 2003. Guest performers have included pianist Lang Lang and violinist Joshua Bell. The TSO presents about three concerts weekly at Roy Thomson Hall from September through May when it is not on tour. ⊠ *Roy Thomson Hall, 60 Simcoe St., Entertainment District, Toronto, Ontario, Canada* ☎ 416/598–3375 ⊕ *www.tso.ca* Ⓜ *St. Andrew.*

University of Toronto. Performances by professors and students of the University of Toronto Faculty of Music and visiting artists, ranging from symphony to jazz to full-scale operas, take place September through May, at little or no cost, in two spaces: the 815-seat **MacMillan Theatre** and the 490-seat **Walter Hall** auditorium. ⊠ *University of Toronto Faculty of Music, Edward Johnson Bldg., 80 Queen's Park Crescent,*

Queen's Park, Toronto, Ontario, Canada ☎416/978–3744 ⊕*www. music.utoronto.ca* Ⓜ *Museum.*

CONTEMPORARY AND EXPERIMENTAL MUSIC

★ **The Music Gallery.** Toronto's go-to spot for experimental music, the self-titled "center for creative music" presents an eclectic selection of avant-garde and experimental music from world and classical to jazz and avant-pop in a relaxed environment. Seeing a show in the dramatic main venue, **St. George the Martyr Church,** is recommended, though there are several other settings. ⊠*St. George the Martyr Church, 197 John St., 1 block north of Queen St., Queen West, Toronto, Ontario, Canada* ☎416/204–1080 ⊕ *www.musicgallery.org* Ⓜ *Osgoode.*

OPERA

Canadian Opera Company. Founded in 1950, the COC has grown into the largest producer of opera in Canada. From the most popular operas to more modern or rarely performed works, the COC has proven trustworthy and often daring. Versions of Giuseppe Verdi's *La Traviata* and Richard Wagner's *The Flying Dutchman* were considered radical by many. The COC often hosts world-renowned performers, and it pioneered the use of scrolling supertitles, which allow the audience to follow the libretto in English in a capsulized translation that appears above the stage. Tickets sell out quickly. Tours (C$20 for adults; C$15 for seniors/students) of the COC's opera house, the magnificent **Four Seasons Centre for the Performing Arts,** are given most weekends and some weekdays; check the Web site for details. ⊠ *Four Seasons Centre for the Performing Arts, 145 Queen St. W, at University Ave., Queen West, Toronto, Ontario, Canada* ☎416/363–8231 ⊕ *www.coc.ca* Ⓜ *Osgoode.*

Opera Atelier. Since its opening in 1985, Opera Atelier has been dedicated to staging 17th- and 18th-century baroque operas, with extravagant sets and costumes and original instruments. Performances are at the Elgin Theatre. ⊠ *189 Yonge St., at Queen St. E, Dundas Square Area, Toronto, Ontario, Canada* ☎416/703–3767 ⊕ *www.operaatelier. com.*

MAJOR VENUES

It's not uncommon for a concert hall to present modern dance one week, a rock- or classical-music concert another week, and a theatrical performance the next. Arenas double as sports stadiums and venues for the biggest names in music and the occasional monster-truck rally or other spectacle.

Air Canada Centre. Most arena shows are held here rather than at the larger Rogers Centre due to superior acoustics. Past performances at the 20,000-capacity arena have included Alicia Keyes, Tom Petty, the American Idol Tour, and Cirque du Soleil. ⊠ *40 Bay St., at Gardiner Expressway, Harbourfront, Toronto, Ontario, Canada* ☎416/815–5500 ⊕ *www.theaircanadacentre.com* Ⓜ *Union.*

★ **Elgin and Winter Garden Theatre Centre.** This jewel in the crown of the Toronto arts scene consists of two former vaudeville halls, built in

1913, one on top of the other. It is the last operating double-decker theater complex in the world and a Canadian National Historic Site. Until 1928, the theaters hosted silent-film and vaudeville legends like George Burns, Gracie Allen, and Edgar Bergen with Charlie McCarthy. Today's performances are still surrounded by magnificent settings: Elgin's dramatic gold-leaf-and-cherub-adorned interior and the Winter Garden's *A Midsummer Night's Dream*–inspired decor, complete with tree branches overhead. These stages host Broadway-caliber musicals, comedians, jazz concerts, operas, and Toronto International Film Festival screenings. The Elgin, downstairs, has about 1,500 seats; the 1,000-seat Winter Garden is upstairs. Guided tours (C$12) are given Thursday at 5 pm and Saturday at 11 am. ⊠ *189 Yonge St., at Queen St. E, Dundas Square Area, Toronto, Ontario, Canada* ☎ *855/622-2787 tickets, 416/314–2871 tours* ⊕ *www.heritagetrust.on.ca/ewg* Ⓜ *Queen.*

HARBOURFRONT CENTRE

Harbourfront Centre. When looking for cultural events in Toronto, always check the schedule at the Harbourfront Centre. A cultural playground, it has an art gallery (the Power Plant), two dance spaces, a music garden co-designed by Yo-Yo Ma, and chockablock festivals and cultural events, some especially for kids and many of them free. ⊠ *235 Queen's Quay W, at Lower Simcoe St., Harbourfront, Toronto, Ontario, Canada* ☎ *416/973–4000* ⊕ *www.harbourfrontcentre.com* ⊘ *Hrs vary; check Web site or call* Ⓜ *Union.*

Fodor's Choice ★ **Massey Hall.** Near-perfect acoustics and handsome, U-shape tiers have made Massey Hall a great place to enjoy music since 1894, when it opened with a performance of Handel's *Messiah*. It's always been cramped, and the 2,753 seats are not terribly comfortable, but this grand old venue remains a venerable place to catch big-time solo acts like Neil Young and Gilberto Gil, comedians, indie bands, and occasional dance troupes. Every December Massey Hall hosts a Sing-Along *Messiah*, where the audience is seated by voice part and joins the choir in singing Handel's masterpiece; tickets start at C$26 and the event usually sells out. ⊠ *178 Victoria St., at Shuter St., Dundas Square Area, Toronto, Ontario, Canada* ☎ *416/872–4255* ⊕ *www.masseyhall.com* Ⓜ *Queen.*

Rogers Centre. Toronto's largest performance venue, with seating for up to 55,000, is the spot for the biggest shows in town. The former SkyDome has hosted the Rolling Stones, U2, and Cher, though the acoustically superior Air Canada Centre is the more widely used arena venue. ⊠ *1 Blue Jays Way, at Spadina Ave., Harbourfront, Toronto, Ontario, Canada* ☎ *416/341–3663* ⊕ *www.rogerscentre.com* Ⓜ *Union.*

★ **Roy Thomson Hall.** Toronto's premier concert hall, home of the Toronto Symphony Orchestra (TSO), also hosts visiting orchestras, popular entertainers, and Toronto International Film Festival red-carpet screenings. The 2,630-seat auditorium opened in 1982 and is named for the billionaire newspaper magnate known as Lord Thomson of Fleet. ⊠ *60 Simcoe St., at King, Entertainment District, Toronto, Ontario, Canada*

In addition to producing numerous works by Canadian artists, the Toronto Dance Theatre collaborates with choreographers from throughout the United States and Europe.

☎416/872–4255 *tickets, 416/593–4822 tours* ⊕*www.roythomson. com* Ⓜ *St. Andrew.*

Sony Centre for the Performing Arts. Almost anything but the most lavish opera or musical can be accommodated in the cavernous 3,191-seat hall, such as recent performances by Janet Jackson, the Merchants of Bollywood, and the Mariinsky Ballet performing *Swan Lake.* When this theater opened in 1960 as the O'Keefe Centre, it showcased the world premiere of *Camelot,* starring Julie Andrews, Richard Burton, and Robert Goulet; a 2010 renovation restored original elements of the design and made technological improvements. The season is roughly October through May. ✉ *1 Front St. E, at Yonge St., Old Town, Toronto, Ontario, Canada* ☎ *855/872–7669 tickets, 416/368-6161* ⊕*www. sonycentre.ca* Ⓜ *Union, King.*

DANCE

Toronto's rich dance scene includes pretty *Giselle* interpretations and edgy, emotionally charged modern-dance performances.

The National Ballet of Canada. Canada's homegrown and internationally recognized classical-ballet company was founded in 1951 by Celia Franca, an English dancer from the Sadler's Wells tradition, and is supported by infusions of dancers trained at its own school. The season runs from November through June. *Sleeping Beauty, Swan Lake, Onegin,* and *The Nutcracker* are included in the company's repertory. Karen Kain, former National Ballet prima ballerina, became the Artistic Director back in 2005. ✉ *Four Seasons Centre for the Performing*

Arts, 145 Queen St. W, Queen West, Toronto, Ontario, Canada ☎ *416/345–9595, 866/345–9595 outside Toronto* ⊕ *www.national. ballet.ca* Ⓜ *Osgoode.*

Harbourfront Centre. This venue has two theaters for dance. The **Fleck Dance Theatre** was built specifically for modern dance in 1983. The proscenium stage hosts some of the best local and Canadian modern and contemporary companies, in addition to some international acts. The **Enwave Theatre** welcomes these same types of dance performances as well as plays and concerts. It has excellent acoustics. Both theaters are small (446 and 422 seats, respectively) so you're never far from the stage. ✉ *Harbourfront Centre, 207 Queen's Quay W, at Lower Simcoe St., Harbourfront, Toronto, Ontario, Canada* ☎ *416/973–4000* ⊕ *www.harbourfrontcentre.com* Ⓜ *Union.*

DISTILLERY DISTRICT

Distillery District. Today the brick buildings and cobblestone walkways of the Distillery District are a popular backdrop for movies, and the pedestrian-only area is a nerve center for arts in the city, with dance and theater companies, galleries, restaurants, shops, and festivals. The Gooderham and Worts Distillery was founded in Toronto in 1832 and closed in 1990; the buildings are a National Historic Site. ✉ *55 Mill St., south of Front St. and east of Cherry St., Old Town, Toronto, Ontario, Canada* ⊕ *www. thedistillerydistrict.com.*

★ **Toronto Dance Theatre.** The oldest contemporary dance company in the city, TDT has created more than 100 original works since its beginnings in the 1960s, over a third of which use original scores by Canadian composers. Two or three pieces are performed each year in its home theater in Cabbagetown, and one major production is performed at the Harbourfront Centre's Fleck Dance Theatre. The company tours internationally. ✉ *80 Winchester St., 1 block east of Parliament St., Greater Toronto, Toronto, Ontario, Canada* ☎ *416/967–1365* ⊕ *www. tdt.org* Ⓜ *Castle Frank.*

FILM

Toronto has a devoted film audience. The result is a feast of riches—commercial first- and second-run showings, independent films and documentaries, cult classics, myriad festivals, and lecture series for every taste. For movie times, contact the theaters directly, or check Cinema-Clock (⊕ *www.cinemaclock.com*) or newsweeklies *NOW* (⊕ *www. nowtoronto.com*) and *The Grid* (⊕ *www.thegridto.com*), online or free on newsstands. Advance tickets are sold through the larger theaters' Web sites.

FIRST-RUN AND MAINSTREAM MOVIES

Polson Pier Drive-in Theatre. For an old-fashioned treat, park your car at this downtown drive-in that locals still refer to by its former name, the Docks. Open May to September (except for major electrical storms), it shows first-run double features on Friday, Saturday, and Sunday evenings. The gates open at 8:30pm, and films start at sundown, usually around 9:30. Purchase tickets on-site (C$15 adults);

on Sunday, admission is C$25 per carload. Cash only. ⊠ *176 Cherry St., just east of Parliament St., Harbourfront, Toronto, Ontario, Canada* ☎ *416/465–4653* ⊕ *www. polsonpier.com.*

Scotiabank Theatre. In the heart of the Entertainment District, this megaplex with 14 screens, including an IMAX theater, shows all the latest blockbusters and is the place to see films with impressive special effects. Tickets are C$13; a few dollars more for 3-D and IMAX movies. ⊠ *259 Richmond St. W, at John St., Entertainment District, Toronto, Ontario, Canada* ☎ *416/368–5600* ⊕ *www.cineplex.com* Ⓜ *Osgoode.*

The Varsity and Varsity VIP. The 12 screens here show new releases. The smaller, licensed VIP screening rooms (ages 19 and up, C$18.75) have seat-side waitstaff ready to take your concession-stand orders. Tickets start at C$12.75. ⊠ *Manulife Centre, 3rd fl., 55 Bloor St. W, at Bay St., Yorkville, Toronto, Ontario, Canada* ☎ *416/961–6303* ⊕ *www. cineplex.com* Ⓜ *Bay or Bloor.*

INDEPENDENT, FOREIGN, AND REVIVAL FILMS

Bloor Cinema. Classic, cult, independent, and second-run movies have been the Bloor's bread and butter but new owners intend to expand on documentary offerings (it hosts a monthly Doc Soup series and is the home of the annual Hot Docs film festival). Tickets are C$9, and the first ticket includes a six-month membership that reduces the price of subsequent shows to C$5. Festival screenings and some special presentations are pricier. At this writing, it's closed for a much-needed renovation. Call ahead to confirm that it's reopened. ⊠ *506 Bloor St. W, at Bathurst St., The Annex, Toronto, Ontario, Canada* ☎ *416/516–2330* ⊕ *www.bloorcinema.com* Ⓜ *Bathurst.*

Cumberland 4. An excellent selection of international and nonmainstream new films is shown at this beloved four-screen cinema. Admission is C$11.99. ⊠ *159 Cumberland St., just east of Avenue Rd., Yorkville, Toronto, Ontario, Canada* ☎ *416/964–9359* Ⓜ *Bay.*

Harbourfront Centre. In July and August, free movies are screened outdoors as part of the Free Flicks program. Documentaries, frequently accompanying summer festivals, cultural events, and retrospectives, are presented ad hoc throughout the year. ⊠ *235 Queen's Quay W, at Lower Simcoe St., Harbourfront, Toronto, Ontario, Canada* ☎ *416/973–4000* ⊕ *www.harbourfrontcentre.com* Ⓜ *Union.*

The Revue. This beloved neighborhood movie house is operated by the nonprofit Revue Film Society. Onscreen are documentaries, classics (cult and non-), foreign films, some first-run movies, silent films, and the occasional oddity like *Giant Killer Shark: The Musical.* Admission is C$10, or buy a C$6 six-month membership for benefits that include discount C$7 tickets. ⊠ *400 Roncesvalles Ave., at Howard Park Ave.,*

Greater Toronto, Toronto, Ontario, Canada ☎ *416/531–9959* ⊕ *www. revuecinema.ca* Ⓜ *Dundas West.*

The Royal. This fully-restored 1939 single-screen theater shows indie documentaries, features, and art films on a state-of-the-art digital projector. ✉ *608 College St., at Clinton St., Little Italy, Toronto, Ontario, Canada* ☎ *416/466-4400* ⊕ *www.theroyal.to* Ⓜ *506 streetcar across College St.*

TIFF Bell Lightbox. Operated by the Toronto International Film Festival (TIFF) organization, this state-of-the-art five-screen, five-story complex, opened in 2010, shows classic and avant-garde films, director retrospectives, actor tributes, national cinema spotlights, exclusive limited runs, and new documentaries and artistic films. Tickets are about C$10–C$15. ✉ *350 King St., at John St., Entertainment District, Toronto, Ontario, Canada* ☎ *416/968–3456* ⊕ *www.tiff.net/tiffbelllightbox* Ⓜ *St. Andrew.*

THEATER

Toronto has the third-largest theater scene in the world, following London and New York. Here you can see Broadway shows as well as a range of smaller Canadian and international productions from reproduced "straight" plays to experimental performances.

For reviews, news, and schedules, check ⊕ *www.stage-door.com* (a wealth of information—this is where industry types browse), the *Globe and Mail* Arts section (⊕ *www.theglobeandmail.com/arts*), and the free newsweeklies.

COMMERCIAL THEATERS

For more large-theater venues see Major Venues.

Canon Theatre. This 1920 vaudeville theater is one of the most architecturally and acoustically exciting live theaters in Toronto. Today it hosts big-budget musicals, such as *Wicked* and *Billy Elliot,* and occasional short runs by dance troupes and other performances. The theater itself is one of the most beautiful in the world and was refurbished in 1989 in preparation for the Canadian debut of *The Phantom of the Opera,* Canada's longest-running stage musical, which closed in 1999. Designed by world-renowned theater architect Thomas Lamb, it has columns, a grand staircase, gold-leaf detailing, and crystal chandeliers. ✉ *244 Victoria St., 1 block south of Dundas St. E, Dundas Square Area, Toronto, Ontario, Canada* ☎ *416/364–4100 theater, 416/872–1212, 800/461–3333 tickets* ⊕ *www.mirvish.com* Ⓜ *Dundas, Queen.*

Princess of Wales. State-of-the-art facilities and wonderful murals by American artist Frank Stella grace this 2,000-seat theater, built by father-and-son producer team Ed and David Mirvish in the early 1990s to accommodate the technically demanding musical *Miss Saigon.* Big-budget musicals like *The Sound of Music* and plays such as *Twelve Angry Men* are showcased. In 2012, Princess of Wales will host the Tony winner for Best Drama, *War Horse.* ✉ *300 King St. W, at John St., Entertainment District, Toronto, Ontario, Canada* ☎ *416/351–9011* *theater, 416/872–1212, 800/461–3333 tickets* ⊕ *www.mirvish.com* Ⓜ *St. Andrew.*

Royal Alexandra. The most historic of the Mirvish theaters, the "Royal Alex" has been the place to be seen in Toronto since 1907. The 1,500 plush red seats, gold plasterwork, and baroque swirls and flourishes make theatergoing a refined experience. Programs are a mix of blockbuster musicals and dramatic productions, some touring before or after Broadway appearances. Second-balcony seats are firmer than those in the first balcony. *Rock of Ages,* a hit on Broadway in 2009, opened here in 2010. ✉ *260 King St. W, Entertainment District, Toronto, Ontario, Canada* ☎ *416/593–1840 theater, 416/872–3333, 800/461–3333 tickets* ⊕ *www.mirvish.com* Ⓜ *St. Andrew.*

Toronto Centre for the Arts. Large-scale musicals are performed in the 1,800-seat Main Stage at this arts center, making it one of the city's major theater venues. Past shows have included *Show Boat, My Fair Lady, Jersey Boys, and American Idiot.* The 200-seat Studio Theatre and 1,032-seat George Weston Recital Hall host smaller plays and classical- and world-music concerts. ✉ *5040 Yonge St., north of Sheppard Ave. E, Greater Toronto, Toronto, Ontario, Canada* ☎ *416/733–9388, 416/870–8000 tickets* ⊕ *www.tocentre.com* Ⓜ *North York Centre.*

SMALL THEATERS AND COMPANIES

Seasons at most of these smaller theaters are September or October through May or June, though some special performances might be scheduled in summer. Soulpepper is open year-round.

Buddies in Bad Times. Canada's largest LGBT theater company presents edgy plays and festivals, as well as specialty after-hours events (burlesque, stand-up). Many shows are pay what you can. ✉ *12 Alexander St., just east of Yonge St., Church–Wellesley, Toronto, Ontario, Canada* ☎ *416/975–8555* ⊕ *www.buddiesinbadtimes.com* Ⓜ *Wellesley.*

Canadian Stage. Canadian- and European-inspired plays that incorporate dance, photography, video, and other media are at the heart of this company's mission, but it is known also for its excellent Dream in High Park Shakespeare productions. ⇨ *See Summer Theater box.* Big, mainstream productions are in the **Bluma Appel Theatre** (✉ *27 Front St. E*) at the St. Lawrence Centre for the Arts, and edgier and new works are at the **Berkeley Street Theatre** (✉ *26 Berkeley St., at Front St. E*). ☎ *416/368–3110, 877/399–2651* ⊕ *www.canadianstage. com* ☼ *Mon.–Sat.*

Factory Theatre. This is the country's largest producer of exclusively Canadian plays. Many of the company's shows are world premieres that have gone on to tour Canada and win prestigious awards. ✉ *125 Bathurst St., at Adelaide St., Entertainment District, Toronto, Ontario, Canada* ☎ *416/504–9971* ⊕ *www.factorytheatre.ca* ☼ *Box office open daily, 1–7 pm* Ⓜ *511 Bathurst streetcar to Adelaide St., 501 Queen or 504 King streetcars to Bathurst St.*

Hart House Theatre. The main theater space of the U of T since 1919, Hart House mounts four emerging-artist and student productions per season (September through April). At least one musical and one Shakespeare

DID YOU KNOW?

After being shuttered for decades, the restored Elgin and Winter Garden Theatre Centre is now a dazzling venue for everything from major musical theater productions to Toronto International Film Festival premieres.

SUMMER THEATER

Summer is the off-season for non-commercial theaters, but—lucky for us—there's no rest for the weary thespians. To avoid getting stuck with a stinker, read reviews for individual festival plays in local newspapers.

Toronto Fringe Festival. More than 140 theater companies descend for the Toronto Fringe Festival, the city's largest theater festival, which takes place over 10 days in late June/early July. New and developing works by emerging (and some established) artists are the norm. Tickets are C$11 or less per show. The most popular shows are given extended runs in the Best of the Fringe Festival. ☎ *416/966–1062* ⊕ *www. fringetoronto.com.*

SummerWorks Theatre Festival. More than 40 plays, performances, concerts, and happenings deemed sufficiently forward-thinking and provocative are staged at the Factory Theatre, Theatre Passe Muraille, and other venues around town as part of the 11-day SummerWorks Theatre Festival in August. Tickets are C$10 per show. ☎ *416/628–8216* ⊕ *www. summerworks.ca.*

Dream in High Park. Every summer, one of Shakespeare's most popular plays is performed under the stars at Dream in High Park, in an outdoor amphitheater. Productions are usually knockouts and run from July to late August, weather permitting. Performances are pay what you can, with a suggested C$20 donation. Performances are Tuesday through Sunday at 8; the box office opens at 6 pm. Tickets are on a first-come, first-served basis. It gets cold in this leafy park, so bring layers and a blanket to sit on; picnicking is allowed. ⊠ *High Park, main entrance off Bloor St. W, at High Park Ave., Greater Toronto, Toronto, Ontario, Canada* ☎ *416/367–1652* ⊕ *www. canadianstage.com* 🎫 *Pay what you can; free for children under 14* Ⓜ *High Park.*

play are always part of the program. ⊠ *7 Hart House Circle, off Welles-ley St. university entrance, Queen's Park, Toronto, Ontario, Canada* ☎ *416/978–8849* ⊕ *www.harthousetheatre.ca* Ⓜ *Museum, St. George, Queen's Park.*

Ⓒ **Young People's Theatre.** Productions like *In This World,* a teen-oriented production that touches on race, feminism, and classism, and *Hana's Suitcase,* the story of a young girl orphaned in the Holocaust, do not condescend or compromise on dramatic integrity and are as entertaining for adults as for kids. ⊠ *165 Front St. E, between Jarvis and Sherbourne sts., Old Town, Toronto, Ontario, Canada* ☎ *416/862-2222* ⊕ *www. youngpeoplestheatre.ca* ☉ *Hrs vary; check Web site for details* Ⓜ *King.*

★ **Soulpepper Theatre Company.** Established in 1997 by 12 of Canada's leading theater actors and directors, this repertory theater company produces classic plays year-round, reimagining the works of Henrik Ibsen, Anton Chekhov, and Samuel Beckett. The company makes its home in the Young Centre for the Performing Arts in the Historic Distillery District. ⊠ *55 Mill St., Bldg. 49, Distillery District, Old Town, Toronto, Ontario, Canada* ☎ *416/866-8666* ⊕ *www.soulpepper.ca* ☉ *Perfor-*

mance hours vary; box office (located in Atrium) open Tues.–Sat. 1–8 Ⓜ *504 King streetcar to Parliament St.*

★ **Tarragon Theatre.** The natural habitat for indigenous Canadian theater is in this old warehouse and railroad district. The main stage is 205 seats and presents plays by new and established Canadian playwrights. Maverick companies often rent the smaller of the Tarragon's theaters (100 seats) for interesting experimental works. ✉ *30 Bridgman Ave., 1 block north of Dupont St., The Annex, Toronto, Ontario, Canada* ☎ *416/531–1827* ⊕ *www.tarragontheatre.com* Ⓜ *Dupont.*

Théâtre Français de Toronto. High-quality French-language drama—with English supertitles—is performed at this theater, whose French and French-Canadian repertoire ranges from classical to contemporary. A children's play and a teen show are part of the seven-play season. ✉ *Berkeley Street Theatre, 26 Berkeley St., 2nd fl., at Front St. E, Old Town, Toronto, Ontario, Canada* ☎ *416/534–6604, 800/819–4981* ⊕ *www.theatrefrancais.com* Ⓜ *King then 504 King streetcar eastbound to Ontario.*

Theatre Passe Muraille. Toronto's oldest alternative theater company, established in 1968, has long been the home of fine Canadian collaborative theater and has launched the careers of many Canadian actors and playwrights. ✉ *16 Ryerson Ave., near Queen and Bathurst sts., Queen West, Toronto, Ontario, Canada* ☎ *416/504–7529* ⊕ *www. passemuraille.on.ca* Ⓜ *Osgoode, 501 Queen streetcar to Bathurst.*

NIGHTLIFE

Downtown—in the Entertainment and Financial districts and Old Town—bars and pubs cater to theatergoers and weekday worker bees. They can be dead on weekends after dark, however—especially in the Entertainment District—until 11 pm rolls around and the big loft-style dance clubs get going. To hang with locals at their neighborhood joints, head to Little Italy or the Annex, where university students mix with residents of the surrounding Victorian-lined streets. Gay nightlife centers around Church and Wellesley streets northeast of the downtown core. Everyone under 40 ends up on Queen West at some point, patronizing the once-bohemian, now-established arty bars and cafés. Ladies who lunch meet for midday martinis in swanky Yorkville and later clink glasses at the tony lounges. Throughout the city are dedicated music venues, bars, and supper clubs that specialize in jazz, Latin, blues, rock, hip-hop, and everything in between.

In this section, we've covered the places that have cemented their place in the city's scene, but new hot spots are always emerging. Check local news outlets *(see "What's On Now" in the Planning section)* to get the latest.

NIGHTLIFE KNOW-HOW

BARS

Establishments in Toronto that serve alcohol must also serve some kind of food. This might account for the fact that many bars in the city are also restaurants. (If they have to build a kitchen anyway, they might as well put it to good use.) Getting just drinks is within your rights at any hour, but at these resto-bars you may be asked to sit at the bar rather than at a table before 10 or 11 pm. This is not to say that all bars serve proper meals: some get around the law with meager offerings like chips and microwavable cups of Mr. Noodles, or by striking a deal with a neighboring pizza joint.

Several bars are also music venues that either have a separate space (with cover only for that space) or charge a cover for the bar (maybe C$5–C$10) on performance nights.

It's not unusual for smaller bars to be cash-only.

DANCE CLUBS

The majority of Toronto's big dance clubs are in the Entertainment District, specifically along Richmond and Adelaide between University and Spadina. But you can find more intimate spaces on Ossington, Queen West, and in the Church and Wellesley area (the "Gay Village"). Always call ahead or check Web sites to get on the guest list to avoid a wait at the door. Doors at clubs usually open at 10 but don't get busy until after 11 or midnight. Cover charges of C$10–C$20 are standard. Most clubs are open until 2 or 3 am. Dress codes are usually in effect but aren't over the top; avoid sneakers, shorts, and casual jeans and you should be fine. Some of the classier lounges in the theater and business districts cater to suit- and stiletto-clad clientele.

The club scene can be fickle, with new venues opening and closing all the time. Our choices have been going strong for years, but for the flavor of the month, special events, and DJ bookings, check weekly papers.

MUSIC VENUES

Toronto is a regular stop for top musical performers from around the world. Most venues have covers that range from C$5 to C$10. Tickets are often available on **Ticketmaster** (⊕ www.ticketmaster.ca). Record shops **Rotate This!** (⊠ 801 Queen St. W ☎ 416/504–8447 ⊕ www.rotate. com) and **Soundscapes** (⊠ 572 College St. ☎ 416/537–1620 ⊕ www. soundscapesmusic.com) also sell tickets.

North by Northeast (NXNE). Each June, Toronto hosts North by Northeast, an annual five-day festival that brings more than 600 musicians to the indoor and outdoor venues around the city. It's affiliated with the similar South by Southwest festival in Austin, Texas. Tickets and passes are available on the Web site and go on sale as early as mid-April. (Significant early-bird discounts apply.) Note that even the all-shows wristband doesn't guarantee entry; unless you have a priority pass (C$200) you'll have to line up among the plebes for highly anticipated bands, sometimes hours in advance. ⊠ Toronto, Ontario, Canada ☎ 416/863–6963 ⊕ www.nxne.com.

CANADA'S NATIVE STARS

Few know that "America's sweet-heart" Mary Pickford hailed from Toronto. And many famous Hollywood or TV actors, Grammy-winning musicians, and other industry types who have made it big in the U.S. were born in Toronto or started out here.

Famous names in the music world who first made their mark in Toronto include Neil Young, Glenn Gould, Joni Mitchell, Robbie Robertson (of The Band), K'naan, Feist, and the bands Rush, the Cowboy Junkies, the Barenaked Ladies, the Tragically Hip, and Broken Social Scene.

Actors who called Toronto home before being "discovered" Stateside include Christopher Plummer, Rachel McAdams, Margot Kidder, Eric McCormack, Will Arnett, Sarah Polley, Catherine O'Hara, John Candy, Rick Moranis, Howie Mandel, Mike Myers, and Jim Carrey. Additionally, directors David Cronenberg, Sidney Olcott, and Norman Jewison are former or present Torontonians.

Toronto's major arena venues are the Air Canada Centre (home of the Maple Leafs and Raptors), the Rogers Centre (home of the Blue Jays; formerly the SkyDome), and the outdoor summer-only Molson Canadian Amphitheatre on the waterfront with city skyline views. *For large-venue shows see Major Venues in Performing Arts.*

GAY AND LESBIAN NIGHTLIFE

Much of Toronto's gay and lesbian nightlife is centered on Church and Wellesley streets. You can easily cruise up Church from Alexander to a couple of blocks north of Wellesley and pop into whichever bar is most happening that night.

There are plenty of LGBT-friendly places outside the Church Street strip. Queen Street West, for example, is sometimes called Queer West, due to the number of not-exclusively-gay-but-gay-friendly bars and restaurants like the Beaver, the Drake, the Gladstone, and Mitzi's Sister.

Publications catering to the gay community include *X-Tra* (⊕ *www. xtra.ca*), free at various venues and at paper boxes around town, and *Fab* (⊕ *www.fabmagazine.com*), a free monthly magazine distributed at shops and restaurants. Both have information on nightlife, issues, and events.

Nightlife listings are organized by neighborhood.

HARBOURFRONT, THE FINANCIAL DISTRICT AND OLD TOWN

The historic brick buildings of Toronto's oldest district mingle with office towers in this downtown neighborhood, popular for weeknight drinks with coworkers and midday power-broker lunches. Many of the city's hotels are concentrated here.

Since 2000, Steam Whistle has been producing a local-favorite pilsner in its downtown Toronto brewery.

HARBOURFRONT

In general, this area is quiet after dark, but a nightlife scene is slowly emerging as more condos are erected and the waterfront is developed. Waterfront concerts take place here in summer, dinner cruises leave from the Harbourfront, and this is the location of Toronto's largest dance club: the Guvernment.

BARS, PUBS, AND LOUNGES

Real Sports Bar & Grill. No hole-in-the-wall sports bar, this sleek 25,000-square-foot space adjacent to the Air Canada Centre lights up with 199 high-definition flat-screen TVs, and amazing sightlines from every club-style booth, table, or stool at one of the two bars. Head to the second floor to watch a game on the 2.5-story-tall projection screen. For popular sporting events, or any day or night the Leafs or Raptors play, it's best to get a reservation (accepted up to three weeks in advance), though the bar does reserve a third of its seats for walk-in traffic an hour before face-off. ☒ *15 York St., at Bremner Blvd., Harbourfront, Toronto, Ontario, Canada* ☎ *416/815–7325* ⊕ *www.realsports.ca/bar* Ⓜ *Union.*

DANCE CLUBS

The Guvernment. If you want to get your grind on in a sea of revelers, this is the place. Each of the eight lounges and dance clubs in this mega-complex has its own themed decor and DJ. In the main club pulsing lasers and thumping electronic beats permeate the 22,000 square feet of dance space. The chic rooftop Skybar has one of the city's best skyline views. The complex is generally open Friday and Saturday nights, but access might be limited by ticketed concerts or events. All of the spaces

CLOSE UP

Beer: The National Drink

The brewing industry has been part of Ontario's heritage since 1840, when Thomas Carling opened his Brewing & Malting Company to supply the British army and the early pioneers. By the 1870s brewing had become a modern industry and maltsters were important businessmen. From the mid-1800s to mid-1900s, there were more than 300 breweries across the province. Prohibition and the Temperance League in 1916 closed most of the small, family-run operations, but even when Prohibition was repealed, the era of the small brewery was over. Restrictive distribution laws, the Depression, and organized, big breweries that delivered good, well-advertised product soon led to consolidation.

BREWERIES
The past few decades have seen a resurgence of small, craft breweries. Two breweries in Toronto give tours.

Mill Street Brewery, in the Distillery District, makes Ontario's only certified organic lager and a seasonal Helles Bock. It is open for sampling daily, with free tours weekdays at 3 pm and weekends at 3 and 5. A brewpub is on-site. ✉ *55 Mill St., Old Town, Toronto, Ontario, Canada* ☎ *416/681–0338* ⊕ *www.millstreetbrewery.com.*

The Steam Whistle Brewery brews an authentically crafted pilsner and offers tours (C$10) of its historic premises Monday–Thursday 1–5, Friday and Saturday noon–5, and Sunday noon–4. It has tastings and hosts other special events. ✉ *The Roundhouse, 255 Bremner Blvd., Old Town, Toronto, Ontario, Canada* ☎ *416/362–2337* ⊕ *www.steamwhistle.ca* Ⓜ *Union.*

BREWPUBS
Classy **Bar Volo** (see full review) is a relaxed place for a beer on busy Yonge Street.

Beer Bistro (see full review) has a long beer list and also a brew-inspired menu.

Bier Markt (see full review) has an awe-inspiring keg room and a loyal after-five clientele.

C'est What? has a wide selection of exclusively Canadian craft brews. ✉ *67 Front St. E, at Church, Old Town, Toronto, Ontario, Canada* ☎ *416/867–9499* ⊕ *www.cestwhat.com* Ⓜ *King.*

Smokeless Joe, a tiny bar half below street level, has one of the best beer selections in Canada, averaging 200 choices, and a sidewalk patio open in nice weather. ✉ *125 John St., Entertainment District, Toronto, Ontario, Canada* ☎ *416/728–4503.*

5

are usually accessible for one cover (C$10–C$25) on Saturday. Take a taxi to this one—it's a desolate after-hours walk. ✉ *132 Queen's Quay E, at Jarvis, Harbourfront, Toronto, Ontario, Canada* ☎ *416/869–0045* ⊕ *www.theguvernment.com* Ⓜ *Union.*

THE FINANCIAL DISTRICT
After happy hour, this business- and high-rise-dense part of town quiets down. Bars and restaurants here are tony affairs, equally suited to schmoozing clients and blowing off steam after a long day at the office.

BARS, PUBS, AND LOUNGES

Beer Bistro. A classy downtown resto-bar, this spot has more than 100 beers from around the world, including Belgian lambics, produced through an age-old, natural fermentation process. Look for beer in the food as well: in sauces, glazes, bread, pizza dough, and even ice cream. ⊠ *18 King St. E., at Yonge St., Financial District, Toronto, Ontario, Canada* ☎ *416/861–9872* ⊕ *www.beerbistro.com.*

> ### A PRE- OR POST-SHOW TIPPLE
>
> The strip of lounges and restaurants on Wellington Street East, just west of Church Street (of which Pravda is one), are all ideal stop-ins before or after theater, symphony, or opera performances downtown. They have an air of sophistication, and as you're already dressed for the occasion, why not?

Fodor's Choice
★

Canoe. Though it's primarily a restaurant, Canoe, on the 54th floor of the Toronto-Dominion Bank tower, is worth a trip just for a drink at the bar and a panoramic view of the lake. It has what might be the city's best Niagara wine selection and an extensive list of international bottles, as well as cocktails and beer. It's popular with finance types from the neighboring towers, who suit the swank surroundings. Go just before sunset to make the most of the view. ⊠ *66 Wellington St. W, between York and Bay sts., Financial District, Toronto, Ontario, Canada* ☎ *416/364–0054* ⊕ *www.oliverbonacini.com* ⊗ *Mon.–Fri. 11:45 am–10:30 pm* ⊗ *Closed Sat. and Sun.* Ⓜ *King, Union.*

OLD TOWN

On weeknights, an after-work crowd frequents the easygoing bars and restaurants in Toronto's historic district. Weekends see a fair number of suburbanites living it up.

BARS, PUBS, AND LOUNGES

Bier Markt. With more than 100 beers from 24 countries, including 40 on tap, this enormous restaurant/bar has a corner on the international beer market, but the best thing about it is the oversized sidewalk patio on the Esplanade, ideal for an afternoon brew. The lines are ridiculous on weekends—do as the locals do and go midweek instead. ⊠ *58 The Esplanade, just west of Church St., Old Town, Toronto, Ontario, Canada* ☎ *416/862–7575* ⊕ *www.thebiermarkt.com* Ⓜ *Union, King.*

★ **C'est What?** This casual, subterranean pub is known for its beer selection; on tap alone are six house beers and 35 Canadian microbrews. It's an especially good choice in winter, when you can cozy up next to the fireplace and order a quintessentially Canadian *poutine* (fries over cheese curds with gravy) or other pub grub. An eclectic mix of local bands—indie, pop, and jazz—plays later in the evening. ⊠ *67 Front St. E, at Church St., Old Town, Toronto, Ontario, Canada* ☎ *416/867–9499* ⊕ *www.cestwhat.com* Ⓜ *King.*

Foundation Room. Descend into this half-below-street-level Middle Eastern–inspired, incense-infused lounge with mirrored and exposed-brick walls, Moroccan lanterns, and banquettes with red-velvet pillows. Enjoy quality mixed drinks, wine, or a pomegranate martini to a soundtrack of mellow house, tribal, R&B, and world music. If you're

The Drake Hotel's Corner Café draws tourists and local hipsters with its bistro menu, home-baked treats, fresh juices, and full bar.

in the mood for a beer, move on—there's only a handful of bottles and no draft. ⊠ *19 Church St., at Front St. E, Old Town, Toronto, Ontario, Canada* ☎ *416/364–8368* ⊕ *www.foundationroom.ca* Ⓜ *King, Union.*

★ **Mill Street Brew Pub.** There may not be a better place in the city for a brewery and pub than in the brick-laned pedestrian-only Distillery District. Sixteen house-brewed beers are on tap, and five are also sold bottled at the on-site store and in Toronto-area shops: an organic lager, coffee porter (smells like coffee, tastes like porter), Tankhouse pale ale, Belgian Wit (wheat), and blonde Stock Ale. The pub serves dressed-up pub fare: beer-braised ribs, lobster grilled cheese, Kobe beef sliders, and beer-steamed mussels. Alfresco tables are prime real estate in warm weather. ⊠ *55 Mill St., at Trinity Street, Distillery District, Toronto, Ontario, Canada* ☎ *416/681–0338* ⊕ *www.millstreetbrewpub.ca* Ⓜ *504 King streetcar to Parliament St.*

Pravda Vodka Bar. A deliberately faded elegance, like a Communist-era club gone rough around the edges, permeates Pravda. Huge paintings of Mao Tse-tung adorn the brick walls, and crystal chandeliers run the length of the two-story room with exposed ductwork. Weekday happy-hour specials draw after-work clientele to lounge on well-worn leather sofas, around low wooden tables, or in a red-velvet-curtained VIP bottle-service area upstairs. Some 75 to 100 vodkas from around the globe are always on the menu, as are vodka flights, martinis, Czech and Russian beers, and caviar, smoked fish, and pierogi. ⊠ *44 Wellington St. E, between Church and Yonge sts., Old Town, Toronto, Ontario, Canada* ☎ *416/863–5244* ⊕ *www.pravdavodkabar.com* Ⓜ *King.*

DANCE CLUBS

The Courthouse. With its lofty ceilings, leather couches, professional go-go dancers working the poles, and oversize fireplaces, this second-floor club—open to the public only on Saturday—is like a 1940s Hollywood mansion on acid. The cocktail crowd is upscale, with many a guy in a tie (though a button-up will do) and ladies in heels and dresses. Stairs lead up to the second-story dance floor and to a mezzanine lounge that overlooks the scene. It has its off nights. ✉ *57 Adelaide St. E, at Church St., Old Town, Toronto, Ontario, Canada* ☎ *416/214–9379* ⊕ *www.libertygroup.com* Ⓜ *King.*

> ### TORONTO ARTS ILLUMINATED
>
> For 10 days in June, **Luminato** packs in 100 or more events spanning the arts from plays to tango lessons, from puppetry to poetry, and from art installations to funk bands. The festival attracts some big names such as Joni Mitchell, the Mark Morris Dance Group, and the Kronos Quartet. ☎ *416/368–3100* ⊕ *www.luminato.com.*

THE ENTERTAINMENT DISTRICT

Traditionally this was Toronto's center for dance clubs cranking out house music. A few of the more popular clubs are still going strong (especially along Richmond), but this area is transitioning as condos are erected and professionals in their 30s and 40s move in. It's also home to three of the big Broadway-style theaters and tourist-oriented pre-show restaurants with bars.

BARS, PUBS, AND LOUNGES

C Lounge. The spa theme of this ultrachic lounge hits you in the form of fruity aromatherapy the moment you walk through the door. Dance music blasts in the bar area inside, but the best part is the back patio, where soft ambient music allows quiet conversation around the shallow-water pool surrounded by beach chairs, coconut palms, and lantern-lit cabanas with couches. It's open Friday, Saturday, and Monday nights. ✉ *456 Wellington St. W, just west of Spadina, Entertainment District, Toronto, Ontario, Canada* ☎ *416/260–9393* ⊕ *www.libertygroup.com* Ⓜ *504 King or 510 Spadina streetcar.*

Wayne Gretzky's Toronto. The pregame Jays and Leafs fans and the post-comedy-club crowd from Second City next door flock to this sports bar and Continental restaurant. When he's in town, the eponymous hockey icon and owner can often be seen in the crowd. The sports bar downstairs has Gretzky memorabilia, 18 flat-screen TVs (broadcasting all sports, not just hockey) and pub-style grub. On the cabana-chic rooftop patio (open from 11 am May through September), considered one of the best in town, a faux waterfall babbles, strings of white lights twinkle, and partygoers order barbecue and buckets of mini Coronas and make themselves heard over the blasting music. ✉ *99 Blue Jays Way, at Mercer St., Entertainment District, Toronto, Ontario, Canada* ☎ *416/979–7825* ⊕ *www.gretzkys.com* ☉ *Mon.–Wed. 11:30 am–1 am, Thurs.–Sat. 11:30 am–2am, Sun. 11:30 am–midnight* Ⓜ *St. Andrew.*

COMEDY CLUBS

Fodor'sChoice **The Second City.** Since it opened in 1973, Toronto's Second City—the
★ younger sibling of the Second City in Chicago—has been providing
some of the best comedy in Canada. Regular features are sketch comedy, improv, and revues. Seating is cabaret-style with table service and
is assigned on a first-come, first-served basis. Doors open at 7:30. Weekend shows tend to sell out. Tickets are C$12–C$29. ⊠ *51 Mercer St., 1
block south of King, Entertainment District, Toronto, Ontario, Canada*
☎ *416/343–0011* ⊕ *www.secondcity.com* Ⓜ *St. Andrew.*

Yuk Yuk's. Part of a Canadian comedy franchise, this venue headlines
stand-up comedians on the rise (Jim Carrey and Russell Peters performed here on their way up), with covers usually between C$12 and
C$25. Admission is C$4 on Tuesday, for amateur night. The small space
is often packed; getting cozy with your neighbors and sitting within
spitting distance of the comedians is part of the appeal. Booking a
dinner-and-show package guarantees better seats. ⊠ *224 Richmond St.
W, 1½ blocks west of University Ave., Entertainment District, Toronto,
Ontario, Canada* ☎ *416/967–6425* ⊕ *www.yukyuks.com* Ⓜ *Osgoode.*

DANCE CLUBS

The Fifth Social Club. This is what you get when you cross a New York–
style warehouse loft with a club playing Top 40, rock, R&B, Latin, and
retro tunes. Professionals (ages 25 to 45), some dressed to the nines in
Armani suits and Versace dresses (though "dressy" jeans are permitted),
provide the scenery. Couches tucked into corners create cozy conversation areas with bottle service, but it's spendy and you'll have to reserve
a week or more in advance for these. The lack of a patio makes this
a better cool- and cold-weather venue. It's open Friday and Saturday
(C$15 cover). Email ahead to ✑ RSVP@thefifth.com to reserve a spot
on the guest list and bypass lines. ⊠ *225 Richmond St. W, 2 blocks west
of University Ave., Entertainment District, Toronto, Ontario, Canada*
☎ *416/979–3000* ⊕ *www.thefifth.com* Ⓜ *Osgoode.*

CHINATOWN

Aside from some long-established music clubs, Chinatown isn't a hot
spot for late-night revelry. But its central location makes it ideal for a
post-pub-crawl bite.

MUSIC

FOLK AND **Grossman's Tavern.** The old and raunchy vibe at Grossman's makes it
BLUES ideal for the blues. There are R&B bands nightly and Dixieland jazz
on Saturday afternoon. ⊠ *379 Spadina Ave., 1 block south of College
St., Chinatown, Toronto, Ontario, Canada* ☎ *416/977–7000* ⊕ *www.
grossmanstavern.com* Ⓜ *505 Spadina or 506 College streetcar.*

The Silver Dollar Room. Some of the top blues acts around play here, as
well as rock bands. The bar is dark and the viewing area narrow, but
the blues-loving clientele is friendly, and you may strike up a conversation with the musicians between sets. ⊠ *486 Spadina Ave., at College
St., Chinatown, Toronto, Ontario, Canada* ☎ *416/763–9139* ⊕ *www.
silverdollarroom.com* Ⓜ *505 Spadina or 506 College streetcar.*

QUEEN WEST

To an outsider, Queen West, with its mix of young owner-operated clothing boutiques, decades-old appliance and antiques stores, dive bars, and hipper-than-thou establishments, might seem to be a neighborhood undergoing a metamorphosis. But it has arrived: firmly grounded in bohemian chic. Ossington Street is the up-and-comer, an offshoot of Queen Street with a similarly arty vibe.

BARS, PUBS, AND LOUNGES

★ **Czehoski.** Creative types who've graduated beyond exclusively working-class beers move on to more sophisticated—but still irreverent—pastures like Czehoski. One of Queen West's coolest restaurant/bars was shaped from a former Czech-Polish butcher shop, and the deli counter inside is now the first-floor bar. On three levels, Czehoski is a carefully orchestrated mix of polished brass, splintery wood, and tongue-in-cheek "objets d'art" like rows of Jameson bottles. It's a full-scale restaurant, but mid-afternoon and late nights are popular with the drinks-only crowd. The tucked-away second-story patio of wooden benches and umbrellas is charming but gets crowded. Drinks and food cater to discerning and adventurous palates. ✉ *678 Queen St. W, at Euclid, Queen West, Toronto, Ontario, Canada* ☎ *416/366–6787* ⊕ *www.czehoski. com* Ⓜ *510 Queen streetcar to Bathurst St.*

★ **The Drake.** A hotel, restaurant, art gallery, café, and music venue all in one, the Drake is high-style hip that appeals to ages 20 to 50, depending on the entertainment. The Underground, downstairs, fills with a younger crowd for indie bands. The sound system is great, and the stark walls are usually decorated with art or projections. Live jazz is performed in the main-floor Drake Lounge, where scenesters sip cocktails and order snacks or dinner. Escape to the rooftop Sky Yard, with potted plants and heat lamps, year-round. ✉ *1150 Queen St. W, 2 blocks east of Gladstone Ave., West Queen West, Toronto, Ontario, Canada* ☎ *416/531–5042* ⊕ *www.thedrakehotel.ca* Ⓜ *501 Queen streetcar.*

Gladstone Hotel. In a restored Victorian hotel, the Gladstone draws a young, stylish crowd that appreciates karaoke (Friday through Saturday), queer night on Wednesday, and frequent indie, jazz, or bluegrass bands, spoken word, and art shows. It has a more everyman vibe than the Drake, its competitor two blocks to the east. The ballroom café is the main space, with tall ceilings, exposed brick walls, and a long dark-wood bar—dinner is served until 10, and a latenight menu from 10 to midnight. The Melody Bar hosts karaoke and bands. The tiny Art Bar has exhibitions, performances, and private events. There are also galleries on the 2nd, 3rd, and 4th floors. ✉ *1214 Queen St. W, at Dufferin, Queen West, Toronto, Ontario, Canada* ☎ *416/531–4635* ⊕ *www.gladstonehotel.com* Ⓜ *501 Queen streetcar to Dufferin St.*

Reposado Bar. The Toronto bar buzz is officially centered on Ossington Avenue, where watering holes, shops, and galleries have sprung up like wildflowers over the past few years. One of the first (in 2007) and still going strong is this classy tequila bar. The dark wood, large windows, big back patio, and live jazz (most nights no cover) set the tone for a serious list of tequilas meant to be sipped, not slammed, and

JAZZ FESTIVALS

Late June and early July bring music lovers to Toronto for the **Toronto Jazz Festival**. The 2011 bill included Aretha Franklin, The Roots, Jessye Norman, and Bela Fleck. Performances are at various venues around town. Concerts are priced individually, but you can buy a three- or five-show pass for a 15% or 20% discount on Mainstage shows. ☎ *416/928–2033* ⊕ *www. torontojazz.com.*

Held in late July, the 10-day **The Beaches International Jazz Festival** in the east Toronto Beach neighborhood showcases jazz, Latin, R&B, funk, soul, and world-music performers like eclectic R&B-pop-reggae group Jay Douglas and the All Stars and "blusion" pianist-saxophonist Deanna Bogart at its Woodbine Park and Kew Gardens stages. Musicians and food vendors also line 2 km of Queen Street East, which is closed to traffic for the event. All performances are free. ☎ *416/698–2152* ⊕ *beachesjazz.com* Ⓜ *501 Queen streetcar to Woodbine.*

Mexican nibbles like tequila-cured salmon with crostini. ⊠ *136 Ossington Ave., between Queen and Dundas Sts., Queen West, Toronto, Ontario, Canada* ☎ *416/532–6474* ⊕ *www.reposadobar.com* ☉ *Sun.–Fri., 6 pm–2 am; Sat. 2 pm–2 am* Ⓜ *505 Dundas or 501 Queen streetcars, or Ossington Subway/Bus.*

Ultra. At this dark and sultry lounge you can relax on a low black-leather chaise with a fancy cocktail or opt for a dinner of global fusion fare. The low-lit black-on-red decor is fabulous, and the rooftop patio is one of the city's best. Light snacks (such as mini Kobe burgers) are served as well. It has an undefined "style" code; you should get by just fine with casual-chic, but suits and ties are common on weeknights. DJs spin Top 40, dance music, and mash-ups on Thursday, Friday, and Saturday (C$10–C$20 cover) to get people dancing. Bottle service is available. Enter through the big red doors on Queen Street. ⊠ *314 Queen St. W, just east of Spadina, Queen West, Toronto, Ontario, Canada* ☎ *416/263–0330* ⊕ *www.ultratoronto.com* ☉ *Closed Sun. and Mon.* Ⓜ *Osgoode; 501 Queen or 510 Spadina streetcars.*

COMEDY CLUBS

★ **The Rivoli.** Solid up-and-coming solo and sketch-comedy acts perform Sunday through Tuesday. The ratio of chuckles to groans is good. Some later-famous comedians (Mike Myers, Samantha Bee) have performed here. Entry is pay-what-you-can. ⊠ *332 Queen St. W, at Spadina Ave., Queen West, Toronto, Ontario, Canada* ☎ *416/596–1908* ⊕ *www. rivoli.ca* Ⓜ *Osgoode.*

MUSIC

JAZZ, LATIN, AND FUNK

★ **The Rex Hotel Jazz & Blues Bar.** Legendary on the Toronto jazz circuit since it opened in the 1980s, the Rex has two live shows every night plus afternoon shows on weekends. Shows range from free to C$10. The kitchen serves diner fare. ⊠ *194 Queen St. W, at St. Patrick St., Queen West, Toronto, Ontario, Canada* ☎ *416/598–2475* ⊕ *www.therex.ca* ☉ *Daily 8 am–2 am* Ⓜ *Osgoode.*

POP AND
ROCK

The Cameron House. A sign behind the bar here reads "This is paradise." If your idea of paradise is oversize papier-mâché ants on the walls and grungy velvet sofas, well, sure. An eclectic bill of alt-rock, country, jazz, and everything in between is showcased in the cramped back room of this bar. Crowds can be heavy on weekends; weeknights can be virtually dead, but it all depends on the band. ⊠ *408 Queen St. W, at Cameron St., Queen West, Toronto, Ontario, Canada* ☎ *416/703–0811* ⊕ *www. thecameron.com* Ⓜ *Osgoode; 501 Queen streetcar.*

★ **Horseshoe Tavern.** Since 1947, this club has evolved from a legendary country-music venue (Charlie Pride, Tex Ritter, Hank Williams, and Loretta Lynn) to a just-as-legendary club that welcomes an eclectic mix of new alternative rock, roots, blues, punk, and rockabilly bands six nights a week. This is the place to catch young bands on the rise. ⊠ *370 Queen St. W, at Spadina Ave., Queen West, Toronto, Ontario, Canada* ☎ *416/598–4753* ⊕ *www.horseshoetavern.com* Ⓜ *Osgoode.*

Mitzi's Sister. It's a bit of a dive, but you'd feel out of place ordering anything but one of the Ontario microbrews on tap, which makes Mitzi's the perfect venue for the alt-, prog-, and folk rock, punk, and country bands that play nearly every night. It's the sister restaurant of brunch fave Mitzi's Café, around the corner on Sorauren. ⊠ *1554 Queen St. W, between Sorauren and Fuller aves., Queen West, Toronto, Ontario, Canada* ☎ *416/532–2570* ⊕ *www.mitzis.ca* Ⓜ *504 Queen streetcar.*

The Rivoli. Along the Queen Street strip, the Rivoli has long been a major showcase for the more daring arts in Toronto. A back room functions as a performance space, with progressive and indie rock, improvisational comedy troupes, and more. Bands have a cover charge, usually C$5–C$10. Asian-influenced cuisine and good steak are served in the dining room. The walls are lined with work (all for sale) by up-and-coming local artists. There's also a bar, and upstairs, a pool hall. ⊠ *332 Queen St. W, at Spadina Ave., Queen West, Toronto, Ontario, Canada* ☎ *416/596–1908, 416/597–0794* ⊕ *www.rivoli.ca* ⊙ *11:30 am–2:45 am* Ⓜ *Osgoode.*

THE ANNEX

Along Bloor between Spadina and Bathurst, the Annex is an established neighborhood of leafy side streets with large Victorian houses that attracts university students and young professionals to its mix of true-blue pubs and well-loved lounges.

BARS, PUBS, AND LOUNGES

Madison Avenue Pub. On the edge of the U of T campus and often filled to the gills with college students from fall to spring, the boisterous "Maddy" takes up two Victorian houses, with six levels of food and drink. It typifies an English pub, with lots of brass, exposed brick, and dartboards. A piano bar, pool tables, and plasma-screen TVs are also part of the scene. The five patios (some heated) are lively in summer, when squeezing your way to one of the 12 bars can become blood sport. Next door is a 23-room boutique hotel called "The Madison Manor." ⊠ *14–18 Madison Ave., just north of Bloor St. W, The Annex, Toronto, Ontario, Canada* ☎ *416/927–1722* ⊕ *www.madisonavenuepub.com*

⊘ *Mon.–Sat. 11:30 am–2 am, Sun. 11:30 am–midnight.* Ⓜ *Spadina.*

Victory Cafe. In a brick Victorian on a side street, the Victory feels sufficiently removed from the bustle of Bloor. It's a neighborhood favorite for its straightforward pub food, microbrewed beers, cozy booth seating, and front patio in summer. The vibe is always low-key and local. ✉ *581 Markham St., 1 block south of Bloor St. W, The Annex, Toronto, Ontario, Canada* ☎ *416/516–5787* ⊕ *www.victorycafe.ca* ⊘ *Mon.–Fri. 3 pm–2 am, Sat.–Sun. 11 pm–2 am* Ⓜ *Bathurst.*

> **HOTEL BARS**
>
> Don't want to stray far from your home away from home at night? Opt for a hotel with nightlife in-house, like the hip bar-and-live-music combo at the Drake or the Gladstone, on Queen West, or the classy martini lounges at the Four Seasons (Avenue) or the Park Hyatt (the Roof Lounge), both in Yorkville.

MUSIC

JAZZ, LATIN, AND FUNK
Trane Studio. Always a worthwhile night out for jazz—occasionally with a Latin or Afro-Cuban bent—the intimate brick-walled Trane Studio features accomplished Canadian musicians as well as impressive upstarts. Caribbean-influenced snacks and dinners are served. ✉ *964 Bathurst St., 3 blocks north of Bloor St. W, The Annex, Toronto, Ontario, Canada* ☎ *416/913–8197* ⊕ *www.tranestudio.com* Ⓜ *Bathurst.*

POP AND ROCK
★ **Lee's Palace.** Some of the most exciting young bands in rock, indie, and punk are served up at this midsize club with a psychedelic graffiti facade on the edge of the University of Toronto campus. Grab a table or watch the show from the sunken viewing area. ✉ *529 Bloor St. W, 1½ blocks east of Bathurst St., The Annex, Toronto, Ontario, Canada* ☎ *416/532–1598* ⊕ *www.leespalace.com* Ⓜ *Bathurst.*

YORKVILLE

The trendy bars of Yorkville tend to draw a well-heeled clientele for excellent drinks, food, and views.

BARS, PUBS, AND LOUNGES

Avenue. This high-end lounge in the Four Seasons Toronto hotel is modern and subdued, with neutral colors, sofas around low glass-topped tables, and a 20-foot onyx bar. Drinks include custom-made martinis, such as the Absolutely Fabulous—strawberry-, mint-, and lavender-infused vodka with a berry cordial, strawberry puree, and fresh lime (C$18). The drinks and food—which is heavy on sushi—are pricey in this buzzy space, but what can you expect from one of the poshest hotels in the country? The attentive service can feel somewhat precious. ✉ *21 Avenue Rd., at Cumberland Rd., Yorkville, Toronto, Ontario, Canada* ☎ *416/928–7332* ⊕ *www.fourseasons.com/toronto/dining/avenue* ⊘ *Mon.–Sat. noon–1 am, Sunday open for brunch 10:30–2:30 and for evening service from 4:30–10 pm* Ⓜ *Bay.*

★ **Hemingways.** One of the few Toronto pubs that isn't overtaken by rowdy sports fans or students, Hemingways is a homey bastion in a sea of

Yorkville swank. The three-story complex, with indoor and outdoor spaces—front and back—is a mishmash of booths, tables, several bars, mirrors, artsy posters, and books. It has a full pub menu, and free appetizers are doled out most nights at around 6. About three-quarters of the over-30 professionals who frequent this place are regulars. ⊠ *142 Cumberland St., just east of Avenue Rd., Yorkville, Toronto, Ontario, Canada* ☎ *416/968–2828* ⊕ *www.hemingways.to* Ⓜ *Bay.*

180 Panorama. Black-leather furniture, glamorous chandeliers, floor-to-ceiling windows, and tented patios combine for a hip, comfortable night out. ■TIP➔ **The 51st-floor patio is the highest in Toronto and is a great perch for enjoying the nightscape.** The south-facing patio has a view of downtown, the CN Tower, and the lake. It is an ideal spot for celebrity sightings, and there is an excellent selection of cocktails, martinis, and tapas—and a decadent chocolate s'more fondue for two. A C$5 cover charge applies Friday and Saturday nights. ⊠ *Manulife Centre, 51st fl., 55 Bloor St. W, at Bay St., Yorkville, Toronto, Ontario, Canada* ☎ *416/967–0000* ⊕ *www.eatertainment.com* Ⓜ *Bay.*

Fodor's Choice
★
The Roof Lounge. Such Canadian literary luminaries as Margaret Atwood and Mordecai Richler have used the 18th-floor Roof Lounge as a setting in their writings. The tiny bar is chic and refined without stuffiness or pretension and has dark wood and leather accents. Martinis and cosmopolitans are the specialties, though the menu also includes a nice selection of single malts and tequilas, tapas, and light meals. In warm weather you can choose a Cuban cigar from the menu of seven south-of-the-border stogies ranging in price from C$8 to C$250 and smoke on the adjoining patio, which affords lovely views of the downtown skyline and lake. The bar is cozily petite and does not accept reservations, so arrive in the late afternoon on weekends to avoid a wait. ⊠ *Park Hyatt Hotel, top fl., 4 Avenue Rd., Yorkville, Toronto, Ontario, Canada* ☎ *416/925–1234* ⊕ *www.parktoronto.hyatt.com* Ⓜ *Bay or St. George.*

DANCE CLUBS

LATIN DANCE CLUBS
★
Babalúu Supperclub. This supper club in the upscale Yorkville area combines the luxury of a tony lounge with the sizzle of sexy Latin rhythms. ■TIP➔ **Free one-hour beginner salsa lessons are offered nightly at 9 or 9:30.** It's open Wednesday through Sunday and cover prices vary (C$7–C$14 after 9 pm); ladies get in free on Thursday. The Latin food ranges from good to *muy sabroso.* ⊠ *136 Yorkville Ave., lower level, just east*

TORONTO COMEDIANS

Since the Second City opened, Toronto has been a comedic hub. Gilda Radner, John Candy, Dan Aykroyd, Dave Thomas, Martin Short, Eugene Levy, Catherine O'Hara, and Rick Moranis all cut their teeth here or on SCTV, a TV offshoot of the theater and precursor to *Saturday Night Live.* Toronto native Lorne Michaels cast Aykroyd and Radner in the first season of *SNL.* Mike Myers, Dave Foley, Bruce McCulloch, and Mark McKinney started at the Bad Dog Theatre. Jim Carrey and Howie Mandel debuted at Yuk Yuk's, and Samantha Bee frequented the Rivoli before joining *The Daily Show.*

of Avenue Rd., Yorkville, Toronto, Ontario, Canada ☎ *416/515–0587* ⊕ *www.babaluu.com* Ⓜ *Bay.*

MUSIC

JAZZ, LATIN, AND FUNK

Pilot Tavern. On Saturday from 3:30 to 6:30, this low-key (circa 1944) Toronto mainstay fills to the gills for mainstream and Dixieland jazz with a side of pints and pub grub. The rest of the time, there's more elbow room. ✉ *22 Cumberland St., just west of Yonge St., Yorkville, Toronto, Ontario, Canada* ☎ *416/923–5716* ⊕ *www.thepilot.ca* Ⓜ *Bay.*

CHURCH–WELLESLEY

The "Gay Village," the "gayborhood," or just plain old "Church and Wellesley"—whatever you call it, this strip of bars, restaurants, shops, and clubs is a fun, always-hopping hangout for the LGBT crowd or anyone with an open mind.

GAY AND LESBIAN NIGHTLIFE

BARS, PUBS, AND LOUNGES

Pegasus on Church. A mixed crowd of all different ages (though 30-plus is the norm), styles, and genders comes to this no-attitude second-floor lounge to meet, shoot pool, and, above all, play the interactive Internet game NTN Trivia. Friday and Saturday are DJ-hosted video dance parties; on other nights the music is mixed by the bartender of the day, and each one has a loyal following. ✉ *489B Church St., just south of Wellesley, Church–Wellesley, Toronto, Ontario, Canada* ☎ *416/927–8832* ⊕ *www.pegasusonchurch.com* Ⓜ *Wellesley.*

★ **Woody's.** A predominantly upscale, professional male crowd (20s to 40s) frequents this cavernous pub. DJs mix every night. Check out weekly events like the Best Chest and Best Butt contests and the drag shows at 6 and 11 each Sunday. The exterior of Woody's was used on the television show *Queer as Folk.* ✉ *467 Church St., at Maitland St., Church–Wellesley, Toronto, Ontario, Canada* ☎ *416/972–0887* ⊕ *www.woodystoronto.com* Ⓜ *Wellesley.*

DANCE CLUBS

★ **Crews & Tangos.** Downstairs is Crews, a gay and lesbian bar with a stage for karaoke or drag shows (depending on the night), a dance floor in back with a DJ spinning house beats, and a sizable back patio. Tangos, upstairs, has a bar and a small dance floor that gets packed with 20- to 30-something guys and gals kicking it to old-school hip-hop and '80s beats. The male–female ratio is surprisingly balanced and the drag shows are lots of fun. Usually a C$5 cover on weekends. ✉ *508 Church St., Church–Wellesley, Toronto, Ontario, Canada* ☎ *416/972–1662* ⊕ *crewsandtangos.com.*

★ **Fly.** Some of the biggest and best DJs from around the world have spun records at the original "Babylon" from television's *Queer as Folk.* An impressive sound system, light show, and 10,000 square feet have won this queer-positive club several Best Dance Club in Toronto awards. The hot—and generally young—clientele doesn't hurt, either. It's one of the best dance spots in the city, gay club or not. Cover ranges from C$10 to C$20. ✉ *8 Gloucester St., just east of Yonge St., Church–Wellesley, Toronto, Ontario, Canada* ☎ *416/410–5426* ⊕ *www.flynightclub.com* Ⓜ *Wellesley.*

5

The North by Northeast music and film festival showcases up-and-coming independent bands and filmmakers from around the world.

Zipperz/Cellblock. This easygoing gay bar and club caters to a more mature crowd than many places in the "Gay Village." At the piano bar in front you can join in on classic tunes; the dance club in the back rocks with a DJ on weekends and drag shows some weekdays. It's open daily; no cover. ⊠ *72 Carlton St., at Church St., Church–Wellesley, Toronto, Ontario, Canada* ☎ *416/921–0066* ⊕ *www.zipperzcellblock. ca* Ⓜ *College.*

DUNDAS SQUARE AREA

With more neon lights than anywhere else in the city, and a big central square used for outdoor concerts and films, Yonge–Dundas Square is decidedly commercial. But remnants of its past remain in Victorian houses on side streets, and there are some worthwhile bars ideal for a drink before or after a show at Massey Hall and the Canon and Elgin theaters.

BARS, PUBS, AND LOUNGES

Bar Volo. Despite its location on a busy thoroughfare, classy Bar Volo has a relaxed, brick-walled, wood-beamed, old-world atmosphere. A side patio is ideal for people-watching. It has unusual draft beers, wines from around the globe, a dinner menu of pizza, pasta, sandwiches and cheeses, and lots of beer-related events. ⊠ *587 Yonge St., Dundas Square Area, Toronto, Ontario, Canada* ☎ *416/928–0008* ⊕ *www.barvolo.com* Ⓜ *Wellesley or Bloor.*

The Queen and Beaver Public House. Toronto's British heritage thrives at this classy bar with a full restaurant that opened in 2009. The black-and-white photos on the walls reveal its true passion: soccer. A Manchester United game is never missed, though NHL and other sporting events are also shown in the library-like "sports bar." On weekend mornings when an early game is on, they'll open—sometimes as early as 7 am. The wine list is admirable for a pub; the beer selection is surprisingly small and focused on Ontario microbrews. Dressed-up British staples—available in the bar or ground-floor dining room—range from Scotch eggs to a killer hand-chopped-beef burger. ⊠ *35 Elm St., between Yonge and Bay sts., Dundas Square Area, Toronto, Ontario, Canada* ☎ *647/347–2712* ⊕ *www.queenandbeaverpub.ca* ⊙ *Daily 11:30 am–11 pm.* Ⓜ *Dundas.*

GREATER TORONTO

Still within the downtown core but a bit farther from the major hotel centers are neighborhoods like the Danforth, Little Portugal (just west of Little Italy), Roncesvalles Village, and Leslieville (on Queen Street East) where you'll find friendly pubs, hipster hangouts, and a few excellent music venues.

DANCE CLUBS

LATIN DANCE CLUBS **Lula Lounge.** Latin-music lovers of all ages dress up to get down to live Afro-Cuban, Brazilian, and salsa music at this Little Portugal hot spot. Pop and rock musicians also perform occasionally. Dinner-and-a-show tickets are available on weekends and include a salsa lesson on Saturday. Lula is also an arts center, with dance and drumming lessons and a multitude of festivals and cultural events. No running shoes on weekends. ⊠ *1585 Dundas St. W, 1½ blocks west of Dufferin St., Greater Toronto, Toronto, Ontario, Canada* ☎ *416/588–0307* ⊕ *www.lula.ca* Ⓜ *505 Dundas streetcar.*

MUSIC

FOLK AND BLUES ★ **Hugh's Room.** The biggest names in folk, bluegrass, and blues love to play this venue because the audiences here love to listen. The supper-club-like venue has a full menu at cabaret-style tables, but it's the intimate performances that are the draw. Many shows sell out, so book early. The best tables are held for those who make dinner reservations. If you're not having dinner, arrive at least an hour early to snag a good spot at a bar table. ⊠ *2261 Dundas St. W, just south of Bloor St. W, Greater Toronto, Toronto, Ontario, Canada* ☎ *416/531–6604* ⊕ *www. hughsroom.com* ⊙ *On performance days, box office open noon–7 pm. Otherwise open Mon.–Sat. noon–5 pm. Matinees at 1 pm, evening performances at 8:30 pm, unless noted* Ⓜ *Dundas West.*

POP AND ROCK **Opera House.** This late-19th-century vaudeville theater retains some of its original charm, most notably in its proscenium arch over the stage. The 850-capacity venue hosts internationally touring acts of all genres. Past performers include Yo La Tengo, the Buzzcocks, and K-OS. ⊠ *735 Queen St. E, 1 block east of Broadview, Greater Toronto, Toronto, Ontario, Canada* ☎ *416/466–0313* ⊕ *www.theoperahousetoronto.com* Ⓜ *Broadview Ave. to 504 streetcar south.*

CABBAGETOWN
MUSIC
POP AND ROCK | **Phoenix Concert Theatre.** A wide variety of music—often of the indie-pop, -folk, or -rock ilk, but with forays into hip-hop, jazz, soul, and more—is presented at this popular concert venue with two stages, the Main Room and the more intimate Parlour. ✉ *410 Sherbourne St., between Wellesley and Carlton sts., Cabbagetown, Toronto, Ontario, Canada* ☎ *416/323–1251* ⊕ *www.phoenixconcerttheatre.com* ⊙ *hrs vary, open for concerts; private bookings also available* Ⓜ *Sherbourne; 506 Carlton streetcar.*

LESLIEVILLE
This area of Queen Street was up-and-coming for years, and is now a bonafide reason to cross the DVP (Don Valley Parkway), thanks to a flurry of small but excellent restaurants, artisanal food shops, niche design stores, and relaxed labor-of-love bars catering to a discerning and artistic local community.

BARS, PUBS, AND LOUNGES
Rasputin Vodka Bar. The Russian Empire is a streetcar ride away at this no-pretenses vodka bar whose mismatched barware, chandeliers, and well-worn Victorian sofas create the illusion that the entire place was smuggled out of the old country. More than 40 varieties of the clear stuff is on the menu, as are creative cocktails and Eastern European nosh (gravlax, cabbage rolls). DJs spin dance music on weekends. ✉ *780 Queen St. E, Leslieville, Toronto, Ontario, Canada* ☎ *416/469–3737* ⊕ *www.rasputinvodkabar.com* Ⓜ *Queen, then 501 streetcar east.*

Swirl. This itty-bitty, bespoke wine bar with flirty Parisian flair was carved out of a petite second-story one-bedroom apartment. The pretty decor is quirkily shabby-chic, with wooden farmhouse chairs set at reclaimed antique sewing tables. Everything is compact, including the well-chosen, reasonably priced wine list (glasses start at C$6; bottles are C$30–C$40 on average), the handful of interesting beers, and the food (pâté, pickled quail eggs, chocolate cake), most of it pre-made and served in pickling jars. ✉ *946½ Queen St. E(2nd fl.), near Carlaw Ave., Leslieville, Toronto, Ontario, Canada* ☎ *647/351–5453* ⊕ *www.swirltoronto.com* Ⓜ *Queen, then 501 streetcar east.*

LITTLE ITALY
College Street between Bathurst and Ossington isn't so much an old-school Italian neighborhood these days as it is a prime destination for bars and restaurants of all cuisines. Casual (but rarely rowdy) student-friendly pubs mix with candlelit martini bars. The party often spills out onto the streets on weekends.

BARS, PUBS, AND LOUNGES
Café Diplomatico. Holding court over a central Little Italy corner since 1968, Diplomatico is popular for one reason: its big sidewalk patio with umbrella-shaded tables, one of the best in the city for people-watching. The food and drink are ho-hum (apart from good Italian desserts), with garden-variety beers on tap and a few so-so wines. It's really all about the outdoor space, which is open from 8 am daily and has one of the

PATIO FEVER

Torontonians are patio-mad once warm weather hits. Can you blame them, after a long, often brutal winter where they wait outside for streetcars in the path of Arctic-fed winds? Patios open in April or May as weather permits or by Victoria Day (May 24) weekend at the latest. Here are some favorites:

Bier Markt (⊠ 58 The Esplanade): A downtown location near most of the city's office buildings, a low-key vibe, a big sidewalk patio, and a long beer list make this a sweet spot during happy hour.

Cabana (⊠ 11 Polson St.): A 41,000-square-foot rooftop restaurant/bar at Polson Pier on the shores of Lake Ontario. Opens at noon, which is just about the right time for a locally brewed Steam Whistle pilsner in the sun.

Café Diplomatico (⊠ 594 College St.): Perfect for soaking up *la bella vita* on Little Italy's main strip is Diplomatico's sidewalk patio, open from morning until last call.

The Drake (⊠ 11 S. Queen St. W): Even jaded hipsters who criticize the Drake's trendy-lounge-in-the-'hood persona can't resist this swish rooftop patio overlooking Queen Street with throw pillows and potted palms.

Wayne Gretzky's (⊠ 99 Blue Jays Way): The roof patio atop the NHL star's restaurant juxtaposes love seats, palm trees, and sparkling lights with a boisterous crowd decompressing after Blue Jays games or comedy shows at next door's Second City.

Also see full reviews.

few neighborhood kitchens serving after midnight. ⊠ *594 College St., at Clinton St., Little Italy, Toronto, Ontario, Canada* ☎ *416/534–4637* ⊕ *www.diplomatico.ca* Ⓜ *506 College streetcar.*

Kalendar. A slice of French bistro style in Little Italy, Kalendar is ideal for a romantic tête-à-tête or a small group of friends. It has a bit of everything: dinner, appetizers, dessert, coffee, and an eclectic menu of wine, beer, single-malt scotches, brandies, cognacs, cocktails, and aperitifs. It's dark and cozy inside, with candlelight, red walls, and gilt-framed mirrors. Café tables spill out onto a sidewalk patio, popular from noon till night. ⊠ *546 College St., at Euclid St., Little Italy, Toronto, Ontario, Canada* ☎ *416/923–4138* ⊕ *www.kalendar.com* Ⓜ *506 College streetcar.*

Souz Dal. The type of place where you'd expect to find a scholarly chap hunched over a book by Charles Baudelaire by candlelight, Souz Dal is sophisticated but low-key, with decor inspired by the onion-dome cupolas in the Russian city of Souzdal (Suzdal). The music is smooth (think bossa nova), and specialty drinks, such as the Caramilk (vanilla vodka, caramel liqueur, crème de cacao), are for those with a sweet tooth. It has a small back patio and specials every night, such as C$5 mojito Mondays. ⊠ *636 College St., at Grace St., Little Italy, Toronto, Ontario, Canada* ☎ *416/537–1883* ⊕ *www.souzdal.com* ⊙ *Daily 8 pm–3 am* Ⓜ *506 College streetcar.*

MUSIC

FOLK AND BLUES

Free Times Cafe. This casual restaurant specializes in Jewish, Middle Eastern, and Canadian food, with many vegetarian and organic options. There's live acoustic and folk music every night of the week on its back-room stage, plus a highly popular traditional Jewish brunch called "Bella! Did Ya Eat?" complete with live klezmer and Yiddish music every Sunday. ⊠ *320 College St., at Major St., Queen's Park, Toronto, Ontario, Canada* ☎ *416/967–1078* ⊕ *freetimescafe.com* ☉ *Daily 10 am–2 am* Ⓜ *Queen's Park.*

JAZZ, LATIN, AND FUNK

Orbit Room. At this icon on College Street you can drink by lava lamp at the bar or take a turn on the compact dance floor accompanied by jazz, jazzy rock, funk, roots reggae, and R&B. Alex Lifeson, guitarist for the rock band Rush, is a co-owner. ⊠ *580A College St., 2nd fl., Little Italy, Toronto, Ontario, Canada* ☎ *416/535–0613* ⊕ *www.orbitroom. ca* ☉ *Daily 9 pm–2 am* Ⓜ *506 College streetcar to Euclid.*

POP AND ROCK

Mod Club Theatre. Excellent indie shows occasionally appear in this sexy black-on-black midsize space with great sight lines and killer acoustics and lighting. Past shows have included RJD2 and Calexico, but upstart Canadian indie rockers are frequent guests. ⊠ *722 College St., at Crawford St., Little Italy, Toronto, Ontario, Canada* ☎ *416/588–4663* ⊕ *www.themodclub.com* Ⓜ *506 College streetcar.*

Shopping

WORD OF MOUTH

"Walk up to Queen St. for some quirky boutique shopping along with a bistro lunch . . . there are countless artists, jewelry booths, and fun shops."

—garyt22

Updated by
Shannon Kelly
and Nina
Callaway

Toronto prides itself on having some of the finest shopping in North America. Indeed, most of the world's name boutiques have branches here, especially in the Yorkville area, where you can find such luxury labels as Tiffany & Co., Gucci, and Cartier. For those a little leaner of wallet, you can join in one of Torontonians' favorite pastimes: bargain hunting. Locals wear discount threads like badges of honor and stretch their dollar at Winners—where overstocked and liquidated designer pieces and last-season fashions are slashed to a fraction of their original retail prices.

Toronto has a large arts-and-crafts community, with numerous art galleries, custom jewelers, clothing designers, and artisans. Sophisticated glass sculpture and Inuit art are ideal as gifts or for your own home. Music stores all over Toronto stock their shelves with international hits as well as homegrown talent like Feist, Broken Social Scene, Tokyo Police Club, K'naan, Shania Twain, and a host of lesser-known pop, rap, hip-hop, folk, opera, and country artists. Bookstores such as Indigo have lounge areas where you can sip a coffee from the in-store café while perusing books by Canadian authors such as Alice Munro, Ann-Marie MacDonald, and Rohinton Mistry.

When it comes to department stores, all roads lead to Holt Renfrew on Bloor Street West, the epicenter of Toronto's designer shopping. A mere block east is the more mid-price department store The Bay. A second Bay can be found across from Eaton Centre, a sprawling shopping complex with multilevel parking in the heart of the city.

THE
ANNEX
Student central:
cafés and
used-bookstores

YORKVILLE
Big fashions names,
upscale *everything*

CHINATOWN
AND
KENSINGTON
MARKET
Ethnic bargains
galore, crowded on
weekends

DUNDAS
SQUARE AREA
Mega-mall Eaton
Centre and busy
Yonge Street

QUEEN WEST
Vintage stores,
Canadian designer
boutiques, and bistros

FINANCIAL
DISTRICT
Underground
chain stores in
the PATH

OLD TOWN
Furnitures
stores,
art dealers

QUEEN'S
PARK

University
of
Toronto

Queen's
Park

Ontario
Legislative
Building

Queen's
Park

Grange
Park

City Hall

Nathan
Phillips
Square

Toronto
Coach
Terminal

St.
Patrick

CHURCH-
WELLESLEY

ENTERTAINMENT
DISTRICT

Spadina

St.
George

Bloor-Yonge

Museum

Wellesley

College

Dundas

Queen

Osgoode

Union

Cumberland St.
Hazelton Ave.
Bloor St. W.
Avenue Rd.
Charles St. E.
Madison Ave.
Spadina Ave.
Sussex Ave.
Spadina
Hoskin Ave.
Isabella St.
Gloucester St.
Dundonald St.
Wellesley St. E.
Brunswick Ave.
Huron St.
Sussex Mews
Spadina Ave.
Robert St.
Major St.
Willcocks St.
St. George St.
Queen's Park Cir. W.
Queen's Park Cir. E.
St. Joseph St.
Bay St.
Yonge St.
Charles St. E.
Wellesley St. W.
Grosvenor St.
Alexander St.
Carlton St.
College St.
College St.
Huron St.
Beverley St.
Henry St.
University Ave.
Elizabeth St.
Bay St.
Yonge St.
Church St.
Gerrard St. W.
Cecil St.
Baldwin St.
D'Arcy St.
McCaul St.
St. George St.
Dundas St. W.
Dundas St. W.
Gould St.
Dundas St. E.
Beverley St.
St. Patrick St.
Simcoe St.
Chestnut St.
Shuter St.
Sullivan St.
Soho St.
James St.
Mutual St.
Church St.
Renfrew Pl.
Pullan Pl.
Queen St. W.
Queen St. E.
Richmond St. E.
Peter St.
Duncan St.
John St.
Widmer St.
Nelson St.
York St.
University Ave.
Bay St.
Adelaide St. E.
Pearl St.
King St. W.
King St. E.
Mercer St.
Wellington St. W.
Wellington St. W.
Front St. W.
Front St. W.
The Esplanade
Spadina Ave.
York St.
Bay St.
Yonge St.
Brennner Blvd.
Gardiner Expy.
Lake Shore Blvd. E.

0   1/4 mile
0   400 meters

PLANNING

HOURS

Most shops open by 10 am Monday to Saturday and close at 6 or 7 pm Monday to Thursday, 8 or 9 pm Friday, and as early as 6 pm Saturday. On Sunday, most downtown shops open noon to 5 pm. There are, however, exceptions. Large chain stores downtown often stay open weeknights until 9 or 10 pm, and boutiques in areas that draw a younger, hipper crowd, such as in Queen West and the Annex, stay open later.

SALES

The biggest sale day of the year is Boxing Day, the first business day after Christmas, when nearly everything in the city is half price. In fact, clothing prices tend to drop even further as winter fades. Summer sales start in late June and continue through August.

SHIPPING

Nearly all stores that sell larger items like sculpture and furniture will ship to anywhere in the U.S. or Canada.

TAXES

A hefty rate of 13% Harmonized Sales Tax is levied on most goods and services.

TOP SHOPPING EXPERIENCES

Blast from the Past: Vintage buffs will bite off more than they can chew in Toronto. Kensington Market is overflowing with dusty old togs and funky retro fashions. For more upscale vintage wear, there are a number of boutiques in West Queen West and Ossington that restore stylish treasures such as 1940s black-beaded dresses and vintage Dior cocktail frocks. For something totally different, the clothing at Preloved boutique has been crafted into new designs from recycled throwaways.

Luxury Lanes: Toronto's answer to Chicago's Magnificent Mile runs along Bloor Street West, between Yonge Street and Avenue Road. Along this strip you'll find Hermès, Gucci, Louis Vuitton, Bulgari, and Canada's largest luxury department store, Holt Renfrew. For a low-key, but no less glamorous, shopping experience, duck into the streets to the north—Cumberland Street and Yorkville Avenue—to check out the smaller designer boutiques, high-end suit stores, and exclusive shoe shops.

Unique Local Designers: For a unique shopping experience in Toronto, head west—to West Queen West and Ossington—to browse shops stocked entirely by local designers. You'll find home accessories at Urban Mode, art at YYZ Artists' Outlet, and an ever-growing list of clothing boutiques including Comrags, Fashion Crimes, Girl Friday, and Virginia Johnson—just take a stroll down Queen Street West and up Ossington Avenue to make a day of it. Nella Cucina has kitchenware signed by local chefs. All the Best Fine Foods has edible goodies from Toronto bakeries, and the local designer at Lilliput Hats in Little Italy has your head covered.

Shopping listings are organized by neighborhood.

HARBOURFRONT, THE FINANCIAL DISTRICT, AND OLD TOWN

HARBOURFRONT

Shopping in the Harbourfront area is primarily limited to the tourist-oriented shops in Queen's Quay Terminal, where you can find some unique gifts, albeit at elevated prices.

DEPARTMENT STORES AND SHOPPING CENTERS

Queen's Quay Terminal. Incoming ships once unloaded their fishy cargo at the terminal, which now hosts a collection of unique boutiques, crafts stalls, food stores, and more. This is a great place to buy gifts, though you won't find any deals. It's an easy walk from Union Station in summer, and a quick streetcar ride in winter. Parking is expensive, but there are some free spots in the area. ⊠ *207 Queen's Quay W, at York St., Harbourfront, Toronto, Ontario, Canada* ☎ *416/203–0510 security desk/main number* ⊕ *www.qqterminal.com* ☉ *Daily 10–6* Ⓜ *Union.*

THE FINANCIAL DISTRICT

Toronto's Financial District has a vast underground maze of shopping warrens that burrow between and underneath its office towers. The tenants of this Underground City are mostly the usual assortment of chain stores, with an occasional surprise. Marked PATH, the walkways (the underground street system) make navigating the subterranean mall easy. The network runs roughly from the Fairmont Royal York hotel near Union Station north to the Atrium at Bay and Dundas.

CLOTHING

MEN'S CLOTHING **Moores the Suit People.** Browse through thousands of discounted Canadian-made dress pants, sport coats, and suits, including many famous labels. Sizes run from extra short to extra tall and from regular to oversize; the quality is solid and the service is good. ⊠ *100 Yonge St., at King St., Financial District, Toronto, Ontario, Canada* ☎ *416/363–5442* ⊕ *www.mooresclothing.com* ☉ *Weekdays 9–8, Sat. 9–6, Sun. 11–5* Ⓜ *King.*

Stagioni. This 2,500-square-foot store has great deals on Italian designer suits, which the proprietors buy in bulk from factories in Italy. ⊠ *20 Toronto St., at Adelaide St. E, Financial District, Toronto, Ontario, Canada* ☎ *416/365–7777* ⊕ *www.stagionimens.com* ☉ *Weekdays 10–6, Sat. 10–3* Ⓜ *King.*

OLD TOWN

If you were to devote a day to shopping, eating, and lounging, Old Town—home to both the Distillery District and St. Lawrence Market—is the place to do it. Antiques, specialty foods, art, furniture, housewares, sweets, books, and more are tucked into the many historic brick buildings.

ART AND CRAFTS GALLERIES

Corkin Gallery. With work by contemporary artists such as Iain Baxter& and David Urban, this gallery is one of the most fascinating in town. See hand-painted photos, documentary photos, fashion photography, and mixed-media art. ⊠ *55 Mill St., Bldg. 61, Old Town, Toronto, Ontario,*

THE ANNEX

London St.

Lowther Ave.

Albany Ave.

Howland Ave.

Madison Ave.

Spadina Ⓜ

Ⓜ St. George

Hazelton Ave.

Cumberland St.

Avenue Rd.

Bloor St. W.

Bloor St. W.

Ⓜ Museum

Lennox St.

Croft St.

Borden St.

Brunswick Ave.

Sussex Mews

Sussex Ave.

Huron St.

St. George St.

Herrick St.

Harbord St.

Robert St.

Spadina Ave.

Hoskin Ave.

QUEEN'S PARK

Queen's Park

Ulster St.

Euclid Ave.

Croft St.

Lippincott St.

Major St.

Willcocks St.

University of Toronto

King's

Queen's Park Cir. W.

Queen's Park Cir. E.

College Cir.

Russell St.

Ontario Legislative Building

College St.

Bellevue Ave.

Augusta Ave.

LITTLE ITALY

Palmerston Blvd.

Markham St.

Bathurst St.

Oxford St.

Nassau St.

Huron St.

Beverley St.

Henry St.

College St.

Queen's Park Ⓜ

University Ave.

Gerrard St. W.

KENSINGTON MARKET

Cecil St.

Baldwin St.

Elm St.

Wales Ave.

Kensington Ave.

CHINATOWN

D'Arcy St.

St. Patrick Ⓜ

See Queen West Map

Dundas St. W.

Chestnut St.

Alexandra Park

Denison St.

Augusta Ave.

Grange Park

Sullivan St.

Beverley St.

McCaul St.

St. Patrick St.

Simcoe St.

Carr St.

Tecumseth St.

Bathurst St.

Wolseley St.

QUEEN WEST

Butwer St.

Soho St.

Renfrew Pl.

Pullan Pl.

Ⓜ Osgoode

Queen St. W.

Richmond St. W.

Spadina Ave.

Peter St.

Duncan St.

University Ave.

Nelson St.

Adelaide St. W.

Widmer St.

John St.

ENTERTAINMENT DISTRICT

Pearl St.

King St. W.

York St.

Downtown Toronto Shopping

Mercer St.

Wellington St. W.

❶ ❷ ❸ ❹ ❺ ❻ ❼ ❽ ❾ ❿ ⓫ ⓬ ⓭ ⓮ ⓯ ㉔

6

KEY

Ⓜ Subway Stops

Canada ☎ *416/304–1050* ⊕ *www.corkingallery.com* ⊙ *Tues.–Sat. 10–6, Sun. noon–5* Ⓜ *King, then streetcar 504 east.*

Fodor'sChoice
★

Sandra Ainsley Gallery. The glass-sculpture gallery within the historic Gooderham and Worts complex on Mill Street has large and small pieces. Rotating displays have included works by artists such as Jon Kuhn and Martin Blank. ✉ *Distillery District, 55 Mill St., Bldg. 32, Old Town, Toronto, Ontario, Canada* ☎ *416/214–9490* ⊕ *www.sandraainsleygallery.com* ⊙ *Tues.–Sat. 10–6, Sun. noon–5; hrs may vary by exhibition* Ⓜ *King 504 streetcar.*

BOOKS

★ **Nicholas Hoare.** This lovely bookstore is beloved by writers and readers alike and specializes in British authors, history, biography, and fiction. It occasionally has author appearances and book signings. ✉ *45 Front St. E, at Church St., Old Town, Toronto, Ontario, Canada* ☎ *416/777–2665* ⊕ *www.nicholashoare.com* ⊙ *Mon.–Sat. 10–6, Sun. noon–6* Ⓜ *King.*

CLOTHING

MEN'S AND
WOMEN'S
CLOTHING

Lileo. Part emporium, part gallery, this is the place to go for men's and women's forward-looking fashion and lifestyle accessories—many of which are exclusive or were created in limited edition for the store. ■TIP→ **Stop by the juice bar/restaurant Livia to keep your energy up while you shop.** ✉ *55 Mill St., Bldg. 35, Distillery District, Toronto, Ontario, Canada* ☎ *416/413–1410* ⊕ *www.lileo.ca* ⊙ *Mon.–Sat. 10–7, Sun. 10–6* Ⓜ *King, then streetcar 508 east.*

DEPARTMENT STORES AND SHOPPING CENTERS

Fodor'sChoice
★
SHOPPING
VILLAGE

Distillery District. Some of the city's most interesting boutiques, art studios, performance spaces, and restaurants populate the restored Victorian brick buildings of this cobblestone-laned heritage village. On a sunny day there's no better destination for rummaging through the stylish shops like Soma chocolatier, A Taste of Quebec, Corktown jewelry, and the Sandra Ainsley Gallery. ✉ *55 Mill St., east of Parliament St., Old Town, Toronto, Ontario, Canada* ☎ *416/364–1177* ⊕ *www.thedistillerydistrict.com* ⊙ *Hrs vary, but most shops are open at least: Mon.–Wed. 10–7, Thurs.–Sat. 10–8, Sun. 11–5* Ⓜ *508 Lakeshore or 504 King streetcar.*

FOOD

FOOD
MARKETS

St. Lawrence Market Complex. Nearly 70 vendors occupy the historic permanent indoor market and sell items such as fish, meats, produce, caviar, and crafts. The building, on the south side of Front Street, was once Toronto's first city hall. ■TIP→ **The best time to visit is early on Saturday from 5 am, when there's a farmers' market in the building on the north side.** ✉ *91 Front St. E, at Jarvis St., Old Town, Toronto, Ontario, Canada* ☎ *416/392–7219* ⊕ *www.stlawrencemarket.com* ⊙ *Tues.–Thurs. 8–6, Fri. 8–7, Sat. 5–5; farmers' market Sat. 5–3* Ⓜ *Union Station.*

FOOD SHOPS

Soma. Satisfy your sweet tooth just by inhaling the delicate wafts of chocolate, dried fruits, and roasted nuts in this gourmet chocolate shop in the Historic Distillery District that specializes in microbatch, fair-trade chocolate. Big sellers include crystallized Australian ginger dipped in dark Venezuelan chocolate, spiced chai tea truffles, and gelato. For something different, try the Bicarin, a thick mixture of melted chocolate, espresso, and whipped cream. ✉ *55 Mill St., Bldg. 48, Old Town, Toronto, Ontario, Canada* ☎ *416/815–7662* ⊕ *www.somachocolate. com* ⊗ *Mon.–Sat. 10–8, Sun. 11–6* Ⓜ *King, then streetcar 508 east.*

A Taste of Quebec. Goût de terroir from the province of Quebec is the specialty of this rustic-chic shop. Pick up artisanal cheeses, handmade dry sausages, pâtés, maple butter, homemade *tourtière* (meat pies), mustards, oils, and flavored salts. ✉ *Distillery District, 55 Mill St., Bldg. 32, Old Town, Toronto, Ontario, Canada* ☎ *416/364–5020* ⊕ *www. atasteofquebec.com* ⊗ *Tues.–Thurs. 11–6, Fri. 11–7, Sat. 10–6, Sun. 11–5* Ⓜ *508 Lakeshore or 504 King streetcar.*

HOME DECOR AND FURNISHINGS

★ **UpCountry.** This 12,000-square-foot store holds a unique mix of furniture collections that reflect leading-edge design principles. Well-made and reasonably priced, the upholstered sofas and chairs are built in small runs by Canadian manufacturers. ✉ *310 King St. E, at Parliament St., Old Town, Toronto, Ontario, Canada* ☎ *416/366–7477* ⊕ *www. upcountry.com* ⊗ *Mon.–Wed. and Sat. 10–6, Thurs. and Fri. 10–7. Sun. noon–5* Ⓜ *King.*

JEWELRY

Corktown Designs. Seventy percent of the reasonably priced jewelry at this Distillery District shop is Canadian-designed, and all of it is unique and handmade. Pieces range from inexpensive glass-and-silver pendants to Swiss-made stainless steel rings and pricier pieces set with pearls and other semiprecious stones. ✉ *Distillery District, 55 Mill St., Bldg. 59, Old Town, Toronto, Ontario, Canada* ☎ *416/861–3020* ⊕ *www. corktowndesigns.com* ⊗ *Mon. 10–6, Tues. and Wed. 10–7, Thurs.–Sat. 10–9, Sun. 11–6* Ⓜ *508 Lakeshore or 504 King streetcar.*

THE ENTERTAINMENT DISTRICT

King Street East is tops for furniture hunters, beginning at Jarvis Street and continuing almost until the Don River. Sofas and chairs take center stage, seducing even the mildly curious. Between the furniture stores are custom framing shops, art dealers, and cafés to refresh the weary shopper.

ANTIQUES AND INTERIORS

Fodor's Choice ★ **Toronto Antiques on King.** The 16,000 square feet of this shop provide ample opportunity for browsing pre- or post-show (the Princess of Wales theater is next door) among the cabinets, shelves, and bins overflowing with porcelain, silver tea sets, Majelica pottery, Lalique vases, collectibles, and antique maps. It's also Toronto's leading purveyor of vintage and estate jewelry. Take the stairs beside Dunn's Deli. ✉ *284 King St. W (2nd fl.), at John St., Entertainment District, Toronto, Ontario, Canada* ☎ *416/260–9057* ⊕ *www.cynthiafindlay* ⊗ *Tues.– Sun. 10–6* Ⓜ *St. Andrew.*

BOOKS

SPECIAL-
INTEREST
BOOKSTORES

Open Air Books and Maps. More than 10,000 travel books, oodles of atlases and road maps, and titles on nature, history, and food has made this jam-packed jumble of a bookshop the ideal place to feed your wanderlust since 1974. The entrance is below street level, through an unmarked black door. ⊠ *25 Toronto St., at Adelaide St. E, Entertainment District, Toronto, Ontario, Canada* ☎ *416/363–0719* ☯ *Weekdays 10–6, Sat. 10–5:30* Ⓜ *King.*

Swipe Books on Advertising & Design. Books on advertising, art, and architecture—from green homes to an ode to sans-serif typefaces—pack the shelves of this aesthetically pleasing store, fittingly located in the arty 401 Richmond heritage building. Part of the store is devoted to modern gifts, like Gijs Bakker fruit bowls and exquisitely carved and painted toy blocks. ⊠ *401 Richmond St. W, at Spadina Ave., Ste. 121, Entertainment District, Toronto, Ontario, Canada* ☎ *416/363–1332, 800/567–9473* ⊕ *www.swipe.com* ☯ *Weekdays 10–7, Sat. 11–6* Ⓜ *Osgoode; 501 Queen or 510 Spadina streetcar.*

SPORTING GOODS

Fodor's Choice
★

Mountain Equipment Co-op. MEC (rhymes with "check"), the much-beloved Toronto spot for anyone remotely interested in camping, sells wares for minor and major expeditions. It's also a go-to spot for cycling gear. A baffling assortment of backpacks allows you to choose anything from a schoolbag to a globe-trotting sack. For C$5, you get lifetime membership to the co-op. ■ TIP→ Try out the rappelling goods on the climbing wall. ⊠ *400 King St. W, at Charlotte St., Entertainment District, Toronto, Ontario, Canada* ☎ *416/340–2667* ⊕ *www.mec.ca* ☯ *Mon.–Wed. 10–7, Thurs. and Fri. 10–9, Sat. 9–6, Sun. 11–5* Ⓜ *St. Andrew.*

CHINATOWN, KENSINGTON MARKET, AND QUEEN WEST

CHINATOWN

While Chinese-Canadians have made Spadina Avenue their own from Queen Street north to College Street, Spadina's basic bill of fare is still "bargains galore." Its collection of inexpensive Chinese clothing stores, Chinese restaurants, ethnic food and fruit shops, and eateries (not only Chinese, but also Vietnamese, Japanese, and Thai) give you your money's worth. Take the (north–south) Spadina streetcar or the (east–west) College or Queen streetcars to Spadina Avenue.

ART AND CRAFTS GALLERIES

Bau-Xi Gallery. Paul Wong, an artist and dealer from Vancouver, founded this gallery across the street from the Art Gallery of Ontario. The paintings and sculpture are a window on contemporary Canadian art, and much of it is affordable. Down the street at 324 Dundas St. W is Bau-Xi Photo, showing both Canadian and international fine art photography. ⊠ *340 Dundas St. W, at McCaul St., Chinatown, Toronto, Ontario, Canada* ☎ *416/977–0600* ⊕ *www.bau-xi.com* ☯ *Mon.–Sat. 10–5:30, Sun 11–5:30* Ⓜ *St. Patrick.*

TORONTO'S GALLERIES

Toronto is Canada's cosmopolitan art center, with a few hundred commercial art galleries carrying items as varied as glass sculpture, Inuit designs, and multimedia pieces. Queen West and Ossington Avenue showcase edgy art; Yorkville and the historic Distillery District offer more mainstream talent. Some buildings are almost entirely dedicated to art galleries, like the building that houses YYZ at ✉ *401 Richmond St. W.* Naturally, the area around the Art Gallery of Ontario is saturated with contemporary art galleries, most of which offer affordable pieces by Canadian artists.

To find out about special art exhibits, check the Saturday edition of the *Globe and Mail* entertainment section, as well as *NOW* and *The Grid*—free weekly local newspapers on culture distributed on Thursday—or *Toronto Life* magazine. The Web site of *Canadian Art* magazine (⊕ *www. canadianart.ca*) is also a good source of information on gallery happenings. ■TIP→ **Most galleries are open Tuesday through Saturday from 10 to 5 or 6, but call to confirm.**

6

GIFTS

shopAGO. The store attached to the Art Gallery of Ontario has an overwhelming selection of curiosities, from books on maximal architecture to colorful dollhouses to prints of celebrated paintings. Adults and kids can shop side by side among the books and fun educational toys. ✉ *317 Dundas St. W., at McCaul St., Chinatown, Toronto, Ontario, Canada* ☎ *416/979–6610* ⊕ *www.ago.net/shop* ☉ *Tues., Thurs–Sun. 11:30–6, Wed. 11:30–9* ☉ *Closed Mon.* Ⓜ *St. Patrick.*

KENSINGTON MARKET

Tucked behind Spadina west to Bathurst Street, between Dundas and College streets to the south and north, is this hippie-meets-hipster collection of inexpensive vintage-clothing stores, cheap ethnic eateries, coffee shops, head shops, and specialty food shops specializing in cheeses, baked goods, fish, dry goods, health food, and more. ■TIP→ **Be warned—this area can be extraordinarily crowded on weekends; do not drive.** Take the College streetcar to Spadina or Augusta, or the Spadina streetcar to College or Nassau.

CLOTHING

MEN'S CLOTHING **Tom's Place.** Find bargains aplenty on brand-name suits like Calvin Klein, Armani, and DKNY. Tom Mihalik, the store's owner, keeps his prices low and carries some women's clothes as well. ✉ *190 Baldwin St., at Augusta Ave., Kensington Market, Toronto, Ontario, Canada* ☎ *416/596–0297* ⊕ *www.toms-place.com* ☉ *Mon.–Wed. 10–6, Thurs. and Fri. 10–7, Sat. 9–6, Sun. noon–5* Ⓜ *St. Patrick, then streetcar 505 west.*

VINTAGE CLOTHING ★ **Courage My Love.** The best vintage store in Kensington Market is crammed with the coolest retro stuff, from sunglasses to sundresses, plus an ample supply of cowboy boots for guys and gals, all at low prices. Not everything is secondhand here: there's a wall of sparkly

Indian-inspired clothing, lots of costume jewelry, and a selection of unique buttons. ⊠ *14 Kensington Ave., at Dundas St. W, Kensington Market, Toronto, Ontario, Canada* ☎ *416/979–1992* ⊘ *Weekdays 11:30–6, Sat. 11–6, Sun. 1–5* Ⓜ *St. Patrick, then streetcar 504 west.*

FOOD

FOOD
MARKETS
Fodor's Choice
★

Kensington Market. This outdoor market occupying a cluster of city blocks just west of Chinatown has a vibrant ethnic mix of casual restaurants and shops selling everything from cheese, coffee, nuts, and spices to vegan Chinese food, Latin American standbys, and Caribbean takeout. Vintage-clothing lovers delight in the shops tucked into houses lining the streets. ■TIP➔ Saturday is the best day to go, preferably by public transit; parking is difficult. ⊠ *Bounded roughly by August Ave., College St., Spadina Ave., and Dundas St. W, Kensington Market, Toronto, Ontario, Canada* ☎ *No phone* ⊕ *www.kensington-market.ca* ⊘ *Hrs vary by shop* Ⓜ *506 College, 510 Spadina, or 505 Dundas streetcar.*

QUEEN WEST

If it's funky or fun, it's found on Queen West. Beginning at University Avenue and heading west, the chockablock stores progress from large chains (Zara, Aritzia, Urban Outfitters) to increasingly independent one-off boutiques closer to Bathurst and beyond. With its collection of vintage stores, Canadian designer boutiques, bars and bistros, Queen West sets the pace for Toronto's street style. Come summer, street vendors and buskers around Spadina create a carnival atmosphere.

ANTIQUES AND INTERIORS

Quasi Modo. This quirky collection of 20th- and 21st-century furniture and design includes Herman Miller lounge chairs and Noguchi lamps. ⊠ *789 Queen St. W, at Manning Ave., Queen West, Toronto, Ontario, Canada* ☎ *416/703–8300* ⊕ *www.quasimodomodern.com* ⊘ *Mon.–Sat. 10–6, Sun. noon–5* Ⓜ *Osgoode, then streetcar 501 west.*

ART AND CRAFTS GALLERIES

Gallery Moos. German-born Walter Moos opened his gallery in 1959 to promote Canadian and European art. He's a discerning, reliable dealer who's had Picassos, Chagalls, Mirós, and Dufys, as well as work by such internationally admired Canadians as Gershon Iskowitz, Ken Danby, Sorel Etrog, and Jean-Paul Riopelle. ⊠ *622 Richmond St. W, at Bathurst St., Queen West, Toronto, Ontario, Canada* ☎ *416/504–5445* ⊕ *www.gallerymoos.com* ⊘ *Tues.–Sat. 11–6* Ⓜ *Bathurst then streetcar 511 south.*

Stephen Bulger. This gallery focuses on historical and contemporary Canadian photography, with Canadian and international artists such as André Kertész and Larry Towell. ⊠ *1026 Queen St. W, at Shaw St., Queen West, Toronto, Ontario, Canada* ☎ *416/504–0575* ⊕ *www.bulgergallery.com* ⊘ *Tues.–Sat. 11–6* Ⓜ *Osgoode, then streetcar 501 west.*

Wynick/Tuck Gallery. Many of the contemporary Canadian artists displayed here have become well-established, attesting to this gallery's influence. ⊠ *401 Richmond St. W, Suite 128, at Spadina Ave., Queen West, Toronto, Ontario, Canada* ☎ *416/504–8716* ⊕ *www.*

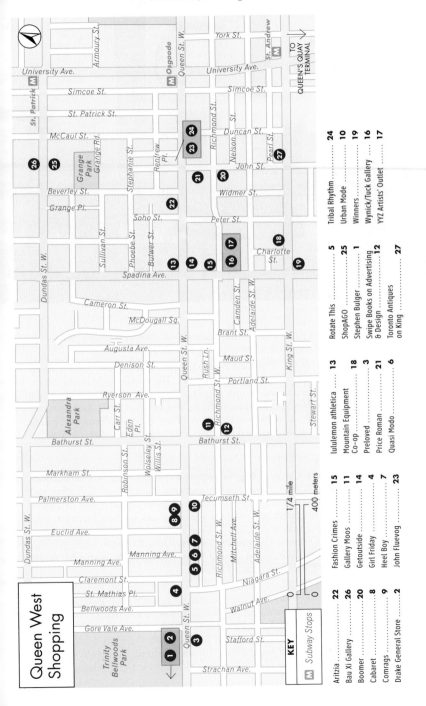

Queen West Shopping

KEY

M Subway Stops

The curios displayed at the Drake General Store make entertaining souvenirs.

wynicktuckgallery.ca ⊘ *Tues.–Sat. 11–5, Summer hours Wed.–Sat. noon–5* Ⓜ *Osgoode, then streetcar 501 west.*

YYZ Artists' Outlet. There are two exhibition spaces here: one for visual art and one for time-based conceptions. The visual might contain two- and three-dimensional paintings and sculptures, whereas the time-based area might have performances, films, and videos. ✉ *401 Richmond St. W, Suite 140, at Spadina Ave., Queen West, Toronto, Ontario, Canada* ☎ *416/598–4546* ⊕ *www.yyzartistsoutlet.org* ⊘ *Tues.–Sat. 11–5* Ⓜ *Osgoode, then 501 streetcar west.*

AUCTIONS

Waddington's. Canada's biggest auction house has more than 30 auctions every year, as well as many online auctions. They feature Canadian and International fine art, many of them prestigious collector and catalogue auctions. In December and June special shows auction Inuit art, jewelry, and decorative arts. ✉ *275 King St. E., at Princess St., Old Town, Toronto, Ontario, Canada* ☎ *416/504–9100, 877/504–5700* ⊕ *www. waddingtons.ca* ⊘ *Open during previews, check Web site for hours* Ⓜ *Bathurst, then streetcar 511 south.*

CLOTHING

MEN'S CLOTHING

Boomer. One of the best-kept secrets of Toronto men brings together tasteful yet trendy slim-fitting suitings and separates that appeal to fashion-forward guys who eschew stuffy, old-school business attire. Tiger of Sweden, J. Lindeberg, and Hugo Boss populate the racks. ✉ *309 Queen St. W, at John St., Queen West, Toronto, Ontario, Canada* ☎ *416/598–0013* ⊘ *Weekdays 10:30–7, Sat. 10:30–6, Sun. 1–5* Ⓜ *Osgoode, then streetcar 501 west.*

VINTAGE
CLOTHING

Cabaret. Classic Hollywood– and mid-century-Parisian–style gowns (1920s–1970s), handbags, and jewelry fill this sweet little checkerboard-floored shop. For men there's a selection of dapper bowties, hats, and jackets and vintage suits and tuxedos. All items on display have been restored and dry-cleaned. Popular with brides is the store's own line of vintage-inspired couture dresses. ✉ *672 Queen St W, at Palmerston Ave., Queen West, Toronto, Ontario, Canada* ☎ *416/504–7126* ⊕ *www.cabaretvintage.com* ⊙ *Mon.–Wed. and Sat. 11–6, Thurs. and Fri. 11–7, Sun 1–5* Ⓜ *501 Queen or 511 Bathurst streetcar.*

> **THE GARMENT DISTRICT**
>
> Between Queen West and West Queen West, SoHo-style industrial lofts house a collection of textile shops stocking leathers, furs, and fabrics of every color under the sun. You can still see remnants of the goth fad that swept through this area in the 1990s in the smattering of macabre clubs and lounges.

Tribal Rhythm. A few vintage gems and pretty silk scarves may be found among the army jackets, cub scout uniforms, and '70s polyester shirts and cowgirl attire, but most of the inventory is simply fun, kitschy, and kooky. Imported Thai and Indian trinkets, rows of body jewelry, tiaras, and wigs are part of the charming and eclectic mix. ✉ *248 Queen St. W, below street level, at John St., Queen West, Toronto, Ontario, Canada* ☎ *416/595–5817* ⊙ *Mon.–Sat. 11–7, Sun. noon–6* Ⓜ *Osgoode; 501 Queen streetcar.*

WOMEN'S
CLOTHING

Comrags. Designers Joyce Gunhouse and Judy Cornish have supplied the city with close to 30 years of sophisticated women's clothing designs. They aptly describe their store as "country farmhouse meets urban industrial." ✉ *654 Queen St. W, at Palmerston Ave., Queen West, Toronto, Ontario, Canada* ☎ *416/360–7249* ⊕ *www.comrags.com* ⊙ *Mon.–Wed. 11–6, Thurs. and Fri. 11–7, Sat. 10–6, Sun. noon–5* Ⓜ *Osgoode, then 501 streetcar west.*

Fashion Crimes. Part romantic, part funk, this Queen West haven of glam party dresses and dreamy designs has a display case packed full of elegant baubles and sparkling tiaras. Designer and owner Pam Chorley also has a pint-size label for girls called Misdemeanours. ✉ *322½ Queen St. W, at Spadina Ave., Queen West, Toronto, Ontario, Canada* ☎ *416/592–9001* ⊕ *www.fashioncrimes.ca* ⊙ *Mon.–Thurs. 10–8, Fri. 10–9, Sat. 10–7, Sun. noon–6* Ⓜ *Osgoode, then streetcar west 501.*

Girl Friday. Designer Rebecca Nixon sells sweet and stylish designs with a retro glam look. Another branch is located in Little Italy. ✉ *740 Queen St. W, at Claremont St., Queen West, Toronto, Ontario, Canada* ☎ *416/364–2511* ⊕ *www.girlfridayclothing.com* ⊙ *Mon.–Thurs. noon–7, Fri. and Sat. 11–7, Sun. noon–6* Ⓜ *501 Queen streetcar.*

lululemon athletica. This bright and airy store is a perfect match for yoga-centric items from this coveted Canadian brand such as specialized yoga sports bras, top-of-the-line yoga mats, and stretchy yoga and gym togs. Check out other Toronto-area branches online. ✉ *342 Queen W, at Spadina Ave., Queen West, Toronto, Ontario, Canada* ☎ *416/703–1399*

6

⊕ *www.lululemon.com* ⊗ *Mon.– Fri. 11–7, Sat. 10-7, Sun. 11–6* Ⓜ *Osgoode, then streetcar 501 west.*

Mendocino. Score the best of the mid-price, super-trendy lines here—those polished looks you find in *InStyle* magazine. This is a great stop if you have a limited amount of time and want to pack a lot in as you can peruse the day and evening lines from both Canadian and international designers. ⊠ *131 Bloor St. W, at Avenue Road, in Yorkville, Toronto, Ontario, Canada* ☎ *416/927–8618* ⊕ *www. mendocino.ca* ⊗ *Daily 10–7, Sat. 10-6, Sun. 11-5* Ⓜ *Bay.*

Preloved. Former models and fashion insiders stock this shop by combing used and vintage markets, and then reconstructing their finds into new unique designs.

> ## A SHOE THING
>
> If you've literally worn out your shoe leather, consider hitting up Queen Street West between John and Spadina for a new pair of kicks. This strip is packed with shoe and sneaker stores for ladies and gents that stock a wide variety of styles at mostly mid-range prices. In winter consider uber-comfy Canadian-made Sorel boots, designed to keep tootsies toasty; in summer browse La Canadienne sandals. Our favorite shops are those covered in this chapter (Getoutside, John Fleuvog, and—a bit farther west—Heel Boy), but you can also find a Crocs shop and boutiques stocked with Camper, Vans, Tsubo, and more.

⊠ *881 Queen St. W, at Trinity Bellwoods Park, Queen West, Toronto, Ontario, Canada* ☎ *416/504–8704* ⊕ *www.preloved.ca* ⊗ *Mon.–Wed. 11–6, Thur. and Fri. 11–7, Sat. 11–6, Sun. 12–6* Ⓜ *Osgoode, then streetcar 501 west.*

Price Roman. Edgy career and evening wear—think bias-cut dresses and asymmetrical hemlines—come in surprising fabric choices here, like Asian brocades and various silks. ⊠ *162 John St., at Queen St. W, Queen West, Toronto, Ontario, Canada* ☎ *416/979–7363* ⊕ *www. priceroman.com* ⊗ *Weekdays noon–7, Sat. noon–6, other times by appt. only.* Ⓜ *Osgoode.*

GIFTS

Drake General Store. Only-in-Canada gifts like Mountie napkins, Hudson Bay Company wool blankets, totem-pole stacking mugs, supersoft Toronto-made Shared tees, and poutine bowls are tucked into every nook and cranny of this offbeat shop. Giftware extends from the unusual but beautiful (whimsical Rob Ryan dishware and pewter-and-ceramic moosehead shot glasses) to the singularly strange (preserved lemons, knitted mustache pins). Additional locations are at Bathurst and King streets and in Rosedale. ⊠ *1144 Queen St. W, at Beaconsfield Ave., Queen West, Toronto, Ontario, Canada* ☎ *416/531–5042* ⊕ *drakegeneralstore.myshopify.com* ⊗ *Mon.–Wed. 11–7, Thurs.–Sat. 11–9, Sun. 11–6.*

HOME DECOR AND FURNISHINGS

Urban Mode. Modern and trend-oriented furniture and home decor include colorful plastic desk accessories in interesting shapes, sleek stainless-steel tabletop accoutrements, and funky wine racks. Most are

Canadian-designed. ⊠ *145 Tecumseth St., at Queen St. W, Queen West, Toronto, Ontario, Canada* ☎ *416/591–8834* ⊕ *www.urbanmode.com* ☾ *Mon.–Sat. 11–6* Ⓜ *Osgoode, then streetcar 501 west.*

MUSIC

Rotate This. Music buyers in the know come here for underground and independent music from Canada, the United States, and beyond. It has CDs, LPs, some magazines, concert tickets, and other treats. ⊠ *801 Queen St. W, at Manning Ave., Queen West, Toronto, Ontario, Canada* ☎ *416/504–8447* ⊕ *www.rotate.com* ☾ *Mon. and Sat. 11–7, Tues.–Fri. 11–8, Sun. noon–6:30* Ⓜ *Osgoode, then streetcar 501 west.*

SHOES

Getoutside. Get your funky street-wear fix here. There are styles for men and women, as well as an entire wall of sneakers. ⊠ *437 Queen St. W, at Spadina Ave., Queen West, Toronto, Ontario, Canada* ☎ *416/593–5598* ⊕ *www.getoutsideshoes.com* ☾ *Mon.–Sat. 10–9, Sun. 11–8* Ⓜ *Osgoode, then streetcar 501 west.*

★ **Heel Boy.** A tried and true spot for cool and cute footwear for both sexes, Heel Boy stocks the most unique styles by well-known brands like Camper, Ugg, TOMS, Colcci, and Dolce Vita, as well as eco-chic bags by Canadian company Matt and Nat. ⊠ *773 Queen St. W, at Euclid St., Queen West, Toronto, Ontario, Canada* ☎ *416/362–4335* ⊕ *www. heelboy.com* ☾ *Weekdays 11–9, Sat. 10–7, Sun. noon–6* Ⓜ *501 Queen or 511 Bathurst streetcar.*

John Fluevog. Fluevog began in Vancouver, infusing good quality with fun, flair, and cutting-edge design, and is now an international shoe star. Stores can be found all over the United States, in Australia, and, luckily, on Queen Street West. ⊠ *242 Queen St. W, at John St., Queen West, Toronto, Ontario, Canada* ☎ *416/581–1420* ⊕ *www.fluevog.com* ☾ *Mon.–Wed. and Sat. 11–7, Thurs. and Fri. 11–8, Sun. noon–6* Ⓜ *Osgoode, then streetcar 501 west.*

THE ANNEX AND YORKVILLE

THE ANNEX

In a neighborhood near the University of Toronto campus populated by academics, students, and '60s hippies, a mix of restored and run-down Victorians and brick low-rises house cafés and bistros, used-book and music stores, and the occasional fashion boutique, like Risqué. At the Annex's outer edge (Bloor and Bathurst) is Honest Ed's, a tacky discount megastore lit with more than 20,000 flashing lightbulbs that is (to the chagrin of some locals) a neighborhood landmark.

BOOKS

Bakka Phoenix. Canada's oldest science fiction and fantasy bookstore, opened in 1972, Bakka Phoenix has several thousand new and used titles for adults, young adults, and children, as well as some graphic novels and DVDs (*Doctor Who* and the like). Knowledgeable staff is always on hand to give advice. ⊠ *84 Harbord St., at Spadina Ave., The Annex, Toronto, Ontario, Canada* ☎ *416/963–9993* ⊕ *www.*

bakkaphoenixbooks.com ⊗ *Weekdays 11–7, Sat. 11–6, Sun. noon–5*
Ⓜ *Spadina; 510 Spadina streetcar.*

BMV. An impressive selection of new and used books is shelved side by side over two floors at BMV (which stands for "Books Magazines Video"). The staff is knowledgeable and helpful. Another branch is located in the Dundas Square Area. ⊠ *471 Bloor St. W., at Brunswick Ave., The Annex, Toronto, Ontario, Canada* ☎ *416/967–5757* ⊗ *Mon.– Wed. 10am–11pm, Thu.–Sat. 10am–midnight, Sun. noon–8* Ⓜ *Spadina.*

Book City. Find good discounts—especially on publishers' remainders—a knowledgeable staff, and a fine choice of magazines at branches of this late-night Toronto chain, usually open until 10 or 11. Five locations are scattered around the city. ⊠ *501 Bloor St. W, at Brunswick Ave., The Annex, Toronto, Ontario, Canada* ☎ *416/961–4496* ⊕ *www.bookcity. ca* ⊗ *Mon.–Sat. 9:30 am–10 pm, Sun. 11 am–10 pm* Ⓜ *Bathurst, Spadina.*

Toronto Women's Bookstore. Titles focus on women and minorities and include the latest fiction by women, feminist works on women's political issues, literary criticism, and lesbian topics. Along with hard-to-find magazines, journals, and zines, a new cafe and back garden patio are a draw. ⊠ *73 Harbord St., at Spadina Ave., The Annex, Toronto, Ontario, Canada* ☎ *416/922–8744* ⊕ *www.womensbookstore.com* ⊗ *Mon.–Fri. 10–7, Sat. 11–6, Sun. 12–5* Ⓜ *Spadina.*

CLOTHING

WOMEN'S
CLOTHING

Risqué. Trendy young dresses, blouses, jumpers, and jeans by primarily Canadian designers as well as inexpensive accessories fill this boutique. The colorful, of-the-moment selections change weekly. ⊠ *404 Bloor St. W, at Brunswick Ave., The Annex, Toronto, Ontario, Canada* ☎ *416/960–3325* ⊗ *Weekdays 11–7, Sat. 11–6, Sun. noon–6* Ⓜ *St. George.*

KITCHENWARE AND TABLETOP

Nella Cucina. Shop alongside Toronto chefs for quality kitchen novelties and supplies: cheese knives, seafood shears, cast-iron cookware, espresso machines and parts, or unique showpieces like locally made salvaged-wood platters. A teaching kitchen upstairs hosts classes, from Italian cooking to knife skills. ⊠ *876 Bathurst St., at London St. The Annex, Toronto, Ontario, Canada* ☎ *416/922–9055* ⊕ *nellacucina.ca* ⊗ *Weekdays 9–6, Sat. 10–6* Ⓜ *Bathurst.*

LINGERIE

Secrets From Your Sister. The art of the brassiere is taken seriously at this bra-fitting boutique. Knowledgeable (but pretension-free) staff are on hand for advice. Fittings can be arranged on the spot at least one hour before closing and must be reserved in person. A session usually lasts about 30 minutes. Or simply peruse the massive selection of prêt-à-porter undergarments, including sports, fashion, strapless, seamless, and nursing bras in wide-ranging sizes and fits. There's a second location near Yonge and Eglinton uptown. ⊠ *560 Bloor St. W, at Bathurst St., The Annex, Toronto, Ontario, Canada* ☎ *416/538–1234* ⊕ *www. secretsfromyoursister.com* ⊗ *Weekdays 11–7, Sat. 10–6, Sun. noon–6.*

Yorkville
Shopping

Davenport Rd.
Bernard Ave.
Webster
Belmont St.
Tranby Ave.
Boswell Ave.
Elgin Ave.
Lowther Ave.
Hazelton Lanes
Scollard St.
Yorkville Ave.
Prince Arthur Ave.
110 Bloor St. West
Cumberland St.
St. George
Bloor St. W.
131 Bloor St. West
Charles St. W.
Bay
Bloor St. E.
Bloor–Yonge
Asquith Ave.
Davenport Rd.
Isabella St.

0   1/8 mi
0   200 meters

KEY

Ⓜ   Subway Stops

MUSIC

Sonic Boom. More than 1,500 daily arrivals fill the rows of this bright and cavernous store with a dizzying array of both used and new CDs, vinyl records, and DVDs. They carry many albums of local musicians—if the timing is right, you might catch one of those bands giving a live performance inside the store. ✉ *512 Bloor St. W, at Albany Ave., The Annex, Toronto, Ontario, Canada* ☎ *416/532–0334* ⊕ *www.sonicboommusic.com* ⊗ *Daily 10–midnight* Ⓜ *Bathurst.*

YORKVILLE

In the 1960s Yorkville was Canada's hippie headquarters. Today it's a well-heeled shopping and dining destination: the place to find high-end everything. From Yonge Street to Avenue Road, Bloor Street is a virtual runway for fashionistas, with world-reknowned designer shops like Bulgari, Prada, Chanel, and quality chains (Williams Sonoma, Roots). Also here is Holt Renfrew, Canada's ultimate luxury department store, and William Ashley, a china store like no other. Running parallel to Bloor, east of Avenue Road, are pedestrian-friendly streets with tony cafés and smaller designer stores that are fun to browse even if you're not buying.

Stanley Wagman Antiques. Stanley Wagman carries a large selection of art-deco pieces and lighting, as well as Louis XVI furniture and accessories. This is the place to find exquisite marble fireplaces, and it reputedly has the biggest selection of lighting in Canada. It also ships worldwide. ✉ *224 Davenport Rd., at Avenue Rd., Yorkville, Toronto, Ontario, Canada* ☎ *416/964–1047* ⊗ *Weekdays 10–6, Sat. noon–4* Ⓜ *Dupont, Bay.*

ART AND CRAFTS GALLERIES

Feheley Fine Arts. Browse contemporary and even avant-garde Canadian Inuit art—a far cry from the traditional whale carvings and stone-cut prints you may expect—at this family-owned gallery founded in 1964. ✉ *14 Hazelton Ave., at Yorkville Ave., Yorkville, Toronto, Ontario, Canada* ☎ *416/323–1373* ⊕ *www.feheleyfinearts.com* ⊗ *Tues.–Sat. 10–5:30* Ⓜ *Bay.*

Loch Gallery. This intimate gallery in an old Victorian house almost exclusively exhibits representational historic and contemporary Canadian painting and sculpture. Artists include bronze sculptor Leo Mol and painters Jack Chambers and John Boyle. ✉ *16 Hazelton Ave., at Yorkville Ave., Yorkville, Toronto, Ontario, Canada* ☎ *416/964–9050* ⊕ *www.lochgallery.com* ⊗ *Tues.–Sat. 10–5* Ⓜ *Bay.*

AUCTIONS

Sotheby's. The Toronto outpost of the international auction house focuses on Canadian art. Auctions happen twice yearly—the end of May and end of November—and are held at the Royal Ontario Museum. ✉ *9 Hazelton Ave., at Yorkville Ave., Yorkville, Toronto, Ontario, Canada* ☎ *416/926–1774, 800/263–1774* ⊕ *www.sothebys.com* ⊗ *Weekdays 9–5:30* Ⓜ *Bay.*

BOOKS

SPECIAL-
INTEREST
BOOKSTORES

Cookbook Store. This store has the city's largest selection of books and magazines on cooking and wine and holds frequent book signings. Owners and staff are so knowledgeable they seem to have read every book on the shelves. ✉ *850 Yonge St., at Yorkville Ave., Yorkville, Toronto, Ontario, Canada* ☎ *416/920–2665, 800/268–6018* ⊕ *www.cook-book.com* ⊙ *Weekdays 10–7, Sat. 10–6, Sun. noon–5* Ⓜ *Bloor-Yonge.*

Theatrebooks. An astounding collection of performing-arts books spans theater, film, opera, dance, television, and media studies. ✉ *11 St. Thomas St., at Bloor St. W, Yorkville, Toronto, Ontario, Canada* ☎ *416/922–7175, 800/361–3414* ⊕ *www.theatrebooks.com* ⊙ *Weekdays 10–7, Sat. 10–6, Sun. noon–5* Ⓜ *Bay.*

> **SHOP AND GO: YORKVILLE**
>
> Make a stop at the corner of Bellair and Cumberland Street for a snack at **MBCo**—a cappuccino, perhaps, or a smoothie, lemon tart, or delectable sandwich—to fuel your shopping adventures. The entrance is on Cumberland, behind Roots. ✉ *100 Bloor St. W, at Bellair St., Yorkville, Toronto, Ontario, Canada* ☎ *416/961–6266* ⊕ *www.mbco.ca.*

CLOTHING

CHILDREN'S CLOTHING

Jacadi. The city's prettiest and priciest children's clothes are stocked here, in vibrant colors and fine fabrics from Paris, designed by stylish French women. ✉ *87 Avenue Rd., in Hazelton Lanes, Yorkville, Toronto, Ontario, Canada* ☎ *416/923–1717* ⊕ *www.jacadi.com* ⊙ *Mon.–Wed. and Fri. 10–6, Thur. 10–7, Sun. 12–5* Ⓜ *Bay or Cumberland.*

MEN'S CLOTHING ★

Harry Rosen. This miniature department store is dedicated to the finest men's fashions, with designers such as Hugo Boss, Armani, and Zegna. The casual section stocks preppy classics. ✉ *82 Bloor St. W, at Bellair St., Yorkville, Toronto, Ontario, Canada* ☎ *416/972–0556* ⊕ *www.harryrosen.com* ⊙ *Mon.–Wed. 10–7, Thurs. and Fri. 10–9, Sat. 10–6, Sun. noon–6* Ⓜ *Bloor-Yonge.*

Perry's. These are the suit professionals. Have one custom-made from a broad range of fabrics, or buy off the rack from a collection of some of the finest ready-to-wear suits, which are made by Samuelsohn and Jack Victor (both from Montréal). ✉ *1250 Bay St., at Cumberland St., Yorkville, Toronto, Ontario, Canada* ☎ *416/923–7397* ⊕ *www.perrysmenswear.com* ⊙ *Mon.–Wed. 9–6, Thu.–Fri. 9–7. Occasionally open on Sunday.* Ⓜ *Bay.*

Stollerys. From wool to linen to salespeople with round spectacles holding measuring tapes, walking into this department store is like stepping into a tailor shop in 1900s England, only on a grander scale. Choose from four floors of carefully conservative clothing. ✉ *1 Bloor St. W, at Yonge St., Yorkville, Toronto, Ontario, Canada* ☎ *416/922–6173* ⊕ *www.stollerys.com* ⊙ *Mon.–Sat. 10–6, Sun. noon–5* Ⓜ *Bloor-Yonge.*

MEN'S AND WOMEN'S CLOTHING

Club Monaco. The bright and airy flagship store of this successful chain, now owned by Ralph Lauren, has homegrown design basics: midprice sportswear and career clothes. ✉ *157 Bloor St. W, at Avenue Rd., Yorkville, Toronto, Ontario, Canada* ☎ *416/591–8837* ⊕ *www.clubmonaco.com* ⊙ *Mon.–Wed. 10–8, Thurs. and Fri. 10–9, Sat. 10–8, Sun. noon–6* Ⓜ *Museum or Bay.*

M0851. This is the place to go for all things leather. Sort through leather and denim jackets, pants, bags, and luggage—all of them the brand's

6

Toronto's fashionistas flock to Holt Renfrew for the latest couture.

own Montréal-made designs. You can even have leather furniture, such as chairs and four-seater couches, made to order. ✉ *23 St. Thomas St., at Bloor St. W, Yorkville, Toronto, Ontario, Canada* ☎ *416/920–4001* ⊕ *www.m0851.com* 🕙 *Mon.–Wed. and Sat. 10–6, Thurs. and Fri. 10–7, Sun. noon–5* Ⓜ *Bay.*

Over the Rainbow. This denim center carries every variety of cut and flare: the trendy, the classic, and the questionable fill the shelves. ✉ *101 Yorkville Ave., at Hazelton Ave., Yorkville, Toronto, Ontario, Canada* ☎ *416/967–7448* ⊕ *www.rainbowjeans.com* 🕙 *Mon.–Wed. 10–6, Thurs. and Fri. 10–8, Sat. 10–7, Sun. noon–6. In Summer, extended hours on Tues. and Wed. 10–8* Ⓜ *Bay.*

★ **Roots.** Torontonians' favorite leather jackets, bags, and basics come from this flagship store. Hours vary according to season, so call ahead to confirm. Branches are in several other Toronto neighborhoods; check out other locations on the Web site. ✉ *100 Bloor St. W, at Bellair St., Yorkville, Toronto, Ontario, Canada* ☎ *416/323–3289* ⊕ *www.canada.roots.com* 🕙 *Mon.–Fri. 9–9, Sat. 9–8, Sun. 10–8* Ⓜ *Bay.*

WOMEN'S **Chanel.** Coco would have loved the largest Chanel boutique in Canada.
CLOTHING The lush surroundings showcase most of the line, including the bags and accessories. ✉ *131 Bloor St. W, at Avenue Road, Yorkville, Toronto, Ontario, Canada* ☎ *416/925–2577* ⊕ *www.chanel.com* 🕙 *Mon.–Sat. 10–6, Sun. noon–5* Ⓜ *Bay.*

Escada. The spacious store carries the designer Escada line of chic Italian creations. ✉ *110 Bloor St. W, at Bellair St., Yorkville, Toronto, Ontario, Canada* ☎ *416/964–2265* ⊕ *www.escada.com* 🕙 *Mon.–Wed. 10–6, Thurs.–Fri. 10–7, Sat. 10–6, Sun. noon–5* Ⓜ *Bay.*

Hermès. The Parisian design house caters to the upscale horse- and hound-loving set, selling its classic sportswear, handbags, and accessories. ⊠ *130 Bloor St. W, at Avenue Rd., Yorkville, Toronto, Ontario, Canada* ☎ *416/968–8626* ⊕ *www.hermes.com* ⊗ *Mon.–Sat. 10–6* Ⓜ *Museum or Bay.*

★ **Hugo Nicholson.** The selection of evening wear by Oscar de la Renta, Christian Dior, Alaia, Carolina Herrera, Alexander McQueen and more is vast and exclusive. The service offered by the owners, the Rosenstein sisters, is old-school, with exacting alterations, a selection of accessories, and home delivery. ⊠ *55 Avenue Rd., in Hazelton Lanes, Yorkville, Toronto, Ontario, Canada* ☎ *416/927–7714* ⊕ *www.hugonicholson. com* ⊗ *Mon.–Sat. 10–6* Ⓜ *Bay.*

Pink Tartan. Ontario-born designer Kimberly Newport-Mimran opened this, her flagship store, in 2011 after selling her sophisticated sportswear in high-end shops around the globe. Expect tailored Oxford shirts, classic little black dresses, and crisp, snug-fitting trousers in expensive fabrics, as well as objets d'art, shoes, and accessories hand-picked by the designer. ⊠ *77 Yorkville Ave. (entrance on Bellair St.), near Bay St., Yorkville, Toronto, Ontario, Canada* ☎ *416/976–7700* ⊕ *www. pinktartan.com* ⊗ *Mon.–Wed. and Sat. 10–6, Thurs. and Fri. 10–7, Sun. noon–5* Ⓜ *Bay.*

Prada. The avant-garde designs are overshadowed only by the brilliant celadon interior of the store and the traffic-stopping window displays. ⊠ *131 Bloor St. W, Unit 5, at Bellair St., Yorkville, Toronto, Ontario, Canada* ☎ *416/513–0400* ⊕ *www.prada.com* ⊗ *Mon.–Sat. 10–6* Ⓜ *Museum.*

DEPARTMENT STORES AND SHOPPING CENTERS

The Bay. The modern descendant of the Hudson's Bay Company, which was chartered in 1670 to explore and trade in furs, the Bay carries mid-price clothing, furnishings, housewares, and cosmetics, including designer names as well as The Bay's own lines. Another store is located on Yonge Street, connected to Eaton Centre by a covered skywalk over Queen Street. ⊠ *44 Bloor St. E, at Yonge St., Yorkville, Toronto, Ontario, Canada* ☎ *416/972–3333* ⊕ *www.thebay.com* ⊗ *Mon.–Wed. 10–7, Thurs. and Fri. 10–9, Sat. 9–7, Sun. noon–6* Ⓜ *Bloor-Yonge.*

Fodor's Choice ★ **Hazelton Lanes.** A stroll through the two floors of Hazelton Lanes, the country's most upscale shopping mall, with more than 60 stores, is an experience. Stores include fashion-forward TNT Woman and Man (TNT is short for The Next Trend); Hugo Nicholson's exquisite, one-of-a-kind evening wear; Fabrice's unique, semiprecious jewelry, personally chosen and imported from Paris by the owner; Jacadi's Parisian kidswear; Brown's designer shoes; and Toronto's only Whole Foods Market. ⊠ *55 Avenue Rd., at Yorkville Ave., Yorkville, Toronto, Ontario, Canada* ☎ *416/968–8600* ⊕ *www.hazeltonlanes.com* ⊗ *Mon.–Wed., Fri., and Sat. 10–6, Thurs. 10–7, Sun. noon–5* Ⓜ *Bay.*

Fodor's Choice ★ **Holt Renfrew.** This multilevel national retail specialty store is the style leader in Canada. It is the headquarters for Burberry, Canali, Chanel, Donna Karan, Armani, and Gucci as well as cosmetics and fragrances from London, New York, Paris, and Rome. ■**TIP**→ Concierge service

City Chains

Below are some of the city's most interesting national and international chains.

Anthropologie. Feminine and ethnic-inspired clothing, housewares, and accessories attract fashionistas looking for mass-produced pieces with one-of-a-kind appearance. ✉ 80 Yorkville Ave., west of Bay St., Yorkville, Toronto, Ontario, Canada ☎ 416/964–9700 ⊕ www.anthropologie.com ⊘ Mon.–Sat. 10–7, Sun. noon–6 Ⓜ Bay.

Aritzia. Young urban women come here for modern funky pieces by lines such as TNA, Wilfred, and the house line Talula. There are other locations throughout the city. ✉ 280 Queen St. W, at John St., Queen West, Toronto, Ontario, Canada ☎ 416/977–9919 ⊕ www.aritzia.com ⊘ Weekdays 11–8, Sat. 11–7, Sun. noon–7 Ⓜ Osgoode, then streetcar 501 west Osgoode ✉ Eaton Centre, 220 Yonge St., Dundas Square Area, Toronto, Ontario, Canada ☎ 416/204–1318 ⊘ Weekdays 10–9, Sat. 9:30–7, Sun. 11–6 Ⓜ Queen Dundas or Queen Street ✉ 50 Bloor St. W, at Yonge and Bloor St., Yorkville, Toronto, Ontario, Canada ☎ 416/934–0935 ⊘ Mon.–Wed. 10–8, Thurs. and Fri. 10–9, Sat. 10–7, Sun. noon–6 Ⓜ Bay Bloor-Yonge.

Indigo. A huge selection of books, magazines, and CDs is stocked at this store, which has a Starbucks and occasional live entertainment. ✉ 55 Bloor St. W, Yorkville, Toronto, Ontario, Canada ☎ 416/925–3536 ⊕ www.chapters.indigo.ca ⊘ Sun.–Thurs. 9 am–10 pm, Fri. and Sat. 9 am–11 pm Ⓜ Bay ✉ 220 Yonge St., Eaton Centre, Dundas Square Area, Toronto, Ontario, Canada ☎ 416/591–3622 ⊘ Weekdays 10–9:30, Sat. 9:30–7, Sun. 11–6 Ⓜ Dundas, Queen.

Winners. Toronto's best bargain outlet has designer lines at rock-bottom prices. The Yonge Street branch, below the elegant Carlu event center, is enormous, but there are a dozen branches of this store scattered all over the city. ✉ 57 Spadina Ave., at King St. W, Entertainment District, Toronto, Ontario, Canada ☎ 416/585–2052 ⊕ www.winners.ca ⊘ Weekdays 9:30–9, Sat. 9:30–6, Sun. noon–6 Ⓜ St. Andrew ✉ 444 Yonge St., Dundas Square Area, Toronto, Ontario, Canada ☎ 416/598–8800 ⊘ Weekdays 8:30–9:30, Sat. 9:30–8, Sun. 11–7 Ⓜ College ✉ 110 Bloor St. W, at Bay St., Yorkville, Toronto, Ontario, Canada ☎ 416/920–0193 ⊘ Weekdays 9:30–9, Sat. 9:30–7, Sun. 11–6 Ⓜ Bay.

Zara. The Spanish chain consistently attracts crowds craving gorgeous knockoffs of the hottest runway trends. See more Toronto locations at online. ✉ 50 Bloor St. W, at Yonge St., Yorkville, Toronto, Ontario, Canada ☎ 416/916–2401 ⊕ www.zara.com ⊘ Mon.–Wed. and Sat. 10–8, Thurs. and Fri. 10–9, Sun. 11–6 Ⓜ Bloor ✉ 220 Yonge St., in Eaton Centre, Dundas Square Area, Toronto, Ontario, Canada ☎ 647/288–0333 ⊘ Weekdays 10–9, Sat. 9:30–7, Sun. 11–6 Ⓜ Queen, Dundas ✉ 341 Queen St. W, Queen West, Toronto, Ontario, Canada ☎ 647/288–0545 ⊘ Mon.–Wed. 10–8, Thurs. and Fri. 10–9, Sat. 11–8, Sun. 11–6 Ⓜ Osgoode.

and personal shoppers are available, but just browsing makes for a rich experience. ✉ *50 Bloor St. W, at Bay St., Yorkville, Toronto, Ontario, Canada* ☎ *416/922–2333* ⊕ *www.holtrenfrew.com* ⊗ *Mon.–Wed. 10–6, Thurs. and Fri. 10–8, Sat. 10–7, Sun. noon–6* Ⓜ *Bay.*

FOOD

FOOD SHOPS **Pusateri's.** From humble beginnings as a Little Italy produce stand, Pusateri's has grown into Toronto's deluxe supermarket, with in-house-prepared foods, local and imported delicacies, and desserts and breads from the city's best bakers. ✉ *57 Yorkville Ave., at Bay St., Yorkville, Toronto, Ontario, Canada* ☎ *416/785–9100* ⊕ *www.pusateris.com* ⊗ *Mon.–Wed., Sat. 8–8, Thurs. and Fri 8–9, Sun 8–7* Ⓜ *Bay.*

JEWELRY

Cartier. The famous jewel box caters to Toronto's elite and has a good selection of the jewelry designer's creations, including the triple-gold-band Trinity Ring and the diamond-studded Tortue Watch. ✉ *131 Bloor St. W, at Avenue Rd., Yorkville, Toronto, Ontario, Canada* ☎ *416/413–4929* ⊕ *www.cartier.com* ⊗ *Mon.–Sat. 10–6* Ⓜ *Bay.*

★ **Fabrice.** The owner of this shop has a good eye for pearls, semiprecious stones, and gold and silver designs. She lives in Paris and ships one-of-a-kind pieces from France and other fashion capitals to the delight of discerning Torontonians. ✉ *55 Avenue Rd., in Hazelton Lanes, Yorkville, Toronto, Ontario, Canada* ☎ *416/967–6590* ⊕ *www.fabricetoronto. com* ⊗ *Mon.–Sat. 10–6, Sun. noon–5* Ⓜ *Bay.*

Royal De Versailles. Don't let the front-door security scare you away from some of the most innovatively classic jewelry designs in town. ✉ *101 Bloor St. W, at St. Thomas St., Yorkville, Toronto, Ontario, Canada* ☎ *416/967–7201* ⊗ *Tues.–Sat. 10:30–5* Ⓜ *Bay.*

Tiffany & Co. Perfect for breakfast or any other time, it's still the ultimate for variety and quality in classic jewelry. ✉ *85 Bloor St. W, at Bay St., Yorkville, Toronto, Ontario, Canada* ☎ *416/921–3900, 800/265–1251* ⊕ *www.tiffany.ca* ⊗ *Mon.–Wed. 10–7, Thurs. and Fri. 10–8, Sat. 10–6, Sun. noon–5* Ⓜ *Bay.*

CLOTHING

SWIMWEAR **Shan.** Montréal designer Chantal Levesque founded this label in 1985, and now stocks locations in more than 20 countries with her creative couture swimwear, swimwear accessories and wraps. There's a separate collection for men. ✉ *38 Avenue Rd., at Prince Arthur Ave., Yorkville, Toronto, Ontario, Canada* ☎ *416/961–7426* ⊕ *www.shan. ca* ⊗ *Mon.–Wed. and Sat. 10–6, Thurs. and Fri. 10–7, Sun. noon–5* Ⓜ *Bay or Museum.*

KITCHENWARE AND TABLETOP

William Ashley. Ashley's has an extensive collection of china patterns that range from Wedgwood to Kate Spade and can often secure those it doesn't carry. Crystal and china are beautifully displayed. Prices are decent—and sales frequent—on expensive names such as Waterford. The store is happy to pack and ship all over the world. ✉ *55 Bloor St. W, at Bay St., Yorkville, Toronto, Ontario, Canada* ☎ *416/964–2900* ⊕ *www.williamashley.com* ⊗ *Mon.–Wed. and Sat. 10–6, Thurs. and Fri. 10–7:30, Sun. noon–5* Ⓜ *Bay.*

MUSIC

Song & Script. Broadway musicals are this store's specialty, and it carries a huge range of songbooks and CDs. You can also find classical and pop sheet music. Personal service has been the key since it opened in 1964, and if what you're after isn't in stock, the staff will happily find and order it for you. The shop is in the Cumberland Terrace shopping center; the closest entrance is on Bay Street. ⊠ *2 Bloor St. W, at Yonge St., Yorkville, Toronto, Ontario, Canada* ☎ *416/923–3044* ⊕ *www.songandscript.ca* ☉ *Weekdays 9–6, Sat. 9:30–6, Sun. noon–5* Ⓜ *Bay.*

> **POSH PICNICKING IN YORKVILLE**
>
> Designer labels and swish restaurants aside, Yorkville is a foodie's paradise. Browse a wide array of fine cheeses in All the Best Fine Foods, the impressive delicatessen at Pusateri's, and the dazzlingly diverse salad bar at Whole Foods, then park yourself in one of Cumberland Street's many green spots for a picnic and people-watching.

SHOES

Brown's. The excellent selection of shoes here can make your heart race. You'll find the latest punky Steve Maddens next to a vampish Manolo Blahnik. Brown's also carries handbags and boots. ⊠ *55 Avenue Rd., in Hazelton Lanes, Yorkville, Toronto, Ontario, Canada* ☎ *416/968–1806* ☉ *Mon.–Wed., Fri., and Sat. 10–6, Thurs 10–7, Sun 12–5* Ⓜ *Bay.*

David's. The collection is always elegant, if somewhat subdued—designers usually include Marc Jacobs, Kate Spade, Salvatore Ferragamo, Lorenzo Banfi, Christian Louboutin, Manolo Blahnik, Jimmy Choo, and Chloe. ⊠ *66 Bloor St. W, at Bay St., Yorkville, Toronto, Ontario, Canada* ☎ *416/920–1000* ⊕ *www.davidsfootwear.com* ☉ *Mon.–Wed. and Sat. 9:30–6:30, Thurs. and Fri. 9:30–8, Sun. noon–6* Ⓜ *Bay.*

Specchio. This is the place for fine Italian shoes and boots on the cutting edge of style, for every season. The store always seems to have your size in the back. ⊠ *1240 Bay St., at Cumberland St., Yorkville, Toronto, Ontario, Canada* ☎ *416/961–7989* ⊕ *www.specchioshoes. com* ☉ *Mon.–Wed. 10:30–6:30, Thurs. and Fri. 10:30–8, Sat. 10–6, Sun. noon–6* Ⓜ *Bay.*

SPORTING GOODS

★ **Nike.** The store's two floors display everything the famous brand-name has to offer, from athletic equipment to sneakers. ⊠ *110 Bloor St. W, at Bellair St., Yorkville, Toronto, Ontario, Canada* ☎ *416/921–6453* ⊕ *www.nike.com* ☉ *Mon.–Fri. 10–8, Sat. 10–7, Sun. 11–6* Ⓜ *Bay.*

DUNDAS SQUARE AREA

Dundas Square is the go-to place for chain stores like Gap, Zara, Roots, and Aritzia, electronics giants Future Shop and Best Buy, and cheap souvenir shops, which line Yonge Street to the north. The mammoth Eaton Centre shopping mall, which opens up into the square, has more than 230 stores (Coach, Banana Republic, and the Apple Store, to name a few) and is anchored by The Bay and Sears at either end.

DEPARTMENT STORES AND SHOPPING CENTERS

Fodor's Choice ★ **Eaton Centre.** This block-long complex with exposed industrial-style ceilings is anchored at its northern end (Dundas Street) by Sears, and a Times Square–style media tower on top of a gigantic anchor store, Sweden's popular H&M. Across the street from the southern end is Canadian department store The Bay. ■ TIP→ Prices at Eaton Centre increase with altitude—Level 1 offers popularly priced merchandise, Level 2 is directed to the middle-income shopper, and Level 3 sells more expensive fashion and luxury goods. The complex is bordered by Yonge Street on the east and James Street and Trinity Square on the west. ⊠ *220 Yonge St., Dundas Square Area, Toronto, Ontario, Canada* ☎ *416/598–8560* ⊕ *www.torontoeatoncentre.com* ⊙ *Weekdays 10–9, Sat. 9:30–7, Sun. 11–6* Ⓜ *Dundas, Queen.*

CLOTHING

MEN'S AND WOMEN'S CLOTHING **Danier Leather.** Suede and leather street wear and dressy attire, made in Canada from the finest hides, are the draw here. The latest trends are up front but bargains can be found in the back. There are four locations and an outlet branch around the city, check their Web site for locations. ⊠ *218 Yonge St., at Queen, Dundas Square Area, Toronto, Ontario, Canada* ☎ *416/598–1159* ⊕ *www.danier.com* ⊙ *Mon.–Fri. 9–9, Sat. 9:30–7, Sun. 11–6* Ⓜ *Queen.*

Urban Outfitters. The young and trendy scan the racks here for the latest "it" piece. Prices are comparatively high considering the clothes' often low quality. Don't miss the quirky, modern housewares and oddball coffee-table books. ⊠ *235 Yonge St. W, north of Queen St., Dundas Square Area, Toronto, Ontario, Canada* ☎ *416/214–1466* ⊕ *www. urbanoutfitters.com* ⊙ *Mon.–Sat. 10-9, Sun 11–7pm* Ⓜ *Dundas, Queen.*

GREATER TORONTO

ROSEDALE

One of Toronto's most exclusive neighborhoods, Rosedale is the city's best place to find upscale antiques and interiors shops, such as Absolutely, purveyor of French-provincial wares. If the thought of freight charges dissuades you from serious spending, you can take home packable gourmet food from All the Best or accessories from Hollace Cluny or Putti.

ANTIQUES AND INTERIORS

Absolutely. A mixture of whimsical trinkets as well as English campaign furniture and French architects' drafting tables are sold at this shop. There's also an extensive collection of antique boxes made of materials ranging from horn to shagreen (a type of leather). ⊠ *1132 Yonge St., at MacPherson Ave., Greater Toronto, Toronto, Ontario, Canada* ☎ *416/324–8351* ⊕ *www.absolutelyinc.com* ⊙ *Mon.–Sat. 10–6* Ⓜ *Rosedale.*

Belle Époque. Find very French, very Euro-pop modern furnishings here, especially colorful, mirrored, and laquered furniture. Its slogan is "edgy euro . . . be hip on a budget," and in addition to home decor and garden ornaments, it also sells fashion accessories. ⊠ *1066 Yonge*

St., at Roxborough St., Greater Toronto, Toronto, Ontario, Canada ☏ *416/925–0066* ⊕ *www.belleepoque.ca* ⊙ *Mon.–Sat. noon–6:30* Ⓜ *Rosedale.*

Putti. Sort through shabby-chic European and domestic antiques and reproduction furniture and home accessories in shades of pastels, white, silver, and gold, as well as bath and garden products at this luxurious store. Prices are a bit steep. ⊠ *1104 Yonge St., at Roxborough St., Rosedale, Greater Toronto, Toronto, Ontario, Canada* ☏ *416/972–7652* ⊙ *Mon.–Sat. 10–6, Sun. noon–5* Ⓜ *Rosedale.*

FOOD

FOOD SHOPS **All the Best Fine Foods.** Stop here for imported cheeses and good local breads and pastries, as well as high-quality prepared foods and condiments. Locally made goodies include Summer Kitchen preserves, Soma chocolate, and Kozlick's mustard. ■ TIP→ One of Toronto's largest LCBOs (the province-controlled liquor store) is a half-block north, making this an especially convenient picnic-supply stop. ⊠ *1099 Yonge St., at Marlborough Ave., Rosedale, Greater Toronto, Toronto, Ontario, Canada* ☏ *416/928–3330* ⊕ *www.allthebestfinefoods.com* ⊙ *Weekdays 8–7, Sat. 8:30–6, Sun. 10–5* Ⓜ *Summerhill.*

HOME DECOR AND FURNISHINGS

The Art Shoppe. The block-long, two-story shop is chock-full of eclectic highbrow furniture ranging from antique Louis XV armoires to modern Italian leather sofas, artfully arranged in multiple museumlike showrooms. ⊠ *2131 Yonge St., just south of Eglinton Ave., Greater Toronto, Toronto, Ontario, Canada* ☏ *416/487–3211* ⊕ *www.theartshoppe.com* ⊙ *Mon.–Wed., Fri., and Sat. 9:30–6, Thurs. 9:30–9* Ⓜ *Eglinton.*

Hollace Cluny. Mid-century modern is the focus of this home shop that carries Knoll and other clean-lined furnishings and accents. ⊠ *1070 Yonge St., at Roxborough St., Rosedale, Greater Toronto, Toronto, Ontario, Canada* ☏ *416/968–7894* ⊕ *www.hollacecluny.ca* ⊙ *Mon.–Sat. 10–6* Ⓜ *Rosedale.*

SHOES

Mephisto. These walking shoes have been around since the 1960s and are made entirely from natural materials. Passionate walkers swear by them and claim they never, ever wear out—even on cross-Europe treks. ⊠ *1177 Yonge St., at Summerhill Ave., Greater Toronto, Toronto, Ontario, Canada* ☏ *416/968–7026* ⊕ *www.mephisto-toronto. com* ⊙ *Mon.–Wed., Sat. 10–6, Thu. and Fri. 10–7, Sun. noon–5* Ⓜ *Summerhill.*

RONCESVALLES VILLAGE AND LITTLE PORTUGAL

The main drag in Roncesvalles Village, an upper-middle-class neighborhood near High Park, is lined with unique bookstores, clothing shops, restaurants, and cafés, and vestiges of a once-dominant Polish community. Little Portugal, near Queen West and Little Italy, is evolving, with hip vintage stores and galleries popping up monthly on and near the uber-cool Ossington strip.

ARTS AND CRAFTS GALLERIES

LE Gallery. Work by contemporary and edgy emerging and "mid-career" artists are on display here. Owner/director Wil Kucey's taste for graffiti and street art is apparent in many of the shows. ✉ *1183 Dundas St. W, Little Portugal, Greater Toronto, Toronto, Ontario, Canada* ☎ *416/532–8467* ⊕ *le-gallery.ca* ⊙ *Wed.–Sun. noon–6* Ⓜ *505 Dundas streetcar.*

Olga Korper Gallery. Many important Canadian and international artists, such as Lynne Cohen, Paterson Ewen, John McEwen, and Reinhard Reitzenstein, are represented by this trailblazing yet accessible gallery, which displays art from the 1960s on. It's a good place for contemporary collectors and art enthusiasts alike. ✉ *17 Morrow Ave., off Dundas St. W., Greater Toronto, Toronto, Ontario, Canada* ☎ *416/538–8220* ⊕ *www.olgakorpergallery.com* ⊙ *Tues.–Sat. 10–6* Ⓜ *Dundas West, then streetcar east.*

CLOTHING

Red Canoe. Canadiana and aviation-themed clothing and accessories at this unique shop include RCAF (Royal Canadian Air Force) hats and jackets, '70s retro CBC (Canadian Broadcasting Corporation) tees and messenger bags, and beaded beaver-pelt-lined moose-hide moccasins handmade in northern Saskatchewan. Red Canoe merchandise is also sold in Pearson Airport, Kensington Market's Blue Banana, and Queen West's Design Republic. ✉ *1356 Dundas St. W, at Rusholme Rd., Little Portugal, Greater Toronto, Toronto, Ontario, Canada* ☎ *416/205–1271* ⊕ *www.redcanoebrands.com* ⊙ *Weekdays 9–5* Ⓜ *505 Dundas streetcar.*

Virginia Johnson. This Toronto designer, well known for her simple and distinctively illustrated printed textiles, first paints her simple, inspired-by-nature designs (animals, flowers) with watercolors and then has them silk-screened or block-printed onto the clothing, shawls, and home textiles you see displayed in this cheery boutique. Her collections can be found all over the world: in Barney's in NYC and Japan and in the UK's Fenwick's. ✉ *132 Ossington St., at Dundas St. W, Little Portugal, Greater Toronto, Toronto, Ontario, Canada* ☎ *416/516–3366* ⊕ *www. virginiajohnson.com* ⊙ *Tues.–Sat. 11–6* Ⓜ *501 Queen or 505 Dundas streetcar.*

VINTAGE
CLOTHING
I Miss You. A new addition to the up-and-coming Ossington Street area in 2008, Julie Yoo's immaculately restored picks in this upscale vintage shop, which she finds at estate sales and auctions, include familiar names such as Pucci, Dior, and Yves Saint Laurent, as well as other random treasures from the 1940s, '50s, and '60s. Accessorize with an Hermès scarf, a pair of gold pin-up heels, or a snakeskin clutch. ✉ *63 Ossington Ave., at Queen St. W, Little Portugal, Greater Toronto, Toronto, Ontario, Canada* ☎ *416/916–7021* ⊕ *imissyouvintage.avl.1stdibs.com* ⊙ *Tues.–Sat. noon–6, Sun. noon–5. Extended summer hours open Fri. and Sat. till 7 pm, Sun. till 6 pm.* ⊙ *Monday* Ⓜ *King, then streetcar 508 west.*

YONGE AND EGLINTON

Jokingly called "Young and Eligible," this northerly nabe is a somewhat sterile but lively high-rise hot spot for chain stores, movie megaplexes, and Irish pubs.

CLOTHING

CHILDREN'S CLOTHING **Hatley.** This company began as a cottage business in rural Quebec 20 years ago, with a line of aprons depicting cute farm animals. Now this mainly children's boutique is stocked with quirky, nature-inspired clothing covered in insects, animals, trees, and flowers—designs inspired by the Canadian wilderness. ⊠ *2648 Yonge St., at Craighurst Ave., Greater Toronto, Toronto, Ontario, Canada* ☎ *416/486–4141* ⊕ *www. hatleystore.com* ⊙ *Mon.–Sat. 10–6, Sun. noon–5* Ⓜ *Either Lawrence or Eglington, then 97 Bus.*

WOMEN'S CLOTHING
★ **Want.** With its inventory direct from Los Angeles, Want has goods you probably won't come across elsewhere in Toronto. The focus is on flirty dresses, which run from fun and sporty to black-tie, in bold colors and prints. ⊠ *1454 Yonge St., at St. Clair St., Greater Toronto, Toronto, Ontario, Canada* ☎ *416/934–9268* ⊕ *www.want.ca* ⊙ *Weekdays 10–7, Sat. 10–6, Sun. noon–5* Ⓜ *St. Clair.*

SPORTING GOODS

Sporting Life. The first off the mark with the latest sportswear trends, this is the place to get couture labels like Juicy, La Coste, and Burberry—or to snag snowboard gear and poll the staff for advice on where to use it. A second "bikes and boards store" is down Yonge Street. ⊠ *2665 Yonge St., north of Eglinton Ave., Greater Toronto, Toronto, Ontario, Canada* ☎ *416/485–1611* ⊕ *www.sportinglife.ca* ⊙ *Weekdays 9:30–9, Sat. 9–6, Sun. 10–6* Ⓜ *Eglinton.*

THE DANFORTH, LESLIEVILLE, AND THE BEACH

The Danforth, along Danforth Avenue (the eastern continuation of Bloor Street) has a mishmash of health-conscious stores like the Big Carrot, yoga studios, low-key pubs, and one-off clothing and novelty stores. Take the Bloor subway line to Broadview or Chester.

Along Queen Street East are the neighborhoods of Leslieville—a bustling thoroughfare once noted for antiques and junk shops where hip clothing boutiques and brunch spots are now popping up—and the Beach, a relaxed upper-middle-class hood with casual-clothing stores, gift and antiques shops, and bars and restaurants, all a few blocks from Lake Ontario beachfront.

FOOD

FOOD SHOPS **Big Carrot Natural Food Market.** This large health-food supermarket carries good selections of organic produce, health and beauty aids, and vitamins. There's a vegetarian café and organic juice bar on-site and freshly prepared foods for takeout. ⊠ *348 Danforth Ave., at Hampton Ave., Greater Toronto, Toronto, Ontario, Canada* ☎ *416/466–2129* ⊕ *www. thebigcarrot.ca* ⊙ *Weekdays 9–9, Sat. 9–8, Sun. 11–6* Ⓜ *Chester.*

Suckers Candy Co. It's like stepping into a comic book. More than 500 different suckers; retro and novelty candy from Canada, the United States, and the United Kingdom; gourmet cotton candy in eight different flavors; and custom-made loot bags and baskets will assuage

6

any sweet tooth. This place is fun for all ages and open until midnight on Saturday. ✉ *450 Danforth Ave., at Chester Ave., Greater Toronto, Toronto, Ontario, Canada* ☎ *416/405–8946* ⊕ *www.suckerscandyco. com* ⊗ *Mon.–Wed., 10–10, Fri. 10 am–midnight, Sat. 10 am–1 am, Sun. 11–10. Hours vary by season, call to confirm.* Ⓜ *Chester.*

HOME DÉCOR AND FURNISHINGS

Seagull Classics Ltd. Victorian and Tiffany-style lamps as well as art deco–inspired forms are among this store's unusual selection of lighting, as well as some furniture. ✉ *1974 Queen St. E, at Waverley St., Greater Toronto, Toronto, Ontario, Canada* ☎ *416/690–5224* ⊕ *www. seagullclassics.com* ⊗ *Mon.–Wed. and weekends 10–6, Thurs. and Fri. 10–9* Ⓜ *Queen, then streetcar 501 east.*

KITCHENWARE AND TABLETOP

The Cook's Place. Even the most cosmopolitan chef should find something to take home in this immense selection of cookware, including baking pans and hard-to-find gadgets and utensils. Don't miss the fascinating "wall of stuff." ✉ *501 Danforth Ave., Greater Toronto, Toronto, Ontario, Canada* ☎ *416/461–5211* ⊕ *www.thecooksplace. com* ⊗ *Mon.–Wed., Sat. 10–6, Thu.–Fri. 10–9, Sun. 1–5* Ⓜ *Chester.*

LITTLE ITALY

Primarily a destination for its Italian eateries, cafés, and gelato shops and young-leaning bars, Little Italy also has a few gift shops, bookstores, and the odd specialty store.

CLOTHING

WOMEN'S CLOTHING

Lilliput Hats. Wide-brimmed hats decorated with silk orchids in vibrant shades, fascinators, close-fitting cloches, a practical straw hat that packs flat, outrageous or tailored hats—all can be found in handmade, off-the-rack, or to-order head coverings. Karyn Gingrais opened here in 1990 and has a huge following. Brides-to-be and their moms are well served. ✉ *462 College St., at Bathurst St., Little Italy, Toronto, Ontario, Canada* ☎ *416/536–5933* ⊕ *www.lilliputhats.com* ⊗ *Weekdays 10–6, Sat. 11–6, Sun. by appt. or chance.* Ⓜ *Queen's Park, then streetcar 506 west.*

MUSIC

Soundscapes. Crammed with pop, rock, jazz, blues, folk, ambient, psychedelic, garage, avant-garde, and electronic titles, this shop satisfies hipsters as well as fans of early Americana. Selections and organization reflect a love of music and its ever-expanding history. ✉ *572 College St., at Manning Ave., Little Italy, Toronto, Ontario, Canada* ☎ *416/537–1620* ⊕ *www.soundscapesmusic.com* ⊗ *Daily 10 am–11 pm* Ⓜ *College or Queen's Park, then streetcar 506 west.*

Side Trips from Toronto

WORD OF MOUTH

Niagara-on-the-Lake has bicycle tours of the wineries. Book a bed-and-breakfast so you have a place to rest your head should you end up a little tipsy . . . If you like the outdoors, Algonquin Park is beautiful. Take a camera. . . . And Niagara Falls, while definitely touristy, is still pretty magnificent.

—cigarbas

SIDE TRIPS FROM TORONTO

TOP REASONS TO GO

★ **The Falls:** Niagara Falls' amazing display of natural power is Ontario's top attraction. See them from both the U.S. and Canadian sides.

★ **Shakespeare and Shaw:** A couple of long-dead British playwrights have managed to make two Ontario towns boom from May through October with the Shakespeare Festival in Stratford and the Shaw Festival in Niagara-on-the-Lake.

★ **Wineries:** The Niagara Peninsula has an unusually good microclimate for growing grapes; most of the more than 60 wineries have tastings.

★ **The great outdoors:** Ski at resorts north of Toronto; canoe backcountry rivers in Algonquin Provincial Park; hike or bike the Niagara-to-Lake-Huron Bruce Trail or the Niagara Parkway along the Niagara River.

★ **Edible Ontario:** Niagara-on-the-Lake and Stratford are both renowned for their skilled chefs who serve culinary masterpieces created with farm-fresh ingredients.

1 Niagara Falls. South of Toronto near the U.S. border, the thundering falls are an impressive display of nature's power.

2 The Niagara Wine Region. The temperate Niagara region bordering Lake Ontario is the ideal growing climate for all kinds of produce, including grapes. Wineries stretch along the shores of Lake Ontario south of Toronto to the pretty Victorian-style town of Niagara-on-the-Lake, at the junction of Lake Ontario and the Niagara River.

3 Stratford. An acclaimed Shakespeare Festival brings this rural town alive from April through October. Overwhelmingly popular, it has become Stratford's raison d'etre, with a multitude of inns and locavore restaurants growing up around it. Frequent outdoor music and arts festivals color the squares and parks all summer.

4 Southern Georgian Bay. North of Toronto is a series of lakes and summer homes, ski resorts, and the small towns that serve them.

5 The Muskokas. This area north of the city is known for its lakes and vacation cottages. Tackle the four-hour drive to Algonquin Provincial Park and you're rewarded with pristine forested land for canoeing, camping, and moose-spotting.

ONTARIO

Algonquin Provincial Park • 60
124
69 Parry Sound
11
60
Huntsville
The Massasauga Provincial Park
Dorset
5
400
Haliburton
Bracebridge
118
11
Queen Elizabeth II Wildlands Provincial Park
Georgian Bay Islands National Park
Gravenhurst
Penetanguishene
Midland 12
11
35
Nottawasaga Bay
93
Orillia
Lake Simcoe
12
4
Collingwood
Barrie
7
35
400
89
12
48
115
Newmarket
9
404
35
Richmond Hill
Markham
Oshawa
401
10
407
401
Brampton
Toronto
Lake Ontario
403 Mississauga
QEW
Guelph
401
407
Oakville
Cambridge
8
Burlington
Niagara-on-the-Lake
CANADA
USA
24
Hamilton
St. Catharines
2
Niagara Pkwy.
104
403
Grimsby
QEW
55
NEW YORK
Brantford
Beamsville
Vineland
Niagara Falls (US)
6
Welland
Niagara Falls
78
24
3
140
90
Port Dover
Buffalo
Lake Erie
90 219

GETTING ORIENTED

Wedged between three Great Lakes—Ontario, Huron, and Erie—and peppered with thousands of smaller lakes, southern Ontario is a fertile area of farmland, wineries, forests, and waterways. Within a two-to-four-hour drive north, west, or southwest of Toronto are small towns, beaches, ski resorts, and rural farmland that feel light-years away from the city lights. Toronto sits at the eastern edge of Southern Ontario, a region that makes up no more than 15% of the province but is home to nearly 95% of the population and most of its major attractions. Head north and you hit the Muskokas and Algonquin, west for Stratford, and south–southwest to Niagara Falls and the Niagara Wine Region.

7

NIAGARA FALLS

Niagara Falls has inspired visitors for centuries, and the allure hasn't dimmed for those who want to marvel at this natural wonder.

Above: Niagara Falls is as dramatic by night as by day; top right: Visitors get close to the falls on the *Maid of the Mist*; bottom right: Parks and walking trails surround the falls on the American side.

Missionary and explorer Louis Hennepin described the falls in 1678 as "an incredible Cataract or Waterfall which has no equal." Nearly two centuries later, Charles Dickens declared, "I seemed to be lifted from the earth and to be looking into Heaven."

Countless daredevils have been lured here. In 1859, 100,000 spectators watched as the French tightrope walker Charles Blondin successfully crossed Niagara Gorge, from the American to the Canadian side, on a three-inch-thick rope. From the early 18th century, dozens went over in boats and barrels. Nobody survived until 1901, when schoolteacher Annie Taylor emerged from her barrel and asked, "Did I go over the falls yet?" Stunts were outlawed in 1912.

The depiction of the thundering cascades in the 1953 Marilyn Monroe film *Niagara* is largely responsible for creating modern-day tourism. And though the lights of the arcades, tacky souvenir shops, and casinos shine garishly bright for some, views of the falls themselves are unspoiled.

NIGHT LIGHTS

See **Fireworks Over the Falls** on Fridays, Sundays, and holidays at 10 pm from mid-May to early September (and on Friday during the Winter Festival of Lights).

Between early November and late January, the **Winter Festival of Lights** illuminates the Niagara Parkway, with 125 animated lighting displays and 3 million tree and ground lights. ⊕ *www. wfol.com.*

WAYS TO EXPLORE

Whatever angle you choose to view the falls from, remember to bring your camera. *See Exploring for full details on some tours.*

By Air: Niagara Helicopters Ltd. does 12-minute sightseeing flights over the whirlpool, gorge, and all three falls, plus winery trips. ⊠ *3731 Victoria Ave., Ontario* ☎ *905/357–5672, 800/281–8034* ⊕ *www.niagarahelicopters.com* ✉ *C$132/ person.*

The **Whirlpool Aero Car** cable car crosses the gorge over the Niagara River whirlpool.

By Boat: The **Maid of the Mist** is an oldie but a goody. Adrenaline-fueled Whirlpool Jet Boat Tours in Niagara-on-the-Lake plow headfirst into the Class-V Niagara River rapids on an hour-long ride.

By Bus: Take an authentic, red London double-decker bus with **Double Deck Tours.** Fares include admission to Journey Behind the Falls, *Maid of the Mist*, and the Whirlpool Aero Car. Tickets and departures are at the *Maid of the Mist* building. ☎ *905/374–7423* ⊕ *www.doubledecktours.com* ✉ *C$68 online* ⊙ *Mid-May–mid-Oct. at 11 am; also 10:15 am and 1:15 pm in July and Aug.*

By Foot: Stroll the Niagara Parkway promenade, stand on the Table Rock Centre terrace, and walk over the Rainbow Bridge. The **White Water Walk** is the closest you'll get to the rapids from land; **Journey Behind the Falls** is a walk through tunnels behind the falls.

Worth a border crossing, **Cave of the Winds** takes you 175 feet into the gorge to an observation deck less than 20 feet from thundering Bridal Veil falls. ⊠ *Departures from Goat Island, Niagara Falls State Park, New York, USA* ☎ *716/278–1730* ⊕ *www.niagarafallsstatepark.com* ✉ *$11* ⊙ *May–Oct.; tours start at 9 am.*

IN ONE DAY

If you have only a day in Niagara Falls, walk the waterfront promenade and go on a *Maid of the Mist* tour. (Plan for wet shins and shoes.) Also consider the Whirlpool Aero Car, a cable-car ride over the whirlpool, or the Whitewater Walk, to see the rapids up close. Dinner within view of the falls, which are colorfully lit at night, is a relaxing end to a full day.

7

THE AMERICAN SIDE

Canada has the superior views and a more developed waterfront, with better restaurants. In contrast, the American waterfront is lined with parks, ideal for hiking and picnicking. Because you're behind the falls here, rather than facing them, views are limited. Stick to Canada for most of your visit, but if you have more time, cross the Rainbow Bridge on foot to get close to Bridal Veil Falls on a Cave of the Winds tour from Goat Island.

WINE REGION KNOW-HOW

WHAT'S IN A VQA

Ontario may not be famed for its wines—yet—but the Niagara Peninsula alone has more than more than 70 wineries and has been producing wine commercially since the early 1970s. Four decades on, the region is coming into its own with some of the world's best wines of origin.

Canadian wine is regulated by the Vintners Quality Alliance, a government-sanctioned wine authority whose strict standards are on par with regulatory agencies in France and Italy. Many Niagara wineries proudly declare their vintages VQA; in fact, 65% of all VQA wines in Ontario are Niagara wines. To be deemed VQA is no small honor: Wines must meet rigorous standards—including being made entirely from fresh, quality-approved Ontario-grown grapes (no concentrates) and approved grape varieties, passing laboratory testing, and approval by an expert tasting panel prior to release. Look for the VQA stamp on the label.

The position of the Niagara appellation, wedged between Lake Ontario and the Niagara Escarpment, creates a microclimate that regulates ground and air temperature and allows for successful grape-growing (today more than 30 varietals) in an otherwise too-cold province. Winds off Lake Ontario are directed back by the escarpment, preventing cold air from settling. Heat stored in lake waters in summer keeps ground temperatures warmer longer into winter. In spring, the cold waters keep the grounds from warming too fast, protecting buds from late-spring frosts. Some say that the slightly colder climate means a more complex-tasting grape. Indisputably it *does* provide perfect conditions for producing some of the world's best ice wine.

NIAGARA WINE TOURING BASICS

THE ONTARIO WINE ROUTE
Niagara wineries along the Ontario Wine Route are well marked by blue signs between Grimsby and Niagara Falls.

■TIP→ For a full map of the wine route, pick up the free Official Guide to the Wineries of Ontario, updated annually and available at wineries and tourist attractions or directly from the Wine Council. ☎ 905/684–8070 ⊕ www.winesofontario.org.

TIMING AND COSTS
Most wineries are open year-round, with limited hours in winter. Tastings begin between 10 and noon. Reservations may be needed for tours in summer.

Tastings usually cost C$1–C$2 per wine, or up to C$7 for more expensive wines. The larger wineries do regular public tours; at smaller operations you may be able to arrange a tour in advance. Tasting and/or tour fees are often waived if you buy a bottle of wine.

ORGANIZED TOURS
Crush on Niagara wine-tour packages include overnight stays, meals, and winery tours. ☎ 905/562–3373, 866/408–9463 ⊕ www.crushtours.com.

Grape and Wine Tours runs day trips and one- or two-night wine-tour packages. ☎ 905/562–9449, 866/562–9449 ⊕ www.grapeandwinetours.com.

Niagara Wine Tours International leads guided bike, van, and coach tours along the Wine Route and has bike rentals. ☎ 905/468–1300, 800/680–7006 ⊕ www.niagaraworldwinetours.com.

Zoom Leisure. One of the most popular bike rental stores in the area because of its convenient location, Zoom Leisure has organized cycling/winery tours and custom guided and self-guided tours. ✉ 431 Mississauga St., Niagara-on-the-Lake, Ontario ☎ 905/468–2366, 866/811–6993 ⊕ www.zoomleisure.com.

EVENTS
The Niagara Wine Festival group organizes three big events in Niagara. The largest, with an annual half million attendees is the eponymous, 10-day **Niagara Wine Festival**, in September, celebrating the grape harvest. The three-week **Niagara Ice Wine Festival**, in January, is a nod to Niagara's specialty, ice wine. The three-weekend **Niagara New Vintage Festival**, in June, is a wine-and-culinary event. ☎ 905/688–0212 ⊕ www.niagarawinefestival.com.

ONTARIO'S ICE WINES: SWEET SIPPING

Ontario is the world's leading producer of ice wine. It's produced from ripe grapes left on the vine into the winter. When grapes start to freeze, most of the water in them solidifies, resulting in a fructose-laden, aromatic, and flavorful center. Ice-wine grapes must be picked at freezing temperatures before sunrise and basket-pressed immediately. By nature ice wine is sweet, and when well made it smells of dried fruits, apricots, and honey and has a long, refreshing finish. Vidal grapes are ideal for ice wine, due to their thick skin and resistance to cracking in subzero temperatures. The thin-skinned Riesling yields better results but is susceptible to cracking and ripens much later than Vidal Drink ice wine after dinner, with a not-too-sweet dessert, or alongside a strong cheese. Here in Niagara it also appears in unexpected places such as tea, martinis, chocolate, ice cream, French toast, and glazes for meat and seafood.

Left: A field of Pinot Noir grapes growing in the Niagara Wine Region. Above: Tasting Ice Wine at the Fielding Estate winery.

7

Updated by
Diana Ng

The rush of 700,000 gallons of water a second. The divinely sweet, crisp taste of ice wine. The tug of a fish hooked under a layer of ice. Sure, the big-city scene in Toronto delivers the hustle and bustle you came for, but escaping the city can transport you to another world. The struggle is choosing which world to visit first.

There's Niagara Falls, acres of local vineyards in Niagara-on-the-Lake and the surrounding Wine Region, or the whimsical Cottage Country, with its quiet towns, challenging ski slopes, and lakefront resorts. Two major theater events have long seasons with masterfully orchestrated plays. Or you can hit the outdoors on Bruce Trail, Canada's oldest and longest footpath, which winds from Niagara Falls to Tobermory 885 km (550 mi) north.

If superlatives are what you seek, the mesmerizing and deservedly hyped Niagara Falls, one of—or more technically, three of—the most famous waterfalls in the world, is Ontario's most popular attraction. Worth seeing at least once, it is truly beautiful (say what you will about the showy town behind it).

Oenophile trailblazers should consider Niagara's rapidly developing wine trail. The Niagara Escarpment, hugging Lake Ontario's western shores, is one of the most fertile growing areas in Canada. A lakeshore drive southwest of Toronto yields miles of vineyards and farm-to-table restaurants, culminating in the Victorian white-picket-fence town of Niagara-on-the-Lake, known for its amazing five-star restaurants and hotels and nearly-as-luxurious B&Bs.

Nourish your appreciation for the arts in and around Stratford. Two major theater events, the Stratford Festival and the Shaw Festival (in Niagara-on-the-Lake), have long seasons with masterfully orchestrated plays by William Shakespeare and George Bernard Shaw.

Both outdoors enthusiasts who want to "rough it" and soft-adventure seekers who yearn for a comfortable bed with the glow of a fireplace at night feel the lure of the nearly 3,000-acre Algonquin Provincial Park.

Sunday drivers find solace near Georgian Bay and in the Muskokas, part of Ontario's lake-smattered "Cottage Country," with quiet towns, challenging ski slopes, and waterfront resorts.

PLANNING

WHEN TO GO

With the exception of destinations like wineries and ski resorts, June through September is prime travel season: Stratford and Shaw festivals are in full swing, hours of operation are longer for most attractions, the mist coming from Niagara Falls is at its most refreshing, and patios are open almost everywhere, not to mention the obvious abundance of water activities and amusement parks.

That said, there's fun to be had in wintertime as well. While Muskoka cottage country, Stratford, and some parks in Algonquin become inaccessible ghost towns between November and April (the time most resorts schedule renovations and maintenance), ski resorts and wineries offer many packages and activities. Enjoy tours on and tastings of one of Ontario's most prized exports during Niagara's Icewine Festival, or enjoy the Canadian winter by snowboarding, skiing, ice fishing, and snowmobiling. Travel around the holiday season to take in the beautiful decorations, lights and special events.

GETTING HERE AND AROUND

AIR TRAVEL

Toronto's Pearson International Airport, 30 km (18 mi) north of downtown, is the obvious choice. Downtown Toronto's smaller Billy Bishop Toronto City Airport serves mostly Porter Airlines; it gets you Niagara-bound on the Gardiner Expressway in a matter of minutes. Hamilton International Airport is about halfway between Toronto and Niagara Falls. Buffalo Niagara International Airport is 30 mi from Niagara Falls, Ontario, but border crossings can add time to your trip. Or, if you are fortunate enough to have a private plane, some resorts in Muskoka have their own landing strip.

Air Travel Contacts Buffalo Niagara International Airport ☎ 716/630–6000 ⊕ www.buffaloairport.com. **Hamilton International Airport** ☎ 905/679–1999 ⊕ www.flyhi.ca. **Porter Airlines** ☎ 416/619–8622, 888/619–8622 ⊕ www.flyporter.com. **Toronto Pearson International Airport** ☎ 866/207–1690, 416/776–3000 ⊕ www.gtaa.com.

CAR TRAVEL

You can get by without a car in downtown Niagara Falls and Stratford if you book a hotel close to the action.

Avoid Toronto-area highways during weekday rush hours (6:30 to 9:30 am and 3:30 to 6:30 pm). Traffic between Toronto and Hamilton might crawl along at any hour.

Ontario's only toll road is the east–west Highway 407, north of Toronto. It's expensive (18¢–22¢ per kilometer) and has no tollbooths; you will be billed via mail if the system has your state's license plate information on file.

PLANNING YOUR TIME

Toronto is a great base to begin your explorations of Ontario.

One Day: In a long day you could see a matinee at the Shakespeare festival, hit a ski resort north of Toronto, visit a few Niagara Escarpment wineries, or—with some stamina—see Niagara Falls. All of these destinations require about four hours of driving time round-trip, not accounting for rush-hour traffic jams.

Two Days: A couple of days are sufficient to get a feel for Niagara Falls, Niagara-on-the-Lake, Stratford, or a Muskoka town or two. Alternatively, head up to Collingwood for an overnight snowboarding or skiing trip.

Four Days: You can decide between an intensive outdoorsy trip in the Algonquin area hiking, biking, camping, canoeing, and exploring; or, a relaxing tour of Niagara Falls and Niagara-on-the-lake, with some time spent at spas and wineries, biking, and hitting culinary hot spots.

One Week: Combine Stratford and Niagara, or really delve into the Niagara region. (A week is probably too much for just Niagara Falls or just Niagara-on-the-Lake.) Alternatively, you could spend some serious time communing with nature in Algonquin Park and meandering through quaint Muskoka and Georgian Bay towns.

The Ministry of Transportation has updates for roadwork and winter road conditions.

Car Contacts Ministry of Transportation ☎ 416/235–4686, 800/268–4686 ⊕ www.mto.gov.on.ca.

TRAIN TRAVEL

VIA Rail connects Toronto with Niagara Falls and Stratford. GO Transit, Toronto's commuter rail, has summer weekend service to Niagara Falls. Ontario Northland's Northlander line travels between Toronto and Bracebridge, Gravenhurst, Huntsville, and other northern points.

Train Contacts GO Transit ☎ 888/438–6646, 416/869–3200 ⊕ www.gotransit. com. **Ontario Northland** ☎ 800/461–8558 ⊕ www.ontarionorthland.ca. **VIA Rail** ☎ 888/842–7245 ⊕ www.viarail.ca.

RESTAURANTS

The dining in Stratford and Niagara-on-the-lake is enough to boost a whole other genre of tourism, as there are a number of outstanding restaurants thanks to many chefs being trained in reputable culinary schools in the area, and impeccably fresh ingredients from local farms. Produce, meats, cheeses, beers, and wine are all produced in Ontario, and some restaurants even have their own gardens, vineyards, or farms. In the immediate areas surrounding Niagara Falls, the dining is a little more lackluster, as views, convenience, and glamour take precedent over food, but there are great pubs and upscale restaurants. Reservations are always encouraged, if not essential.

HOTELS

Make reservations well in advance during summer and at ski areas in winter. Prices are higher in peak season and nearer to the tourist centers. In Niagara Falls, for example, hotel rates are determined by proximity to the falls. Taxes are seldom included in quoted prices, but rates sometimes include food, especially in more remote areas such as Muskoka, where many resorts offer meal plans.

Cottage rentals are available through local tourism boards or **At the Cottage.** ⊕ *www.atthecottage.com.*

BBCanada.com can help you locate a B&B and reserve a room. ☎ *800/239–1141* ⊕ *www.bbcanada.com.*

A comprehensive B&B guide listing about 250 establishments is published by the **Federation of Ontario Bed & Breakfast Accommodations.** ⊕ *www.fobba.com.*

Camping, in campgrounds or backcountry, is popular in summer and early fall, especially in the provincial parks to the north of Toronto.

WHAT IT COSTS IN CANADIAN DOLLARS					
	¢	$	$$	$$$	$$$$
Restaurants	under C$8	C$8–C$12	C$13–C$20	C$21–C$30	over C$30
Hotels	under C$75	C$75–C$125	C$126–C$175	C$176–C$250	over C$250

Restaurant prices are based on the median main course price at dinner. Hotel prices are for two people in a standard double room in high season, excluding service and 13% tax.

VISITOR INFORMATION

Ontario Parks ☎ *800/668–2746, 905/754–1958* ⊕ *www.ontarioparks. com.*

Ontario Tourism ☎ *800/668–2746, 905/754–1958* ⊕ *www.ontariotravel. net.*

Niagara Falls Tourism ☎ *800/563–2557* ⊕ *www.niagarafallstourism.com.*

Tourism Niagara ☎ *905/945–5444, 800/263–2988* ⊕ *www.tourismniagara. com.*

NIAGARA FALLS

130 km (81 mi) south of Toronto via the QEW (Queen Elizabeth Way).

Fodor'sChoice **Niagara Falls.** Although cynics have had a field day with Niagara Falls
★ (most memorably, Oscar Wilde called it "the second major disappointment of American married life"), most visitors are truly impressed. The falls are actually three cataracts: the American and Bridal Veil Falls in New York State, and the Horseshoe Falls in Ontario. In terms of sheer volume of water—more than 700,000 gallons per second in summer—Niagara is unsurpassed in North America.

On the Canadian side, you can get a far view of the American Falls and a close-up of the Horseshoe Falls. You can also park your car for the

Clifton Hill's food, shopping, games, rides, and other attractions will keep the whole family entertained.

day in any of several lots and hop onto one of the People Mover buses, which run continuously to all the sights along the river. If you want to get close to the foot of the falls, the *Maid of the Mist* boat takes you near enough to get soaked in the spray.

After experiencing the falls from the Canadian side, you can walk or drive across Rainbow Bridge to the U.S. side. On the American side you can park in the lot on Goat Island near the American Falls and walk along the path beside the Niagara River, which becomes more and more turbulent as it approaches the big drop-off of just over 200 feet.

The amusement parks and tacky souvenir shops that surround the falls attest to the area's history as a major tourist attraction. Most of the gaudiness is contained on Clifton Hill, Niagara Falls' Times Square. Despite these garish efforts to attract visitors, the landscaped grounds immediately bordering the falls are lovely and the beauty of the falls remains untouched.

One reason to spend the night here is to admire the falls illumination, which takes place every night of the year, from dusk until at least 10 pm (as late as 1 am during the summer). Even the most contemptuous observer will be mesmerized as the falls change from red to purple to blue to green to white, and finally all the colors of the rainbow in harmony. .

WHEN TO GO

Water-based falls tours operate only between mid-May and mid-September, and the summer weather combats the chilly falls mist. Fewer events take place in other seasons, and it's too cold in winter to linger on the promenade along the parkway next to the falls, but it's much easier to reserve a window-side table for two at a falls-view restaurant. Clifton Hill and most indoor attractions are open year-round. At any time of year it feels a few degrees cooler on the walkway near the falls.

GETTING HERE AND AROUND

Niagara Falls is easily accessible by car and train from Toronto. VIA Rail and GO (summer only) trains serve Niagara Falls, both stopping at the main rail station, not far from the falls. The nearest airports are in Toronto, Hamilton, and Buffalo, New York. It is possible to use public transportation and cabs to get around, but a car is more flexible and is recommended. There is no public transport between Niagara Falls and Niagara-on-the-Lake, 20 km (12 mi) north.

The four- to eight-lane Queen Elizabeth Way—better known as the QEW—runs from the U.S. border at Fort Erie through the Niagara region to Toronto.

PARKING In Niagara Falls, parking prices increase closer to the falls. It can be triple the price to park along the Niagara Parkway (C$15/day) than it is up the hill near Victoria Street (usually C$5/day). If you park up top, know that the walk down to the falls is a steep one. You might want to take a taxi back up, or hop aboard the Falls Incline Railway, a funicular that operates between the Table Rock Centre and Portage Road behind the Konica Minolta Tower. The trip takes about one minute and costs C$2.50.

SHUTTLES Niagara Transit's two Falls Shuttle lines travel along the Niagara Park-
AND PEOPLE way (late May–mid-October) as far north as the Whirlpool Aero Car
MOVERS entry area and the bus and train stations on Bridge Street and as far south as Marineland, as well as taking major routes through town along Fallsview Boulevard and Stanley Avenue, and past the QEW on Ferry Street/Lundy's Lane. A day pass is C$6, single-trip fare is C$3.50. You can pay the driver; exact fare is required. Otherwise, you can buy a ticket at the bus terminal, at ⊠ *4320 Bridge St., across from the VIA Rail train station.*

From mid-April to mid-October (10–5), air-conditioned People Mover buses travel on a loop route on the Niagara Parkway between the Table Rock Centre and the Whirlpool Aero Car parking lot (9 km [6 mi] north) and, from late June to early September, as far north as Queenston Heights Park, 15 km (9 mi) downriver. A day pass, available from Welcome Centres and at any booth on the system, is C$8 per person per day and includes the Falls Incline Railway. You can get on and off as many times as you wish at well-marked stops along the route.

FIRST THINGS FIRST

Start at the **Table Rock Centre** (⊠ *6650 Niagara Pkwy., about 1 km south of Murray Hill*) for a close-up of Horseshoe Falls. Here you can buy a Niagara Parks Great Gorge Adventure Pass, tickets for the People Mover, and do the Journey Behind the Falls and Niagara's Fury. At the end of the People Mover line, it's easy to hop aboard and do all of the falls-front sights in a northward direction. Starting with the *Maid of the Mist* or a Jet Boat Tour when you arrive is also a good way to get your feet wet—literally.

7

Both the People Mover and Falls Shuttle pick up frequently (every 20 minutes and 30 minutes, respectively) and both are seasonal, but the People Mover operates only between 10 and 5 and only on a limited route along the Niagara Parkway, whereas the Falls Shuttle runs from around 9 am to midnight and has a much more extensive route. If you don't have a car (or you want to avoid pricey Niagara Parkway parking) and you need to get to some farther-flung destinations, consider the Falls Shuttle. The People Mover is convenient for visiting the main Niagara Parks destinations along the Niagara Parkway and makes it easy to hit all of these in a day.

BORDER CROSSINGS
Everyone—including children and U.S. citizens—must have a passport or other approved travel document (e.g. a New York State–issued "enhanced" driver's license) to enter the U.S. Go to the Department of Homeland Security Web site (⊕ *www.dhs.gov*) for the latest information. Avoid crossing the border at high-traffic times, especially Friday and Saturday nights. The Canada Border Agency and the U.S. Customs and Border Protection list border wait times into Canada and into the U.S., respectively, online at ⊕ *www.cbsa-asfc.gc.ca/bwt-taf* and ⊕ *apps.cbp.gov/bwt*. Crossings are at the Peace Bridge (Fort Erie, ON–Buffalo, NY), the Queenston–Lewiston Bridge (Queenston, ON–Lewiston, NY), and the Rainbow Bridge (Niagara Falls, ON–Niagara Falls, NY).

DISCOUNTS AND DEALS

Pick up the free Save-A-Buck coupon booklet for discounts on various tours, attractions, and restaurants. ■TIP→ **Many attractions have significant online discounts and combination tickets.** Bundled passes are available through the tourism board, at Welcome Centres (foot of Clifton Hill and Murray Hill, near Maid of the Mist ticket booth, Table Rock Centre), and at most attractions' ticket windows.

The **Clifton Hill Fun Pass** incorporates entry to six of the better Clifton Hill attractions (including the SkyWheel, Ripley's Believe It or Not! Museum, and the Midway Combo Pass rides) for C$29.95 plus tax. The Midway Combo Pass (C$9.99 plus tax) includes two indoor thrill rides: Ghost Blasters and the FX Ride Theatre.

The **Niagara Falls and Great Gorge Adventure Pass** (C$45; available mid-April–late October) covers admission to Journey Behind the Falls, *Maid of the Mist*, White Water Walk, and Niagara's Fury, plus a number of discounts and two days of unlimited use of both the People Mover and the Falls Incline Railway. It's available from Niagara Parks, as is the **Winter Magic Pass** (C$28; available late October–mid-April), which includes Niagara's Fury, the Butterfly Conservatory, Journey Behind the Falls, and discount coupons.

TOURIST INFORMATION

The main Niagara Falls Tourism center is on Robinson Street near the Skylon Tower.

Open June through August, Welcome Centres are run by Niagara Parks and have tickets for and information about Niagara Parks sights, including People Mover and Falls Incline Railway passes and the Niagara Falls and Great Gorge Adventure Pass. Welcome Centre kiosks are at the

NIAGARA FALLS: PAST AND FUTURE

The story begins more than 10,000 years ago as a group of glaciers receded, diverting the waters of Lake Erie north into Lake Ontario. The force and volume of the water as it flowed over the Niagara Escarpment created the thundering cataracts. Erosion has been considerable since then, more than 7 mi in all, as the soft shale and sandstone of the escarpment have been washed away and the falls have receded. Diversions of the water for power generation have slowed the erosion somewhat, spreading the flow more evenly over the entire crestline of Horseshoe Falls. The erosion is now down to 1 foot or less per year.

At this rate—given effects of power generation and change in riverbed composition—geologists estimate it will be some 50,000 years before the majestic cascade is reduced to rapids somewhere near present-day Buffalo, 20 mi to the south.

foot of Clifton Hill, foot of Murray Hill, and near the *Maid of the Mist* ticket booth; a Welcome Centre booth is inside the Table Rock Centre.

ESSENTIALS

Discounts and Deals Clifton Hill Fun Pass ⊕ www.cliftonhill.com. **Save-A-Buck coupon booklet** ⊕ www.saveabuck.com.

Transportation Contacts GO Transit ☎ 888/438–6646, 416/869–3200 ⊕ www.gotransit.com. **Niagara Falls VIA Rail Canada Train Station** ✉ 4267 Bridge St., Niagara Falls, Ontario ☎ 888/842-7245. **Niagara Falls Transit** ✉ 4320 Bridge St., Niagara Falls, Ontario ☎ 905/356–1179 ⊕ www.niagarafalls. ca. **Peoplemover** ☎ 905/357–9340 ⊕ www.niagaraparks.ca. **VIA Rail** ☎ 888/842–7245 ⊕ www.viarail.ca.

Visitor Information Niagara Falls Tourism ✉ 5400 Robinson St., Niagara Falls, Ontario ☎ 905/356–6061, 800/563–2557 ⊕ www.niagarafallstourism.com. **Niagara Parks** ☎ 905/371–0254, 877/642–7275 ⊕ www.niagaraparks.com.

EXPLORING

TOP ATTRACTIONS

☾ **Clifton Hill.** With haunted houses, more wax museums than one usually sees in a lifetime, and fast-food chains galore, this is undeniably the most crassly commercial district of Niagara Falls. But for kids, the entertainment is endless—especially kids who enjoy arcade games—and the SkyWheel is alluring to all ages. Attractions are typically open late (midnight–2 am in summer, 11 pm off-season), with admission ranging from about C$10 to C$16. For the most part, the right-side-of-street attractions as you face the falls (SkyWheel side) are superior to those on the left side, many of which are looking shabby. *See Discounts and Deals, above, for information about Clifton Hill passes.* It may be cliché, but it's definitely symbolic. Some of the best attractions include: The 175-foot **SkyWheel** (✉ 4950 Clifton Hill ☎ 905/358–4793 ⊕ *www. skywheel.ca* ☾ C$9.99) has enclosed, heated, and air-conditioned gondolas, and views of the Niagara skyline. A 70,000-square-foot, 300-game, entertainment complex, the **Great Canadian Midway** (✉ 4950 Clifton Hill ☎ 905/358–3676) holds arcade games, a bowling alley, air hockey, and food. The collection of oddities at **Ripley's Believe It or Not! Museum** (⊠ *4960 Clifton Hill* ☎ *905/356–2261* ⊕ *www. ripleysniagara.com* ⊠ *C$13.99*) is creepily fascinating. **Movieland Wax Museum** (⊠ *4960 Clifton Hill* ☎ *905/358–3676* ⊕ *www.cliftonhill.com/ attractions/movieland-wax-museum-stars* ⊠ *C$11.99*) has such life-like characters as Justin Bieber, Harry Potter, and Barack and Michelle Obama. Seven thousand square feet of truffles, fudge, and the trademark Kisses, the **Hershey Store** (⊠ *5685 Falls Ave* ☎ *800/468–1714* ⊕ *www. hersheycanada.com/en/discover*) is marked by a six-story chocolate bar at the base of the hill. ☎ *905/358–3676* ⊕ *www.cliftonhill.com.*

Fallsview Casino Resort. Canada's largest gaming and resort facility crowns the city's skyline, overlooking the Niagara Parks with picture-perfect views of the falls. Within the 30-story complex are Canada's first casino wedding chapel, a glitzy theater, spa, shops, plenty of restaurants and, for the gaming enthusiasts, 150 gaming tables and 3,000 slot machines on one of the largest casino gaming floors in the world. The Las Vegas–style Avalon Ballroom showcases a wide array of talents, from Al Pacino to Jon Stewart. ⊠ *6380 Fallsview Blvd., Niagara Falls, Ontario* ☎ *888/325–5788, 905/371–7505* ⊕ *www. fallsviewcasinoresort.com* ⊗ *Daily 24 hrs.*

Ↄ Fodor's Choice ★ **Maid of the Mist.** Boats have been operating for *Maid of the Mist* since 1846, when they were wooden-hulled, coal-fired steamboats. Today, double-deck steel vessels tow fun-loving passengers on 30-minute journeys to the foot of the falls, where the spray is so heavy that ponchos must be distributed. From the observation areas along the falls, you can see those boarding the boats in their blue slickers. ■TIP→ Unless you cower in the center of the boat, your shoes and pants will get wet: wear quick-drying items or bring spares. ⊠ *Tickets and entrance at foot of Clifton Hill on falls side of Niagara Pkwy., Niagara Falls, Ontario* ☎ *905/358–0311* ⊕ *www.maidofthemist.com* ⊠ *C$16.50* ⊗ *Departures every 15 mins May–late Oct.*

Ↄ **Marineland.** A theme park with a marine show, wildlife displays, rides, and aquariums—including a beluga whale habitat with underwater viewing areas where you can pet and feed the whale—Marineland is 1½ km (1 mi) south of the falls. The daily marine shows include performing killer whales, dolphins, harbor seals, and sea lions. Children can pet and feed deer at the Deer Park. Among the many rides are Dragon Mountain, the world's largest steel roller coaster, and Ocean Odyssey. ⊠ *7657 Portage Rd., off Niagara Parkway or QEW (McLeod Rd. exit), Niagara Falls, Ontario* ☎ *905/356–9565* ⊕ *www.marinelandcanada. com* ⊠ *C$41.95* ⊗ *Mid-May–late June and early Sept.–mid-Oct., daily 10–dusk (ticket booths close at 5); late June–early Sept. daily 9–dusk (ticket booths close at 6).*

Niagara Parks Botanical Gardens and School of Horticulture. Professional gardeners have graduated from here since 1936; 100 acres of immaculately maintained gardens are open to the public. Within the Niagara Botanical Gardens, the **Niagara Parks Butterfly Conservatory** (⊠ *2405 Niagara Pkwy.* ⊠ *C$12.25*) houses one of North America's largest collections of free-flying butterflies—at least 2,000 butterflies from 50 species around the world are protected in a climate-controlled, rain forest–like conservatory. ✉ *2565 Niagara Pkwy., Niagara Falls, Ontario* ☎ *905/356–8554, 877/642–7275* ⊕ *www.niagaraparks.com* ⊗ *Gardens daily dawn–dusk; Butterfly Conservatory daily, hrs vary.*

↺ ★ **Skylon Tower.** Rising 775 feet above the falls, this is the best view of the great Niagara Gorge and the entire city. The indoor-outdoor observation deck has visibility up to 130 km (80 mi) on a clear day. Other reasons to visit include amusements for children, a revolving dining room, a gaming arcade, and a 3-D theater that lets you experience the falls up close. Tickets are sometimes as much as 50% off if purchased online. ✉ *5200 Robinson St., Niagara Falls, Ontario* ☎ *905/356–2651, 800/814–9577* ⊕ *www.skylon.com* ⊠ *C$13.91* ⊗ *Mid-June–early Sept., daily 8 am–midnight; early Sept.–mid June, 9 am–10 pm most days.*

★ **Whirlpool Aero Car.** In operation since 1916, this antique cable car crosses the Whirlpool Basin in the Niagara Gorge. This trip is not for the faint-hearted, but there's no better way to get an aerial view of the gorge, the whirlpool, the rapids, and the hydroelectric plants. ✉ *3850 Niagara Pkwy., 4½ km (3 mi) north of falls, Niagara Falls, Ontario* ☎ *905/371–0254, 877/642–7275* ⊕ *www.niagaraparks.com* ⊠ *C$12.25* ⊗ *Early Apr.–mid-Nov., daily, hrs vary.*

White Water Walk. A self-guided route involves taking an elevator to the bottom of the Niagara Gorge, the narrow valley created by the Niagara Falls and River, where you can walk along a 1,000-foot boardwalk beside the Class VI rapids of the Niagara River. The gorge is rimmed by sheer cliffs as it enters the giant whirlpool. ✉ *4330 Niagara Pkwy., 3 km (2 mi) north of falls, Niagara Falls, Ontario* ☎ *905/371–0254, 877/642–7275* ⊕ *www.niagaraparks.com* ⊠ *C$9.50* ⊗ *Early Apr.– late Oct. daily 9–dusk, weather permitting.*

WORTH NOTING

↺ **Bird Kingdom.** A tropical respite from the crowds and Las Vegas–style attractions, Bird Kingdom is the world's largest indoor aviary, with over 400 free-flying birds and more than 35 exotic-bird species in the 50,000-square-foot complex. For creepy-crawly lovers, there are also spiders, lizards, and snakes—including a 100-pound python that you can hold. Check online for a schedule of feeding times. Parking is an additional C$2 per half hour, but there's a public lot behind the building (on Hiram Street) that is C$5 per day. ✉ *5651 River Rd., Niagara Falls, Ontario* ☎ *905/356–8888, 866/994–0090* ⊕ *www.niagarafallsaviary. com* ⊠ *C$16.50* ⊗ *Mid-Oct.–June, daily 10–5; July–early Sept., daily 9–7; early Sept.–mid-Oct., weekdays 10–5, weekends 10–6.*

Casino Niagara. Smaller and more low-key than Fallsview, Casino Niagara also has some older machines, but well-equipped nonetheless: Slot machines, video-poker machines, and gambling tables for games such as blackjack, roulette, and baccarat fill this casino. Multisports wagering and off-track betting are available. Diversions from gambling are also offered. Within the casino are several lounges, a Yuk Yuk's comedy club and an all-you-can-eat buffet restaurant. Valet parking is available. ✉ *5705 Falls Ave., Niagara Falls, Ontario* ☎ *905/374–3598, 888/946–3255* ⊕ *www.casinoniagara.com* ⊗ *Daily 24 hrs.*

7

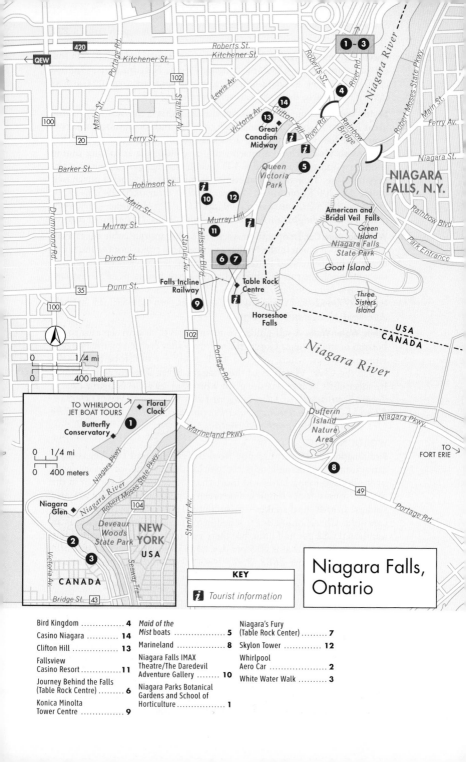

Niagara Falls, Ontario

KEY

i Tourist information

Bird Kingdom **4**
Casino Niagara **14**
Clifton Hill **13**
Fallsview
Casino Resort **11**
Journey Behind the Falls
(Table Rock Centre) **6**
Konica Minolta
Tower Centre **9**

*Maid of the
Mist* boats **5**
Marineland **8**
Niagara Falls IMAX
Theatre/The Daredevil
Adventure Gallery **10**
Niagara Parks Botanical
Gardens and School of
Horticulture **1**

Niagara's Fury
(Table Rock Center) **7**
Skylon Tower **12**
Whirlpool
Aero Car **2**
White Water Walk **3**

OFF THE
BEATEN
PATH

Fort Erie Race Track. Beautifully landscaped with willows, manicured hedges, and flower-bordered infield lakes, the Fort Erie Race Track has dirt and turf horse racing, with the year's highlight being the Prince of Wales Stakes, the second jewel in Canada's Triple Crown of Racing. ✉ *230 Catherine St., off QEW Exit 2, Fort Erie, Ontario* ☎ *905/871–3200* 🖥 *www.forterieracing.com* 🕐 *May–Nov., Sat.–Tues. 9 am to 3 am.*

WORD OF MOUTH

"Cave of the Winds—loved loved loved this. By far the best, most unique way to see the falls. It is a winding stairway down and up, and you end up at one point on what is called the hurricane deck. No kidding! Walking up the stairs approaching the American Falls pouring down on you, it is hard to climb the stairs or even breathe with the sheer force of water coming at you. It was amazing, exhilarating, and terrifying!"
—LizaMarie

Journey Behind the Falls. This 30-to-45-minute tour starts with an elevator ride to an observation deck that provides an eye-level view of the Canadian Horseshoe Falls and the Niagara River. From there a walk through tunnels cut into the rock takes you behind thunderous waterfalls, and you can glimpse the back side of the crashing water through two portals cut in the rock face. ✉ *Table Rock Centre, 6650 Niagara Pkwy., Niagara Falls, Ontario* ☎ *905/371–0254, 877/642–7275* 🖥 *www.niagaraparks.com* 🖼 *Mid-Dec.–mid-Apr. C$11.25, mid-Apr.–Dec. C$14.60* 🕐 *Tours daily beginning at 9 am; hrs vary—call or check Web site for details.*

Konica Minolta Tower Centre. At 525 feet above the base of the falls, the tower affords panoramic views of the Horseshoe Falls and the area from its 25th-floor observation deck. Floors 27 to 30 are accommodations, and Pinnacle Restaurant atop the tower offers pasta, steaks, and seafood dishes. ✉ *6732 Fallsview Blvd., Niagara Falls, Ontario* ☎ *905/356–1501, 800/461–2492* 🖥 *www.niagaratower.com* 🖼 *C$5* 🕐 *Daily 7 am–11 pm.*

Niagara Falls IMAX Theatre/The Daredevil Adventure Gallery. Get the human story behind the falls, from local native tribes' relationship with the waters to the foolhardy folks who went over the edge, with *The Falls Movie: Legends and Daredevils* on the six-story IMAX screen. The Daredevil Adventure Gallery chronicles the expeditions of those who have tackled the falls and has some of the actual barrels they used on display. ✉ *6170 Fallsview Blvd., Niagara Falls, Ontario* ☎ *905/358–3611, 866/405–4629* 🖥 *www.imaxniagara.com* 🖼 *C$14.50* 🕐 *Shows on the hr Nov.–Apr., daily 10–4; May, Sept., and Oct., daily 9–8; June–Aug., daily 9–9.*

Niagara's Fury. Learn how Niagara Falls formed over thousands of years on this 15-minute simulation ride. Standing on a mesh platform surrounded by an uninterrupted 360-degree viewing screen, you feel snow falling, winds blowing, the floor rumbling, and waves crashing as you watch glaciers form, collide, and melt, creating the falls as we know them today. In certain spots you *will* get wet; ponchos are provided. ✉ *Table Rock Centre, 6650 Niagara Pkwy., Niagara Falls, Ontario*

☎ *905/371–0254, 877/642–7275* ⊕ *www.niagaraparks.com* ✉ *C$15*
⊙ *Showtimes daily every 30 mins 10:30–4.*

WHERE TO EAT

Dining in Niagara Falls is still a bit disappointing because of the lack of sophistication that usually comes with a highly touristic area (especially when compared with the neighboring foodie paradise Niagara-on-the-Lake). A view of the falls and convenient location don't come cheap, so prices are rarely what one would consider reasonable. Thankfully, the landscape is slowly changing, and some falls-view restaurants, such as 17 Noir, are hiring creative chefs who are stepping up the quality—though still at a pretty penny. But with views like these, it might be worth it.

$$$$
CONTINENTAL
★

✕ **17 Noir.** The best fine-dining-with-a-view in town, 17 Noir plays up its casino locale without being kitschy. The tall-ceilinged, modern space is inspired by roulette, in a profusion of red, black, and gold, and juxtaposes the traditional steak-house menu. More secluded seating areas wind around the perimeter next to huge windows overlooking the falls, on a raised, illuminated floor on a patio. The menu is seasonal, but you might start out with fresh oysters or roasted beet salad, then move on to Canadian or USDA Prime steak, duck *sous vide* with foie gras and a goat cheese–gooseberry tart, or wild king salmon with cauliflower puree and white balsamic butter reduction. The baby bananas Foster—warm bananas on a bed of streusel topped with caramel and ice cream—is a memorable dessert. Because 17 Noir is accessible only via the casino floor, all diners must be at least 19. ✉ *Fallsview Casino Resort, 6380 Fallsview Blvd., Niagara Falls, Ontario* ☎ *905/358–3255, 888/325–5788* ⊕ *www.fallsviewcasinoresort.com/dining* ⚑ *Reservations essential* ⊙ *Closed Tues. and Wed. No lunch.*

$$$$
ITALIAN
★

✕ **Casa Mia Ristorante.** Fresh, quality ingredients done simply and in generous portions are what make this off-the-beaten-path restaurant, about a 10-minute drive from the falls. A free shuttle service from Niagara Falls hotels whisks guests to this labor of love, owned and operated by the Mollica family. Modern Amalfi Coast–inspired decor brings a seaside terrace indoors, and it all feels miles, not minutes, away from the city's tourist attractions. To start, try a delectable *bresaola* (air-dried salted beef) served with arugula, Parmigiano-Reggiano shavings, and fragrant truffled dwarf peaches, drizzled with balsamic and truffle oils. Move on to tender pieces of shredded duck confit over linguine in a white-truffle–duck-broth reduction. A sommelier is on hand with suggestions from the 300-plus-label cellar. ✉ *3518 Portage Rd., Niagara Falls, Ontario* ☎ *905/356–5410* ⊕ *www.casamiaristorante.com* ⊙ *No lunch weekends.*

$$
AMERICAN

✕ **Edgewaters Tap & Grill.** Inside a former refectory building, this second-floor restaurant operated by Niagara Parks has a huge veranda overlooking the falls, across Niagara Parkway. Secondary to the view, the decor and menu are reflective of those in a diner—standard options of burgers, salads, pasta, and steaks served to small wooden tables. The location is prime and the patio is the perfect place to enjoy the view. Reservations are taken online, and you should make one if you want one of the coveted patio tables closest to the falls. Live amplified music

Rides on the *Maid of the Mist* have been thrilling visitors to Niagara Falls since 1846.

often accompanies dinner in summer. ✉ *Niagara Pkwy. at Murray St., Niagara Falls, Ontario* ☎ *905/356–2217* ⊕ *www.niagaraparks.com/ dining* ☺ *Closed mid-Oct.–early May.*

$$$ ✕ **Lucky's Steakhouse.** Heavy soundproof doors insulate this classy
STEAK 1920s-style steakhouse from the less glamourous and very loud
★   Casino Niagara where it's located. Inside the intimate second-story dining room, all is quiet and comfortably chic, with gleaming hardwood floors, a floor-to-ceiling wine cabinet along one wall, semicircular leather booths, and music provided by some of the greats (Ella Fitzgerald, Frank Sinatra) whose black-and-white portraits adorn the brick walls. Tall windows provide lots of light but, alas, only street views. The menu includes a wide range of choices and prices, from garlic-rubbed thin-crust pizza to surf and turf, but the house specialties are the chops and steaks: filet mignon, prime rib, T-bone, and more. ✉ *Casino Niagara (2nd fl.), 5705 Falls Ave., Niagara Falls, Ontario* ☎ *905/374–3598* ⊕ *www.casinoniagara.com* ☺ No lunch.

$$ ✕ **Napoli Ristorante e Pizzeria.** On busy Ferry Street, Napoli is just a five-
ITALIAN minute drive from Clifton Hill but it's a local joint that manages to be both casual and refined. Sit in the back room if possible, where exposed-brick columns and black-and-white photos of Naples on the walls set the scene for the southern Italian pasta dishes and thin-crust pizzas. The extensive menu includes 10 pizzas with crisp, wafer-thin crusts and generous dollops of tomato sauce, and plenty of pasta dishes and hearty meat dishes to choose from. Start with a garlicky bruschetta before an entrée like homemade roasted sausage with baked polenta and rapini or fettuccine in a red-pepper-spiced oil-and-garlic sauce with anchovies, bread crumbs, and Pecorino. Wines are exclusively Italian or Niagara.

You can order pizzas for pick-up. ✉ *5545 Ferry St., Niagara Falls, Ontario* ☎ *905/356–3345* ⊕ *www. napoliristorante.ca* ⊘ *No lunch.*

$$ \times **Shibuki Japanese Sushi.** In a tourist area of mostly gaudy steak houses and themed restaurants sits this renovated sushi restaurant showing simplicity and refinement. The decor, dominated by wood in the floors, chairs, and tables, and set off by dark walls, gives the space a sense of relaxation and sets the mood for the forthcoming plates of beautifully presented, fresh sushi and sashimi. The tempura battered Shibuki roll of shrimp, avocado, and spicy sauce is a popular item, as are other rolls and standard sushi dishes. ✉ *6175 Dunn St., Niagara Falls, Ontario* ☎ *905/371–2227.*

$$$$ $\times$ **Skylon Tower.** The big draw here is the view from the **Revolving Dining Room:** perched 520 feet above the Horseshoe Falls, it's simply breathtaking. And the atmosphere puts this restaurant above those serving similar cuisine in the area, drawing an eclectic crowd of couples in cocktail attire and families in casual clothes. The menu revolves as well: prime rib with horseradish sauce and chicken cordon bleu have made appearances. **The Summit Suite Buffet Dining Room,** an all-you-can-eat buffet restaurant one level up, doesn't revolve, but has comparable views for slightly less and serves a popular Sunday brunch. A reservation at either restaurant includes free admission to the observation deck, which makes the prices (upward of C$50 per person at the Revolving Dining Room; C$40 prix-fixe at the Summit Suite) a little easier to digest, considering the food is secondary to the view. ✉ *5200 Robinson St., Niagara Falls, Ontario* ☎ *905/356–2651, 800/814–9577* ⊕ *www. skylon.com* ⚶ *Reservations essential* ⊘ *Summit Suite closed Nov.–Apr. but open for Sun. brunch year-round.*

WHERE TO STAY

For expanded hotel reviews, visit Fodors.com.

A room with a view of the falls means staying in a high-rise hotel, usually a chain. Hotels with falls views are clustered near the two streets leading down to the falls, Clifton Hill (and adjacent Victoria Avenue) and Murray Street (and adjacent Fallsview Boulevard), also called Murray Hill. Families gravitate toward Clifton Hill, with its video arcades, chain restaurants, and *Maid of the Mist* docking at the end of the street. Murray Hill, where the Fallsview Casino is, is less ostentatious and closer to the falls.

Niagara Falls has plenty of B&Bs, but they're mediocre compared to those in Niagara-on-the-Lake, 20 km (12 mi) north. All of the hotels we recommend here are within walking distance of the falls.

$$$ ▦ **Country Inn & Suites.** If you're on a budget but not willing to stay at a dingy motor lodge, this seven-story hotel is probably your best

choice. **Pros:** low-cost parking (C$6 a day); breakfast and high-speed Internet included; within walking distance of Clifton Hill. **Cons:** no views to speak of; 15-minute walk down to the falls. ✉ *5525 Victoria Ave., Niagara Falls, Ontario* ☎ *905/374–6040, 800/263–2571* ⊕ *www.countryinns.com/niagarafallson* 🛏 *49 rooms, 59 suites* ⚹ *In-room: a/c, Internet. In-hotel: pool, gym, laundry facilities, business center, parking* ⦿ *Breakfast.*

$$$$ 🏨 **Fallsview Casino Resort.** Like the name suggests, all rooms in this cen-
★ trally located, 30-story hotel tower overlook the Horseshoe or Ameri-
can and Bridal Veil falls. **Pros:** the most glamorous address in Niagara Falls; first-class accommodation; great entertainment. **Cons:** pricey; rooms fill up fast. ✉ *6380 Fallsview Blvd., Niagara Falls, Ontario* ☎ *905/358–3255, 888/946–3255* ⊕ *www.fallsviewcasinoresort.com* 🛏 *289 rooms, 85 suites* ⚹ *In-room: a/c, safe, kitchen, Internet. In-hotel: restaurant, pool, gym, spa, business center, parking.*

$$$$ 🏨 **Great Wolf Lodge.** Instead of the usual casino-and-slot-machine ambi-
ence in other area hotels, you'll find a spectacular water park of 12 slides, seven pools, water fort, outdoor hot tubs, and other fun water facilities for the kids. **Pros:** great variety of water slides and facilities. **Cons:** rooms are mostly open concept, so there is less privacy for the parents. ✉ *3950 Victoria Ave., Niagara Falls, Ontario* ☎ *905/354–4888, 888/878–1818* ⊕ *www.greatwolf.com* 🛏 *406 suites* ⚹ *In-room: Wi-Fi. In-hotel: restaurant, pool, spa, water sports, children's programs.*

$$$ 🏨 **Sheraton on the Falls.** Just steps from the Niagara Parkway and *Maid of the Mist* ticket booth is this 22-story tower at the corner of Clifton Hill, and it's the most polished option in that area. **Pros:** at the bottom of Clifton Hill and very close to the falls; updated rooms; breakfast overlooking all three falls is a great start to the day. **Cons:** no views from rooms below sixth floor; expensive Wi-Fi and parking. ✉ *5875 Falls Ave., Niagara Falls, Ontario* ☎ *905/374–4445, 888/229–9961* ⊕ *www.sheratononthefalls.com* 🛏 *660 rooms, 10 suites* ⚹ *In-room: a/c, Wi-Fi. In-hotel: restaurant, pool, gym, spa, business center, parking, some pets allowed.*

$$$ 🏨 **Sterling Inn & Spa.** Unique among the chain options in Niagara Falls
★ is this boutique hotel in a converted 1930s milk factory—hence the bottle-shaped building face. **Pros:** big rooms; modern design; AG restaurant serves good locally sourced cuisine. **Cons:** no views; subterranean restaurant; north of Victoria Avenue opposite the top of Clifton Hill, about a 20-minute walk to the base of Clifton Hill. ✉ *5195 Magdalen St., Niagara Falls, Ontario* ☎ *289/292–0000, 877/783–7772* ⊕ *www.sterlingniagara.com* 🛏 *41 rooms* ⚹ *In-room: a/c, Internet, Wi-Fi. In-hotel: restaurant, gym, spa, business center, parking, some pets allowed* ⦿ *Breakfast.*

BIKING AND HIKING

Niagara Parks Commission. The Niagara Parks Commission has information on hiking and biking trails, local parks, restaurants, and the Niagara Gorge. ☎ *905/371–0254, 877/642–7275* ⊕ *www.niagaraparks.com.*

Ontario Trails Council. Ontario Trails Council has information and maps about hikes in the province. ☎ *877/668–7245, 613/389–7678* ⊕ *www.ontariotrails.on.ca.*

Niagara Glen. The 82.5-acre Niagara Glen nature reserve has 4 km (2.5 mi) of hiking trails through forested paths that pass giant boulders left behind as the falls eroded the land away thousands of years ago. Some trails are steep and rough, and the Glen has an elevation change of more than 200 feet. ⊕ *www.niagaraparks.com/nature-trails.*

Niagara River Recreation Trail. From Fort Erie to Niagara-on-the-Lake, this recreation trail is 56 km (35 mi) of bicycle trails along the Niagara River. The 29-km (18-mi) route between Niagara Falls and Niagara-on-the-Lake is paved. The trail is divided into four sections, each with site-specific history: Niagara-on-the-Lake to Queenston; Queenston to the Whirlpool Aero Car; Chippawa to Black Creek; and Black Creek to Fort Erie. ⊕ *www.niagaraparks.com/nature-trails.*

NIAGARA WINE REGION

Ontarians have been growing Concord grapes for (sweet) wine in the Niagara region since the 1800s, but experiments with European *Vitis vinifera* species between the 1950s and 1970s led to more serious wine production. Today, the Niagara Peninsula is Canada's largest viticultural area, accounting for nearly 80% of the country's growing volume. More than 60 wineries reside here, either north of St. Catharines spread out across the largely rural Niagara Escarpment, or south of St. Catharines, in close proximity to pretty, Victorian-tinged Niagara-on-the-Lake.

But wine-tasting isn't the only game in the Peninsula. Niagara-on-the-Lake draws theatergoers to its annual Shaw Festival and food lovers to its unparalleled restaurants. The Niagara Escarpment is a prime Sunday-drive destination, with winding country roads, the charming town of Jordan, and a couple of diamond-in-the-rough restaurants.

NIAGARA-ON-THE-LAKE

15 km (9 mi) north of Niagara Falls and 130 km (80 mi) south of Toronto.

The hub of the Niagara wine region is the town of Niagara-on-the-Lake (sometimes abbreviated NOTL). Since 1962 this town of 14,000 residents has been considered the southern outpost of fine summer theater in Ontario because of its acclaimed Shaw Festival. As one of the country's prettiest and best-preserved Victorian towns, Niagara-on-the-Lake has architectural sights, shops, flower-lined streets and plentiful ornamental gardens in summer, quality theater nearly year-round, and some of the best chefs and hoteliers in the country.

WHEN TO GO

The town is worth a visit at any time of the year for its inns, restaurants, and proximity to the wineries (open year-round), but the most compelling time to visit is from April through November, during the Shaw Festival, and when the weather allows alfresco dining. Wine-harvesting tours and events take place in the fall and, for ice wine, in December and January. Be warned that the tiny town can get packed over Canadian and American holiday weekends in summer: parking will be scarce, driving slow, and you might have to wait for tastings at wineries.

GETTING HERE AND AROUND

From Buffalo or Toronto, Niagara-on-the-Lake is easily reached by car via the QEW. NOTL is about a two-hour drive from Toronto, a bit far for just a day trip. From Niagara Falls or Lewiston, take the Niagara Parkway. There's no public transport in Niagara-on-the-Lake or to Niagara Falls, 15 km (9 mi) south.

Niagara-on-the-Lake is a very small town that can easily be explored on foot. Parking downtown can be nightmarish in peak season. Parking along the main streets is metered, at C$1 or C$1.50 per hour. On most residential streets parking is free but still limited.

TOURS

Sentineal Carriages conducts year-round tours in and around Niagara-on-the-Lake. Catch a carriage at the Prince of Wales hotel or make a reservation for a pick-up. The private, narrated tours are C$45 for 15 minutes, C$65 for 30 minutes, and C$90 for 45 minutes (prices are per carriage).

ESSENTIALS

Tour Contacts Sentineal Carriages ☎ *905/468–4943* ⊕ *www.sentinealcarriages.ca.*

Visitor Information Niagara-on-the-Lake Chamber of Commerce and Visitor & Convention Bureau ⊠ *26 Queen St., Niagara-on-the-Lake, Ontario* ☎ *905/468–1950* ⊕ *www.niagaraonthelake.com.*

TOP EXPERIENCE: WINERIES

Château des Charmes. Founded in 1978, this is one of Niagara's first wineries, and one of the two largest family-owned wineries in Niagara (Peller is the other). Originally from France, the Bosc family were pioneers in cultivating European varieties of grapes in Niagara. Wines here consistently win awards, and the winery is particularly known for its chardonnay and Gamay Noir Droit, made from a grape variety that was accidentally created through a mutation. The wine is proprietary, and this is the only winery allowed to make it. Château des Charmes is pioneering again and in the process of developing brand-new wholly Canadian grape varieties. ⊠ *1025 York Rd., Niagara-on-the-Lake, Ontario* ☎ *905/262–4219* ⊕ *www.chateaudescharmes.com* 🖭 *Tastings C$1–C$7, depending on wine; tours C$5* ⊘ *Daily 10–6; tours at 11 and 3.*

Frogpond Farm. Ontario's only certified-organic winery is a small, family-owned affair with exclusively organic wines. The setting is truly farm-like: sheep and guinea hens mill about outside while you taste. With only eight varieties, all VQA and including a nice ice wine, you can become an expert in this label in one sitting. The wines are available on-site, online, at selected restaurants in Ontario; the cabernet franc is available at the LCBO. ⊠ *1385 Larkin Rd. (Line 6), Niagara-on-the-Lake, Ontario* ☎ *905/468–1079, 877/989–0165* ⊕ *www.frogpondfarm.ca* 🖭 *Tastings free* ⊘ *Retail and tastings May–Oct., daily 11–6; Nov.–Apr., Tues.–Sat. 11–5.*

★ **Hillebrand Estates Winery.** With more than 300 wine awards, this winery—one of Niagara's first and largest—produces many excellent varieties. Its reds (especially Trius Red and Trius Cabernet Franc) are some of the best in Niagara, consistently taking top prizes at competitions; the Trius Brut is another gold medalist. After the half-hour cellar and vineyard tour are three complimentary tastings. Another dozen themed tours and regular events include a seminar where you can blend your own Trius Red and chef-hosted meals at their terrific restaurant. Book in advance for tours. ⊠ *1249 Niagara Stone Rd., Niagara-on-the-Lake, Ontario* ☎ *905/468–7123, 800/582–8412* ⊕ *www.hillebrand. com* ⌂ *Tastings C$2, C$5 (ice wine). Tours C$10–C$15* ⊘ *Sun.–Thurs. 10–6, Fri. and Sat. 10–9. Tours daily every hr on hr 11–5.*

Jackson-Triggs Niagara Estate Winery. An ultramodern facility, this famous winery blends state-of-the-art wine-making technology with age-old, handcrafted enological savvy, as evidenced by the stainless steel trough by the entrance. A multitude of tours, workshops, and events are offered. The hourly public tour is a great introduction to winemaking and includes three tastings and a mini-lesson in wine tasting. Its premium award-winning VQA wines can be sipped in the tasting gallery and purchased in the retail boutique. ⊠ *2145 Niagara Stone Rd., Niagara-on-the-Lake, Ontario* ☎ *905/468–4637, 866/589–4637* ⊕ *www.*

jacksontriggswinery.com 🖳*Tastings C$1 (C$5–C$7 ice wine). Tours C$5* ⊗ *June–Sept., daily 10:30–6:30; Oct.–May., Sun.–Fri 10:30–5:30, Sat. 10:30–6:30. Tours June–Sept., daily every hr on the hr; Oct.–May, daily at 10:30, 12:30, and 2:30.*

Konzelmann Estate Winery. An easygoing winery with a friendly staff and sociable tasting bar, Konzelmann has garnered praise (and awards) from various authoritative sources like the *Wall Street Journal*, for its fruitier wines in particular, and it's known for high-quality ice wines, one of which made *Wine Spectator*'s top 100 wines list in 2008, the first Canadian wine ever to make the list. Konzelmann's vineyards border Lake Ontario, and the winery has a viewing platform with vistas of the vines and water. The retail shop is well stocked with wine-related gifts. ✉ *1096 Lakeshore Rd., Niagara-on-the-Lake, Ontario* ☎ *905/935–2866* ⊕ *www.konzelmann.ca* 🖳*Public tours C$5* ⊗ *May–Oct., daily 10–6; Nov.–Apr., Mon.–Sat. 10–5, Sun. 11–5. Public tours May–Sept., daily at 11 and 1; specialty tours by appointment.*

★ **Stratus.** Standing out from a vast landscape of single varietal wines, Stratus specializes in assemblage: combining multiple varieties of grapes to create unique blends. Established in 2000, and emerging on the Niagara wine scene in 2005, they continue to perfect what has traditionally been a recipe for disaster for winemakers. A fine example is the Stratus White, a mix of six grape varieties, that's complex and unlike anything you've ever tasted (in a good way). Sip all three assemblage wines (white, red, and ice wine) and a handful of single varietals in the modern glass-walled tasting room, installed in Canada's first LEED-certified building. ✉ *2059 Niagara Stone Rd., Niagara-on-the-Lake, Ontario* ☎ *905/468–1806* ⊕ *www.stratuswines.com* 🖳*Tastings C$10 (4 wines)* ⊗ *May–Dec., daily 11–5; Jan.–Apr., Wed.–Sun., noon–5.*

EXPLORING

★ **Queen Street.** You can get a glimpse of the town's rich architectural history walking along this single street, with Lake Ontario to your north, and it is the core of NOTL's commercial portion. At the corner of Queen and King streets is Niagara Apothecary. This high-style, mid-Victorian building was an apothecary from 1866 to 1964. The Court House is situated across the street. It became the Town Hall in 1862. Presently, it houses a small 327-seat theatre during Shaw Festival. At No. 209 is the handsome Charles Inn, formerly known as Richardson-Kiely House, built in 1832 for Charles Richardson, who was a barrister and member of Parliament.

Niagara Historical Society & Museum. In connected side-by-side buildings—one the 1875 former Niagara High School building and the other the first building in Ontario to have been erected as a museum, in 1906—this extensive collection relates to the often colorful history of the Niagara Peninsula from earliest times through the 19th century. The museum also leads guided walking tours of the town (C$5). ✉ *43 Castlereagh St., Niagara-on-the-Lake, Ontario* ☎ *905/468–3912* ⊕ *www.niagarahistorical.museum* 🖳*C$5* ⊗ *May–Oct., daily 10–5; Nov.–Apr., daily 1–5.*

☼ **Fort George National Historic Site.** On
Fodor's Choice   a wide stretch of parkland south
★   of town sits this fort that was built
in the 1790s but lost to the Yan-
kees during the War of 1812. It
was recaptured after the burning
of the town in 1813 and largely
survived the war, only to fall into
ruins by the 1830s. Thankfully, it
was reconstructed a century later,
and you can explore the officers'
quarters, the barracks rooms of
the common soldiers, the kitchen,
and more. Staff in period uniform
conduct tours and reenact 19th-
century infantry and artillery drills.
✉ *Queens Parade, Niagara Pkwy.,
Niagara-on-the-Lake,   Ontario*
☎ *905/468–4257* ⊕ *www.pc.gc.
ca/lhn-nhs/on/fortgeorge/index.aspx* 🎫 *C$11.70 (C$5.90 parking)*
☼ *May–Oct., daily 10–5, Apr. and Nov. weekends 10–5.*

> ### 1812 BICENTENNIAL
>
> The Niagara region, then part of
> British-owned Upper Canada, saw
> lots of action during the War of
> 1812. Today battle reenactments,
> fife and drum displays, and shoot-
> ing and marching competitions
> take place at Niagara forts and
> other historic sites in summer.
> For the 2012 bicentennial of the
> war, Niagara Parks and other local
> organizations are refurbishing bat-
> tle sites and planning events. For
> schedules, check the War of 1812
> Bicentennial Web site (⊕ *www.
> visit1812.com*).

St. Mark's Church. One of Ontario's oldest Anglican churches, this was
built in 1804, and St. Mark's parish is even older, formed in 1792.
The stone church still houses the founding minister's original library of
1,500 books, brought from England. During the War of 1812, American soldiers used the church as a barracks, and still-visible rifle pits
were dug in the cemetery. The church is open for concerts, lectures, and
Sunday services only. ✉ *41 Byron St., Niagara-on-the-Lake, Ontario*
☎ *905/468–3123* ⊕ *www.stmarks1792.com.*

☼ **Whirlpool Jet Boat Tours.** A one-hour thrill ride, these tours veer around
★   and hurdle white-water rapids that follow Niagara canyons up to the
wall of rolling waters, just below Niagara Falls. Children must be at least
six years old for the open-boat Wet Jet Tour and four years old for the
covered-boat (dry!) Jet Dome Tour; minimum height requirements also
apply. Tours depart from Niagara-on-the-Lake or Niagara Falls, Ontario
(June–August only) and Lewiston, NY. ✉ *61 Melville St., Niagara-
on-the-Lake, Ontario* ☎ *905/468–4800, 888/438–4444* ⊕ *www.
whirlpooljet.com* 🎫 *C$59* ☼ *Mid-Apr.–mid-Oct., weather-permitting.*

WHERE TO EAT

George Bernard Shaw once said, "No greater love hath man than the
love of food," and Niagara-on-the-Lake, which hosts a festival devoted
to the playwright, is a perfect place to indulge your epicurean desires.
Many eateries serve fine produce and wines from the verdant Niagara
Peninsula, and the glut of high-end options fosters fierce competition.
A number of inns and wineries here have restaurants. Especially in
summer, make reservations whenever possible. Many restaurants serve
dinner only until 9.

$$$ ✕ **Fans Court.** Authentic Chinese food is a welcome change of pace in
CHINESE   this Victorian-flavored town packed with restaurants serving mostly

Niagara-on-the-Lake, in the heart of the Niagara wine region, has gained fame for its fine wines and food, beautiful setting, and the annual summer Shaw Festival.

Continental or British pub cuisine. Delicate Cantonese dishes are prepared in the small dining room set back from busy Queen Street. Favorites such as lemon chicken, black-pepper-and-garlic beef, and shrimp and scallops sautéed with vegetables and served in a crunchy noodle basket are delicious and not overly "Canadianized." The yellow walls are hung with a few framed Chinese prints, but the plastic patio furniture out front cries for an update. ⊠ *135 Queen St., Niagara-on-the-Lake, Ontario* ☎ *905/468–4511.*

$$$$
INTERNATIONAL
Fodor's Choice
★

✕ **Hillebrand Winery Restaurant.** Niagara-on-the-Lake's first winery restaurant is still one of its best. After a complimentary winery tour and tasting, you can continue to indulge in the spacious, light-filled dining room with big double doors framing vineyards almost as far as the eye can see. The menu of locally inspired cuisine changes every six weeks. Tasting menus are available to try such culinary masterpieces as wild spring salmon with cranberry bean cassoulet, and Maritime harvested scallop with pressed Tamworth pork head. Earl Grey crème brûlée is just one delicious dessert from the pastry chef. Lunch is more economic and just as luxurious as dinner. ⊠ *1249 Niagara Stone Rd., at Hwy. 55, Niagara-on-the-Lake, Ontario* ☎ *905/468–7123, 800/582–8412* ⊕ *www.hillebrand.com.*

$$
BRITISH
★

✕ **Olde Angel Inn.** You can request a Yorkshire pudding to accompany any meal at this tavern just off Queen Street, which should tip you off to its British leanings, played out further in the decor: a warren of rooms with creaky floors and worn (or well-loved, depending on how you see it) wooden tables and chairs, low ceilings and exposed beams, and convivial chatter throughout. In Ontario's oldest operating inn (it's believed to have opened in 1789) the Olde Angel sets out pub fare such

Peller Estates Winery, known for its award-winning Rieslings and ice wines, provides visitors an elegant experience, from winery tours to tastings to fine dining.

as shepherd's pie, bangers and mash, and steak-and-kidney pie. Entrées change periodically but always include the house specialty, prime rib of beef au jus. Twenty-six domestic and imported (European) brews are on tap. The pub has live music, ranging from Celtic to 1970s covers, on Friday and Saturday beginning at 9:30. ⊠ *224 Regent St., Niagara-on-the-Lake, Ontario* ☎ *905/468–3411* ⊕ *www.angel-inn.com.*

$$$$
CONTINENTAL
Fodor's Choice
★

✕ **Peller Estates Winery Restaurant.** Frequently cited as the best restaurant in Niagara-on-the-Lake—an impressive feat in a town with many excellent restaurants—Peller manages refinement without arrogance and has a superior view to its main competitor, Hillebrand. The stately Colonial revival dining room is anchored by a huge fireplace at one end and has windows running the length of the room overlooking a large patio and the estate vineyards. A menu of ever-changing expertly prepared entrées often weaves the Peller Estates wine into modern Canadian cuisine, such as the perfectly cooked cabernet fig glazed lamb and succulent ice-wine roasted duck breast. Tasting menus are available at lunch and dinner. Inventive desserts have included a honey-lemon soufflé with cardamom crème anglaise. ⊠ *290 John St. E, Niagara-on-the-Lake, Ontario* ☎ *905/468–4678* ⊕ *www.peller.com* ⚞ *Reservations essential.*

$$$
ITALIAN

✕ **Ristorante Giardino.** The real treat at this modern Italian restaurant is to sit on the large patio out front, set back from Queen Street across the lawn under the shade of tall trees, and nibble on antipasti such as thin-sliced smoked duck breast and classic caprese salad (with tomatoes and mozzarella). The menu is seasonal, always with fresh (made daily) pasta, grilled fish, chicken, veal, and lamb. A light fish course like the grilled rainbow trout with white wine and caper butter sauce is perfect for spring and summer. Make time to indulge in the kitchen's classic

Italian desserts. Find the perfect bottle from the extensive wine list to go with the meal. ⊠ *Gate House Hotel, 142 Queen St., Niagara-on-the-Lake, Ontario* ☎ *905/468–3263* ⊕ *www.gatehouse-niagara.com* ⊘ *Closed Jan.–mid-Mar.*

$$$$
CANADIAN ✕ **Tiara Restaurant at Queen's Landing.** Niagara-on-the-Lake's only waterfront restaurant, the regal Tiara sits beside a marina with a view

DID YOU KNOW?

The moderate climate of the Niagara region doesn't benefit only grapes: about 40% of Canada's apples and 70% of its peaches as well as berries, cherries, and pears are grown in an area smaller than Rhode Island.

of the Niagara River beyond the sailboat masts. The elegant, amber-hued Georgian-meets-contemporary dining room is buttoned up but accented by a pretty stained-glass ceiling and near-panoramic windows that give nearly every table a water view. The outdoor tables next to the marina, however, are the ones to request to go with the exquisite French-influenced menu which consists of pan-seared diver scallops and *sous vide* pork belly, as well as roasted lamb loin with celery root and almond puree. Round out the meal with chocolate truffles and fruit jellies. ⊠ *155 Byron St., Niagara-on-the-Lake, Ontario* ☎ *905/468–2195, 888/669–5566* ⊕ *www.vintage-inns.com* ⩍ *Reservations essential.*

$$$
ECLECTIC ✕ **Zee's Grill.** For alfresco dining, it's hard to beat Zee's huge wraparound patio with heat lamps across from the Shaw Festival Theatre. More informal than most similarly priced restaurants in town, Zee's has a seasonal menu that brings panache to homegrown comfort foods, such as seared rainbow trout with Jerusalem artichoke ravioli and crispy leeks or grilled beef tenderloin with double-smoked bacon hash and cabernet *jus*. Appetizers follow the same philosophy—elegant, yet whimsical—as represented by a lobster poutine of butter poached lobster in a classic herbed Hollandaise sauce, and the duck confit pâté en croûte of confit duck leg, baked in a pastry shell served with chutney. Breakfast is served daily. ⊠ *92 Picton St., Niagara-on-the-Lake, Ontario* ☎ *905/468–5715* ⊕ *www.zees.ca* ⩍ *Reservations essential* ⊘ *No lunch Dec.–mid-Apr.*

WHERE TO STAY
For expanded hotel reviews, visit Fodors.com.

In terms of superior lodging, you're spoiled for choice in Niagara-on-the-Lake and it's hard to go wrong with any of the properties within the town's historic center. Prices are high, but hotels sometimes offer significant deals online.

Niagara-on-the-Lake may be Canada's B&B capital, with more than 100 to its name. Their service and quality can rival some of the priciest hotels.

For B&B listings, contact **Niagara-on-the-Lake Bed & Breakfast Association.** ☎ *905/468–0123, 866/855–0123* ⊕ *www.niagarabedandbreakfasts.com.*

The **Niagara-on-the-Lake Historic Bed & Breakfasts** Web site maintains a list of historic B&Bs, all built before 1850 and all within two blocks from Queen/Picton Street, the center-of-town shopping and dining strip. ⊕ *www.historicbb.com.*

$$$ ★ ⊡ **The Charles Inn.** An air of old-fashioned civility permeates this 1832 Georgian gem. **Pros:** historic details with modern touches; highly lauded restaurant; impeccably decorated. **Cons:** some historic "quirks" like variable water temperature; some verandas are connected (i.e. shared with neighbors). ⊠ *209 Queen St., Niagara-on-the-Lake, Ontario* ☎ *905/468–4588, 866/556–8883* ⊕ *www.charlesinn.ca* ⌁ *12 rooms* ⌂ *In-room: a/c, Internet, Wi-Fi. In-hotel: restaurant, parking* ⦿ *Breakfast.*

> **BREAKFAST BASICS**
>
> At local inns and B&Bs, breakfasts are often lavish multicourse affairs. But be wary of lodging that does not include it, as it's tough to find breakfast outside hotel restaurants that tend to charge an arm for eggs and a leg for toast.

$$$$ Fodor'sChoice ★ ⊡ **Harbour House.** The closest hotel to the waterfront in town is this luxurious and romantic boutique hotel with a contemporary-cottage theme just a block from the river. **Pros:** staff cater to every need; approachable luxury; full breakfast included. **Cons:** virtually no public spaces; no restaurant, gym, or spa on-site; a few rooms without water views. ⊠ *85 Melville St., Niagara-on-the-Lake, Ontario* ☎ *905/468–4683, 866/277–6677* ⊕ *www.harbourhousehotel.ca* ⌁ *28 rooms, 3 suites* ⌂ *In-room: a/c, Internet, Wi-Fi. In-hotel: business center, parking* ⦿ *Breakfast.*

$$ ⊡ **Moffat Inn.** A central location on Picton Street next to the Prince of Wales hotel, reasonable prices, and expert management make this 1835 stucco inn a real find. **Pros:** great location at reasonable price; impeccably clean; upscale linens. **Cons:** rooms small and not as posh as other area hotels; floral-on-floral decor may be off-putting to some. ⊠ *60 Picton St., Niagara-on-the-Lake, Ontario* ☎ *905/468–4116, 888/669–5566* ⊕ *www.moffatinn.com* ⌁ *23 rooms, 1 2-bedroom apartment* ⌂ *In-room: a/c, Wi-Fi. In-hotel: restaurant, parking.*

$$ ★ ⊡ **Olde Angel Inn.** Though established in the late 1700s, this coach-house inn burned down during the War of 1812 and was rebuilt in 1816. **Pros:** excellent price at the heart of town; on-site English-style tavern *(⇨ Where to Eat)*. **Cons:** historic inn means poor soundproofing, which is a problem for rooms over the pub; dedicated parking for cottages only. ⊠ *224 Regent St., Niagara-on-the-Lake, Ontario* ☎ *905/468–3411* ⊕ *www.angel-inn.com* ⌁ *3 rooms, 2 2-bedroom suites, 2 2-bedroom cottages* ⌂ *In-room: a/c, kitchen. In-hotel: restaurant, bar, parking.*

$$$$ Fodor'sChoice ★ ⊡ **Pillar and Post.** A two-story hotel six (long) blocks from the heart of town, this building has been a cannery, barracks, and basket factory in its 100-plus-year history. **Pros:** exceptional staff; unaffected mix of historic and modern; cool spa and pool. **Cons:** not as central as some other hotels (a brisk 20-minute walk to Queen/Picton Street); no elevator to second-floor rooms. ⊠ *48 John St., Niagara-on-the-Lake, Ontario* ☎ *905/468–2123, 888/669–5566* ⊕ *www.vintage-hotels.com* ⌁ *122 rooms* ⌂ *In-room: a/c, safe, Internet, Wi-Fi. In-hotel: restaurant, bar, pool, gym, spa, parking, some pets allowed.*

$$$$ ⊡ **Prince of Wales.** A visit from the Prince of Wales in 1901 inspired the name of this venerable hostelry that still welcomes the occasional

The Prince of Wales hotel pampers guests with old-fashioned luxury and elegance.

royal guest or film star (aka Hollywood royalty). **Pros:** nice spa; over-the-top-elegant public spaces; highly trained staff at your beck and call. **Cons:** some views of the parking lot; rabbit warren of corridors can be confusing; breakfast not included. ⊠ *6 Picton St., Niagara-on-the-Lake, Ontario* ☎ *905/468–3246, 888/669–5566* ⊕ *www.vintage-hotels.com* ↪ *110 rooms* ⚒ *In-room: a/c, safe, Wi-Fi. In-hotel: restaurant, bar, pool, gym, spa, parking, some pets allowed.*

$$$$ ⊞ **Queen's Landing.** About half of the rooms at this Georgian-style brick mansion have knockout views of the fields of historic Fort George or the marina—ask for one when making a reservation. **ros:** elegant, historic look; excellent service. **Cons:** pricy; breakfast not included. ⊠ *155 Byron St., Niagara-on-the-Lake, Ontario* ☎ *905/468–2195, 888/669–5566* ⊕ *www.vintage-hotels.com* ↪ *138 rooms, 4 suites* ⚒ *In-room: a/c, safe, Wi-Fi. In-hotel: restaurant, bar, pool, gym, parking, some pets allowed.*

$$$$ ⊞ **Riverbend Inn & Vineyard.** Surrounded by its own private vineyard, this
★ restored 1860s Georgian-style, off-white, green-shuttered mansion is formal in style: it's fronted by a grand portico, and an enormous original 19th-century crystal chandelier greets you in the lobby. **Pros:** charming atmosphere, especially out on the patio if the weather permits. **Cons:** no elevators. ⊠ *16104 Niagara Pkwy., Niagara-on-the-Lake, Ontario* ☎ *905/468–8866, 888/955–5553* ⊕ *www.riverbendinn.ca* ↪ *19 rooms, 2 suites* ⚒ *In-room: a/c, Internet. In-hotel: restaurant, bar, parking.*

$$$ ⊞ **Shaw Club Hotel & Spa.** Clean lines, neutral colors, and modern elements like steel and glass give Shaw Club an edgy and hip vibe over its competitors, in a town that's largely Georgian or Victorian in style. **Pros:** hip cosmopolitan style unique in the region; ideal location just

across the street from Shaw Festival Theatre; easygoing staff. **Cons:** small rooms; Standard and Annex rooms lack the wow factor of the rest of the hotel. ⊠ *92 Picton St., Niagara-on-the-Lake,* *Ontario* ☎ *905/468–5711, 800/511–7070* ⊕ *www.shawclub.com* 🛏 *29 rooms, 1 suite* ⚹ *In-room: a/c, Internet, Wi-Fi. In-hotel: gym, spa, business center, parking, some pets allowed* ❙◎❙ *Breakfast.*

> **DID YOU KNOW?**
>
> The Shaw Festival is the only theater festival in the world that specializes in the plays of George Bernard Shaw and plays written during and about the period of Shaw's life.

NIGHTLIFE AND THE ARTS

Fodor's Choice
★
Shaw Festival. Niagara-on-the-Lake remained a sleepy town until 1962, when local lawyer Brian Doherty organized eight weekend performances of two George Bernard Shaw plays, *Don Juan in Hell* and *Candida*. The next year he helped found the festival, whose mission is to perform the works of Shaw and his contemporaries, including Noël Coward, Bertolt Brecht, J. M. Barrie, J. M. Synge, and Anton Chekhov. Now, the festival has expanded to close to a dozen plays, running from April to October, including some contemporary plays by Canadian playwrights, and one or two musicals (which are performed unmiked). All are staged in one of three theaters within a few blocks of one another. The handsome **Festival Theatre,** the largest of the three, stands on Queen's Parade near Wellington Street and houses the box office. The **Court House Theatre,** on Queen Street between King and Regent streets, served as the town's municipal offices from the 1840s until 1969, and is a national historic site. At the corner of Queen and Victoria streets, the **Royal George Theatre** was originally built as a vaudeville house in 1915. The festival is one of the biggest events in the summer. ■TIP➔ Regular-price tickets cost C$30 to C$105, but discounts abound; see "Ways to Save" on the Web site. ⊠ *Shaw Festival Box Office, 10 Queen's Parade, Niagara-on-the-Lake, Ontario* ☎ *905/468–2172, 800/511–7429* ⊕ *www.shawfest.com.*

SHOPPING

Niagara-on-the-Lake's historic Queen Street is lined with Victorian storefronts housing art galleries, women's clothing stores, and tea and sweets shops.

Greaves Jams & Marmalades. Since the company began in 1927, Greaves Jams & Marmalades has been making jams, jellies, and marmalades from mostly local produce using family recipes. The spreads have no preservatives, pectin, or additives. The brand has expanded into an operation with an online store, and its jams are often served for afternoon tea in upscale hotel restaurants. ⊠ *55 Queen St., Niagara-on-the-Lake, Ontario* ☎ *905/468–7831* ⊕ *www.greavesjams.com.*

EN ROUTE

From midsummer to late fall, the Niagara Peninsula's roadside fruit and vegetable stands and farmers' markets are in full bloom, with an abundance of berries, peaches, and cherries, as well as late-summer vegetables like corn and field tomatoes. Some of the best stands are on Highway 55, between Niagara-on-the-Lake and the QEW, and along

Lakeshore Road, between Niagara-on-the-Lake and St. Catharines, some with pick-your-own options.

There are many fruit stands and produce markets along the streets of Niagara-on-the-Lake, but just outside of the area is the mother lode that dwarfs the others. **Harvest Barn Country Markets,** in a barn with a red-and-white-striped awning, sells regional fruits and vegetables and tempts with its fresh-baked goods: sausage rolls, bread, and fruit pies. After shopping for fresh and local ingredients, satisfy your hunger with lunch at the deli, or soup and salad bar, and join locals at the picnic tables. It's open year-round. ⊠ *1822 Niagara Stone Rd./Hwy. 55, Niagara-on-the-Lake, Ontario* ☎ *905/468–3224* ⊕ *www.harvestbarn.ca.*

THE NIAGARA ESCARPMENT

Vineland is 102 km (63 mi) southeast of Toronto and 41 km (25 mi) west of Niagara-on-the-Lake.

The Niagara Peninsula north of St. Catharines is known as Niagara Escarpment or the Twenty Valley, for the huge valley where the region's main towns of Jordan, Vineland, and Beamsville are. This area is much less visited than Niagara-on-the-Lake, and the wineries more spread out. Peach and pear trees, hiking trails, and long stretches of country road are the lay of the land. Aside from wine-tasting, you can also visit the cute-as-a-button town of Jordan.

WHEN TO GO

Unlike Niagara-on-the-Lake, this area doesn't get overcrowded in summer, the ideal season for puttering along the country roads. Many restaurants, cafés, and shops have abbreviated hours between mid-September and late May. Most wineries do open for tastings in winter, but call ahead to be sure and to check on driving conditions, as some of these spots are on steep or remote rural roads.

GETTING HERE AND AROUND

Aside from booking a structured winery tour, getting behind the wheel yourself is the only way to visit the attractions in this region. This area is about 75 minutes from Toronto and 45 minutes from Niagara-on-the-Lake and is a feasible day trip.

ESSENTIALS

Visitor Information Twenty Valley Tourism Association ⊠ *3720 19th St., Jordan, Ontario* ☎ *905/562–3636* ⊕ *www.twentyvalley.ca.*

TOP EXPERIENCE: WINERIES

Fodor'sChoice ★ **Cave Spring Cellars.** On Jordan's Main Street, Cave Spring is one of the leading wine producers in Canada, with Ontario's oldest wine cellars, in operation since 1871. Go for the Riesling, chardonnay, and ice wine. It shares ownership with Inn on the Twenty and On the Twenty restaurant (next door) and produces custom blends for the latter. ⊠ *3836 Main St., Jordan, Ontario* ☎ *905/562–3581* ⊕ *www.cavespring.ca* 🍷 *Tastings C$1–C$4* ☺ *Nov.–May, Sun.–Thurs. 10–5, Fri. and Sat., 10–6; June, Sept., and Oct., daily 10–6; July and Aug., Sun.–Thurs. 10–6, Fri. and Sat. 10–7.*

7

Fielding Estate. Two Adirondack chairs by the cedar framed entrance set the tone for the warm and charming winery within. Inside the modern West Coast–style cedar building with corrugated tin roof and massive stone chimney, Fielding has envious views of vineyards and Lake Ontario from huge picture windows and a big stone fireplace for chilly days. A young team—husband-and-wife owners and two winemakers—has been making quick strides here. The vineyard produces a low yield that enables flavours to be concentrated. Try the 2008 sauvignon blanc or 2007 Viognier, both prizewinners. ⊠ *4020 Locust La., Beamsville, Ontario* ☎ *888/778–7758, 905/563–0668* ⊕ *www.fieldingwines. com* 🖃 *Tastings C$5 (3 wines)* ⊗ *May–Oct., daily 10:30–6; Nov.–Apr., daily 10:30–5:30.*

Tawse. Eco-friendly and partially geothermally powered, Tawse is so committed to producing top-notch pinot noir that it installed a six-level gravity-flow system to avoid overhandling the delicate grape. The investment seems to be paying off, especially with the first-class 2007 Cherry Avenue Pinot Noir and 2008 Quarry Road Gewurztraminer. The rural hillside winery is modern, its big stainless-steel vats visible from the tasting room. Don't leave empty handed because tasting fees are waived if you buy two or more bottles. ⊠ *3955 Cherry Ave., Vineland, Ontario* ☎ *905/562–9500* ⊕ *www.tawsewinery.ca* 🖃 *Tastings C$5 (3 wines)* ⊗ *May–Oct., daily 10–6, Nov.–Apr., daily 10–5.*

★ **Vineland Estates Winery.** One of Ontario's most beautiful wineries occupies 75 acres that were once a Mennonite homestead established in 1845. The original buildings have been transformed into the visitor center and production complex. Several tour and tasting options are available, including a wine and cheese tour and tasting for C$15, and ice-wine tour and tasting for C$25. The excellent Restaurant@Vineland Estates Winery *(see Where to Eat)* serves lunch and dinner, and you can find a guesthouse and a B&B cottage on the property. ⊠ *3620 Moyer Rd., 40 km (25 mi) west of Niagara-on-the-Lake, Vineland, Ontario* ☎ *905/562–7088, 888/846–3526* ⊕ *www.vineland.com* 🖃 *Tastings C$3* ⊗ *Most days 10–6; call or check Web site for details. Public tours mid-May–Oct., daily at 11 and 3; Nov.–mid-May, weekends at 3. Private tours by request.*

EXPLORING

Jordan Village. Charming Main Street Jordan, aka Jordan Village, is a small enclave of cafés and shops selling antiques, garden supplies, and artisanal foods. The Inn on the Twenty, the On the Twenty Restaurant, and Cave Spring Cellars are also here. Just a few blocks long, Jordan Village can be fully explored in a morning or afternoon. Home store **Chic** (⊠ *3836 Main St., Unit 9* ☎ *905/562-0083* ⊕ *www.chicbyjansen. com*) is worth a wander to gawk at unique reproductions of European furniture and art, like Siberian fox throws and a bronze bear the size of an actual bear cub, even if you can't afford a C$4,000 cedar canoe. Gardeners love the **Copper Leaf** (⊠ *3845 Main St.* ☎ *905/562-0244* ⊕ *www.thecopperleaf.com*) for its fine and unique garden accessories and plants. ✛ *Off QEW Exit 55 (Jordan Rd.); follow Jordan Rd. south 3 km (1.9 mi), take right onto Fourth Ave.; follow signs to Cave Spring*

Cellars from here;, Jordan, Ontario ☎ *No phone* ⊕ *www.jordanvillage. com.*

WHERE TO EAT

$$$$
CANADIAN
Fodor's Choice
★

✕ **Inn on the Twenty Restaurant.** The huge windows framing the Twenty Valley conservation area are reason enough to dine at this restaurant on Jordan's boutiques-lined Main Street. Many come from far away to enjoy a meal at what is known as one of the best restaurants around Toronto. Regional specialties and local and organic produce are emphasized on a seasonal menu that has included Wellington County oxtail rillette served with garlic crostini, two mustards, three pickles and frisée salad; and wild Huron trout with potato "mille-feuille" in spring leek cream. The dining room reminiscent of the French and Italian countryside is lovely, with a soaring ceiling, whitewashed exposed beams, and a view of the gardens. Cave Spring Cellars, which has a shop next door, provides many of the wines. ⊠ *3836 Main St., off QEW Exit 55 or 57 (follow Cave Spring Cellars signs), Jordan, Ontario* ☎ *905/562–7313* ⊕ *www.innonthetwenty.com.*

$$$$
CANADIAN
Fodor's Choice
★

✕ **Restaurant@Vineland Estates Winery.** Exquisite progressive Canadian food and venerable wines are served by an enthusiastic staff on this bucolic property with three 19th-century Mennonite stone buildings. Sit on the large outdoor patio overlooking vineyards and Lake Ontario beyond or in the glassed-in restaurant, where many of the tables have a similar panoramic view. The menu is locally sourced and seasonal; salmon from Canada is seared and rests upon sautéed greens and fingerling potatoes blanketed under olive and caper rémoulade. Carnivorous cravings are answered with rare-seared venison haunch with wild rice and juniper *jus*. Desserts, like spiced pumpkin cheesecake served with mascarpone gelato is the perfect demonstration of simplicity and innovation. ⊠ *3620 Moyer Rd., Vineland, Ontario* ☎ *905/562– 7088, 888/846–3526* ⊕ *www.vineland.com* ☾ *Closed Mon. and Tues., Jan.–Apr.*

WHERE TO STAY

For expanded hotel reviews, visit Fodors.com.

$$$$

⌂ **Inn on the Twenty.** Seven of the 24 suites in the main building of this Main Street Jordan inn are 600-square-foot, two-story affairs. **Pros:** large rooms; impeccably decorated; central location for the Twenty Valley. **Cons:** not as much to do in Jordan as in surrounding areas. ⊠ *3845 Main St., off QEW Exit 55 or 57 (follow Cave Spring Cellars signs), Jordan, Ontario* ☎ *905/562–5336, 800/701–8074* ⊕ *www. innonthetwenty.com* ⇌ *28 suites* ⌂ *In-room: a/c, Internet, Wi-Fi. In-hotel: restaurant, spa, business center, parking, some pets allowed* ⍓ *Breakfast.*

BIKING AND HIKING

★ **Bruce Trail.** Canada's oldest and longest footpath, the Bruce Trail stretches 885 km (550 mi) along the Niagara Escarpment, with an additional 400 km (250 mi) of side trails. It takes in scenery from the orchards and vineyards of the Niagara Escarpment—one of Canada's 15 UNESCO World Biosphere Reserves—to the craggy cliffs and bluffs at Tobermory, 370 km (230 mi) north of Niagara-on-the-Lake. You can access the hiking trail at just about any point along the route; the main trail is marked with white blazes, the side trails with blue blazes. Northern parts of the trail are remote.

Consult the *Bruce Trail Reference Guide,* available from the Bruce Trail Conservancy when hiking this trail. ☎ *905/529–6821, 800/665–4453* ⊕ *www.brucetrail.org .*

STRATFORD

145 km (90 mi) west of Toronto.

In July 1953 Alec Guinness, one of the world's greatest actors, joined with Tyrone Guthrie, probably the world's greatest Shakespearean director, beneath a hot, stuffy tent in a quiet town about a 90-minute drive from Toronto. This was the birth of the Stratford Shakespeare Festival, which now runs from April to late October or early November and is one of the most successful and admired festivals of its kind.

Today Stratford is a city of 32,000 that welcomes more than 500,000 visitors annually for the Stratford Shakespeare Festival alone. But Shakespeare is far from the only attraction. The Stratford Summer Music Festival (July and August) is another highlight, shopping in the enchanting city core is a favorite pastime, and with more amazing restaurants than you could hope to try in one visit, dining out in Stratford could be a reason to return.

WHEN TO GO

The festival runs from mid-April through late October or early November. Most visitors choose their travel dates based on the play(s) they want to see. About half of the city's restaurants and B&Bs close off-season; the city is quiet in the colder months, but shops and art galleries stay open, hotels have reduced rates, and you'll rub elbows with locals rather than visitors.

GETTING HERE AND AROUND

Ontario's main east–west highway, the 401, which traverses the province all the way from Michigan to Québec, is the main route from Toronto to Kitchener-Waterloo; from there, Highway 7/8 heads to Stratford. Traffic-free driving time is about two hours. VIA Rail has daily service to downtown Stratford from Toronto's Union Station; the trip is about two hours.

Stratford is an ideal town for cruising via bicycle. Totally Spoke'd rents cruisers, mountain bikes, and tandem bikes (C$35–C$45/day; C$20–C$30/half day).

ESSENTIALS

Bicycle Rental Totally Spoke'd ⊠ *29 Ontario St., Stratford, Ontario* ☎ *519/273–2001* ⊕ *www.totallyspoked.ca.*

Train Information Stratford Train Station ⊠ *101 Shakespeare St., Stratford, Ontario* ☎ *888/842–7245.* **VIA Rail** ☎ *888/842–7245* ⊕ *www.viarail.ca.*

Visitor Information Stratford Shakespeare Festival ⊠ *55 Queen St., Stratford, Ontario* ☎ *519/273–1600, 800/567–1600* ⊕ *www.stratfordfestival.ca.*

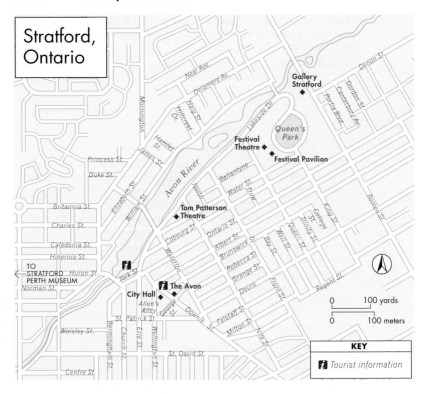

Stratford, Ontario

Stratford Tourism Alliance ✉ *47 Downie St., Stratford, Ontario* ☎ *519/271–5140, 800/561-7926* ⊕ *www.welcometostratford.com.*

EXPLORING

Gallery Stratford. Regular exhibits of Canadian visual art and, in summer, of local artists' work are displayed here. Great for groups of all ages. ✉ *54 Romeo St., Stratford, Ontario* ☎ *519/271–5271* ⊕ *www.gallerystratford.on.ca* 🎟 *C$5* ⊗ *Mid-May.–Sept., Tues.–Sun. 10–5; Oct.–mid-May., Tues.–Sun. 11–3.*

QUICK BITES

The humble potato rises to become a star at Boomer's Gourmet Fries, equipped with a take-out window and a handful of stools at a counter. Toppings of every ilk can be found here, like veg chili, hickory sticks, and salsa. The imaginative pairings apply to burgers as well, with options like bruschetta and goat cheese and the luau (grilled pineapple and ham) on the menu. Fish-and-chips is done simply with cod. Try one of the many unique and delicious takes on a Canadian "delicacy," *poutine:* the traditional version is fries topped with cheese curds and gravy. ✉ *26 Erie St., Stratford, Ontario* ☎ *519/275–3147.*

★ **Stratford Perth Museum.** You can brush up on Stratford and Perth County history with permanent displays and changing exhibits that cover such topics as hockey in Stratford, the city's railroad, and the settlement of the area in the early 1800s. There are hiking trails and picnic areas on the property. ✉ *4275 Huron Rd., Stratford, Ontario* ☎ *519/393–5311* ⊕ *www. stratfordperthmuseum.ca* 📧 *By donation, suggested C$5* ⊙ *May–Aug., Tues.–Sat. 10–4, Sun. and Mon. noon–4; Sept.–Apr., Tues.–Sat. 10–4, closed Sun. and Mon.*

WHERE TO EAT

For a tiny town, Stratford is unusually endowed with excellent restaurants. Perth County is a locavore's dream of farmers' markets, dairies, and organic farms. The proximity of the Stratford Chefs School supplies a steady stream of new talent, and the Shakespeare festival ensures an appreciative audience.

$$$
CONTINENTAL
★

✕ **Bijou.** A husband-and-wife team, both Stratford Chefs School grads, operates this small, self-professed "culinary gem." The chalkboard menu changes daily, and nearly everything on it is locally sourced. Two- or three-course prix-fixe dinners have French, Italian, and Asian influences: duck confit steamed in cabbage leaves with French lentils and bok choy may be an option for your main course. For dessert, there might be a Ontario peach tarte tatin with black-pepper ice cream and basil syrup. The small entrance, next to the Stratford Hotel, is easy to miss: to get here, cross the parking lot on Erie Street, or pass through Allen's Alley, off Wellington Street. ✉ *105 Erie St., Stratford, Ontario* ☎ *519/273–5000* ⊕ *www.bijourestaurant.com* 📧 *Reservations essential* ⊙ *May–Oct., closed Mon., no lunch Tues.–Thurs.; Nov.–Apr. closed Sun.–Thurs., no lunch.*

$$$$
FRENCH
★

✕ **Church Restaurant and Belfry.** Constructed in 1873 as a congregational church, the building has most of the original architecture in place, but today white tablecloths gleam in the afternoon light that pours through the stained-glass windows. Some say the Church, the formal ground-floor dining room, is pretentious; others call it divine, but it's undeniable that the artfully plated modern French meals—spice-crusted loin of elk with pickled Niagara cherries and hazelnuts—are complex production numbers. The menu usually includes lamb and always includes at least one fish entrée. The bistro-style and slightly less expensive Belfry ($$$), upstairs, has more down-to-earth but still-stylish food, such as ice wine–glazed quail with double-smoked bacon, *boudin noir* (blood sausage), and baby vegetables. ✉ *70 Brunswick St., Stratford, Ontario* ☎ *519/273–3424* ⊕ *www.churchrestaurant.com* ⊙ *Church closed Mon. and Jan.–Mar. Belfry closed Sun. and Mon. and Jan.–Mar.*

CLOSE UP

Bringing the Bard to Ontario

In addition to presenting world-class plays, the Stratford Shakespeare Festival holds classes for children.

The origins of Stratford are modest. After the War of 1812, the British government granted a million acres of land along Lake Huron to the Canada Company, headed by a Scottish businessman. Surveyors came to a marshy creek surrounded by a thick forest and named it "Little Thames," noting that it might make "a good mill-site." It was Thomas Mercer Jones, a director of the Canada Company, who renamed the river the Avon and the town Stratford. The year was 1832, 121 years before the concept of a theater festival would take flight and change Canadian culture.

For years Stratford was considered a backwoods hamlet. Then came the first of two saviors of the city, both of them also (undoubting) Thomases. In 1904 an insurance broker named Tom Orr transformed Stratford's riverfront into a park. He also built a formal English garden, where flowers mentioned in the plays of Shakespeare—monkshood to sneezewort, bee balm to bachelor's button—bloom grandly to this day.

Next, Tom Patterson, a fourth-generation Stratfordian born in 1920, looked around; saw that the town wards and schools had names like Hamlet, Falstaff, and Romeo; and felt that some kind of drama festival might save his community from becoming a ghost town. The astonishing story of how he began in 1952 with C$125 (a "generous" grant from the Stratford City Council), tracked down Tyrone Guthrie and Alec Guinness, and somehow, in little more than a year, pasted together a long-standing theater festival is recounted in his memoirs, *First Stage: The Making of the Stratford Festival.*

Soon after it opened, the festival wowed critics worldwide with its professionalism, costumes, and daring thrust stage. The early years brought giants of world theater to the tiny town of some 20,000: James Mason, Alan Bates, Christopher Plummer, Jason Robards Jr., and Maggie Smith. Stratford's offerings are still among the best of their kind in the world— the next-best thing to seeing the Royal Shakespeare Company in sister city Stratford-upon-Avon, in England— with at least a handful of productions every year that put most other summer arts festivals to shame. *For planning information see The Arts.*

$$$ ╳ **Down the Street Bar and Restaurant.** Funky and eclectic, this bistro-
ECLECTIC bar is the hottest place in town and a go-to spot for Festival actors.
Chatter and jazz tunes are the soundtrack in the whimsical bordello-
meets-Macbeth space, decorated with low-hung chandeliers and red
rococo-style wallpaper and drapes—even the ceilings are red. The sea-
sonal menu of only eight entrées is as playful as the decor, ranging from
rib eye with herb shallot butter to sweet chili-fried tofu with coconut
curry rice noodles. A "late-night" menu of dressed-up sandwiches,
burgers, and antipasti is served 'til midnight. On tap is a comprehen-
sive selection of imported beers and microbrews. ⊠ *30 Ontario St.,
Stratford, Ontario* ☎ *519/273–5886* ⊕ *www.downthestreet.ca* ⋐ *Reser-
vations essential* ☯ *Closed Mon. Closed Sun. mid-Oct.–mid-June. No
lunch mid-Oct.–mid-May.*

$$$$ ╳ **The Old Prune.** A converted 1905 house holds a number of charming
CANADIAN gray-purple dining rooms with white table linens surrounded by a tidy
courtyard. Chef Bryan Steele, who is also senior cookery instructor at
Stratford Chefs School, coaxes fresh local ingredients into innovative
dishes with the best of what's available globally. Dishes change with
the harvest but have included Lake Huron whitefish meunière with
asparagus, cinnamon cap mushrooms; and spring risotto with Parme-
san, crispy egg, wild leek pesto. The owners proudly source their lamb
from small family-owned Church Hill Farm, just 30 km (18 mi) away.
The restaurant has a sommelier on staff and has a strong wine list, with
many Ontario options. Desserts are made fresh for each meal. ⊠ *151
Albert St., Stratford, Ontario* ☎ *519/271–5052* ⊕ *www.oldprune.on.ca*
⋐ *Reservations essential* ☯ *Closed Nov.–mid-May and Mon. No lunch.*

$$ ╳ **Pazzo Ristorante and Pizzeria.** A corner of Stratford's main crossroads
ITALIAN is home to one of the city's best and most convivial Italian restaurants.
Have a drink and people-watch at the bar or on the patio. Upstairs
is the Ristorante, with hearty regional-Italian–Continental mains and
house-made pastas, such as pork hock ravioli with pea puree. The three-
course lunch for about C$22 is a steal. Downstairs, in the partially
subterranean brick-and-stone-walled pizzeria, go for the straightforward pasta dishes or the thin-crust pizzas—the two favorites are the
Soprano, with calabrese, portobello mushrooms, and Asiago; and the
Medici, with hot peppers, tomatoes, pesto, black olives, and fresh garlic. It's a popular meeting place after the play, and the service is quick
and friendly. ⊠ *70 Ontario St., Stratford, Ontario* ☎ *519/273–6666*
⊕ *www.pazzo.ca* ☯ *Ristorante closed Mon. and Nov.–mid-May (pizzeria open year-round).*

$$$$ ╳ **Rundles Restaurant.** At Stratford's top choice for sophisticated haute
CONTINENTAL cuisine the look is summery and modern: brick is exposed, windows
Fodor's Choice are unadorned and panoramic, and, with a theatrical flourish, flowing
★ white silk scarves hang from primitive stone masks. Diners have five
to seven choices for each course (appetizer, entrée, and dessert) on the
prix-fixe menu. Offerings change frequently, but regulars would protest the removal of the braised duck confit or, for dessert, the lemon
tart with orange sorbet. The more relaxed **Sophisto-Bistro**, at the same
location, has two- and three-course dinners at slightly less lofty prices
that might include hot-smoked trout salad with fingerling potatoes in

7

a hot bell pepper cream or, for dessert, poached apples and candied apple ice cream. Considerable artistry is lavished on preparation and presentation. ⊠ *9 Cobourg St., Stratford, Ontario* ☎ *519/271–6442* ⊕ *www.rundlesrestaurant.com* ✍ *Reservations essential* ⊘ *Closed Oct.–May (may vary; check Web site for exact dates) and Mon. No lunch weekdays.*

$$$ ✕ **Sun Room.** Stir-fries and noodle dishes were joined by Continental
ECLECTIC choices when new owners took over this Stratford institution in 2010. Additional options draw from the bounty of nearby wine and food producers, such as Perth County pork tenderloin stuffed with caramelized apple and chèvre from C'est Bon Cheese (in St. Mary's) or pan-seared elk with a red-wine jus and blue-potato hash. Save room for dessert: the popular sun-dried-cherry crème brûlée is still on the menu. The casual dining room is modernized with painted black tables, globe lights, high-back leather chairs, and artwork by Stratford Festival set designer John Pennoyer on the walls. Service is welcoming. ⊠ *55 George St., Stratford, Ontario* ☎ *519/271–0331* ⊕ *www.sunroomstratford.com* ✍ *Reservations essential* ⊘ *Closed Sun. No lunch Mon.*

$$ ✕ **York Street Kitchen.** Locals come to this casual spot across from the
CAFÉ waterfront for the signature generously portioned and juicy sandwiches
★ and, for dinner, homemade comfort dishes, such as meat loaf with Yukon Gold mashed potatoes or lamb potpie, but especially for the breakfast served daily: favorites are the French toast with homemade apple compote and the Canadiana sandwich with peameal bacon, mustard, tomato, and egg on a toasted kaiser roll. A build-your-own-sandwich menu (¢) is available for lunch and at the take-out window in summer. The bright dining room is decorated with vibrant-patterned vinyl tablecloths. During festival season the lines form early. ⊠ *41 York St., Stratford, Ontario* ☎ *519/273–7041* ⊕ *www.yorkstreetkitchen.com.*

WHERE TO STAY

For expanded hotel reviews, visit Fodors.com.

Stratford has a wide range of atmospheric B&Bs on the outskirts of downtown, and trendier boutique hotels are scattered around the center. Room rates are discounted substantially in winter, sometimes by more than 50%.

The **Stratford Area Bed & Breakfast Association** conducts regular inspections of area B&Bs and maintains a list of those that pass muster. ☎ *519/272–2961* ⊕ *www.sabba.ca.*

$$ 🏠 **Avery House.** This 1874 Gothic Revival brick home transformed into an impeccably decorated B&B has an eclectic interior. **Pros:** continually updated; affable host; big breakfasts. **Cons:** communal dining and set breakfast time (9:30) not everyone's cup of tea; on a busy road; ground-floor unit's bathroom isn't directly en suite. ⊠ *330 Ontario St., Stratford, Ontario* ☎ *519/273–1220, 800/510–8813* ⊕ *www.averyhouse. com* ➭ *5 rooms, 1 suite* ⚷ *In-room: a/c, no TV, Wi-Fi. In-hotel: business center, parking, some age restrictions* ⊘ *Closed intermittently Nov.–May; call ahead* ⎪⎰⎪ *Breakfast.*

$$ 🏠 **Festival Inn.** This is Stratford's largest hotel, east of town in a commercial area, a 10-minute drive from the theaters. **Pros:** fair prices;

recently renovated rooms; exceptional staff. **Cons:** slightly out of town on a commercial strip. ⊠ *1144 Ontario St., Stratford, Ontario* ☎ *519/273–1150, 800/463–3581* ⊕ *www.festivalinnstratford.com* ↩ *169 rooms* ⚹ *In-room: a/c, Internet. In-hotel: restaurant, bar, pool, parking* ⦿ *Breakfast.*

$$$ ⛫ **Foster's Inn.** Two doors away from the Avon and Studio theaters, this brick building dates to 1906 and has a bit of history—it once housed the International Order of Odd Fellows, a fraternal organization that started in the United Kingdom. **Pros:** great deals in winter; excellent locale; full breakfast menu at restaurant. **Cons:** fills up fast in summer; sometimes a two-night minimum stay required. ⊠ *111 Downie St., Stratford, Ontario* ☎ *519/271–1119, 888/728–5555* ⊕ *www.fostersinn. com* ↩ *9 rooms* ⚹ *In-room: a/c, Wi-Fi. In-hotel: restaurant, bar.*

$$$ ⛫ **Queen and Albert B&B Inn.** A 1901 storefront, now bright blue with a striped awning, is the unique facade of this residential-neighborhood B&B, a 10-minute walk to Stratford's main shopping and eating strip. **Pros:** friendly host; large rooms; two rooms with a shared balcony. **Cons:** mattresses and linens could be more luxurious; no elevator and only one ground-floor room, which has twin beds and is not as impressively decorated as upper-floor rooms. ⊠ *74 Queen St., Stratford, Ontario* ☎ *519/272–0589* ⊕ *www.queenandalbert.com* ↩ *4 suites* ⚹ *In-room: a/c, Wi-Fi. In-hotel: business center, parking, some age restrictions* ⦿ *Breakfast.*

$$$ ⛫ **Stewart House Inn.** The interior of this elegant 1870s home draws on
★ the Victorian period but with modern conveniences. **Pros:** exceptional service; in-house massage; private breakfast tables. **Cons:** not as central as some other inns; ground-floor Garden Room available only in summer. ⊠ *62 John St. N, Stratford, Ontario* ☎ *519/271–4576, 866/826–7772* ⊕ *www.stewarthouseinn.com* ↩ *6 rooms* ⚹ *In-room: a/c, Wi-Fi. In-hotel: pool, parking* ⦿ *Breakfast.*

$ ⛫ **Swan Motel.** The original 1960s motel sign still marks this single-story tawny-brick motel 3 km (2 mi) south of downtown. **Pros:** one of the best deals in town; warm hosts; on a private lot backed by farmland. **Cons:** basic rooms with parking-lot views; not walkable to downtown. ⊠ *960 Downie St., Stratford, Ontario* ☎ *519/271–6376* ⊕ *www.swanmotel.ca* ↩ *24 rooms* ⚹ *In-room: a/c, Wi-Fi. In-hotel: pool, parking* ⊙ *Closed Nov.–May.*

$$$ ⛫ **The Three Houses.** On a quiet residential street, this elegant and taste-
★ fully decorated trio of two Edwardian houses and one Victorian has been frequented by the likes of Kevin Spacey, Julie Andrews, and Christopher Plummer. **Pros:** star appeal; exquisite decorative taste; heated pool. **Cons:** irregular hours in winter; sometimes entire house is rented out to film crews. ⊠ *100 Brunswick St., Stratford, Ontario* ☎ *519/272–0722* ⊕ *www.thethreehouses.com* ↩ *6 suites* ⚹ *In-room: a/c, Wi-Fi. In-hotel: pool, parking* ⦿ *Breakfast.*

THE ARTS

★ **Stratford Summer Music.** For five weeks in July and August, Stratford Summer Music brings musicians—from string quartets to Mexican mariachi bands—to indoor and outdoor venues around town. Outdoor performances, like those sounding from a barge on the Avon River, are free.

The award-winning Festival Theatre, the largest of the Stratford Shakespeare Festival's four venues, has been staging great drama for theater lovers since 1957.

Series may include Saturday-night cabaret at the Church restaurant and classical-music lunches at Rundles. Some performances do sell out, so get tickets in advance. ☎ 519/271–2101 ⊕ *www.stratfordsummermusic.ca.*

Fodor'sChoice
★
Stratford Shakespeare Festival. One of the two largest classical repertory companies in the world—England's Royal Shakespeare Company is the other—the Festival presents not only Shakespeare plays, but also works by other dramatists (including new plays) and popular musicals and musical revues in its four theaters.

Throughout the season, with the height of the festival between July and September, 12 to 16 productions are mounted. The Festival also offers numerous concerts, workshops, tours, lectures, and talks, such as Meet the Festival, where the public can ask questions of actors and artists. The festival has both matinees and evening performances (and many visitors do see two plays per day). Theaters are closed most Mondays. For tickets, information, and accommodations, contact the festival office directly. The 1,800-seat **Festival Theatre** (⊠ *55 Queen St.*), with its hexagonal wooden thrust stage and permanent wooden stage set, is the largest and the oldest of the Festival's theaters—in its first incarnation in 1953 it was just a stage under a tent. The 1,100-seat **Avon Theatre** (⊠ *99 Downie St.*) has a traditional proscenium stage. The **Tom Patterson Theatre** (⊠ *111 Lakeside Dr.*) has a long, runway-style thrust stage and 496 steeply stacked seats. The petite **Studio Theatre** (⊠ *34 George St. E*), with only 260 seats, is the go-to space for experimental and new works; built in 2002, it has a modern appearance and a hexagonal thrust stage. ⊠ *55 Queen St., Stratford, Ontario* ☎ *519/273–1600, 800/567–1600* ⊕ *www.stratfordfestival.ca.*

SHOPPING

Downtown Stratford is a great place for daytime distractions and is utterly devoid of chain stores. Ontario Street alone is lined with quaint bookstores stocking great local reads, chocolatiers, myriad colorful housewares and women's clothing shops, and catch-all gift stores.

The Theatre Store. In two locations (at the Avon and Festival theaters), this is the place for Shakespeare finger puppets, every Shakespeare play ever written, original costume sketches, soundtracks to the musicals, and Bard-themed children's books. Visit their online store if you miss the chance to go in person. ⊠ *Avon Theatre, 100 Downie St., Stratford, Ontario* ☎ *519/271–0055* ⊕ *https://store.stratfordfestival.ca* ⊠ *Festival Theatre, 55 Queen St., Stratford, Ontario* ☎ *519/271–0055.*

Watson's Chelsea Bazaar. At this brimming curio shop you might find a cat curled up among the reasonably priced china, glassware, French soaps, kitchen gadgets, and other bric-a-brac. The Bradshaw family has owned a store at this location in various forms (it used to be a high-end china hall) since the 1800s. ⊠ *84 Ontario St., Stratford, Ontario* ☎ *519/273–1790.*

EN ROUTE The tiny village of St. Jacobs, in Mennonite country 50 km (30 mi) northeast of Stratford, has a main street lined with quilt shops, fresh-from-the-farm food stores, and restaurants whose menus feature locally raised and grown meat and produce.

St. Jacobs Farmers' Market. The St. Jacobs Farmers' Market, just outside of town, has hundreds of indoor and outdoor booths with homemade foods straight from the farm: preserves, pies, smoked meats, and cheeses—plus flea-market fare like crafts and handmade furniture. Don't miss the fresh hot apple fritters, a made-to-order treat worth queuing up for. ⊠ *878 Weber St. N, Waterloo, Ontario* ☎ *519/747–1830* ⊕ *www.stjacobs.com* ⊙ *Early Sept.–mid-June Thurs. and Sat. 7–3:30; mid-June–early Sept. Tues. 8–3, Thurs. and Sat. 7–3:30; also Sun. 10–4 seasonally; call ahead.*

DISCOUNT TICKETS

Regular Stratford Festival tickets are around C$50 to C$110, but there are many ways to pay less. Spring previews and some fall performances are discounted 30%. Savings of 30% to 50% can be had for students and seniors, and theatergoers aged 18 to 29 can buy seats online for C$25 for select performances two weeks prior. Also available are early-ordering discounts, rush seats, and family and group discounts.

SOUTHERN GEORGIAN BAY

Collingwood is 150 km (90 mi) north of Toronto on Hwys. 400 and 26. Midland is 145 km (90 mi) north of Toronto on Hwys. 400 and 93.

The southern shores of Lake Huron's Georgian Bay are home to waterfront towns and beaches that are popular getaways for Torontonians in summer. Ski resorts—Blue Mountain is the most popular—draw city folk as well once the snow falls and become biking and adventure resorts in summer. The region's largest city is Barrie (population 130,000), on the shore of Lake Simcoe, originally a landing place for the area's aboriginal inhabitants and, later, for fur traders. Today it's a big-box-store-filled suburb and one of Toronto's farther-flung bedroom communities. More interesting are the quiet towns of Midland and Penetanguishene (also called Penetang by locals), occupying a small corner of northern Simcoe County known as Huronia, on a snug harbor at the foot of Georgian Bay's Severn Sound. These are docking grounds for trips to the Georgian Bay Islands National Park. To the west, the attractive harbor town of Collingwood, on Nottawasaga Bay, is at the foot of Blue Mountain, the largest ski hill in the province.

WHEN TO GO
After Labour Day and before Victoria Day weekend (late May), few tourist attractions apart from ski resorts are open.

GETTING HERE AND AROUND
Georgian Bay towns and attractions are west of Highway 400, either via Highway 26 toward Collingwood or well marked off Highway 400 north of Barrie. These towns and regions are 2½ to 4 hours from Toronto and are generally long weekend or even weeklong trips from the city.

■TIP→ If you are heading north of Barrie in winter, go with a four-wheel-drive vehicle. Resorts, especially, are usually well off the highway and may require navigating twisting backcountry routes.

ESSENTIALS
Tourism Information **Southern Georgian Bay Chamber of Commerce and Tourism Information** ☎ *705/526–7884, 800/263–7745* ⊕ *www.southerngeorgianbay.on.ca.* **Georgian Bay Coastal Route** ⊕ *www.visitgeorgianbay.com.*

EXPLORING
Sainte-Marie among the Hurons. A Jesuit mission was originally built on this spot in 1639. The reconstructed village, which was once home to a fifth of the European population of New France, was the site of the first European community in Ontario; it had a hospital, farm, workshops, and a church. Workers also constructed a canal from the Wye River. A combination of disease and Iroquois attacks led to the mission's demise. Twenty-two structures, including two native longhouses and two wigwams, have been faithfully reproduced from a scientific excavation. Staff members in period costume demonstrate 17th-century trades, share native stories and legends, and grow vegetables—keeping the working village alive. ⊠ *16164 Hwy. 12 W, 5 km (3 mi) east of Hwy. 93, Midland, Ontario* ☎ *705/526–7838* ⊕ *www.saintemarieamongthehurons.on.ca* 🖼 *Late-Apr.–mid-May and mid-/late Oct., C$10; mid-May–early-Sept., C$12* ☉ *Late Apr.–mid-May and mid-/late Oct., weekdays 10–5; mid-May–early-Sept., daily 10–5; last entry at 4:45.*

Martyrs' Shrine. On a hill overlooking Sainte-Marie among the Hurons, a twin-spired stone cathedral was built in 1926 to honor the eight missionaries stationed in Huronia who were martyred between 1642 and 1649. In 1930 all eight were canonized by the Roman Catholic Church.

PLANNING YOUR OUTDOOR ADVENTURE

The Ontario Tourism Marketing Partnership's Web site (⊕ *www. ontariotravel.net*) is a one-stop-shop for information on outdoor adventures from cycling to snowmobiling. It also publishes a free outdoor-adventure guide. The nonprofit Ontario Trails Council (☎ 877/668–7245 ⊕ *www.ontariotrails.on.ca*) has information on every trail and trail sport in the province; click the Central tab for the Muskokas and Georgian Bay. *For Georgian Bay cruises, see Georgian Bay Islands National Park, in the Southern Georgian Bay section. For Algonquin Park tours, see the "Dogsledding and Moose-spotting" feature in the Algonquin Provincial Park section.*

CAMPING

Peak season in Ontario parks is June through August. Reserve a campsite if possible, though all provincial parks with organized camping have some sites available on a first-come, first-served basis.

Ontario Parks. For detailed information on parks and campgrounds provincewide, to make campground reservations, or to get the *Ontario Parks Guide*, visit the Ontario Parks Web site. ⊕ *www.ontarioparks.com.*

FISHING

Ministry of Natural Resources. Fishing licenses are required for Ontario and may be purchased from Ministry of Natural Resources offices and from most sporting-goods stores, outfitters, and resorts. A C$9.68 Outdoors Card, good for three years, is also required for fishing beyond a day (Canadian residents always need the Outdoors Card). For non-Canadians, the most restrictive (i.e. cheapest) one-day fishing license is C$20.75 (C$12.38 for Canadians); eight-day and one-year licenses are also available. All prices include taxes. ☎ 800/667–1940 ⊕ *www.mnr.gov.on.ca.*

Go Fish Ontario (⊕ *www. gofishinontario.com*), operated by Ontario Tourism, is an excellent planning tool for fishing trips.

SKIING

Ski resorts with downhill runs are concentrated north and west of Barrie. *See recommended resorts in the Sports and the Outdoors section, below.* The central Ontario region also has more than 1,600 km of cross-country ski trails.

Ontario Snow Resorts Association. Ski Ontario has information on the condition of slopes across the province. ☎ 800/668–2746 ⊕ *www. skiontario.ca.*

Also check the **Ontario Parks Ski Report** (⊕ *www.parkreports.com/ skireport*) online.

✉ *16163 Hwy. 12 W, Midland, Ontario* ☎ *705/526–3788* ⊕ *www. martyrs-shrine.com* 🎫 *C$4* ⊙ *Mid-May–mid-Oct., daily 8:30–9.*

Huronia Museum. Nearly one million artifacts on native and Maritime history are on display at the museum building and Huron/Ouendat village. Visitors can expect a contemporary art and extensive photography pieces, in addition to native art and archaeological collections. ✉ *549 Little Lake Park, P.O. box 638, Midland, Ontario* ☎ *705/526–2844, 800/263–7745* ⊕ *huroniamuseumtest.wordpress.com* 🎫 *C$8.60* ⊙ *May–Oct., daily 9–5; Nov.–Apr., weekdays 9–5.*

Georgian Bay Islands National Park. A series of 63 islands in Lake Huron's Georgian Bay, the park can be visited only via boat. Organized boat tours with the park or private companies operate from the weekend closest to May 24 through mid-October, weather permitting. The park's campground, on Beausoleil Island, was refurbished in 2010. The only way to explore one of the islands on foot is to book a trip on the park's Daytripper boat, bring your own boat, or take a water taxi in Honey Harbour (contact the park for details).

The park's own water taxi, the **DayTripper** (☎ *705/526–8907* ⊕ *www. pc.gc.ca/georgianbay* ⌂ *C$15.70* ⊙ *June–early Oct.; call for schedules*), makes the 15-minute trip to Beausoleil Island, which has hiking trails and beaches, from Honey Harbour, 15 km (9 mi) north of Port Severn at Highway 400 Exit 156. The *DayTripper 2* offers weekend crossings to the Northern section of Beausoleil Island.

Two companies do cruises through the Georgian Bay but don't allow you to disembark on any of the islands.

The 300-passenger *Miss Midland*, operated by **Midland Tours** (☎ *705/ 549–3388, 888/833–2628* ⊕ *www.midlandtours.com* ⌂ *C$27*), leaves from the Midland town dock and offers 2½-hour sightseeing cruises daily mid-May to mid-October. The company can arrange departures from Toronto, which includes time to explore the town of Midland.

From the Penetanguishene town dock, **Penetanguishene 30,000 Island Cruises** (☎ *705/549–7795, 800/363–7447* ⊕ *www.georgianbaycruises. com* ⌂ *C$20–C$27*) takes passengers on Penetanguishene Harbour and the Georgian Bay islands tours, including 1½- and 2½-hour cruises of Penetanguishene Harbour and 3½-hour cruises of the 30,000 islands of Georgian Bay, on the 200-passenger MS *Georgian Queen*. Lunch and dinner cruises are available. Captain Steve, the owner and your tour guide, has operated these tours—a family business—since 1985. Cruises depart one to three times daily in July and August; less frequently (but usually Saturday, Sunday, and Wednesday) in May, June, September, and October. ✉ *Town and park welcome center: off Hwy. 400 Exit 153 or 156, Port Severn, Ontario* ☎ *705/526–9804* ⊕ *www.pc.gc.ca/ georgianbay* ⌂ *C$5.80* ⊙ *Late May (Victoria Day weekend)–early Oct.*

♺ **Scenic Caves Nature Adventures.** Explore ancient caves, hike along craggy hilltop trails, get a thrill on zip-line rides, or brave the suspension foot-bridge, 25 meters (82 feet) above the ground with amazing views of the bay, 300 meters (985 feet) below. Hiking boots or sneakers are required. ✉ *Scenic Caves Rd., Collingwood, Ontario* ☎ *705/446–0256* ⊕ *www.sceniccaves.com* ⌂ *C$20.80* ⊙ *May, June, Sept., Oct., Mon.– Fri. 9–5, Sat. and Sun. 9–6. July and Aug., daily 9–8. Last admission 2 hrs before close.*

WHERE TO STAY

For expanded hotel reviews, visit Fodors.com.

$$$$
Fodor's Choice
★

🖼 **Blue Mountain Resort.** The largest ski resort in Ontario, and only getting bigger, this huge property near Collingwood revolves around its brightly painted Scandinavian-style alpine "village" with several blocks of shops, restaurants, bars, a grocery, and a plaza with live music. **Pros:** just a skip and a hop from the pedestrian village where all shops and restaurants are located; wide range of accommodation; excellent skiing. **Cons:** Blue Mountain Inn needs renovation; other accommodations pricey in season. ✉ *108 Jozo Weider Blvd., Blue Mountains, Ontario* ☎ *705/445–0231, 877/445–0231* ⊕ *www.bluemountain.ca* ⮑ *Blue Mountain Inn: 93 rooms, 2 suites; Westin Trillium House: 222 suites; Mosaïc: 85 suites; Village Suites: 447 suites* ⬧ *In-room: a/c, safe, kitchen, Internet, Wi-Fi. In-hotel: restaurant, bar, golf course, pool, tennis court, gym, spa, beach, water sports, children's programs, business center, parking.*

$$ 🏨 **Horseshoe Resort.** Most modern guest rooms at this lodge on a 1,600-acre property have down comforters; some have views of the valley and golf course. **Pros:** free Wi-Fi; fun programs for kids. **Cons:** dull and outdated room decor. ✉ *East of Hwy. 400 Exit 117, Ontario* ☎ *705/835–2790, 800/461–5627* ⊕ *www.horseshoeresort.com* ⮑ *56 rooms, 45 suites* ⬧ *In-room: a/c, Wi-Fi. In-hotel: restaurant, bar, golf course, pool, tennis court, gym, spa, children's programs, parking.*

SPORTS AND THE OUTDOORS

Most ski resorts have a multitude of summer activities, such as mountain biking, golf, and adventure camps.

Fodor'sChoice ★ **Blue Mountain Resort.** The province's highest vertical drop, 720 feet, is at Blue Mountain Resort. Ontario's most extensively developed and frequented ski area has 34 trails, 22 of which are available after dark for night skiing, served by high-speed six-person lifts; quad, triple, and double lifts; and magic carpets. ✉ *Off Hwy. 26, follow signs 7 km [4 mi] west of Collingwood, Ontario 705/445–0231, 416/869–3799 from Toronto* ⊕ *www.bluemountain.ca.*

Horseshoe Resort. One of the few resorts to offer snowboarding, tubing, snowmobiling, snowshoeing, and cross-country and downhill skiing trails and facilities is Horseshoe Resort, about an hour's drive north of Toronto, off Highway 400. The resort has a terrain park, competition-level half-pipe and 26 alpine runs, 15 of which are lit at night, served by six lifts and a magic carpet. The vertical drop is only 304 feet, but several of the runs are rated for advanced skiers. Winter sports is only half the fun. Treetop trekking, horseback riding, and other summer adventures are available as well. ✉ *Horseshoe Valley Rd., R.R. 1, Ontario* ☎ *705/835–2790, 800/461–5627* ⊕ *www.horseshoeresort.com.*

⟳ **Mount St. Louis Moonstone.** Skiers and snowboarders can take advantage of 40 runs at Mount St. Louis Moonstone, 26 km (16 mi) north of Barrie. The majority of slopes are for beginner and intermediate skiers, though there's a sprinkling of advanced runs. The resort's Kids Camp, a day-care and ski-school combination, attracts families. Inexpensive cafeterias within the two chalets serve decent meals. No overnight lodging is available. ✉ *Off Hwy. 400 Exit 131, 24 Mount St. Louis Rd., R.R. 4, Coldwater, Ontario* ☎ *705/835–2112, 877/835–2112* ⊕ *www. mslm.on.ca.*

THE MUSKOKAS

Outcroppings of pink and gray granite, drumlins of conifer and deciduous forest, and thousands of freshwater lakes formed from glaciers during the Ice Age characterize the rustic Muskoka region north of Toronto. Called Muskoka for Lake Muskoka, the largest of some 1,600 lakes in the area, this region is a favorite playground of those who live in and around Toronto. Place names such as Orillia, Gravenhurst, Haliburton, Algonquin, and Muskoka reveal the history of the land's inhabitants, from Algonquin tribes to European explorers to fur traders. This huge 4,761-square-km (1,838-square-mi) swath of land and lakes is also referred to colloquially as Cottage Country. (In Ontario, "cottage" is broadly used to describe any vacation home, from a fishing shack to a near-mansion.) The area became a haven for the summering rich and famous during the mid–19th century, when lumber barons who were harvesting near port towns set up steamship and rail lines, making travel to the area possible. Since then, Cottage Country has attracted urbanites who make the pilgrimage to hear the call of the loon or swat incessant mosquitoes and black flies. A few modern-day celebrities are reported to have cottages here as well. For the cottageless, overnight seasonal camping in a provincial park is an option, as is a stay in a rustic lodge or posh resort.

Tourism Information Haliburton County Tourism ☎ 705/296–1777, 800/461–7677 ⊕ www.haliburtoncounty.ca. **Muskoka Tourism** ☎ 705/689–0660, 800/267–9700 ⊕ www.discovermuskoka.ca.

GRAVENHURST

74 km (46 mi) north of Barrie on Hwy. 11.

Gravenhurst is a town of approximately 10,000 and the birthplace of Norman Bethune, a surgeon, inventor, and political activist who is a Canadian hero. The heart of town is the colorful Muskoka Wharf, with its boardwalk along the water, restaurants, steamship docks, vacation condos, and plaza that hosts festivals and a Wednesday farmers' market from mid-May to early October. Still, Gravenhurst is a tiny town and can be seen in a day or even an afternoon.

WHEN TO GO

As with everywhere in the Muskokas, Gravenhurst comes alive in the summer months, with many attractions opening only after Victoria Day and closing between Labour Day and mid-October, as the weather dictates. However, area resorts do plan winter activities—snowshoeing, sleigh rides, and the like—and restaurants are open (with shorter off-season hours) year-round.

GETTING HERE AND AROUND

From Toronto, take Highway 400 north, which intersects with the highly traveled and often congested Highway 11. Gravenhurst is about 70 km (40 mi) north of the junction on Highway 11. Driving time in good traffic is a bit over two hours. Ontario Northland buses and trains operate six days a week between Toronto's Union Station and downtown Gravenhurst; travel time is 2 hours 10 minutes.

ESSENTIALS

Transportation Information Ontario Northland ☎ *800/461–8558* ⊕ *www. ontarionorthland.ca.* **Gravenhurst Bus and Railway Station** ✉ *150 Second Ave., Gravenhurst, Ontario* ☎ *705/687–2301.*

Visitor Information Gravenhurst Chamber of Commerce ✉ *685-2 Muskoka Rd. N, Gravenhurst, Ontario* ☎ *705/687–4432* ⊕ *www.gravenhurstchamber.com.*

EXPLORING

Bethune Memorial House. An 1880-vintage frame structure, this National Historic Site honors the heroic efforts of field surgeon and medical educator Henry Norman Bethune (1890–1939), who worked in China during the Sino-Japanese War in the 1930s and trained thousands to become medics and doctors. There are period rooms and an exhibit tracing the highlights of his life. The house has become a shrine of sorts for Chinese diplomats visiting North America. ✉ *235 John St. N, Gravenhurst, Ontario* ☎ *705/687–4261* ⊕ *www.pc.gc.ca/lhn-nhs/ on/bethune/index.aspx* 🎟 *C$3.90* ⊙ *June–Aug., daily 10–4; Sept. and Oct., Sat.–Wed. 10–4; Nov.–May, by appointment.*

♺ ★ **Muskoka Steamships Cruises.** In warm weather, cruises tour the Muskoka lakes on historic and reproduction vessels. Excursions range from one to eight hours and include lunch and dinner cruises, sightseeing cruises, and themed trips, like the murder-mystery cruise and, for kids, a cruise with a magic show. The restored 128-foot-long, 99-passenger *RMS Segwun* (the initials stand for Royal Mail Ship) is North America's oldest operating steamship, built in 1887, and is the sole survivor of a fleet that provided transportation through the Muskoka Lakes. The 200-passenger *Wenonah II* is a 1907-inspired vessel with modern technology. Reservations are required. Learn about steamboat history and technology in the **Muskoka Boat and Heritage Centre** with a rotating collection of historic boats that have included a 1924 propeller boat, a 30-foot 1894 steamboat, and gleaming wooden speedboats. ✉ *185 Cherokee La., Muskoka Wharf, Gravenhurst, Ontario* ☎ *705/687–6667, 866/ 687–6667* ⊕ *www.segwun.com* 🎟 *Sightseeing cruises C$18–C$49, lunch and dinner cruises C$49–C$83* ⊙ *June–mid-Oct. by reservation.*

Muskoka Boat & Heritage Centre. Learn about steamboat history and technology in this museum with a rotating collection of historic boats that have included a 1924 propeller boat, a 30-foot 1894 steamboat, and gleaming wooden speedboats. ✉ *275 Steamship Bay Rd., Muskoka Wharf, Gravenhurst, Ontario* ☎ *705/687–2115, 866/687–6667* ⊕ *www.segwun.com* 🎟 *C$6.80* ⊙ *Late June–mid-Oct., Tues.–Fri. 10–6, Sat.–Mon. 10–4; mid-Oct.–late June, Tues.–Sat. 10–4.*

WHERE TO EAT

$$ CAFÉ ✕ **Blue Willow Tea Shop.** The dozen or so petite tables are set with blue-willow-pattern china in this quaint restaurant serving traditional English fare on the Muskoka Wharf overlooking the bay. Afternoon tea—a three-tier platter of shortbread, scones with Devonshire cream, and savory finger sandwiches, plus a pot of tea per person—is served every day from 2 to 4 pm, for C$20. Other than tea, sandwiches, such as grilled bacon and Brie, quiches, and specials like homemade stews are offered for lunch. Popular items on the short dinner menu include

baked fish and chips, prime rib with Yorkshire pudding, and classic bangers and mash. The attached shop sells loose leaf teas and other food items for your own tea party at home. It often opens for special meals on holidays. ✉ *900 Bay St., Muskoka Wharf, Gravenhurst, Ontario* ☎ *705/687–2597* ⊕ *www.bluewillowteashop.ca* ⊗ *Closed Mon. Sept.– June; other hrs vary widely—call ahead.*

$$$$
ECLECTIC
✕ **Elements.** Consistent with the aesthetics of Taboo Resort, Elements offers luxurious and contemporary international cuisine in a structured, modern, and subdued dining room, with sleek black wood veneers, hardwood floors, and a wall of lakefront windows. The Mediterrean, French, and Canadian-inspired menu changes seasonally, but is well-represented by dishes like Thai-style black cod, sea urchin infused scallop and prawn, and Pacific Coast halibut and razor clams with barley risotto. The wine list features more than 350 consignment wines, not available in the LCBO, and includes their own private label. For the highly acclaimed Culinary Theatre (C$95/person; C$150 with wine), bar stools surround the chef's station, giving you an up-close view of the preparation of your meal. Wine classes are offered on Saturdays. ✉ *1209 Muskoka Beach Rd., Gravenhurst, Ontario* ☎ *705/687–2233, 800/461–0236* ⊕ *www.tabooresort.com* ⊲ *Reservations essential* ⊗ *Closed 2nd wk of Dec.–Apr.*

$
CAFÉ
✕ **Marty's World Famous Café.** Duck into this cozy café in the afternoon for what is possibly the best butter tart you've ever tasted. The chalkboard on the wall lists other home-cooked dishes like pies, quiche, and daily soups and sandwiches. Food and decor is simple, natural, and homey, just like the neighborhood. It's located outside of Gravenhurst in Bracebridge. ✉ *5 Manitoba Street, Bracebridge, Ontario* ☎ ⊕ *www.martysworldfamous.com.*

$$$
CANADIAN
★
✕ **North.** Since opening in 2007 in the center of Gravenhurst, North has been praised as one of the best restaurants in Muskoka, serving hearty Canadian fare that makes good use of local meats and produce. The small dining room, with walls lined with paintings by local artists, high-backed dark leather chairs and white tablecloths paired with rustic-looking stained pine floors, has a clean and rustic farm-to-table chic. Chef Alain Irvine's menu changes seasonally but patrons can expect staples such as grilled Angus New York steak with fries, tomatoes in basil oil, and red wine veal glaze; black Angus beef tenderloin and garlic prawn with truffle whipped potato; and fish and chips with house-made tartar sauce; in addition to fresh seafood dishes. Popular dessert includes brownies made with local Muskoka Brewery brown ale. Despite its being one of the classiest establishments in town, the atmosphere is relaxed and the service friendly and attentive. ✉ *530 Muskoka Rd. N, Gravenhurst, Ontario* ☎ *705/687–8618* ⊕ *northinmuskoka.com* ⊗ *Closed Sun. Call for hrs in Nov.–Apr.*

WHERE TO STAY

For expanded hotel reviews, visit Fodors.com.

$$$
⊗
☷ **Bayview-Wildwood Resort.** Seemingly remote but truly only a 20-minute drive south of Gravenhurst, this all-inclusive lakeside resort dates to 1898 and is particularly geared to outdoor types and families.

The Muskoka region north of Toronto is a popular destination for people wanting to escape the faster pace of city life.

Pros: great for families; casual atmosphere; free activities for kids. **Cons:** strict meal times; room decor is passé; noisy cargo trains pass by day and night. ⊠ *1500 Port Stanton Pkwy., R.R. 1, Severn Bridge, Ontario* ☎ *705/689–2338, 800/461–0243* ⊕ *www.bayviewwildwood.com* ⤳ *28 rooms, 26 suites, 16 cottages, 3 houses* ⅊ *In-room: a/c, kitchen, Wi-Fi. In-hotel: restaurant, bar, pool, tennis court, gym, beach, water sports, children's programs, laundry facilities, parking* ⦿ *All-inclusive.*

$$$$
Fodor's Choice
★

⬚ **Taboo Resort, Golf and Spa.** A magnificent 1,000-acre landscape of rocky outcrops and evergreen trees typical of the Muskoka region surrounds this alpine lodge–style, ultra-lux resort. **ros:** fantastic golf course; forest and lake views; excellent spa and restaurant. **Cons:** expensive; too easy to never leave the resort grounds. ⊠ *1209 Muskoka Beach Rd., Gravenhurst, Ontario* ☎ *705/687–2233, 800/461–0236* ⊕ *www. tabooresort.com* ⤳ *79 rooms, 22 suites, 15 Cottage Chalets* ⅊ *In-room: a/c, kitchen, Internet, Wi-Fi. In-hotel: restaurant, bar, golf course, pool, tennis court, gym, spa, beach, water sports, parking* ⦿ *Closed mid-Dec.–Apr.*

SHOPPING

Muskoka Cottage Brewery. You would never guess that in this tiny shop off the main strip of Manitoba St. in neighboring Bracebridge, there's a brewery, tasting room, and retail store for one of the most popular beers in Ontario. For a fun afternoon, arrange for a free tour of the brewery in the back of the complex before tasting a few popular beers like the cream ale and premium lager, or seasonal ales like summer weiss or double chocolate cranberry stout. ⊠ *13 Taylor Rd., Bracebridge, Ontario* ☎ *705/646–1266* ⦿ *Mon.-Sat., 11-5.*

HUNTSVILLE

51 km (32 mi) north of Gravenhurst on Hwy. 11.

Muskoka's Huntsville region is filled with lakes and streams, stands of virgin birch and pine, and deer—and no shortage of year-round resorts. It is usually the cross-country skier's best bet for an abundance of natural snow in southern Ontario. All resorts have trails.

WHEN TO GO

Summer is high season for vacationers in Huntsville, but the town is also ideal for cross-country skiing, ice fishing, and other backcountry winter adventures.

GETTING HERE AND AROUND

From Toronto, take Highway 400 north just past Barrie and then take Highway 11 north about 120 km (75 mi). Without traffic, the trip is about three hours. Ontario Northland trains operate between Toronto's Union Station and Huntsville six days a week; travel time is three hours, and the station is a five-minute drive away, across the bay.

From Gravenhurst, Huntsville is about 55 km (35 mi) north on Highway 11, a 45-minute drive.

ESSENTIALS

Transportation Information Huntsville Bus Station ⌧ *77 Centre St. N, Huntsville, Ontario* ☏ *705/789–6431.* **Huntsville Train Station** ⌧ *26 Station Rd., Huntsville, Ontario* ☏ *No phone.* **Ontario Northland** ☏ *705/789–6431, 800/461–8558* ⊕ *www.ontarionorthland.ca.*

Visitor Information Huntsville/Lake of Bays Chamber of Commerce ⌧ *8 West St. N, Huntsville, Ontario* ☏ *705/789–4771* ⊕ *huntsvillelakeofbays.on.ca.*

WHERE TO EAT

$$$

CANADIAN

★

✕ **The Norsemen Restaurant.** Generations of devotees have returned to this lakeside restaurant in the wooded hills near Huntsville for the warm hospitality and modern Canadian cuisine with French flair, some of whom may even come by canoe or kayak. Built in the 1920s, the lodge became a restaurant in 1970 and is unabashedly rustic and homey: double-sided stone fireplace, locally harvested beams overhead, and oxbows over the doorways. Even the coffee is roasted in-house on a daily basis. Ask to be seated by the screened in porch for a view of the lake to soak in the leisurely evening. Popular and enduring dishes include Ontario rack of lamb and prime rib with Yorkshire pudding. Menu of seven or so entrées include at least one vegetarian option. Round out the meal with fun and modern desserts like s'mores mousse and green-tea poached pear. The extensive wine list is a point of pride. Seatings are between 5:30 and 9:30. ⌧ *1040 Walker Lake Dr., 2 km (1 mi) north of Hwy. 60, Huntsville, Ontario* ☏ *705/635–2473, 800/565–3856* ⊕ *www.norsemen-walkerlake.com* ☾ *Jan.–Mar. closed Sun.–Thurs.; Apr., May, and Sept.–Dec. closed Mon. and Tues.; June–Aug. closed Mon., call to confirm. No lunch.*

WHERE TO STAY

For expanded hotel reviews, visit Fodors.com.

$$$ Deerhurst Resort. This deluxe resort along Peninsula Lake is a 780-acre, self-contained community with restaurants and lodgings to fit every budget and every style, from weddings to corporate events. **Pros:** wide-range of amenities. **Cons:** outdated decor in certain parts of the resort. ⊠ *1235 Deerhurst Dr., just south of Rte. 60, Huntsville, Ontario* ☎ *705/789–6411, 800/461–4393* ⊕ *www.deerhurstresort.com* ☞ *400 rooms* ⟐ *In-room: a/c, Internet, Wi-Fi. In-hotel: restaurant, bar, golf course, pool, tennis court, gym, spa, water sports, parking.*

SKIING

Hidden Valley Highlands Ski Area. Hidden Valley Highlands Ski Area has 35 skiable acres with 13 hills and three quad lifts. It's great for beginner and intermediate skiers, with a couple of black-diamond runs for daredevils. ⊠ *1655 Hidden Valley Rd., off Hwy. 60, 8 km east of town, Huntsville, Ontario* ☎ *705/789–1773* ⊕ *www.skihiddenvalley.on.ca.*

ALGONQUIN PROVINCIAL PARK

35 km (23 mi) east of Huntsville on Hwy. 60.

WHEN TO GO

Most people go to Algonquin in the summer, but the many winter attractions—ice fishing, cross-country skiing, dogsled tours—make it a popular destination in cold months as well. The only time to avoid is the notorious blackfly season, usually sometime in May. The mosquito population is healthy all summer, so pack repellent, pants, and long-sleeved shirts. Algonquin Provincial Park can be done in a weekend, but four days is the average stay; the park is huge and there's a lot of ground to cover.

GETTING HERE AND AROUND

A good four-hour drive from Toronto, Algonquin is most readily reached via Highway 400 north to Highway 60 east. The huge park has 29 different access points, so call to devise the best plan of attack for your visit based on your interests. The most popular entry points are along the Highway 60 corridor, where you'll find all the conventional campgrounds. If you're heading into the park's interior, spring for the detailed Algonquin Canoe Routes Map (C$4.95), available from the park's Web site. The visitor centers, at the park gates, or on the Highway 60 corridor, 43 km (27 mi) east of the west gate, have information on park programs, a bookstore, a restaurant, and a panoramic-viewing deck. ■TIP→ In winter, go with a four-wheel-drive vehicle.

EXPLORING

★ **Algonquin Provincial Park.** Algonquin Provincial Park stretches across 7,650 square km (2,954 square mi), containing nearly 2,500 lakes, 272 bird species, 45 species of mammals, and 50 species of fish and encompassing forests, rivers, and cliffs. The typical visitor is a hiker, canoeist, camper, angler, or all of the above. But don't be put off if you're not the athletic or outdoorsy sort. About a third of Algonquin's visitors come for the day to walk one of the 17 well-groomed and well-signed interpretive trails or to enjoy a swim or a picnic. Swimming is especially good at the Lake of Two Rivers, halfway between the west

7

ADVENTURE TOURS NEAR ALGONQUIN

If planning an Algonquin Park adventure seems daunting, leave it to the pros. Transport from Toronto, meals, and accommodations are included. You might, for example, do a multi-day paddle-and-portage trip, catered with organic meals. Most companies have cabins, some quite luxurious, in Algonquin Park for tour participants; other tours may require backcountry tent camping.

Call of the Wild. Call of the Wild offers guided trips of different lengths—dogsledding and snowmobiling in winter, canoeing and hiking in summer—deep in the park away from the more "touristy" areas. The tour company's in-park Algonquin Eco Lodge is powered only by waterfall. A popular package is a four-day canoe trip and three days relaxing at the lodge. ☎ 905/471-9453, 800/776-9453 ⊕ www.callofthewild.ca.

Northern Edge Algonquin. Northern Edge Algonquin eco-adventure company provides adventurous

learning vacations and retreats with themes such as moose-tracking (via canoe), sea kayaking, yoga, shamanism, and women-only weekends. Home-cooked comfort food is local and organic; lodging ranges from new cabins to tents. ☎ 888/383-8320, ⊕ www. northernedgealgonquin.com.

Voyageur Quest. Voyageur Quest has a variety of adventure wilderness trips year-round in Algonquin Park and throughout northern Ontario, including a number of family-geared vacations. ☎ 416/486-3605, 800/794-9660 ⊕ www. voyageurquest.com.

Winterdance Dogsled Tours. Winterdance Dogsled Tours takes you on half-day, full-day, multiday, and moonlight dogsledding adventures in and near Algonquin Provincial Park. Canoe tours are available in summer, as are kennel visits with the sled dogs. ⊠ 6577 Haliburton Lake Rd., Haliburton, Ontario ☎ 705/457-5281 ⊕ www.winterdance.com.

and east gates along Highway 60. Spring, when the moose head north, is the best time to catch a glimpse of North America's largest land mammal. Getting up at the crack of dawn gives you the best chance of seeing the park's wildlife. Park naturalists give talks on area wildflowers, animals, and birds, and you can book a guided hike or canoe trip. Expeditions to hear wolf howling take place in late summer and early autumn. The **Algonquin Logging Museum** (◷ Mid-June–mid Oct., daily 9–5) depicts life at an early Canadian logging camp with video presentations, re-created camps, and various displays. ⊠ Hwy. 60; main and east gate is west of town of Whitney; west gate is east of town of Dwight, Algonquin Provincial Park, Ontario ☎ 705/633-5572 ⊕ www. algonquinpark.on.ca ⊠ C$13 per vehicle ◷ Apr.–mid-Oct., daily 8 am–10 pm; mid-Oct.–Mar., daily 9–5. Park attractions may have their own operating hrs; call ahead.

WHERE TO EAT

If you'd like wine with dinner, bring your own: park restrictions prohibit the sale of alcohol here.

Highway 60 takes drivers on a scenic route through Ontario's famed Algonquin Provincial Park.

$$$$ ✕ **Arowhon Pines Restaurant.** A meal at this breathtaking, circular log-
CANADIAN cabin restaurant in the heart of Algonquin Park is the highlight of
many visits. A view of the lake is a great accompaniment to the food,
but a towering stone fireplace in the center of the room is an attraction, too. Menu changes daily, but guests can expect hearty Canadian
dishes with local and seasonal ingredients like Northern Ontario trout
with sautéed potatoes and squash, rack of lamb scented with garlic and
rosemary, or roasted loin of pork stuffed with apples and prunes. The
menu always includes plenty of vegetarian options, and other diets are
readily accommodated. Bring your own wine for no corkage fee. Dinners are C$70 prix-fixe for the public. Lunch and breakfast are also
served. ✉ *Algonquin Provincial Park, near west entrance, 8 km north
of Hwy. 60, Algonquin Provincial Park, Ontario* ☎ *705/633–5661,
866/633–5661* ⊕ *www.arowhonpines.com* ⌨ *Reservations essential*
🍴 *BYOB* ☾ *Closed mid-Oct.–late-May.*

$$$$ ✕ **Bartlett Lodge Restaurant.** In the original 1917 lodge building, this small
CANADIAN lakeside pine dining room offers an ever-changing prix-fixe menu of
comtemporary Canadian cuisine, which might kick off with fennel and
mustard rubbed pork belly and move on to pistachio and cherry crusted
Australian rack of lamb or the house specialty, beef tenderloin. Fish and
vegetarian options, such as sweet-potato gnocchi with shaved Gruyère,
are always available. Desserts, included with the meal, all made on-
site, feature cheesecakes, some variation of crème brûlée (perhaps a
chocolate-chili version), and homemade pie. Breakfast is served from
8 am to 9:30 am, and dinner seatings are at 6 pm and 8 pm only. ✉ *Algonquin Park, by boat from Cache Lake Landing, just south of Hwy.
60, Huntsville, Ontario* ✉ *Box 297, Lakeshore Rd. E, Oakville, Ontario*

☎ *705/633–5543, 866/614–5355* ⊕ *www.bartlettlodge.com* ⚓ *Reservations essential* 🍽 *BYOB* ⊗ *Closed late-Oct.–mid-May. No lunch.*

WHERE TO STAY

For expanded hotel reviews, visit Fodors.com.

$$$$ 🏨 **Arowhon Pines.** The stuff of local legend, Arowhon is a family-run wilderness retreat deep in Algonquin Provincial Park known for unpretentious rustic "luxury" and superb dining. **Pros:** all-inclusive swimming, sailing, canoeing, kayaking, hiking, and birding on a private lake in a gorgeous setting; excellent restaurant. **Cons:** limited menu; pricey considering rusticity of cabins; only half the rooms have water views. ✉ *Algonquin Park, near west entrance, 8 km north of Hwy. 60, Algonquin Provincial Park, Ontario* ☎ *705/633–5661, 866/633–5661 toll-free year-round* ⊕ *www.arowhonpines.ca* ➘ *50 rooms in 13 cabins* ⚮ *In-room: no a/c, no TV. In-hotel: restaurant, tennis court, beach, water sports, parking* ⊗ *Closed mid-Oct.–late May* 🍽 *All-inclusive.*

$ 🏨 **Bartlett Lodge.** Smack in the center of Algonquin Provincial Park, this impressive 1917 resort is reached by a short boat ride on Cache Lake (just make your reservation and use the phone at the landing to call the lodge when you arrive), and one of only two that is inside the provincial park. **ros:** completely quiet; each cabin has its own canoe and porch. **Cons:** restaurant is expensive and only offers dinner (or picnic lunches). ✉ *Algonquin Park, by boat from Cache Lake Landing, just south of Hwy. 60, Algonquin Provincial Park, Ontario* ☎ *705/633–5543, 905/338–8908 in winter* ⊕ *www.bartlettlodge.com* ➘ *12 cabins, 2 platform tents* ⚮ *In-room: no a/c, no TV. In-hotel: restaurant, water sports, parking* ⊗ *Closed late Oct.–early May* 🍽 *Some meals.*

SPORTS AND THE OUTDOORS

OUTFITTERS **Algonquin Outfitters.** Algonquin Outfitters is the most well-known outfitter and has multiple locations in and around the park, specializing in canoe trip packages and rentals, outfitting and camping services, sea kayaking, and a water-taxi service to the park's central areas. Stores are at Oxtongue Lake (the main store—near the west Highway 60 park entrance), Huntsville, Opeongo Lake, Bracebridge, Haliburton, and Brent Base on Cedar Lake. Call to confirm equipment rentals. Visit their blog at ⊕ *www.algonquinoutfitters.blogspot.com* for updates on park conditions and other happenings. ✉ *Oxtongue Lake store:, 1035 Algonquin Outfitters Rd., R.R. 1, just north of Hwy. 60, Dwight, Ontario* ☎ *705/635–2243, 800/469–4948* ⊕ *www.algonquinoutfitters. com.*

CLOSE UP

Camping in Algonquin Provincial Park

Algonquin Provincial Park. Campgrounds, backcountry camping, and cabins are all available inside the park. Along the parkway corridor, a 56-km (35-mi) stretch of Highway 60, are eight organized campgrounds. Prices range from C$30.25 to C$40 depending on the location and whether you require electricity. Within the vast park interior you won't find any organized campsites (and the purists love it that way). Interior camping permits are C$11 per person, available from Ontario Parks. Contact Algonquin Park's main number to learn about the guidelines for interior camping before calling Ontario Parks to reserve. In between the extremes of the corridor campgrounds and interior camping are the lesser-known peripheral campgrounds—Kiosk, Brent, and Achray—in the northern and eastern reaches of the park, which you access by long dirt roads. These sites do not have showers, and Brent has only pit toilets. The Highway 60 corridor campsites have showers, picnic tables, and, in some cases, RV hookups.

A bit less extreme than pitching a tent in Algonquin's interior but just as remote is a stay in one of the park-run ranger cabins (C$58–C$135 per person, C$12 each additional adult), which have woodstove or propane heat and, in some cases, mattresses and electricity. Four of the 13 cabins are accessible by car; the rest are reached by canoe, which can take from one hour to two days. Reservations are required for all campsites, cabins, and for interior camping; call the **Ontario Parks reservations line** (☎ 888/668–7275 ⊕ www.ontarioparks.com) ✉ Algonquin Provincial Park, Ontario ☎ 705/633-5572.

Portage Store. If you plan to camp in the park, you may want to contact the Portage Store, which provides extensive outfitting services and guided canoe trips. It rents canoes and sells self-guided canoe "packages" that include all the equipment you need for a canoeing-and-camping trip in the park. Also available are bike rentals, maps, detailed information about routes and wildlife, and an on-site general store and casual restaurant. When you arrive, employees can help you brush up on your paddling and portaging skills. ✉ *Hwy. 60, Canoe Lake, Algonquin Park, Algonquin Provincial Park, Ontario* ☎ *705/633–5622 in summer, 705/789–3645 in winter* ⊕ *www.portagestore.com.*

7

Travel Smart

GETTING HERE AND AROUND

Most of the action in Toronto happens between just north of Bloor and south to the waterfront and from High Park in the west to the Beach in the east. It's easy to get around this area via subway, streetcar, and bus. Service is frequent.

Yonge Street (pronounced "young") is the official dividing line between east and west streets. It's a north–south street that stretches from the waterfront up through the city. Street numbers increase heading away from Yonge in either direction. North–south street numbers increase heading north from the lake.

▌ AIR TRAVEL

Flying time to Toronto is 1½ hours from New York and Chicago and 5 hours from Los Angeles. Nonstop to Toronto from London is about 7 hours.

Most airlines serving Toronto have numerous daily trips. Allow extra time for passing through customs and immigration, which are required for all passengers, including Canadians. The 2½-hour advance boarding time recommended for international flights applies to Canada. The Toronto airport has check-in kiosks for Air Canada flights, which cut back on time spent in line.

Brace yourself for the possibility of weather delays in winter.

All travelers must have a passport to enter or reenter the United States. U.S. Customs and Immigration maintains offices at Pearson International Airport in Toronto; U.S.-bound passengers should arrive early to clear customs before their flight.

Security measures at Canadian airports are similar to those in the United States.

Airline Security Issues Canadian Transportation Agency ☎ *888/222–2592* ⊕ *www. cta-otc.gc.ca.* **Transportation Security Administration** ⊕ *www.tsa.gov.*

NAVIGATING TORONTO

■ The CN Tower can be seen from most anywhere in the city except on very cloudy days. Remember its location (Front and John streets) to get your bearings.

■ Lake Ontario is the ultimate landmark. It's always south, no matter where you are.

■ The subway is the fastest way to get around. Stay at a hotel near a subway line to make navigating the city easier.

■ The streetcar and bus signs can be easy to miss. Look for the red, white, and blue signs with a black streetcar picture on electrical poles near street corners every five blocks or so along the route.

AIRPORTS

Most flights into Toronto land at Terminals 1 and 3 of Lester B. Pearson International Airport (YYZ), 32 km (20 mi) northwest of downtown. There are two main terminals, so check in advance which one your flight leaves from to save hassles. The automated LINK cable-line shuttle system moves passengers almost noiselessly between Terminals 1 and 3 and the GTAA Reduced Rate Parking Lot.

Wi-Fi Internet access is free in both terminals. There are several chain hotels at the airport.

The airport departure tax from Pearson International is C$20 per person (C$8 for connecting passengers), included in the price of your airline ticket.

Porter Airlines—which flies to Boston, Chicago, Halifax, Montréal, Newark, Ottawa, and Québec City—is the only airline operating from Billy Bishop Toronto City Airport (YTZ), often called Toronto Island Airport. The airport departure tax here is C$15 per person and is also included in the ticket price. There are few amenities at this smaller airport, but it is very convenient to downtown.

Airport Information Lester B. Pearson International Airport ☎ 416/776–3000 ⊕ www.gtaa.com. **Billy Bishop Toronto City Airport** ☎ 416/203–6942 ⊕ www.torontoport. com/airport.asp.

GROUND TRANSPORTATION

Although Pearson International Airport is not far from downtown, the drive can take well over an hour during weekday rush hours from 6:30 to 9:30 am and 3:30 to 6:30 pm. Taxis to a hotel or attraction near the lake cost C$49 or more and have fixed rates to different parts of the city. (Check fixed-rate maps at ⊕ www.gtaa. com.) You must pay the full fare from the airport, but it's often possible to negotiate a lower fare going to the airport from downtown with regular city cabs. It's illegal for city cabs to pick up passengers at the airport, unless they are called—a time-consuming process sometimes worth the wait for the lower fare. Likewise, airport taxis cannot pick up passengers going to the airport; only regular taxis can be hailed or called to go to the airport.

A 24-hour Airport Express coach service runs daily to several major downtown hotels and the Toronto Coach Terminal (Bay and Dundas streets). It costs C$21.95 one-way, C$36.25 round-trip. Pickups are from the arrivals levels of the terminals at Pearson. Look for the curbside bus shelter, where tickets are sold.

GO Transit interregional buses transport passengers to the Yorkdale and York Mills subway stations from the arrivals levels. Service can be irregular (once per hour) and luggage space limited, but at C$4.70 it's one of the least expensive way to get to the city's northern sections (or onto the subway line).

Two Toronto Transit Commission (TTC) buses also run from any of the airport terminals to the subway system. Bus 192 (Airport Rocket bus) connects to the Kipling subway station; Bus 58 Malton links to the Lawrence West station. Luggage space is limited and no assistance is given, but the price is only C$3 in exact change (⇨ See Bus Travel).

If you rent a car at the airport, ask for a street map of the city. Highway 427 runs south some 6 km (4 mi) to the lakeshore. Here you pick up the Queen Elizabeth Way (QEW) east to the Gardiner Expressway, which runs east into the heart of downtown. If you take the QEW west, you'll find yourself swinging around Lake Ontario, toward Hamilton, Niagara-on-the-Lake, and Niagara Falls.

From Toronto Island Airport a free ferry operates to the terminal at the base of Bathurst Street; the trip takes less than 10 minutes. Porter Airlines also runs a free shuttle from Union Station to the ferry terminal.

Contacts GO Transit ☎ 416/869–3200, 888/438–6646 ⊕ www.gotransit.com. **Airport Express** ☎ 905/564–6333, 800/387–6787 ⊕ www.torontoairportexpress.com. **Toronto Transit Commission or TTC** ☎ 416/393–4636 ⊕ www.ttc.ca.

TRAVEL TO DOWNTOWN TORONTO FROM PEARSON AIRPORT		
Mode of Transport	Duration	Price
Taxi	45–90 min	C$49
Airport Express bus	45–90 min	C$21.95
GO train	40 min	C$4.70
Car	45–90 min	NA
TTC	40 min	C$3

FLIGHTS

Toronto is served by Air Canada, American, Continental, Delta, United, and US Airways as well as more than a dozen European and Asian carriers with easy connections to many U.S. cities. Toronto is also served within Canada by Air Canada Jazz, WestJet, Porter, and Air Transat, a charter airline.

Airline Contacts Air Canada ☎ 888/247–2262, 514/393–3333 ⊕ www.aircanada. com. **Air Canada Jazz** ☎ 888/247–2262,

514/393–3333 ⊕ www.flyjazz.ca. **Air Transat** ☎ 877/872–6728, 514/636–3630 ⊕ www. airtransat.ca. **American Airlines** ☎ 800/433–7300 ⊕ www.aa.com. **Continental Airlines** ☎ 800/523–3273 for U.S. and Mexico reservations, 800/231–0856 for international reservations ⊕ www.continental.com. **Delta Airlines** ☎ 800/221–1212 for U.S. reservations, 800/241–4141 for international reservations ⊕ www.delta.com. **Porter Airlines** ☎ 888/619–8622, 416/619–8622 ⊕ www. flyporter.com. **United Airlines** ☎ 800/864–8331 for U.S. reservations, 800/538–2929 for international reservations ⊕ www.united. com. **US Airways** ☎ 800/428–4322 for U.S. and Canada reservations, 800/622–1015 for international reservations ⊕ www.usairways. com. **WestJet** ☎ 888/937–8538 ⊕ www. westjet.com.

▌ BOAT TRAVEL

Frequent ferries connect downtown Toronto with the Toronto Islands. In summer, ferries leave every 15 to 30 minutes for Ward's Island, every hour for Centre Island, and every 30 to 45 minutes for Hanlan's Point. Ferries begin operation between 6:30 and 9 am and end between 10 and 11:45 pm. Fares are C$6.50 round-trip.

Boat Information Toronto Islands Ferry ☎ 416/392–8193 ⊕ www.toronto.ca/parks/ island.

▌ BUS TRAVEL

ARRIVING AND DEPARTING

Most buses arrive at the Toronto Coach Terminal, which serves a number of lines, including Greyhound (which has regular service to Toronto from all over the United States), Coach Canada, Ontario Northland, and Can-AR. The trip takes 6 hours from Detroit, 3 hours from Buffalo, and 11 hours from Chicago and New York City. During busy times, such as around holidays, border crossings can add an hour or more to your trip as every passenger must disembark and be questioned.

Information on fares and departure times is available online or by phone. Tickets are purchased at the Toronto Coach Terminal before boarding the buses.

Some Canadian bus lines do not accept reservations, but Coach Canada and Greyhound Canada allow online ticket purchases, which can then be printed out ahead of time or picked up at the station. On most lines, there are discounts for senior citizens (over 60), children (under 12), and students (with ISIC cards). Purchase your tickets as far ahead as possible, especially for holiday travel. Seating is first-come, first-served; arriving 45 minutes before your bus's scheduled departure time usually gets you near the front of the line.

A low-cost bus company, Megabus, runs from Buffalo, New York, to Toronto through Niagara Falls. The further in advance tickets are purchased, the less expensive they are.

WITHIN TORONTO

Toronto Transit Commission (TTC) buses and streetcars link with every subway station to cover all points of the city. ⇨ See *Public Transportation Travel.*

Bus Information Can-AR ☎ 905/738–2290 ⊕ www.can-arcoach.com. **Coach Canada** ☎ 800/461–7661 ⊕ www.coachcanada. com. **Greyhound Lines of Canada Ltd.** ☎ 416/594–1010, 800/661–8747 ⊕ www. greyhound.ca. **Megabus** ☎ 800/461–7661 ⊕ www.megabus.com. **Ontario Northland** ☎ 705/472–4500, 800/461–8558 ⊕ www.ontc. on.ca. **Toronto Coach Terminal** ✉ 610 Bay St., just north of Dundas St. W, Dundas Square Area, Ontario ☎ 416/393–7911 ⊕ http:// torontocoachterminal.com.

▌ CAR TRAVEL

Given the relatively high price of gas, Toronto's notoriously terrible traffic, and the ease of its public transportation system, car travel is recommended only for those who wish to drive to sites and attractions outside the city, such as the Niagara

Wine Region, Niagara Falls, and live theater at Stratford or Niagara-on-the-Lake. The city of Toronto has an excellent transit system that is inexpensive, clean, and safe, and cabs are plentiful.

In Canada your own driver's license is acceptable for a stay of up to three months. In Ontario, you must be 21 to drive a rental car. There may be a surcharge of C$10–C$30 per day if you are between 21 and 25. Agreements may require that the car not be taken out of Canada, including the U.S. side of Niagara Falls; check when booking.

CAR RENTAL

Rates in Toronto begin at C$30 a day and C$150 a week for an economy car with unlimited mileage. This does not include tax, which is 13%. If you prefer a manual-transmission car, check whether the rental agency of your choice offers it; some companies don't in Canada. All of the major chains listed *below* have branches both downtown and at Pearson International Airport.

Contacts Alamo ☎ 800/522–9696 ⊕ *www. alamo.com.* **Avis** ☎ 800/331–1084 ⊕ *www. avis.com.* **Budget** ☎ 800/472–3325 ⊕ *www. budget.com.* **Discount Car and Truck Rental** ☎ 800/263–2355 outside Ontario or in U.S., 416/249–5800 in Toronto, 888/820–7378 in Ontario ⊕ *www.discountcar.com.* **Enterprise** ☎ 416/798–1465, 800/261–7331 ⊕ *www. enterprise.com.* **Hertz** ☎ 800/654–3001 ⊕ *www.hertz.com.* **National Car Rental** ☎ 800/227–7368 ⊕ *www.nationalcar.com.*

GASOLINE

Distances are always shown in kilometers, and gasoline is always sold in liters. (A gallon has 3.8 liters.)

Gas prices in Canada are higher than in the United States and have been on the rise. At this writing, the per-liter price is between C$1.25 and C$1.35 (US$4.73–$5.10 per gallon). Gas stations are plentiful; many are self-service and part of small convenience stores. Large stations are open 24 hours; smaller ones close after the dinner rush. For up-to-date prices and where to find the cheapest gas in the city (updated daily), go to ⊕ *www. torontogasprices.com.*

PARKING

Toronto has green parking-meter boxes everywhere. Parking tickets net the city C$50 million annually, so they are frequently given out. Boxes are computerized; regular rates between C$1 and C$2.50 per half hour are payable with coins—the dollar coin, the two-dollar coin, and nickels, dimes, and quarters are accepted—or a credit card (AE, MC, or V). Parking lots are found under office buildings or on side streets near main thoroughfares.

ROAD CONDITIONS

Rush hours in Toronto (6:30 to 9:30 am and 3:30 to 6:30 pm) are bumper-to-bumper, especially on the 401 and Gardiner Expressway. Avoid them like the plague, particularly when coming into or leaving the city.

ROADSIDE EMERGENCIES

The American Automobile Association (AAA) has 24-hour road service in Canada, provided via a partnership with the Canadian Automobile Association (CAA).

Emergency Services Canadian Automobile Association ☎ 416/221–4300, 800/268–3750 ⊕ *www.caa.ca.*

RULES OF THE ROAD

By law, you are required to wear seat belts and to use infant seats in Ontario. Fines can be steep. Drivers are prohibited from using handheld cellular phones. Right turns are permitted on red signals unless otherwise posted. You must come to a complete stop before making a right turn on red. Pedestrian crosswalks are sprinkled throughout the city, marked clearly by overhead signs and very large painted yellow Xs. Pedestrians have the right of way in these crosswalks; however, Toronto pedestrians rarely heed crosswalk signals, so use caution in driving along downtown streets. The speed limit in most areas of the city is 50 kph

(30 mph) and usually within the 90–110 kph (50–68 mph) range outside the city.

Watch out for streetcars stopped at intersections. Look to your right for a streetcar stop sign (red, white, and blue signs on electrical poles). ⚠ It's illegal to pass or pull up alongside a streetcar stopped at an intersection—even if its doors aren't open—as it might be about to pick up or drop off passengers. Stop behind the streetcar and wait for it to proceed.

Ontario is a no-fault province, and minimum liability insurance is C$200,000. If you're driving across the Ontario border, bring the policy or the vehicle-registration forms and a free Canadian Non-Resident Insurance Card from your insurance agent. If you're driving a borrowed car, also bring a letter of permission signed by the owner.

Driving motorized vehicles while impaired by alcohol is taken seriously in Ontario and results in heavy fines, imprisonment, or both. It's illegal to refuse to take a Breathalyzer test. The possession of radar-detection devices in a car, even if they are not in operation, is illegal in Ontario. Studded tires and window coatings that do not allow a clear view of the vehicle interior are forbidden.

FROM THE U.S.
Expect a wait at major border crossings. The wait at peak visiting times can be 60 minutes. If you can, avoid crossing on weekends and holidays at Detroit–Windsor, Buffalo–Fort Erie, and Niagara Falls, New York–Niagara Falls, Ontario, when the wait can be even longer.

Highway 401, which can stretch to 16 lanes in metropolitan Toronto, is the major link between Windsor, Ontario (and Detroit), and Montréal, Québec. There are no tolls anywhere along it, but you should be warned: between 6:30 and 9:30 each weekday morning and from 3:30 to 6:30 each afternoon, the 401 can become very crowded, even stop-and-go; plan your trip to avoid rush hours. A toll highway, the 407, offers quicker travel;

there are no tollbooths, but cameras photograph license plates and the system bills you, if it has your address. It has access to plates registered in Georgia, Maryland, Maine, Michigan, New York, Ohio, Ontario, Québec, and Wisconsin. If you are not identified then you don't have to pay. The 407 runs roughly parallel to the 401 for a 65-km (40-mi) stretch immediately north of Toronto.

If you're driving from Niagara Falls (U.S. or Canada) or Buffalo, New York, take the Queen Elizabeth Way (QEW), which curves along the western shore of Lake Ontario and eventually turns into the Gardiner Expressway, which flows right into downtown.

Insurance Information Insurance Bureau of Canada ☎ 416/362–2031 ⊕ www.ibc.ca.

▮ PUBLIC TRANSPORTATION

The Toronto Transit Commission (TTC), which operates the buses, streetcars, and subways, is safe, clean, and reliable. There are three subway lines, with 65 stations along the way: the Bloor–Danforth line, which crosses Toronto about 5 km (3 mi) north of the lakefront, from east to west; the Yonge–University line, which loops north and south like a giant "U," with the bottom of the "U" at Union Station; and the Sheppard line, which covers the northeastern section of the city. A light rapid transit (LRT) line extends service to Harbourfront along Queen's Quay.

Buses and streetcars link with every subway station to cover all points of the city. Service is generally excellent, with buses and streetcars covering major city thoroughfares about every 10 minutes; suburban service is less frequent.

TICKETS
The single fare for subways, buses, and streetcars is C$3. An all-day unlimited-use pass (valid from the start of service until 5:30 am the next day) is C$10; five tickets or tokens are available for C$12.50;

10 tickets or tokens are C$25. ■TIP→ On weekends and holidays, up to two adults and four children can use the C$10 day pass—an excellent savings.

Tokens and tickets are sold in each subway station and many convenience stores. All vehicles accept tickets, tokens, or exact change, but you must buy tickets and tokens before you board. With tickets or exact change on the subway, you must use the turnstile closest to the station agent window and drop the ticket or money into the clear receptacle, whereas a token or swipecard can be used at any turnstile. Paper transfers are free; pick one up from the driver when you pay your fare on the bus or streetcar or get one from the transfer machines just past the turnstiles in the subway, then give the driver or station agent the transfer on the next leg of your journey. Note that transfers are time-sensitive from your start point, and TTC staff knows how long it takes to get to your transfer point to prevent misuse.

If you plan to stay in Toronto for a month or longer, consider the Metropass, a prepaid card (C$121) that allows unlimited rides during one calendar month.

TTC TICKET/PASS	PRICE
Single Fare	C$3
Day Pass	C$10
5-Ticket or -Token Pack	C$12.50
10-Ticket or -Token Pack	C$25
Monthly Unlimited Pass	C$121

HOURS AND FREQUENCY

Subway trains run from approximately 6 am to 1:30 am Monday through Saturday and from 9 am to 1:30 am Sunday; holiday schedules vary. Subway service is frequent, with trains arriving every two to five minutes. Most buses and streetcars operate on the same hours as the subway. On weekdays, subway trains get very crowded (especially on the Yonge–University line northbound and the Bloor–Danforth line eastbound) from 8 to 10 am and 4 to 7 pm.

Late-night buses along Bloor and Yonge streets, and as far north on Yonge as Steeles Avenue, run from 1 am to 5:30 am. Streetcars that run 24 hours include those on King Street, Queen Street, and College Street. Late-night service is slower, with buses or streetcars arriving every 30 minutes or so. All-night transit-stop signs are marked with reflective blue bands.

Streetcar lines, especially the King line, are interesting rides with frequent service. Riding the streetcars is a great way to capture the flavor of the city as you pass through many neighborhoods.

STOPS AND INFORMATION

Streetcar stops have a red pole with a picture of a streetcar on it. Bus stops usually have shelters and gray poles with bus numbers and route maps posted. Both buses and streetcars have their final destination and their number on both the front and back and side windows. The drivers are friendly and will be able to help you with your questions.

The free *Ride Guide,* published annually by the TTC, is available in most subways. It shows nearly every major place of interest in the city and how to reach it by public transit. The TTC's telephone information line provides directions in 20 languages.

Smoking is prohibited on all subway trains, buses, and streetcars, a rule that is strictly enforced.

Subway and Streetcar Information Toronto Transit Commission or TTC ☎ 416/393–4636, *416/393–4100 for lost and found* ⊕ *www.ttc.ca.*

▌ TAXI TRAVEL

Taxis can be hailed on the street, but if you need to make an appointment (e.g., for an early-morning airport run) or if you are in a residential neighborhood, it's necessary to call ahead. Taxi stands are rare and usually only at hotels and at the airport.

Taxi fares are C$4 for the first 0.155 km and C25¢ for each 31 seconds not in motion and for each additional 0.155 kilometers. A C$0.25 surcharge is added for each passenger in excess of four. The average fare to take a cab across downtown is C$8–C$9, plus a roughly 15% tip (⇨ see Tipping), when the traffic is flowing normally. The largest companies are Beck, Co-op, Diamond, Metro, and Royal.

■**TIP→ Call ☎ 416/829–4222 to be connected to one of many taxi companies for free via an automated system.**

Taxi Companies Beck ☎ 416/751–5555, 877/883–2325 ⊕ www.becktaxi.com. **Co-op** ☎ 416/504–0663, 877/471–4023 ⊕ www.co-opcabs.com. **Diamond** ☎ 416/366–6868 ⊕ www.diamondtaxi.ca. **Metro** ☎ 416/504–8294. **Royal** ☎ 416/777–9222 ⊕ www.royaltaxi.ca.

▐ TRAIN TRAVEL

Amtrak has service from New York and Chicago to Toronto (both 12 hours), providing connections between its own United States–wide network and VIA Rail's Canadian routes. VIA Rail runs trains to most major Canadian cities; travel along the Windsor–Québec City corridor is particularly well served. Amtrak and VIA Rail operate from Union Station on Front Street between Bay and York streets. You can walk underground to a number of hotels from the station, and there is a cab stand outside its main entrance.

Trains to Toronto may have two tiers of service: business class and reserved coach class. Business class is usually limited to one car, and benefits may include more legroom, meals, free Internet access, and complimentary alcoholic beverages.

To save money, look into rail passes, but be aware that if you don't plan to cover many miles, you may come out ahead by buying individual tickets.

VIA Rail's Canrail pass allows seven one-way trips in coach-class within a 21-day period, between two pre-determined points, with one stopover per trip permitted. Sleeping cars are available, but they sell out very early and must be reserved at least a month in advance during high season (June through mid-October). The SuperSaver pass (high season: C$969; low season: C$606) must be purchased three days prior to the first trip; the more expensive Discounted pass (high season: C$1114; low season: C$697) can be booked up to the day before. There are discounts for youths and senior citizens aged 60 and over.

Children under two travel for free in a parent's seat, and children up to 11 can get their own seat for roughly half the price of an adult ticket.

Major credit cards, debit cards, and cash are accepted.

Reservations are strongly urged for intercity and interprovincial travel and for journeys to and from the United States. If your ticket is lost, it is like losing cash, so guard it closely. If you lose your reservation number, your seat can still be accessed in their reservation system by using your name or the train you have been booked on.

GO Transit is the Greater Toronto Area's commuter rail. (It also runs buses.) The double-decker trains are comfortable and have restrooms.

Train Contacts Amtrak ☎ 800/872–7245 ⊕ www.amtrak.com. **GO Transit** ☎ 416/869–3200, 888/438–6646 ⊕ www.gotransit.com. **Union Station** ✉ 65–75 Front St., between Bay and York sts., Ontario ☎ 416/366–7788 ⊕ www.toronto.ca/union_station. **VIA Rail Canada** ☎ 888/842–7245 ⊕ www.viarail.ca.

ESSENTIALS

■ BUSINESS SERVICES AND FACILITIES

FedEx Office—where you can fax, copy, print, and rent computers—has several locations in Toronto.

Contacts FedEx Kinko's ✉ *357 Bay St., at Temperance St., Financial District, Ontario* ☎ *416/363–2705* ⊕ *www.fedexkinkos. ca* ✉ *505 University Ave., at Dundas St. W, Chinatown, Ontario* ☎ *416/979–8447* ✉ *459 Bloor St. W, at Major St., The Annex, Ontario* ☎ *416/928–0110.*

■ COMMUNICATIONS

INTERNET

Most hotels in Toronto have some Internet access, and more and more are offering Wi-Fi. Chain hotels usually charge around C$12 per day for Wi-Fi. In boutique hotels and B&Bs, Wi-Fi charges are rare. There are many designated Internet cafés around town, or cafés that provide Wi-Fi for customers.

Note that cybercafés frequently change hands and names but often stay in the same location. Rates are usually C$2–C$3 per hour. Two areas are hubs for 24-hour cybercafés: Bloor and Bathurst (heading east) and Church–Wellesley on Yonge. Cybercafes lists more than 4,000 Internet cafés worldwide.

Contacts Cybercafes ⊕ *www.cybercafes.com.*

Internet Cafés iKlick ✉ *614 Yonge St., at Wellesley St., Church-Wellesley, Ontario* ☎ *416/922–0852* ✉ *1453 Queen St. W, at Lansdowne Ave., Queen West, Ontario* ☎ *416/538–3317.* **Netropass** ✉ *836 Yonge St., at Cumberland St., Yorkville, Ontario* ☎ *416/323–3177* ⊕ *www.netropass.com* ✉ *767 Yonge St., Yorkville, Ontario* ☎ *416/923–3737.* **Internet Mart** ✉ *519 Bloor St. W, at Bathurst St., The Annex, Ontario* ☎ *416/538–1498.*

PHONES

The good news is that you can now make a direct-dial telephone call from virtually any point on earth. The bad news? You can't always do so cheaply. Calling from a hotel is almost always the most expensive option; hotels usually add huge surcharges to all calls, particularly international ones. Calling cards usually keep costs to a minimum but only if you purchase them locally. And then there are mobile phones, which are sometimes more prevalent than landlines; as expensive as mobile phone calls can be, they are still usually a much cheaper option than calling from your hotel.

When you are calling Canada, the country code is 1. The country code is 1 for the United States as well, so dialing a Canadian number is like dialing a number long distance in the U.S.—dial 1, followed by the 10-digit number.

CALLING WITHIN CANADA

Local calls in Canada are exactly the same as local calls in the United States. Despite the ubiquitousness of cell phones, pay phones still appear every few blocks and take quarters (C50¢ for the first three minutes). Ask at your hotel whether local calls are free—there may be hefty charges for phone use. Buying a prepaid calling card or renting a cell phone may be worthwhile if you plan to make many local calls.

CALLING OUTSIDE CANADA

Calling to the United States from Canada is billed as an international call, even though you don't have to dial anything but 1 and the 10-digit number. Charges can be $1 per minute or more on cell phones. Prepaid calling cards are the best option.

CALLING CARDS

Prepaid phone cards, which can be purchased at convenience stores, are generally the cheapest way to call the United

States. You can find cards for as little as C\$5 for eight hours of talk time. With these cards, you call a toll-free number, then enter the code from the back of the card. You can buy the cards online before you leave home.

MOBILE PHONES

If you have a multiband phone and your service provider uses the world-standard GSM network (as do T-Mobile, AT&T, and Verizon), you can probably use your phone in Canada. Roaming fees can be steep, however: 99¢ a minute is considered reasonable. And internationally you normally pay the toll charges for incoming calls. It's almost always cheaper to send a text message than to make a call as text messages have a very low set fee (often less than C5¢).

If you just want to make local calls, consider buying a new SIM card (note that your provider may have to unlock your phone for this) and a prepaid service plan in the destination. You'll then have a local number and can make local calls at local rates. If your trip is extensive, you could also simply buy a new cell phone in your destination, as the initial cost will be offset over time. Fido, a Canadian cell-phone company, sells prepaid SIM cards with a rate of C40¢-per-minute for the first five minutes of the day (C20¢-per-minute after that) to the U.S. and long-distance in Canada, but you have to go to a Fido store to buy and install the card.

■TIP→ If you travel internationally frequently, save one of your old mobile phones or buy a cheap one on the Internet; ask your cell phone company to unlock it for you and take it with you as a travel phone, buying a new SIM card with pay-as-you-go service in each destination.

There are plenty of mobile-phone stores in downtown Toronto for renting phones. You can rent cell phones for as little as US\$29 per week with Cellular Abroad, but international rates to the U.S. are 66¢ per minute.

Cellular Abroad rents and sells GSM phones and sells SIM cards that work in many countries. Mobal rents mobiles and sells GSM phones with SIM cards (starting at US\$129) that will operate in 140 countries. Per-call rates vary throughout the world. Planet Fone rents cell phones, but the per-minute rates are expensive.

Contacts Cellular Abroad ☎ 800/287–5072 ⊕ www.cellularabroad.com. **Fido** ✉ 218 Yonge St., between Queen and Dundas, Dundas Square Area, Ontario ☎ 416/597–1436 ⊕ fido. ca ✉ 120 Adelaide St. W, Financial District, Ontario ☎ 416/815–0207. **Mobal.** Mobal ☎ 888/888–9162 ⊕ www.mobalrental.com. **Planet Fone** ☎ 888/988–4777 ⊕ www.planetfone.com.

■ CUSTOMS AND DUTIES

You're always allowed to bring goods of a certain value back home without having to pay any duty or import tax. But there's a limit on the amount of tobacco and liquor you can bring back duty-free, and some countries have separate limits for perfumes; for exact figures, check with your customs department. The values of so-called "duty-free" goods are included in these amounts. When you shop abroad, save all your receipts, as customs inspectors may ask to see them as well as the items you purchased. If the total value of your goods is more than the duty-free limit, you'll have to pay a tax (most often a flat percentage) on the value of everything beyond that limit.

Clearing customs is fastest if you're driving over the border. Unless you're pulled aside or traffic is backed up, you'll be through in a matter of minutes. When arriving by air, wait times can be lengthy—plan on at least 45 minutes. If you're traveling by bus, customs is a slow process as all passengers must disembark, remove their luggage from the bus, and be questioned. Make sure all prescription drugs are clearly labeled or bring a copy of the prescription with you.

American and British visitors may bring in the following items duty-free: 200 cigarettes, 50 cigars, and 7 ounces of tobacco; 1 bottle (1.5 liters or 53 imperial ounces) of wine, 1.14 liters (40 ounces) of liquor, or 24 355-milliliter (12-ounce) bottles or cans of beer for personal consumption. Any alcohol and tobacco products in excess of these amounts are subject to duty fees, provincial fees, and taxes. You can also bring in gifts of no more than C$60 in value per gift.

A deposit is sometimes required for trailers, which is refunded upon return. Cats and dogs must have a certificate issued by a licensed veterinarian that clearly identifies the animal and certifies that it has been vaccinated against rabies during the preceding 36 months. Certified assistance dogs are allowed into Canada without restriction. Plant material must be declared and inspected. There may be restrictions on some live plants, bulbs, and seeds. With certain restrictions or prohibitions on some fruits and vegetables—including oranges, apples, and bananas—visitors may bring food with them for their own use, provided the quantity is consistent with the duration of the visit.

Canada's firearms laws are significantly stricter than those in the United States. All handguns and semiautomatic and fully automatic weapons are prohibited and cannot be brought into the country. Sporting rifles and shotguns may be imported provided they are to be used for sporting, hunting, or competing while in Canada. All firearms must be declared to Canada Customs at the first point of entry. Failure to declare firearms will result in their seizure, and criminal charges may be made. Regulations require visitors to have a confirmed "Firearms Declaration" to bring any guns for sporting, hunting, or competition into Canada; a fee of C$25 applies, good for 60 days. For more information, contact the Canadian Firearms Centre.

Information in Canada Canada Revenue Agency ☎ *800/267-5177 for international*

> ### DID YOU KNOW?
>
> Though Canada is a bilingual country—it has two official languages, French and English—Toronto is the Anglophone center of Canada, and 99% of the people living here will speak to you in English. By law, product labels must also be in French, but you won't find French road signs or hear much French here.

and nonresident inquiries ⊕ *www.cra.gc.ca*.
Canadian Firearms Centre ☎ *800/731-4000* ⊕ *www.cfc-cafc.gc.ca*.

U.S. Information U.S. Customs and Border Protection ⊕ *www.cbp.gov*.

▌ ELECTRICITY

Canada's electrical capabilities and outlet types are no different from those in the United States. Residents of the United Kingdom, Australia, and New Zealand will need adapters to type A (not grounded) or type B (grounded) plugs. Voltage in Canada is 110, which differs from the United Kingdom, Australia, and New Zealand. Newer appliances should be fine, but check with the manufacturer and buy a voltage converter if necessary.

▌ EMERGENCIES

For a complete listing of emergency services, you can always check the Yellow Pages or ask for assistance at your hotel desk. The Dental Emergency Clinic operates from 8 am to midnight. Many Pharma Plus Drugmarts are open until midnight; some branches of Shoppers Drug Mart are open 24 hours.

All international embassies are in Ottawa; there are some consulates in Toronto, including a U.S. consulate. The consulate is open weekdays 8:30–3, but most services are offered only before noon.

Doctors and Dentists Dental Emergency Clinic ⊠ *1650 Yonge St., Greater Toronto, Ontario* ☎ *416/485-7121*.

Foreign Consulates Consulate General of the United States ✉ *360 University Ave., Queen West, Ontario* ☎ *416/595–1700, 416/595–6506 emergency line for U.S. citizens* ⊕ *http://toronto.usconsulate.gov.*

General Emergency Contacts Ambulance, fire, and police ☎ *911.*

Hospitals and Clinics St. Michael's Hospital ✉ *30 Bond St., near Sherbourne and Queen sts., Dundas Square Area, Ontario* ☎ *416/360–4000* ⊕ *www.stmichaelshospital.com.* **Toronto General Hospital** ✉ *200 Elizabeth St., Queen's Park, Ontario* ☎ *416/340–3111, 416/340–3946 for emergencies* ⊕ *www.uhn.ca.*

24-Hour and Late-Night Pharmacies Pharma Plus ✉ *777 Bay St., at College St., Dundas Square Area, Ontario* ☎ *416/977–5824* ⊕ *www.rexall.ca* ☾ *Daily 8 am–midnight* ✉ *63 Wellesley St. E, at Church St., Church-Wellesley, Ontario* ☎ *416/924–7760* ☾ *Daily 8 am–midnight.* **Shoppers Drug Mart** ✉ *465 Yonge St., at College St., Dundas Square Area, Ontario* ☎ *416/408–4000* ⊕ *www.shoppersdrugmart. ca* ☾ *24 hrs* ✉ *388 King St. W, at Spadina Ave., Entertainment District, Ontario* ☎ *416/597–6550* ☾ *Daily 8 am–midnight* ✉ *390 Queen's Quay W, at Spadina Ave., Harbourfront, Ontario* ☎ *416/260–2766* ☾ *Daily 8 am–midnight.*

▌ HEALTH

Toronto does not have any unique health concerns. It is safe to drink tap water. Pollution in the city is generally rated Good to Moderate on the international Air Quality Index. Smog advisories are listed by the Ontario Ministry of the Environment at ⊕ *www.airqualityontario.com.*

HEALTH CARE

Consider buying trip insurance with medical-only coverage. Neither Medicare nor some private insurers cover medical expenses anywhere outside of the United States. Medical-only policies typically reimburse you for medical care (excluding that related to preexisting conditions) and hospitalization abroad, and provide for evacuation. You still have to pay the bills and await reimbursement from the insurer, though.

Another option is to sign up with a medical-evacuation assistance company. A membership in one of these companies gets you doctor referrals, emergency evacuation or repatriation, 24-hour hotlines for medical consultation, and other assistance. International SOS Assistance Emergency and AirMed International provide evacuation services and medical referrals. MedjetAssist offers medical evacuation.

Medical Assistance Companies AirMed International ⊕ *www.airmed.com.* **International SOS Assistance Emergency** ⊕ *www.internationalsos.com.* **MedjetAssist** ⊕ *www.medjetassist.com.*

Medical-Only Insurers International Medical Group ⊕ *www.imglobal.com.* **International SOS** ⊕ *www.internationalsos.com.* **Wallach & Company** ⊕ *www.wallach.com.*

OVER-THE-COUNTER REMEDIES

OTC medications available in Canada are nearly identical to those available in the United States. In some cases, brand names are different, but you'll recognize common brands like Tylenol, Midol, and Advil. Nonprescription medications can be found at drugstores and in some grocery and convenience stores.

▌ HOURS OF OPERATION

Post offices are closed weekends, but post-office service counters in drugstores are usually open on Sunday. When open, hours are generally 8 to 6 or 9 to 7. There is no mail delivery on weekends. The Beer Store, which sells beer only, and the LCBO (Liquor Control Board of Ontario), which sells wine, beer, and liquor, close on holidays.

Most banks are open Monday through Thursday 10 to 5 and Friday 10 to 6. Some are open longer hours and on Saturday. All banks are closed on national holidays. Most have ATMs accessible around the clock.

As in most large North American urban areas, many highway and city gas stations in and around Toronto are open 24 hours, although there's rarely a mechanic on duty Sunday. Smaller stations close at 7 pm.

The variety of museums in Toronto have an array of opening and closing times; it is best to phone ahead or check Web sites. Opening hours of sites and attractions are denoted in this book by a clock icon.

Most retail stores are open Monday through Saturday 10 to 6, and many now open on Sunday (generally noon to 5) as well. Downtown stores are usually open until 9 pm seven days a week. Some shops are open Thursday and Friday evenings, too. Shopping malls tend to be open weekdays from 9 or 10 am to 9 pm, Saturday from 9 am to 6 pm, and Sunday from noon to 5 pm, although many extend their hours pre-Christmas. Corner convenience stores are often open until midnight, seven days a week.

HOLIDAYS

Standard Canadian national holidays are New Year's Day, Good Friday, Easter Monday, Victoria Day (Monday preceding May 25), Canada Day (July 1), Civic Day (aka Simcoe Day in Toronto; first Monday in August), Labour Day (first Monday in September), Thanksgiving (second Monday in October), Remembrance Day (November 11), Christmas, and Boxing Day (December 26).

▌MAIL

Canada's national postal system is called Canada Post. There are few actual post-office buildings in Toronto. Instead, many drugstores have post-office counters that offer full mail services. Check the Canada Post Web site for locations; a red, blue, and white Canada Post sign will also be affixed to the storefront. Post offices are closed weekends, and there is no mail delivery on weekends. During the week most post offices are open from 8 to 6 or from 9 to 7.

You can buy stamps at the post office, railway stations, airports, bus terminals, many retail outlets, and some newsstands. Letters can be dropped into red Canada Post boxes on the street or mailed from Canada Post counters in drugstores or post offices. If you're sending mail to or within Canada, be sure to include the postal code—six digits and letters. Note that the suite number may appear before the street number in an address, followed by a hyphen. The postal abbreviation for Ontario is ON.

Main postal outlets for products and services in the downtown area are the Adelaide Street Post Office; the Atrium on Bay Post Office near the Marriott, the Delta Chelsea Hotel, and the Eaton Centre; and Postal Station "F," one block southeast of the major Bloor–Yonge intersection.

The Canadian postal system is almost identical to the U.S. system. To send regular letters within Canada, just ask for a letter stamp, which is C59¢. Stamps for letters to the United States are C$1.03. Stamps for letters to countries other than the United States are C$1.75. Envelopes that exceed 30 grams (1 ounce) or are oversized cost incrementally more. Letter stamps are also sold in books of 10 or rolls of 100 for domestic and in books of six or rolls of 50 for international.

When sending mail other than a letter weighing less than 30 grams, take your envelope or package to a postal counter in a drugstore or to the post office to have it weighed and priced accordingly.

Mail may be sent to you care of ✉ *General Delivery, Toronto Adelaide Street Post Office, 36 Adelaide Street East, Toronto, ON M5C 1J0.*

Info Canada Post ☎ *416/979-8822, 866/607-6301 in Canada* ⊕ *www.canadapost.ca.*

Main Branches Adelaide Street Post Office ✉ *31 Adelaide St. E, Financial District, Ontario* ☎ *866/607-6301.* **Atrium on Bay Post Office** ✉ *595 Bay St., Dundas Square*

Area, Ontario ☎ *416/506–0911.* **Postal Station "F"** ✉ *50 Charles St. E, Yorkville, Ontario* ☎ *416/413–4815.*

SHIPPING PACKAGES

Customs forms are required with international parcels. Parcels sent regular post typically take up to two weeks. The fastest service is FedEx, which has 24-hour locations at University and Dundas and at Bloor and Spadina. "Overnight" service with Canada Post usually takes two days.

Express Services FedEx ✉ *505 University Ave., at Dundas St. W, Chinatown, Ontario* ☎ *416/979–8447* ⊕ *www.fedex.ca* ✉ *459 Bloor St. W, at Major St., The Annex, Ontario* ☎ *416/928–0110* ✉ *357 Bay St., at Temperance St., Entertainment District, Ontario* ☎ *416/363–2705.*

▮ MONEY

Unless otherwise stated, all prices, including dining and lodging, are given in Canadian dollars. Toronto is the country's most expensive city.

Prices throughout this guide are given for adults. Substantially reduced fees are almost always available for children, students, and senior citizens.

ATMS AND BANKS

Your own bank will probably charge a fee for using ATMs abroad; the foreign bank you use may also charge a fee. Nevertheless, you'll usually get a better rate of exchange at an ATM than at a currency-exchange office or even when changing money in a bank. And extracting funds as you need them is a safer option than carrying around a large amount of cash.

▮**TIP→** PINs with more than four digits are not recognized at ATMs in many countries. If yours has five or more, remember to change it before you leave.

ATMs are available in most bank, trust-company, and credit-union branches across the country, as well as in many convenience stores, malls, and gas stations. The major banks in Toronto are Scotiabank, CIBC, HSBC, Royal Bank of Canada, the Bank of Montréal, and TD Canada Trust.

ITEM	AVERAGE COST
Cup of Coffee	C$1.50
Glass of Wine	C$6–C$9
Glass of Beer	C$3–C$6
Sandwich	C$6–C$8
One-Mile Taxi Ride	C$2.50 (plus initial C$4)
Museum Admission	C$8–C$20

CREDIT CARDS

It's a good idea to inform your credit card company before you travel, especially if you're going abroad and don't travel internationally very often. Otherwise, the credit-card company might put a hold on your card owing to unusual activity—not a good thing halfway through your trip. Record all your credit-card numbers—as well as the phone numbers to call if your cards are lost or stolen—in a safe place, so you're prepared should something go wrong. Both MasterCard and Visa have general numbers you can call (collect if you're abroad) if your card is lost, but you're better off calling the number of your issuing bank as MasterCard and Visa usually just transfer you to your bank; your bank's number is usually printed on your card.

If you plan to use your credit card for cash advances, you'll need to apply for a PIN at least two weeks before your trip. Although it's usually cheaper and safer to use a credit card abroad for large purchases (so you can cancel payments or be reimbursed if there's a problem), note that some credit-card companies *and* the banks that issue them add substantial percentages to all foreign transactions, whether they're in a foreign currency or not. Check on these fees before leaving home so there won't be any surprises when you get the bill.

▮**TIP→** Before you charge something, ask the merchant whether or not he or she plans to do a dynamic currency conversion

(DCC). In such a transaction the credit-card processor (shop, restaurant, or hotel, not Visa or MasterCard) converts the currency and charges you in dollars. In most cases you'll pay the merchant a 3% fee for this service in addition to any credit-card company and issuing-bank foreign-transaction surcharges.

Dynamic currency conversion programs are becoming increasingly widespread. Merchants who participate in them are supposed to ask whether you want to be charged in dollars or the local currency, but they don't always do so. And even if they do offer you a choice, they may well avoid mentioning the additional surcharges. The good news is that you *do* have a choice. And if this practice really gets your goat, you can avoid it entirely thanks to American Express; with its cards, DCC simply isn't an option.

Reporting Lost Cards American Express ☎ *800/297–8500 in the U.S., 336/393–1111 collect from abroad* ⊕ *www.americanexpress. com.* **Diners Club** ☎ *800/234–6377 in the U.S., 303/799–1504 collect from abroad* ⊕ *www.dinersclub.com.* **Discover** ☎ *800/347–2683 in the U.S., 801/902–3100 collect from abroad* ⊕ *www.discovercard.com.* **MasterCard** ☎ *800/627–7309 in the U.S., 636/722–7111 collect from abroad* ⊕ *www.mastercard.com.* **Visa** ☎ *800/847–2911 in the U.S., 303/967–1096 collect from abroad* ⊕ *www.visa.com.*

CURRENCY AND EXCHANGE

U.S. dollars are sometimes accepted—more commonly in the Niagara region close to the border than in Toronto. Some hotels, restaurants, and stores are skittish about accepting Canadian currency over $20 due to counterfeiting, so be sure to get small bills when you exchange money or visit an ATM. Major U.S. credit cards and debit or check cards with a credit-card logo are accepted in most areas. Your credit-card-logo debit card will be charged as a credit card.

The units of currency in Canada are the Canadian dollar (C$) and the cent, in almost the same denominations as U.S.

currency ($5, $10, $20, 1¢, 5¢, 10¢, 25¢, etc.). The $1 and $2 bill are no longer used; they have been replaced by $1 and $2 coins (known as a "loonie," because of the loon that appears on the coin, and a "toonie," respectively). At this writing the exchange rate is US$1.03 to C$1.

Even if a currency-exchange booth has a sign promising no commission, rest assured that there's some kind of huge, hidden fee. (Oh . . . that's right. The sign didn't say no *fee*.) And as for rates, you're almost always better off getting foreign currency at an ATM or exchanging money at a bank.

Google does currency conversion. Just type in the amount you want to convert and an explanation of how you want it converted (e.g., "14 Swiss francs in dollars"), and voilà. Oanda.com also allows you to print out a handy table with the current day's conversion rates. XE.com is a good currency conversion Web site.

Conversion sites Google ⊕ *www.google. com.* **Oanda.com** ⊕ *www.oanda.com.* **XE.com** ⊕ *www.xe.com.*

▌PACKING

You may want to pack light because airline luggage restrictions are tight. For winter, you need your warmest clothes, in many layers, and waterproof boots. A scarf that covers your face is a good idea—winds can be brutal. In summer, loose-fitting, casual clothing will see you through both day and evening events. It's a good idea to pack a sweater or shawl for cool evenings or restaurants that run their air conditioners full blast. Men will need a jacket and tie for the better restaurants and many of the nightspots. Jeans are as popular in Toronto as they are elsewhere and are perfectly acceptable for sightseeing and informal dining. Be sure to bring comfortable walking shoes. Consider packing a bathing suit for your hotel pool and a small umbrella.

PASSPORTS AND VISAS

Anyone who is not a Canadian citizen or Canadian permanent resident must have a passport to enter Canada. Passport requirements apply to minors as well. Anyone under 18 traveling alone or with only one parent should carry a signed and notarized letter from both parents or from all legal guardians authorizing the trip. It's also a good idea to include a copy of the child's birth certificate, custody documents if applicable, and death certificates of one or both parents, if applicable. (Most airlines do not allow children under age five to travel alone, and on Air Canada, for example, children under age 12 are allowed to travel unaccompanied only on nonstop flights. Consult the airline, bus line, or train service for specific regulations if using public transport.) Citizens of the United States, United Kingdom, Australia, and New Zealand do not need visas to enter Canada for a period of six months or less.

PASSPORTS

U.S. passports are valid for 10 years. You must apply in person if you're getting a passport for the first time; if your previous passport was lost, stolen, or damaged; or if your previous passport has expired and was issued more than 15 years ago or when you were under 16. All children under 18 must appear in person to apply for or renew a passport. Both parents must accompany any child under 16 (or send a notarized statement with their permission) and provide proof of their relationship to the child.

■ TIP → Before your trip, make two copies of your passport's data page (one for someone at home and another for you to carry separately). Or scan the page and email it to someone at home and yourself.

If you're renewing a passport, you can do so by mail. Forms are available at passport acceptance facilities and online. The cost to apply for a new passport is $135 for adults, $120 for children under 16; renewals are $110. Allow six weeks for

processing, both for first-time passports and renewals. For an expediting fee of $60 you can reduce this time to about two weeks. If your trip is less than two weeks away, you can get a passport even more rapidly by going to a passport office with the necessary documentation. Private expediters can get things done in as little as 48 hours.

U.S. Passport Information U.S. Department of State ☎ 877/487-2778 ⊕ http://travel.state.gov/passport.

U.S. Passport and Visa Expediters A. Briggs Passport & Visa Expediters ☎ 800/806-0581, 202/338-0111 ⊕ www.abriggs.com. **American Passport Express** ☎ 800/455-5166, 603/559-9888 ⊕ www.americanpassport.com. **Passport Express** ☎ 800/362-8196, 401/272-4612 ⊕ www.passportexpress.com. **Travel Document Systems** ☎ 800/874-5100, 202/638-3800 ⊕ www.traveldocs.com.

RESTROOMS

Toronto is often noted for its cleanliness, which extends to its public restrooms. In the downtown shopping areas, large chain bookstores and department stores are good places to stop. If you dart into a coffee shop, you may be expected to make a purchase. Gas stations downtown do not typically have restrooms. Only a few subway stations have public restrooms; their locations are noted on the subway map posted above the doors in each car on the train.

SAFETY

Toronto is renowned as a safe city, but you should still be careful with your valuables—keep them in a hotel safe when you're not wearing them. Downtown areas are generally safe at night, even for women alone. Most of the seedier parts of the city are on its fringes. However, areas east of Dufferin on Queen Street, College, or Bloor can feel desolate after dark as can most of Dundas Street, though a few pioneer hipster bars are popping up in these areas.

Panhandling happens in Toronto, especially in Queen West and Kensington Market. Jaywalking is not illegal in Toronto and it happens frequently. Be alert when driving or walking—streetcars, jaywalkers, and plentiful bicyclists make downtown navigation somewhat hazardous.

■TIP→ Distribute your cash, credit cards, IDs, and other valuables between a deep front pocket, an inside jacket or vest pocket, and a hidden money pouch. Don't reach for the money pouch once you're in public.

Advisories U.S. Department of State ⊕ travel.state.gov.

▌TAXES

Toronto has a Harmonized Sales Tax (HST) of 13% (the combination of the former 5% national GST and the 8% provincial PST) on most items purchased in shops and on restaurant meals. (Be aware that taxes and tip add at least 30% to your food and beverage total when dining out.) The HST also applies to lodging and alcohol purchased at the Liquor Control Board of Ontario (LCBO). Prices displayed in LCBO stores include tax, so you won't see the extra taxes levied at the register. Other stores that sell wine charge only GST, but as they have to pay the LCBO a 10% tax, it's fair to assume they've marked up their prices accordingly.

▌TIME

Toronto is on Eastern Standard Time (EST), the same as New York. The city is three hours ahead of Pacific Standard Time (PST), which includes Vancouver and Los Angeles, and is one hour behind Atlantic Standard Time, which is found in the Maritime Provinces. The Province of Newfoundland and Labrador is 1½ hours ahead of Toronto.

Timeanddate.com can help you figure out the correct time anywhere.

Time Zones Timeanddate.com ⊕ www.timeanddate.com/worldclock.

▌TIPPING

Tips and service charges are not usually added to a bill in Toronto. In general, tip 15% of the total bill. This goes for food servers, barbers and hairdressers, and taxi drivers. Porters and doormen should get about C$2 a bag. For maid service, leave C$2–C$5 per person a day.

▌VISITOR INFORMATION

The Web site of the City of Toronto has helpful material about everything from local politics to public transit. The monthly magazine Toronto Life and the weekly alternative papers Now and Eye Weekly list the latest art and nightlife events and carry information about dining, shopping, and more. Another site, ⊕ toronto.com, is one-stop shopping for nuts-and-bolts info like traffic or transportation, as well as for cultural events and links to lots of other Toronto Web sites and blogs.

Written by locals, for locals, Blog TO includes commentary on Toronto life and upcoming cultural events.

Official Web sites Canadian Tourism Commission ☎ 604/638–8300 ⊕ www.canadatourism.com. City of Toronto ⊕ www.toronto.ca. Ontario Travel ☎ 800/668–2746 ⊕ www.ontariotravel.net. Tourism Toronto ☎ 416/203–2500, 800/499–2514 ⊕ www.seetorontonow.com.

Other Helpful Web sites Toronto Life ⊕ www.torontolife.com. Toronto.com ⊕ www.toronto.com. NOW ⊕ www.nowtoronto.com. Eye Weekly ⊕ www.eyeweekly.com. Blog TO ⊕ www.blogto.com.

INDEX

PHOTO CREDITS

ABOUT OUR WRITERS

Freelance writer and editor and former Fodor's staffer Shannon Kelly has contributed to many Fodor's guides, including *San Francisco, Brazil,* and *New York City.* Following two cross-continent moves, she has been firmly rooted in Toronto since 2007, exploring the city and the province of Ontario from top to bottom. For this edition she updated our Shopping and Nightlife chapters.

Born in Hong Kong and raised in Toronto, food writer Diana Ng grew up on home-cooked Chinese food as well as a diverse range of authentic ethnic cuisines that the city offers. She has written for canada.com, Wish magazine, Readersdigest.ca, and Canadianliving.com, among others. What she enjoyed most about updating the Where to Eat section was meeting people who are passionate about food and sharing unique dining experiences. She also updated our Side Trips chapter. Currently a lifestyle content producer, freelance writer, and recipe tester, she is constantly checking out new restaurants and ingredients.

Sarah Richards was delighted to settle in one of the world's most multicultural cities after wandering about Asia and Europe for five years. While updating the Exploring, Where to Stay, and Travel Smart chapters for this edition, her favorite day started with a morning stroll through Edwards Gardens followed by an afternoon of devouring the Group of Seven paintings at the McMichael Canadian Art Collection, and ended with drinks and dinner at the Drake Hotel in West Queen West. She has also contributed to past editions of *Fodor's USA, Fodor's Japan,* and *Fodor's Great Britain.*